Food and Wine Festivals and Events Around the World

Development, Management and Markets

C. Michael Hall
and
Liz Sharples

ELSEVIER

AMSTERDAM • BOSTON • HEIDELBERG • LONDON • NEW YORK • OXFORD
PARIS • SAN DIEGO • SAN FRANCISCO • SYDNEY • TOKYO
Butterworth-Heinemann is an imprint of Elsevier

Butterworth-Heinemann is an imprint of Elsevier
Linacre House, Jordan Hill, Oxford OX2 8DP, UK
30 Corporate Drive, Suite 400, Burlington, MA 01803, USA

First edition 2008

British Library Cataloguing in Publication Data
A catalogue record for this book is available from the British Library

Library of Congress Cataloging-in-Publication Data
A catalog record for this book is available from the Library of Congress

ISBN: 978-0-7506-8380-7

For information on all Butterworth-Heinemann publications
Visit our web site at books.elsevier.com

Typeset by Charon Tec Ltd., A Macmillan Company. (www.macmillansolutions.com)

Printed and bound in Hungary
08 09 10 11 12   10 9 8 7 6 5 4 3 2 1

Contents

List of Exhibits

List of Figures

List of Tables

List of Plates

List of Contributors

Wendy Barrie, Consultant, Scottish Food Industry

Liping A. Cai, Department of Hospitality and Tourism, Purdue University, USA

Fiona Crawford, formerly Department of Management, University of Canterbury, Christchurch, New Zealand

Stuart Crispin, School of Management, University of Tasmania, Launceston, Tasmania, Australia

Tim H. Dodd, Texas Wine Marketing Research Institute, Texas Tech University, USA

Jane F. Eastham, Faculty of Organisation and Management, Sheffield Hallam University, England

C. Michael Hall, Department of Management, University of Canterbury, Christchurch, New Zealand and Department of Geography, University of Oulu, Finland

Atsuko Hashimoto, Department of Tourism and Environment, Brock University, St. Catharines, Ontario, Canada

Anne-Marie Hede, School of Hospitality Tourism and Marketing, Faculty of Business and Law, Victoria University, Melbourne, Victoria, Australia

Meg Houghton, School of Sport, Tourism and Hospitality Management, La Trobe University, Victoria, Australia

Na Jiang, formerly Faculty of Organisation and Management, Sheffield Hallam University, England

Lee Jolliffe, Faculty of Business, University of New Brunswick, New Brunswick, Canada

Carol Kalkstein-Silkes, Department of Hospitality and Tourism Management, Purdue University, USA

Xinran Y. Lehto, Department of Hospitality and Tourism Management, Purdue University, USA

Sally Linton, Indiana Wine Grape Council, Food Science Department, Purdue University, USA

Howard Lyons, Faculty of Organisation and Management, Sheffield Hallam University, England

Richard Mitchell, Department of Tourism, University of Otago, Dunedin, New Zealand

Alastair Morrison, Department of Hospitality and Tourism Management, Purdue University, USA

Dirk Reiser, School of Management, University of Tasmania, Launceston, Tasmania, Australia

Ian D. Rotherham, Faculty of Development and Society, Sheffield Hallam University, England

David Scott, Department of Tourism, University of Otago, Dunedin, New Zealand

Liz Sharples, Faculty of Organisation and Management, Sheffield Hallam University, England

David J. Telfer, Department of Tourism and Environment, Brock University, St. Catharines, Ontario, Canada

Jingxue (Jessica) Yuan, Department of Nutrition, Hospitality and Retailing, Texas Tech University, USA

Acknowledgements

As tourism and hospitality education and research has developed so the field of study has also become more specialized. This book is in part testimony to that, but it also demonstrates the way in which a topic such as food events is able to link together a wide range of approaches and interests so as to focus on what is becoming an increasingly important area in the development of sustainable hospitality and tourism.

The present volume builds on our previous work, with respect to wine and food, but also provides some new focal points in research. In addition, many of the chapters also reflect the way in which academic research can be connected with the day-to-day problems facing communities as they seek to develop and sustain the social, environmental and economic resources on which they depend.

We also wish to acknowledge the help and support of a number of people without whom this book would not have been produced. Michael would like to thank Tori Amos, Nick Cave, Bruce Cockburn, Tim Coles, Fiona Crawford, David Duval, Ebba Forsberg, Stefan Gössling, Dieter Müller, Stephen Page, Jarkko Saarinen and Nicola van Tiel and Sandra Wilson for stimulating thoughts and examples on food and wine events while the book was being undertaken, and Jody Cowper for assistance with food research. Special thanks are also due to a number of providors for their physical sustenance: the Canterbury Cheesemongers, Banfields of Beckenham, Johnson's Grocery, the Victoria Markets, the Granville Island Markets and the fine cheesemakers of Vasterbotten.

Liz would like to thank Doreen Blakemore of Newcastle upon Tyne Farmers' Market; Beth Cohen, John Fleming, Graeme Kidd, Phil Maile and all her friends associated with the Ludlow Food Festival; Paul Nicoll, Marianne Blaauboer and Shona

Hendrick of the National Trust and her friends at Slow Food Sheffield who share her passion for good food and celebration.

Liz would also like to dedicate this book to her father, Wesley, who continues to be a great inspiration and to her Mum, Ann, in her 80th year. She would also like to thank her daughters Kathy and Vicky for their patience and understanding throughout the project.

The editors and authors would like to thank Sally North and all the team at Elsevier – Butterworth Heinemann for the ongoing support for this project.

PART I

Context

Food events, festivals and farmers' markets: An introduction

C. Michael Hall and Liz Sharples

Food events, sometimes referred to as hallmark or special events are fairs, festivals, expositions, cultural, consumer and industry events which are held on either a regular or a one-off basis. Hallmark events have assumed a key role in international, national, regional and firm tourism and food and wine marketing and promotion strategies. From a business perspective their primary marketing function is to provide products, sponsors, host communities and other stakeholders with an opportunity to secure high prominence in the marketplace while also adding brand value and building customer and consumer relationships (Hall and Mitchell, 2008).

Events have assumed an important role in tourism and marketing in recent years and have developed their own specialist professional organizations and niche area within tourism and visitor studies. At the same time the study of food and wine tourism, which is sometimes also referred to as gourmet, culinary or gastronomic tourism has also grown in importance (Hall et al., 2000, 2003b). Food events therefore lie at the intersection of these two fields (Figure 1.1). However, because of the nature of food as a product and the daily part it plays in consumption and economic systems, food events are more than just part of food retailing, marketing and promotion but also coincide with a number of other economic, political and

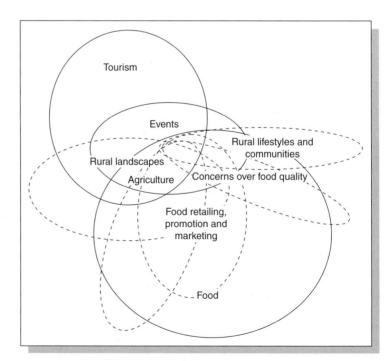

Figure 1.1
The intersections of events, food, tourism

social concerns relating to the nature of contemporary agricultural systems, conservation of rural landscapes, maintenance of rural lifestyles and communities, and concerns over food quality. Because of these factors, food events are *different*.

Food events are therefore not just about external promotion to visitors and/or consumers outside of the host region they also have substantial internal drivers for being conducted which relate to the consumption and production of food from particular locations and communities and to the maintenance of those communities. Food events are therefore strongly connected to senses of place and community pride in the products that they produce. Furthermore, food and the emotions and necessities that surround it, are significant not just for producers but also for consumers in that consumption of particular products may also have implications for identities and lifestyles (Hjalager and Corigliano, 2000; Hall et al., 2003c; Che et al., 2005). There is also widespread agreement that the number of food-related events being held around the developed world is growing rapidly although definitive figures are hard to determine (Payne, 2002; Griffin and Frongillo, 2003).

The purpose of this book is therefore to provide an overview of the food events area via an assessment of key features and issues and presentation of cases and examples of the various events. This first chapter aims to give an introduction to some of the key issues from a management perspective while the following chapter addresses some of the ways within which events are embedded within local food systems and alternative forms of food distribution and marketing.

Food events in a tourism context

Food tourism is defined by Hall and Mitchell (2001, p. 308) as 'visitation to primary and secondary food producers, food festivals, restaurants and specific locations for which food tasting and/or experiencing the attributes of specialist food production regions are the primary motivating factor for travel'. Wine tourism is a subset of food tourism being defined as 'visitation to vineyards, wineries, wine festivals and wine shows for which grape wine tasting and/or experiencing the attributes of a grape wine region are the prime motivating factors for visitors' (Hall, 1996). Such definitions do not mean that any trip to an event is food tourism, rather the desire to experience a particular type of food or the produce of a specific region must be the major motivation for such travel. Indeed, food tourism may possibly be regarded as an example of 'culinary', 'gastronomic', 'gourmet'

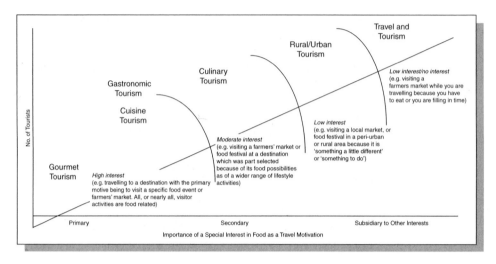

Figure 1.2
Food tourism as a special interest tourism product (*Source*: After Hall and Sharples, 2003)

or 'cuisine' tourism that reflects consumers for who interest in food and wine is a form of 'serious leisure'(Hall and Mitchell, 2001; Hall and Sharples, 2003; Mitchell and Hall, 2003) (Figure 1.2). Such definitional distinctions are significant because they also alert the reader to the potential dimensions of the food tourism market. However, for all these categories described as part of food tourism, food and wine rank as the main or a major travel motivator. Such categories of tourism are therefore defined primarily by the consumer (Hall et al., 2003a).

Food events are dependent on tourism. However, in using tourism in this context we are looking at a more generic notion of travel than the one imbued in terms of popular culture. Tourism can be understood as one form of leisure oriented mobility that ranges in scale from the local to the international (Hall, 2005). Tourism in the context used in this book therefore refers to visitation to events by people from within the immediate environment of the event, and the broader region and beyond therefore encompasses what we may conceive of as day tripping, domestic travel and international tourism.

From the production perspective a number of advantages of events, and food events in particular, can be identified at both a regional and enterprise scale. At a regional scale (Dywer et al., 2000; Chhabra et al., 2003; Lankford and Çela, 2005; Farmers' Market Federation of New York, 2006) advantages include:

● increased visitation to a region;
● retaining travellers within a region;

- economic benefits by attracting funds to a local economy;
- increasing or maintaining employment;
- improving the image of a destination;
- enhancing community pride and assisting in creating a sense of community;
- acting as a catalyst for economic development and tourism development in particular;
- reducing the impacts of seasonality often by extending the visitor season;
- enlivening public space;
- adding value to existing food and rural products; and
- providing social, cultural and health benefits.

At the enterprise level (Telfer and Wall, 1996; Hall and Mitchell, 2001, 2008; Hall et al., 2003b) advantages include:

- creating relationships with customers and consumers. The opportunity for face-to-face contact can lead to positive relationships with consumers which may lead to both direct sales and indirect sales through positive 'word of mouth';
- increasing margins through direct sales to consumer because of the absence of many distribution and intermediary costs;
- increasing consumer exposure to products and increasing opportunities to sample products rather than through normal retail outlets;
- building brand and product awareness and loyalty through establishing links between producer and consumer;
- providing an additional sales outlet. For smaller producers who cannot guarantee volume or consistency of supply, direct sales via event is the only feasible sales outlet;
- providing marketing intelligence on products and customers. Producers can gain instant and valuable feedback on the consumer reaction to their existing products, and are able to trial new additions to their product range; and
- providing opportunities to educate customers. Visits to events can help create awareness and appreciation of specific types of foods and food as a whole, the knowledge and interest generated by this can be expected to result in increased consumption and purchase.

Because food events are usually regarded as part of the supply side of tourism they are often regarded as being a form of tourism product. In one sense they clearly are because, as discussed later in this chapter and throughout the book, they are capable of being managed, marketed and planned in order to provide a particular type of visitor product or serve a range of goals of those who provide the elements that make up the event. However, increasingly, the division between consumption and production in tourism is becoming recognized as a convenient abstraction. Instead, it is increasingly recognized that from a services perspective, tourism is co-produced or co-created between the consumer and the people and firms that enable the visitor experience.

Although tourism is a service industry this does not mean that it is completely intangible. Far from it. Tourism is based on a complex set of infrastructure and physical resources, such as events spaces, market buildings, food products and landscape that have a significant relationship to the places in which they are situated. However, what is being purchased or consumed by the event visitor are the experiences that this infrastructure and set of resources provides, not the infrastructure itself. Because tourism is an experience-based product it means that in order to be able to understand food event phenomenon we need to be able to understand both its consumption and production. This is an almost deceptively simple statement but its implications are enormous: food events cannot be understood by looking at one aspect in isolation, consumption cannot occur without production and vice versa. The inseparability of production and consumption is therefore one of the

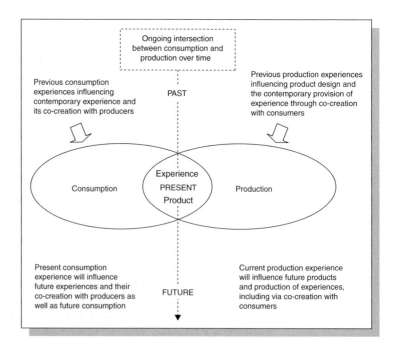

Figure 1.3
Locating the food event experience and product

hallmarks of tourism with the value of the visitor experience therefore being determined by both the consumer and the producer of the experience and the tourism product (Figure 1.3). The inseparability of consumption and production also means that the factors that make up consumption and production are constantly feeding back on one another thereby influencing the development of food event products and their appeal to consumers (Cooper and Hall, 2008).

The fact that food events are co-created between producers and consumers also means that in order to be able to understand the nature and quality of the experience we need to have an appreciation of both the consumption and production elements of food events and how they come together to provide experiences for consumers.

Food events and festivals

Events have long been synonymous with food and particularly with religious and spiritual festivals. Celebrations have long been held in many cultures that celebrate harvest. As Hall and Mitchell (2008) note, wine-related events have their origins in pre-Christian bacchanalia – mystical festivals dedicated to the Roman god of wine (in Greek mythology, Bacchus was known as Dionysus or Eleutherios) that were originally held in mid-March but later extended to be held five times a year. In Christian societies saints days were often used to try and replace pagan festivals though the festivals and events associated with them were often continued (Barkin and James, 1994). In wine-growing countries religious festivals and celebrations are often entwined with the various stages of vine growth: budbreak, flowering, fruit set, veraison and harvest. However, in recent years events have become far more secular in nature although in a number of countries, such as Spain and Italy, wine and food festivals and religious celebrations still go hand-in-hand, while in others while events may still be held on saint's days this fact may not be recognized by visitors (see Exhibit 1.1). Many holidays also have a strong relationship to food. Thanksgiving, sometimes also jokingly referred to as 'Turkey Day' which is celebrated on the fourth Thursday of November in the United States and the second Monday of October in Canada is a traditional holiday to give thanks at the conclusion of the harvest season.

Festivals are a celebration of something the local community wishes to share and which involves the wider public as

Exhibit 1.1 Whitstable Oyster Fair

The town of Whitstable is situated on the South East coastline of England in the county of Kent. It is located just to the north of the historic cathedral city of Canterbury and close to the historic town of Margate. The town has been associated with oysters for hundreds of years and evidence reports that in Norman times Whitstable was an established fishing port. In 1793 the Whitstable Oyster Company was established and from this time the industry expanded bringing work to the town and creating a buoyant economy. By the nineteenth century the oyster industry was so successful that the town acquired the nickname of 'Oysterville'.

A festival associated with fish can be traced back to Norman Times when fishermen and dredgers would celebrate their trade with an annual ceremony. The fishermen then started to hold their celebration at a slack time of year, the close season for Oysters, and the festival became linked to the feast day of St James of Compestella, the patron saint of Oysters, on the 25th July. This traditional focus has continued and the festival now lasts for one week around this time of July.

The exact form of the original festival is unknown but it is likely that it included a blessing of the town, the sea, the boats and the fishermen who worked the fleet, as well as dancing, games and contests. The format today is a little more complex but still contains these basic elements. The programme includes a Food and Produce Fair, an Oyster Parade, the Landing and Blessing of the Catch at Long Beach, Oyster Eating Competitions, Guided History Walks, a Beer Festival and Arts and Music events. The programme caters for all age groups including children.

The festival is now managed by the newly formed Whitstable Oyster Festival Association (WOFA, 2007) which is made up of local residents committed to maintaining the community focus of the event. Sponsorship is primarily local and includes Canterbury City Council. The aims of the WOFA are described in its Constitution as follows:

The Association's objects are to promote, maintain, improve and advance, education, celebration, appreciation and understanding of the culture and heritage of Whitstable and the surrounding areas, through the curation and development of the annual Whitstable Oyster Festival. The Association will do this through the provision of a programme that is accessible, inclusive and participatory, involving residents and visitors of all ages in events that embrace without limitations the arts, heritage, and sport.

Source: Derived from Whitstable Oyster Festival:
http://www.whitstableoysterfestival.co.uk and WOFA: http://www.wofa.org.uk.

participants in the experience. Festivals are 'an event, a social phenomenon, encountered in virtually all human cultures' (Falassi, 1987, p.1) which have five key elements:

1. A sacred or profane time of celebration, marked by special observances.
2. The annual celebration of a notable person or event, or the harvest of an important product.
3. A cultural event consisting of a series of performances of works in the fine arts, often devoted to a single artist or genre.
4. A fair.
5. Generic gaiety, conviviality, cheerfulness.

Festivals are intimately related with the maintenance and celebration of community values. 'Both the social function and the symbolic meaning of the festival are closely related to a series of overt values that the community recognizes as essential to its ideology and worldview, to its social identity, its historical continuity, and to its physical survival, which is ultimately what festival celebrates' (Falassi, 1987, p.2). However, as a result of greater cultural and economic connectedness between places, community food festivals have increasingly taken on a role as a commoditized product that is used externally promoted in order to attract visitors, promote the region or community, or promote consumption of specific food products – all usually with an economic motive (Hall and Mitchell, 2008). This is not to deny that events and festivals still have an important community-based social function but that such celebrations increasingly also have an economic and commercial dimension to them.

Many rural towns, especially in North America, often proclaim themselves as the 'capital' of various food types as a way of celebrating their heritage and food production, while simultaneously using the food as a way of differentiating themselves as a place to visit. For example, in California, Sacramento and Chico both proclaim to the almond capital of the world, while Watsonville is the strawberry capital of the world. Gilroy is the garlic capital of the world and also hosts an annual garlic festival that usually attracts over 100,000 people each year (Exhibit 1.2).

The use of food events and festivals for tourism and economic development purposes has also allowed for renewed public and private investment in community-based food events

Exhibit 1.2 The Gilroy Garlic Festival

The Gilroy Garlic festival is one of the most well-known food festivals in California if not the USA. The first festival was held in August 1979. The festival was founded because Rudy Melone, then President of the local community college, read an article in mid-1978 about a garlic festival in Arleux, France, a small community that claimed to be Garlic Capital of the World, but who believed that Gilroy had claim to the title given the economic importance of garlic to the area. Following a Rotary Club luncheon with members of the garlic industry and local media support for a garlic festival was generated and civic leaders, initially reluctant, started to assist the project. The first festival was an enormous success, far exceeding expectations, and succeeding in raising $19,000 and improving community relations and pride in the local garlic industry. Since then several million dollars have been raised from the more than three million visitors the festival has received.

The festival is organized by the Gilroy Garlic Festival Association which is a non-profit corporation. Its goal is to support the community projects, charitable groups and service organizations of Gilroy. The mission statement of the festival is that it 'is established to provide benefits to local worthy charities and non-profit groups by promoting the community of Gilroy through a quality celebration of Garlic'. In 2006 over 4,000 volunteers from 169 non-profit groups worked 41,763 hours to host the 28th Annual Garlic Festival; $253,000 was distributed to non-profit organizations. From 1979 through 2006 the success of the annual Festival enabled the Association to award over $7.5 million to these groups, as well as assisting other charities which generate funds through booths at the 3-day event.

Source: Derived from Gilroy Garlic Festival: http://www.gilroygarlicfestival.com/.

because of the perceived direct, that is purchasing of local product, and indirect benefits, that is awareness of regional brand, that they bring (e.g. the Whitstable Oyster Fair discussed in Exhibit 1.1). The economic benefits of such events may be substantial even if they retain a community focus. Çela et al. (2007) assessed the economic impact of 11 community-based food festivals in Northeast Iowa (from May to October 2005). The total economic impact of visitors ($n = 22,806$) in local food festivals was estimated to be almost $2.6 million in terms of sales; $1.4 million in terms of personal income; and

generated 51 jobs. The study also found that festival participants were middle-aged, college graduates, affluent and day
trippers and were primarily motivated to specifically attend
the festivals, via word of mouth. However, the focus of food
events will usually depend on the relative mix of their commercial and non-commercial goals, their product focus and their
size and intended visitor reach (scale). Food and wine events
occur over a range of scales not only in terms of the numbers of
people they attract but also their promotional base (i.e. brand,
firm, multi-firm, community or region). Table 1.1 provides an
overview of some of the categories of different food events
with examples.

In addition to public events there are also a substantial
number of private, industry-oriented events that are often
categorized as trade fairs and exhibitions, although some of
these events now also host a day when the general public can
attend to sample. The size of such events varies substantially.
For example, Vinitaly 2007 one of the world's largest wine
trade events had more than 150,000 visitors from more than
100 countries of which 38,000 were international attendees. In
addition, there were more than 2,600 journalists from 52 countries. In terms of numbers of businesses the exhibition attracted
4,300 companies from more than 30 countries (VeronaFiere
Press Office, 2007). The International Wine Competition held
as part of Vinitaly included almost 3,500 wines from 31 different countries (Hall and Mitchell, 2008). Nevertheless, also the
food exhibition market is significant for business-to-business
commerce; the primary focus of the present book is on public
food events.

Public food events

Public food events can be defined (after Ritchie, 1984; Hall,
1992) as one-time or recurring events of limited duration,
developed primarily to enhance the awareness, sales, appeal
and profitability of food and beverage products in the short
and/or long term. Such events rely for their success on uniqueness, status, quality or timely significance to create interest
and attract attention. A primary function of food events is to
provide an opportunity for food products and related destinations to secure a position of prominence in the market for a
short, well defined, period of time in order to make sales.
Significant secondary functions from the demand side include
building and promoting product, firm and destination brand

Table 1.1 Categories of food events

Product focus	Scale in terms of promotion and visitor attraction			
	Local	**Regional**	**National**	**International**
Generic (no local food focus)	Devonport Food and Wine Festival	Abergavenny Food Festival Twin Cities Food and Wine Experience (Minneapolis) Festivale (Launceston)	The BBC Good Food Summer Festival Food and Fun Festival (Reykjavik)	Oktoberfest (Munich and elsewhere) Annual Fiery Foods and BBQ Show (Albuquerque) Kosher World Expo (Anaheim)
Generic (but focussed on local food)	Most farmers' markets (e.g. Airey Inlet, Lyttleton, Otago Farmers' markets)	Exeter Festival of South-West England	Taste of Tasmania	Tasting Australia (Adelaide)
Multiple/themed categories	Wakefield Food, Drink and Rhubarb Festival	Mendocino Crab and Wine Days Waipara Wine and Food Festival	Hokitika Wild Foods Festival	Marlborough Wine and Food Festival
Single categories of product	Whitstable Oyster Festival	Granite Belt Spring Wine Festival Niagara Icewine Festival	Gilroy Garlic Festival National Date Festival (Indio)	World champion chili cookoff (International Chili Society) World Championship Cheese Contest (Madison)
Single specific product/food type	Bluff Oyster Festival The Tualatin Crawfish Festival	Oregon Truffle Festival Elmira Maple Syrup Festival	Best in the West Nugget Rib Cook-off (Sparks) National Buffalo Wing Festival	Annual Zinfandel Festival (San Francisco)

values, maintaining relationships with customers, encouraging new consumers, educating consumers and promoting visitation (Hall and Mitchell, 2008) (see Exhibits 1.3 and 1.4). From the production side secondary functions include promoting improved production methods and quality of product, reducing the length of supply chains, and promoting sustainable agricultural development, particularly with respect to the development of farmers' markets.

Although there may be some commonalities with respect to visitor profiles (e.g. see the discussion in Chapter 13) with respect to farmers–markets–consumers, it is important to note

---

Exhibit 1.3 Wakefield Food, Drink and Rhubarb Festival

The area between Wakefield, Leeds and Morley, in the county of West Yorkshire, is commonly known as the Wakefield Rhubarb Triangle due to the rows of long, low, 'forcing' sheds in this area which produce the 'champagne of rhubarb' according to connoisseurs. Artificially brought on in pitch black, warm, moist conditions the rhubarb that is produced has pink/red stems, and tightly curled yellow leaves, unlike its green outdoor relative. The Wakefield growers produce about nine-tenths of the world's total forced Rhubarb crop. One grower, E. Oldroyd & Sons, in the village of Carlton, was established in 1934, and regularly supplies rhubarb to markets in London, Europe and further afield. The company makes the most of this rich asset and throughout the growing season, particularly during the festival, organize tours of the forcing sheds. The national rhubarb collection, home to 150 varieties of rhubarb, is located at The Harlow Carr Gardens in Harrogate, just North of Wakefield, which is an additional attraction for rhubarb lovers.

Wakefield hosts an annual rhubarb-oriented food festival and attracts food and rhubarb enthusiasts from around the UK and overseas. The festival started in 1999 and at first was just dedicated to the appreciation of Rhubarb. In 2007 the festival organizers decided to extend their offering and the festival now includes a city centre marquee hosting live cookery demonstrations, tasting sessions and a specialist food market. Many of the local restaurants, hotels and pubs are also involved in offering themed rhubarb menus for the duration of the festival and there are tours of Fernandes, the local micro-brewery, to sample their award winning ales, including one based on Rhubarb.

Source: Derived from Campaign For Real Ale:
http://www.camra.org.uk,
Visit Wakefield: http://www.wakefield.gov.uk/ and
Yorkshire Rhubarb: http://www.yorkshirerhubarb.co.uk.

Exhibit 1.4 BBC Good Food Shows

There are increasing linkages between food events and the media, especially specialist food media. One of the biggest food events within the UK is the BBC Good Food Show which is held in November at the National Exhibition Centre in Birmingham. This spectacular event is home to over 500 food producers as part of the Great British Food Festival and presents an impressive range of lectures, master-classes, cookery demonstrations and competitions. The Show has over 10 'theatres' including a 'Supertheatre' sponsored by supermarket chain Sainsbury's and 9 restaurants offering a range of cuisines. The show also includes a speciality food fair organized by Henrietta Green, who organizes a number of Food Lover's fairs throughout the UK, a stand which showcases Ludlow, one the best food festivals in the UK and the Ludlow Slow Food Convivium is also present.

A number of celebrity chefs are involved with the event. In 2007 there was a line up including Rick Stein, Gordon Ramsey, Ainsley Harriet, James Martin and Jamie Oliver. In addition a new activity, the Kids Kitchen Academy, was sponsored by Morrison's supermarket.

The BBC Good Food concept has been so successful in recent years that the show has now been 'rolled out' at several other locations around the UK. Similar shows now take place in London and Glasgow and in the Summer another event takes place in Birmingham. Details of these shows can be found on the main website.

Source: Derived from Good Food Show:
at http://www.bbcgoodfoodshow.com.

that food event attendees do not constitute a single homogeneous market, instead different events attract different audiences. For example, Table 1.2 provides a breakdown of different visitor profiles to wine events and festivals.

Critical factors that determine visitation to a food event include, from the production perspective (Taylor and Shanka, 2002; Hall et al., 2003b, c; Tasslopoulos and Haydam, 2006; Hall and Mitchell, 2008):

- location
- timing
- accessibility
- seasonality of produce
- event facilities, infrastructure, spaces and activities
- appropriate mix of vendors and activities

Table 1.2 Profile of visitors to selected wine events from around the world

Festival	Profile
Breedekloof Outdoor Festival, South Africa	Almost 36.7% of attendees were between 36 and 50 years, almost 32.2% were single, the majority were female (57.4%), and were mostly Afrikaans-speaking (78.1%). The results suggest that the overwhelming majority of the event attendees were domestic visitors primarily from Cape Town. The travelling party to the event consisted mostly of two people (25.9%) and the majority (68.7%) only visited the event for one day (Tasslopoulos and Haydam, 2006).
Rutherglen Winery Walkabout, Australia	31.2% of respondents were aged 18–30 with only a low number of older people (5% of respondents aged 61 and over attended the festival). 22.2% of respondents had family incomes lower than AUS$35,000 (Houghton, 2001).
Tastes of Rutherglen, Australia	In terms of age 31.6% of respondents were 31–40 and 29.8% 41–50. In comparison with the Rutherglen winery walkabout 14% of respondents to this event were aged 61 or over; 10.5% of respondents had family incomes lower than AUS$35,000 (Houghton, 2001).
Vancouver Playhouse International Wine Festival, Canada	19.3% of attendees were aged less than 30 and 4.3% were over 60. The average age of attendees was 39. Females made up 58% of the audience. The average monthly expenditure on wine was CAN$152 and 31.3% of attendees spend between CAN$51–100 on wine a month; 40.5% of attendees were single (Vancouver Playhouse International Wine Festival, 2007).
Wine Marlborough Festival, New Zealand	In 2003, 28.4% of respondents to a festival survey were aged 24 or below. The 2003 survey indicated a significant increase in festival goers in this age group over the previous year, while the 25–34 age group had not changed significantly. There had been a significant decline in numbers in the 40–59 age group. This group almost halved between 2002 and 2003, down from 43.5% to 23.1%; 54.7% of respondents came from outside the Marlborough region, including 10% from overseas; 45.2% of survey respondents were from the Marlborough region (Hall and Mitchell, 2005).
Winter Wine Fest, Australia	52% of visitors were female. 7% were aged between 18 and 24 years old, 42% between 25 and 44, 47% between 45 and 64 and only 4% were 65 years or over; 87% were working full or part-time. In terms of social groups the largest proportion visited with friends (48%), followed by couples (33%), families (15%) and only 4% attended by themselves. Nearly all visitation was domestic primarily from Melbourne (Weiler et al., 2004).

- event planning and programming
- promotion and marketing.

From the consumers' perspective important considerations are (Hall et al., 2003b, c; Brown and Getz, 2005; Çai et al., 2005; Hall, 2005; Hall and Mitchell, 2008):

- travel time in relation to the overall availability of free time of the potential visitor (time budget);
- economic budget of visitor and perceived value of event;
- accessibility;
- motivations, particularly social motivations;
- prior experience and positive recommendations via word of mouth;
- programming;
- perceptions of quality and value;
- the development of trust between consumers and producers is critical for return visitation and positive word of mouth.

These factors are dealt with in more detail in the various chapters in the book while the next chapter looks at some of the economic development and planning aspects in more detail.

Outline and summary

The chapters in the book are broadly divided into five sections. This and the following two chapters provides a broad introduction to food events, with Chapter 2 paying special emphasis to economic and planning issues, especially in relation to the development of local food systems. Chapter 3 by Rotherham picks up on the theme of the connection between food, landscape and events discussed in Chapter 2 and provides an historical account of feasts and events in relation to British regional landscape and culture.

Chapters 4–8 deal with a number of marketing and management issues in food events, with 9–12 examining wine- and beverage-related events. Chapters on branding (Kalkstein et al., Chapter 4), impacts and business-to-business network relations (Hede, Chapter 6), visitor behaviour (Yuan et al., Chapter 10) and visitor profiles (Houghton, Chapter 12) are interspersed with case studies and review chapters on apple and cider festivals (Sharples, Chapter 9), Scottish food events (Barrie, Chapter 5), beer festivals (Sharples and Lyons, Chapter 11), the food festival of the world-famous gastronomic destination of Ludlow in the UK (Sharples and Lyons, Chapter 7), and a study of two food and wine events in Tasmania within the context of the state's broader tourism strategies (Crispin and Reiser, Chapter 8).

Chapters 13–18 focus on farmers' markets as a particular type of food event that is growing in business and community importance. The section is introduced in Chapter 13 by a review of farmers' markets and some of the issues of definition, marketing and development that contextualize the rest of the farmers' market chapters which focus, in turn, on the different local, national and regional contexts in which farmers' markets are embedded. These include New Brunswick, Canada (Jolliffe, Chapter 14); Japan (Telfer and Hashimoto, Chapter 15); Airey Inlet Farmers' Market, Australia (Hede, Chapter 16); Otago Farmers' Market, New Zealand (Mitchell and Scott, Chapter 17) and markets in the UK (Eastham, Chapter 18).

The final two chapters aim to provide a guide to ongoing issues facing food events with Chapter 19 by Lyons suggesting research methods and approaches that can be utilized in food festival research, while the last chapter by Hall and Sharples (Chapter 20) outlines some of the issues faced by food events that will need to be addressed in order to maintain the current level of their development.

Food events have come to enjoy an extremely high public profile in developed countries in recent years. This is partly due to the growth of food as an important expression of contemporary lifestyle and consumption, especially with respect to the way in which it has come to be given a significant role in the media, including specialized food magazines and even television channels. However, it is also related to the increasing concerns that many people feel about where their food comes from with respect to its quality and the impacts of its production and consumption on the economic, social and physical environment. Travelling locally to food events may be one of the most sustainable forms of tourism that currently exist as not only is the environmental effects of consumption reduced, but also, and especially in the case of farmers' markets, production. It is to this sustainable dimension of food events that we will now turn to in the next chapter.

References

Barkin, C. and James, E. (1994). *The Holiday Handbook*. Clarion Books, New York.

Brown, G. and Getz, D. (2005). Linking wine preferences to the choice of wine tourism destinations. *Journal of Travel Research*, 43(3), 266–276.

Çela, A., Knowles-Lankford, J. and Lankford, S. (2007). Local food festivals in Northeast Iowa communities: A visitor and economic impact study. *Managing Leisure*, 12(2/3), 171–186.

Che, D., Veeck, A. and Veeck, G. (2005). Sustaining production and strengthening the agritourism product: Linkages among Michigan agritourism destinations. *Agriculture and Human Values*, 22, 225–234.

Chhabra, D., Sills, E. and Cubbage, F.W. (2003). The significance of festivals to rural economies: Estimating the economic impacts of Scottish Highland Games in North Carolina. *Journal of Travel Research*, 41, 421–427.

Cooper, C. and Hall, C.M. (2008). *Contemporary Tourism: An International Approach*. Elsevier Butterworth Heinemann, Oxford.

Dywer, L., Mellor, R., Mistilis, N. and Mules, T. (2000). A framework for assessing 'tangible' and 'intangible' impacts of festivals and conventions. *Festival Management*, 6, 175–189.

Falassi, A. (ed.) (1987). *Time Out of Time: Essays on the Festival*, University of New Mexico Press, Albuquerque.

Farmers' Market Federation of New York (2006). *The Value of Farmers' Markets to New York's Communities*. Farmers' Market Federation of New York, New York.

Griffin, M.R. and Frongillo, E.A. (2003). Experiences and perspectives of farmers from upstate New York farmers' markets. *Agriculture and Human Values*, 20, 189–203.

Hall, C.M. (1992). *Hallmark Tourist Events*. Belhaven Press, London.

Hall, C.M. (1996). Wine tourism in New Zealand. In Kearsley, G. (ed.) *Tourism Down Under II, Conference Proceedings*. Centre for Tourism, University of Otago, Dunedin, pp. 109–119.

Hall, C.M. (2005). *Tourism: Rethinking the Social Science of Mobility*. Pearson, Harlow.

Hall, C.M. and Mitchell, R. (2001). Wine and food tourism. In Douglas, N., Douglas, N. and Derrett, R. (eds.) *Special Interest Tourism: Context and Cases*. John Wiley & Sons, Australia, Brisbane, pp. 307–329.

Hall, C.M. and Mitchell, R. (2005). Wine Marlborough: A profile of visitors to New Zealand's oldest wine festival. *Journal of Hospitality and Tourism*, 3(1), 77–90.

Hall, C.M. and Mitchell, R.D. (2008). *Wine Marketing: A Practical Approach*. Butterworth-Heinemann, Oxford.

Hall, C.M. and Sharples, E. (2003). "The consumption of experiences or the experience of consumption?: An introduction to the tourism of taste", pp. 1–24 in *Food Tourism Around the World: Development, Management and Markets*, eds Hall, C.M., Sharples, E., Mitchell, R., Cambourne, B. and Macionis, N. Butterworth-Heinemann, Oxford.

Hall, C.M., Sharples, E., Cambourne, B. and Macionis, N. (eds.) (2000). *Wine Tourism Around the World: Development, Management and Markets*. Butterworth-Heinemann, Oxford.

Hall, C.M., Mitchell, R. and Sharples, E. (2003). Consuming places: The role of food, wine and tourism in regional development. In Hall, C.M., Sharples, E., Mitchell, R., Cambourne, B. and Macionis, N. (eds.) *Food Tourism Around the World: Development, Management and Markets*. Butterworth-Heinemann, Oxford, pp. 25–59.

Hall, C.M., Sharples, E., Mitchell, R., Cambourne, B. and Macionis, N. (eds.) (2003a). *Food Tourism Around the World: Development, Management and Markets*. Butterworth-Heinemann, Oxford.

Hall, C.M., Sharples, E. and Smith, A. (2003b). The experience of consumption or the consumption of experiences? Challenges and issues in food tourism. In Hall, C.M., Sharples, E., Mitchell, R., Cambourne, B. and Macionis, N. (eds.) *Food Tourism Around the World: Development, Management and Markets*. Butterworth-Heinemann, Oxford, pp. 314–336.

Hjalager, A.-M. and Corigliano, M.A. (2000). Food for tourists – Determinants of an image. *International Journal of Tourism Research*, 2(4), 281–293.

Houghton, M. (2001). The propensity of wine festivals to encourage subsequent winery visitation. *International Journal of Wine Marketing*, 13(2), 32–41.

Lankford, S. and Çela, A. (2005). *A Study of Place Based Food Tourism in Northeast Iowa Communities*. A Final Report prepared for the Leopold Center for Sustainable Agriculture.

Mitchell, R. and Hall, C.M. (2003). Consuming tourists: Food tourism consumer behaviour. In Hall, C.M., Sharples, E., Mitchell, R., Cambourne, B. and Macionis, N. (eds.) *Food Tourism Around the World: Development, Management and Markets*. Butterworth-Heinemann, Oxford, pp. 60–81.

Payne, T. (2002). *US Farmers Markets – 2000: A Study of Emerging Trends*. Agricultural Marketing Service, United States Department of Agriculture, Washington, DC.

Ritchie, J.R.B. (1984). Assessing the impact of hallmark events: Conceptual and research issues. *Journal of Travel Research*, 23(1), 2–11.

Tasslopoulos, D. and Haydam, N. (2006). A study of adventure tourism attendees at a wine tourism event: A qualitative and quantitative study of the Breedekloof Outdoor Festival, South Africa. In Carlsen, J. (ed.) *World Wine and Travel Summit and Exhibition Academic Stream Proceedings*, 13–17 November 2006, pp. 53–71.

Taylor, R. and Shanka, T. (2002). Attributes for staging successful wine festivals. *Event Management*, 7(3), 165–175.

Telfer, D.J. and Wall, G. (1996). Linkages between tourism and food production. *Annals of Tourism Research*, 23, 635–653.

Vancouver Playhouse International Wine Festival (2007). *Demographics*. Vancouver Playhouse International Wine Festival, Vancouver.

VeronaFiere Press Office (2007). *Wine Exhibition Closes Today. Vinitaly 2007: Business is Here. International Operators up by 15%*. VeronaFiere Press Office, Verona.

Weiler, B., Truong, M. and Griffiths, M. (2004). *Visitor Profiles and Motivations for Visiting an Australian Wine Festival*. Department of Management Working Paper Series 19/04. Melbourne: Department of Management, Monash University.

Food events and the local food system: Marketing, management and planning issues

C. Michael Hall and Liz Sharples

As noted in Chapter 1, food events are different. Their connection to a product which is not only part of everyday life, but also has particular cultural, economic and environmental significance, means that food events have to meet a different range of consumer and producer expectations than other events. Food events are obviously connected to the promotion of food products, but even here the dimension to place of production becomes an important element of branding and quality assurance. Although food events have long been a part of the distribution channel for food and agricultural products, in recent years there has been a significant emphasis placed on their potential to bypass the food retail and distribution channels that are dominated by supermarket chains. As Brown (2005, p. 1) observes:

Supermarkets now dominate food sales in developed countries and are rapidly expanding their global presence. At the same time, international mergers and acquisitions and aggressive pricing strategies have concentrated market power in the hands of a few major retailers.

The market power of retailers is considerable. The top 30 supermarket chains and food companies account for about one-third of global grocery sales and this market share is increasing rapidly as a result of urbanization and the rapid economic growth of two of the world's largest markets, China and India. Wal-Mart, the world's largest company, accounts for more than one-third of US food industry sales. In the UK the top five supermarkets account for 70 per cent or more of grocery sales which is double the share that existed at the end of the 1980s, while throughout Europe there is increasing consolidation in the retail sector (Brown, 2005; Hall and Mitchell, 2008). The 2005 Human Development Report reveals that these 30 supermarket chains are responsible for over one-third of global grocery sales (United Nations Development Programme, 2005, p. 142). Brown (2005) suggests that this proportion is likely to increase in future, with the market compressing to as little as 10 major firms, as the industry continues to consolidate. Despite notable exposure in food retailing literature (Retail World, 2007) outlets such as local grocers are declining in the face of increasing competition from the supermarket retailers (Clarke, 2000). Figure 2.1 indicates the estimated range of market share within four different retail grocery channels on a global basis.

Although estimates of the globalization of retail grocery channels and their dominance by supermarkets vary substantially,

Supermarkets and superstores	Specialist grocers and independents	Convenience outlets	Farmers' markets
60–80%	10–35%	5–20%	5%

Market share range

Figure 2.1
Estimated market share range of world retail grocery channels (*Source*: Friends of the Earth, 2003; Brown, 2005; Fearne et al., 2005; United Nations Development Programme, 2005)

it is nevertheless clear that they do dominate, and that the extent of their domination and their potential gatekeeper role in retail is also growing.

One of the more significant responses to the rise of the retail dominance of supermarket chains and their global supply and distribution channels has been the rise of ethical consumerism. Ethical consumerism is generally associated with the consumption of goods and services the production of which does not result in harm to people, animals or the environment (Rayner, 2002), and covers a range of manifestations of new sustainable consumption and production practices often focused on such concerns as fair trade, organic and free range produce, human rights, environmental sustainability and the production of consumer goods. Another element of ethical consumerism, is a strong stress on 'buying local' as a means not only of potentially reducing how far food has to travel and therefore impacts the environment, but also as a means of showing support for local producers. Events are very significant to such a strategy via the running of farmers' markets. However, localization as a strategic response to the globalization of food chains should not be regarded as a 'ring-fenced' approach to the world. For example, farmers' markets and the other production aspects of local food can be an attraction for tourists and therefore local food systems are tied into the global via the tourism system, while more traditional promotional and distribution networks maintain global linkages to consumers (Figure 2.2).

Both industry and public events can contribute to a region's tourism development by serving to attract visitors from outside of the destination. Industry events attract business visitors and contribute to the development of economic networks. Visitors to industry events and conferences also tend to have an extremely high per day spend. Yet, despite this, the tourism focus on food and wine events tends to be on public events, which are regarded as providing an opportunity for destinations to establish themselves as food tourism destinations,

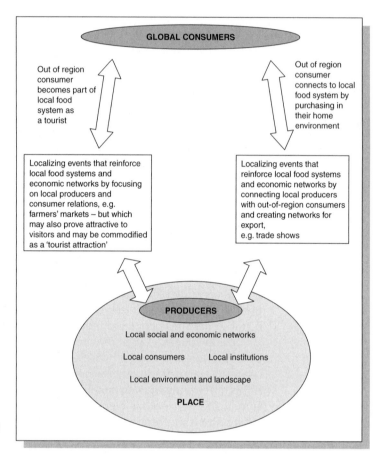

Figure 2.2

Place and producer response to globalization of food production

promote the regional brand and contribute to regional economic development (Brown et al., 2002). For example, in reflecting on the experience of the Breedekloof Outdoor Festival in South Africa, Tasslopoulos and Haydam (2006, p. 69) commented that, 'Wine events provide wine regions with an opportunity to promote the wine and build market identity and, therefore, result in the transition of traditional rural areas into modern service economies'. Nevertheless, it is becoming increasingly recognized that events need to be seen not just as an opportnity to increase visitor numbers or sell produce, but also to seek to build brands at various scales (i.e. region, producer) (Mowle and Merrilees, 2005), often by using the event to increase brand loyalty, and by creating long-term relationships with consumers. However, it is also important for food event organizers to consider the communities in which they are located and connected so as to ensure that an event's potential contribution in terms of community cohesiveness, economic benefits and social incentives are not outweighed by environmental and social costs (Gursoy et al., 2004).

Putting local food systems in place

The focus on place and the local can also be an important element in reinforcing the perception of the quality of produce from the region when being sold via more conventional means. Indeed, it is significant that even given the ethical trend in food retailing that the biggest sellers of ethical foods are supermarkets. With broad distribution networks, expansive retail presence and strong buying power, supermarket chains have become the primary retailers through which ethical products are sold (Corporate Watch, 2004; Fearne et al., 2005; Hughes et al., 2007). Therefore, food events, such as commercial fairs and trade expositions, can help promote local foods and products in order to enable their export out of the region. Indeed, even specialized artisan food and wines that are sold in specialized stores will usually utilize conventional food transport and distribution systems in order to reach the market, with some purchase of artisan foods by consumers also having been initiated as a result of consumers travelling as tourists (Hall and Mitchell, 2001, 2008; Hall et al., 2003).

A local food system refers to deliberate formed systems that are characterized by a close producer–consumer relationship within a designated place or local area. Local food systems support long-term connections; meet economic, social, health and environmental needs; link producers and markets via locally focused infrastructure; promote environmental health; and provide competitive advantage to local food businesses (Food System Economic Partnership, 2006; Buck et al., 2007). According to Anderson and Cook (2000, p. 237):

The major advantage of localizing food systems, underlying all other advantages, is that this process reworks power and knowledge relationships in food supply systems that have become distorted by increasing distance (physical, social, and metaphorical) between producers and consumers. ... [and] gives priority to local and environmental integrity before corporate profit-making.

Buck et al. (2007) argue that the potential benefits of such a system include:

- Bolstering the local economy as less money is diverted to corporations based outside of the region and local businesses satisfy unmet demands, or create new or more efficient systems for the production and movement of foods. 'These opportunities help to strengthen the local economy by growing the agricultural sector, creating jobs, providing more choices for consumers, contributing to the local tax base, and reinvesting local money exchanged for food back into local farms and businesses' (p.3).

- Producers and consumers are linked via efficient infrastructures, which can provide a competitive advantage for local farmers, processors, distributors, retailers and consumers alike, meaning that farmers receive a greater return for their produce as there are fewer intermediaries. 'By sharing the risks and rewards of food production, processing, distribution and retail with other local partners, farmers and businesses can explore opportunities to produce new varieties of foods or expand existing ventures to meet a local or regional need' (p.3).
- Positive effects on community development and revitalization with consumers receiving fresher, healthier food and the opportunity to develop a relationship with the farmers.
- Supporting the viability of small and medium-sized family farms and foster a sense of place, culture, history and ecology within a region as well as helping combat urban sprawl, obesity and hunger.
- Generating environmental benefits particularly as a result of decreased energy and fuel consumption.

Elements of such an approach are well illustrated by Farmers' Markets Ontario (FMO) (2007) on their web site:

Shopping at the Farmers' Market is a healthy decision not only for you, but for your community's economy as well. For every dollar spent at the market, another two dollars ripple through the provincial economy. In Ontario alone, sales at Farmers' Markets total almost $600 million, leading to an economic impact of an astounding $1.8 billion.

For every one person you see working at the market, another two are busy at work back on the farm. As many as 27,000 people in Ontario are directly involved in preparing and selling the products you find at the market.

Furthermore, Farmers' Markets are good for other businesses too. Studies show 60 to 70 percent of market-goers visit neighbouring businesses on their way to and from the market.

A concept closely related to the local food systems idea if that of the 'foodshed' which is associated to the bio-regionally oriented concept of the watershed (Kloppenburg et al., 1996;

Feagan and Krug, 2004). Direct marketing via farmers' markets and food festivals along with other forms of tourism are recognized as integral components of a foodshed. According to Feagan and Krug (2004) in order for a local foodshed to be established, several things need to happen:

- Producers and consumers must be brought closer together to shorten food chains and to build 'community' and foster sustainability.
- There must be public awareness of the nature of the 'costs' associated with the industrial food system so that local consumers and producers will rethink their food production and purchasing decisions.
- The means – mechanisms, places and opportunities – for meeting objectives must be made available.

Interestingly, the example used by Feagan and Krug (2004) of a foodshed was that of Niagara, which also shares the characteristics of successful local food systems identified by Buck et al. (2007): a major metropolitan area within close proximity to fertile farmland. Such a characteristic has also been identified as contributing to successful food tourism destinations (Hall et al., 2003) as well as farmers' markets. Indeed, no matter how 'alternative' a food system may be, it cannot ignore the importance of connecting producers with consumers, and the larger the market of consumers, the easier it is to be successful.

Farmers' markets and other community food events and festivals clearly serve an important role in local food systems. Lyson (2004) also described this as 'civic agriculture', a concept that emphasizes community economic development balanced against the social and environmental objectives of a community. With respect to farmers' markets, Lyson comments that, 'as social institutions and social organizations, farmers' markets can be important components of civic agriculture. They embody what is unique and special about local communities and help to differentiate one community from another' (2004, p. 93).

Farmers' markets and other community based food events are therefore a very significant means to encourage entrepreneurship and business incubation within local food systems and therefore provide a basis for their organizational sustainability. Stalls at farmers' markets may often represent a form of micro-entrepreneurship. In Hilchey et al.'s (1995) study of farmers' markets in the US north-east, they noted that most vendors either did not have a business before they started selling at a farmers' market, nor did they start on a small scale at their residence. Many vendors do not have the capital to open a retail outlet, or they perceived that they have few other marketing options available. They also found that farmers' markets can help vendors hone their skills in areas such as business management, marketing, communication, leadership and entrepreneurship by helping the vendor, improve their understanding of consumer needs, self-confidence in merchandising, co-operating with others, advertising and customer relations, pricing and competing effectively, while also having positive effects on their families. Therefore, farmers' markets can have an extremely important incubation function and provide a rich entrepreneurial environment for starting new businesses or products, or changing the direction of existing businesses (Hilchey et al., 1995). Some similar findings have also been reported in studies of farmers' markets in Australia (Coster and Kennon, 2005) and New Zealand (Guthrie et al., 2006). Farmers' markets can therefore help entrepreneurs overcome start-up barriers by:

Facilitating product development and diversification: Farmers' markets provide a service to vendors in providing information on the likes and dislikes of consumers.
Creating opportunities to add value to products: Value is added to products through processing and/or through packaging, branding and labelling.
Enhancing the customer base: Markets provide vendors an opportunity to expand the size and diversity of their customer base because of a stable market for their products and increased awareness of their business.
Expanding sales and income: Markets provide vendors opportunities to earn extra income above and beyond that available through normal distribution channels and can help to enhance sales at other outlets.

Marketing is a critical element in the hosting and management of successful food events. To modify Kotler and Levy's (1969) definition of marketing in food event terms: marketing is that function of food event management that can keep in touch with the event's participants and consumers (including visitors), read their needs and motivations, develop products that meet these needs and build a communication programme which expresses the event's and associated product's purpose and objectives. Certainly, selling and influencing will be large components of food event marketing; but, properly seen, selling follows rather than precedes the event management's desire to create experiences (products) which satisfy its consumers. Food events, such as farmers' markets, work within local food systems because they are able to connect with the needs of consumers and other relevant stakeholders and actors within the system. As such, they may therefore have a range of benefits beyond that of immediate business and economic returns, although such returns may be substantial. For example, in the UK the National Farmers' Retail and Markets Association (FARMA, 2006) estimate that farmers' markets are worth £220 million annually and estimate that some 10,000 farmers and producers participate annually in farmers' markets. Results of FARMA supported research indicated that a group of five farmers' markets in Gloucestershire/Wiltshire (112 market days) generated an estimated £2.8 million a year in turnover while a group of eight monthly farmers' markets in Surrey (96 market days in total) generated an estimated £2.6 million a year (FARMA, 2006). The role of FARMA in encouraging farmers' markets as an 'alternative' distribution and retail channel for farmers and producers is very clear given that their stated mandate is to champion local food 'through helping to reconnect rural and urban communities, offering business support to emerging enterprises, and encouraging the revival of fresh and distinctive locally produced foods' (FARMA, 2006, p.2). Table 2.1 lists some of the elements of a successful farmers' market as reported by the FMO.

Table 2.1   Characteristics of a community-driven, producer-based farmers' market

- Home grown produce, home made crafts and value-added products, where the vendors are primary producers (including preserves, baked goods, meat, fish, dairy products, etc.).
- There is freshness, abundance, quality.
- Local, from the community, a cottage industry.
- Family oriented and a fun place.
- The producer is the vendor; proud of product; fully knowledgeable.
- The Market is dynamic, friendly, reflects community personality.
- Open-air, seasonal, during the local growing season, usually once or twice a week.
- Championed and supported and/or administered by a local community group.
- Provides opportunity for exchange of information and learning, i.e. building community alliances, good health, nutrition, use of products.
- Product presentation and service training are regularly provided for vendors.
- There is policy guidance for leaders and managers to assist them in working with various community groups in organizing significant events, festivals and other fund-raising efforts.

Source: Derived from Farmers Market Ontario (undated); also see Colihan and Chorney (2004).

Nevertheless, farmers' markets may not always succeed or be appropriate to every producer or community's circumstances (Stephenson et al., 2006). Hilchey et al. (1995) point out that:

- Farmers' markets are not for everyone.
- Farmers' markets alone will not revitalize a central business district.
- Vendors differ in their commitment to entrepreneurship.
- Vendors differ in their visions for their farmers' markets.
- Many vendors want to keep things simple and with little formal organization and outside help.
- Although some market and enterprise successes are dramatic, most are small and incremental.
- Not all promising businesses will be successful and flourish.
- Many vendors and markets are not conceptually aware of, or do not appreciate, the farmers' market 'incubation function'.

Stephenson et al. (2006) note that research suggests that a little over 80% of US farmers' markets may be regarded as self-sustaining or self-supporting. Yet that still leaves a significant number of markets that do not survive. Their study of farmers' markets that had closed, suggested seven factors associated with failure, several of which mirror-wider research on business survivability (Hall and Williams, 2008):

1. Small size.
2. Need for farm products.
3. Collection of insufficient administrative revenue.
4. Manager was either a volunteer or was being paid a low salary.
5. High manager turnover.
6. Years of manager experience and age of market.
7. Effort thresholds for volunteer managers (Stephenson et al., 2006).

A successful food event marketing plan focuses on the development of a marketing process which revolves around activities and decisions in three main areas (Hall and Mitchell, 2008):

- Market segmentation and targeting.
- Market entry strategy, including time and location of event.
- Marketing mix variables.

Market segmentation

No food event can be all things to all people. Thilmany's (2005) guide for planning and developing a farmers' market suggests, 'learn about your customers using indicators such as income, population, success of markets in similar communities and assessing the competition to make sure there are not already too many markets operating in your community' (p. 2). It is therefore essential that any business, community, destination or organization that is planning an event should incorporate an understanding of consumer behaviour into their marketing and promotional strategies. Most importantly, food events should ideally be held as part of a broader marketing strategy with respect to business, community and/or product development rather than being held for their own sake. An attractive market for a food event will be one in which:

- The market segment is of sufficient size to make the event viable.
- The market segment has the potential for growth or, depending on the objectives of keeping to a sustainable size (this is particularly important for events primarily organized by volunteers so as to avoid the potential for volunteer burn-out).
- The market segment is not 'taken' or 'owned' by existing events, so that existing event initiatives will be 'cannibalized'.
- The market segment has a relatively unsatisfied interest, motivation or need that the food event can satisfy (Hall and Mitchell, 2008).

Exhibit 2.1   Wallington Food and Craft Festival

This 2-day food fair is held each October in the grounds of Wallington, one of the National Trust's finest properties in the North-East of England. This eighteenth century Palladian Mansion is set within a 13,000 acre site, which includes several tenant farms producing high-quality beef and lamb (National Trust, 2007a).

The border county of Northumberland, in which Wallington estate lies, is a land of contrasts. A stretch of wild, and mostly undiscovered, coastline rises inland to an area of high rugged moorland, and in the south of the county there is a softer area of rolling hills and pasture land. This varied topography has resulted in the development of a healthy farming and fishing community supplying some of the finest produce in the country. Northumberland is especially well known as a producer of fine salmon, kippers, meat and game.

(Continued)

The National Trust is a champion of local and seasonal food within the UK. Local food is listed as one of four key campaigns at present and information about their food and farming policies can be seen on their web site (National Trust, 2007b). A recent document produced for the North-East region of the National Trust states:

'The National Trust would like to help 'reconnect' the food chain between producers and consumers. Our aim is to show consumers the benefits of local and seasonal food and share the joy it is to prepare and eat food that comes from a known source, and is healthy and tasty. At the same time, we want to see farmers rewarded for producing quality food whilst protecting and enhancing the countryside' (Blaauboer, 2007a).

The introduction of Wallington Farm Shop, which was purpose built and opened in 2002, has been a positive move to achieving these aims. Much of the meat produced on the estate is distributed directly through the shop or visitor restaurant, and the use of the 'Freedom Food' label is a sure way of reassuring customers about the high standards of farming practice that is being maintained.

The unit also sells a range of seasonal vegetables, cheese, jams, chutneys, cakes and baked goods, all grown or produced in the locality.

The farm shop project also sits well with the National Trust's effort to reduce their carbon footprint effect of food miles as part of their Carbon Footprint Project (Blaauboer, 2007b).

The development to hold a food festival was a logical next step for Wallington and in its first year, in 2006, the event attracted nearly 13,000 visitors. This figure was maintained in 2007, but interestingly the number of 'non-members' of the National Trust who attended this year rose from 2,000 to 5,000. This was significant for the organization as its message about local food reached out to a wider audience (Nicoll, 2007).

The event is a showcase for nearly 50 local food producers from the county of Northumberland and the neighbouring county of Cumbria, in the Lake District. The event also features stands selling local arts and crafts such as beeswax candles, jewellery and ceramics.

Jointly planned as a partnership between the National Trust and two regional food groups, Northumbria Larder (2007) and Made in Cumbria (2007) and supported by DEFRA, this event fits well with the National Trust's local food strategy. As well as enjoying cookery demonstrations from several local food 'celebrities', the festival includes educational activities for both adults and children. This year cookery demonstrators included Terry Miller, winner of the ITV television show, Hell's Kitchen and Nick Martin, a champion of local food from Cumbria.

Market entry strategy

Each new food event also needs to develop a market entry strategy. Although many food and wine events are constrained in terms of their location, especially community events that must, by definition, be based within the community, the timing of when an event is held will be crucial to its success in attracting visitors and attendees. The objectives which underlie an event are again crucial to decisions regarding the timing of holding an event. Where there is some flexibility in hosting an event, organizers should consider (a) what other events and competing attractions or activities the food event will be competing with and (b) especially in the case of events that are eternally oriented with respect to visitation, given the seasonality of visitation in a destination and of agricultural production, can the event be utilized to boost visitor arrivals in shoulder-season and off-peak periods or 'down-times' in growing produce? Stephenson et al. (2006) in their analysis of why farmers' markets fail stress the importance of planning new markets carefully in order to ensure success – a recommendation that clearly applies to food events in general:

Market organizers should spend considerable time deciding whether and how to open a new market. Better planning and promotion before a new market is opened may help with some of the issues that arise during the first year of operation. An important part of the planning process is setting a goal for market size in general or a goal by year, so that cash flow can match the scale of the market and appropriate management tools can be provided. Planning for size is the first step in creating a viable organization that will endure challenges and conflicts that occur with growth (Stephenson et al., 2006, p.19).

The marketing mix

The design of an appropriate marketing strategy for an event consists of analysing market opportunities, identifying and targeting market segments, and developing an appropriate market mix for each segment. Key factors are identified below (Colihan and Chorney, 2004; Hall and Mitchell, 2008).

Product/service characteristics

Food and wine event management must understand the difference between the generic needs the event is serving and the specific products or services it is offering. In order to meet the demands of the marketplace, it is essential that organizers focus the food event product/s in light of the needs of specific market segments. Farmers' markets also have to manage a complex relationship between vendors and consumers that is different than most conventional retail outlets. A viable farmers' market must have enough farmer vendors to attract customers, and it must have enough customers to be attractive to farmer vendors and producers (Stephenson et al., 2006). Burns and Johnson (1996, p. 12) describe this situation:

Farmers' markets, unlike retail stores, operate both on the supply side, with the farmers, and on the demand side, with the consumers. However, the overall retail marketing dynamic is operative. Consumers wish to have certain preconceptions met when selecting a retail site. If they are not met, the consumers will stop coming. Farmers will go to markets where they are guaranteed selling space and have exposure to enough customers to allow them to sell the majority of their product in an allotted time. When farmer ... and customer expectations are not met, both farmers and customers will look for alternative markets.

Promotional channels and messages

Promotional programmes for even the most modest local farmers' market or food and wine festival require exactly the same kind of organization, planning, allocation of responsibilities and attention to detail that larger more commercially oriented events require. In promoting events to the market various communication methods are used, including advertising, personal selling, sales promotion and publicity. Promotional methods should be selected on the basis of their capacity to achieve the objectives of the event with respect to target audience and their relative cost.

Price

Although many food events are 'free' in terms of entry costs to participants and visitors, particularly community events, the issues of price are significant at all levels of event management and marketing. Prices may cover costs, maximize profits, subsidize all participants or certain market segments, encourage competition or result in unanticipated consumer reaction. Prices should be set according to a wide range of factors including past history, general economic conditions, ability to pay, revenue potential, costs, level of sponsorship and the competition. Pricing may even be used as a mechanism to appeal to particular markets. Affordability, for example, is of substantial importance in appealing to lower-income groups who may be the target of some urban farmers' markets. Fisher (1999) provided some general recommendations concerning the development and operation of farmers' markets in low-income areas.

Fisher noted that while low-income consumers face many of the same challenges as middle-income consumers concerning a diet based on healthful and nutritious foods, there are also many unique barriers. For example, low-income consumers may be more price-sensitive or have food access issues such as no transportation or grocery store in their neighbourhood. Fisher (1999) outlined five specific guidelines for successful low-income market operations including:

1. Low-income markets may need to be subsidized.
2. Community organizing is an essential component of any successful market in a low-income community.
3. Low-income markets should tailor their product mix to focus on basic foods at affordable prices.
4. Farmers should consider hiring sales staff from the neighbourhood.
5. Transportation issues are a significant barrier for market operation.

Place and methods of distribution

Despite the 'fixed' nature of the majority of food events in the sense that they occur at a specific location, distribution issues are also of significance to organizers. As noted above, the time and place in which food events are held will be a major factor in determining the event's success as well as having potential implications for branding and identity. According to Thilmany (2005, p. 3):

The market should be easy to find, and centrally located, with adequate parking for farmers/vendors and customers. You should realize that most vendors want to drive into their stall to forego the unloading/loading time they would spend setting up a stand-alone display. Consider partnering with a business or area of town that is trying to redevelop or redefine itself as a pedestrian friendly area that is a social hub of the community … they often will help establish markets.

Time and place are actually questions about the most appropriate manner in which to 'distribute' the event product to its current and potential market. As markets increase in size,

they draw both vendors and customers from a larger geographical area. As Burns and Johnson (1996, p.16) observed,
'it appears that as the size of the market increases, the market
becomes more attractive to farmers from a wider geographical
area and the retail (customer) trading area also increases. This
clearly has implications for smaller markets. 'As larger markets
draw farmers from a larger area, this process may also draw
farmers away from markets they perceive as less profitable'
(Stephenson et al., 2006). Furthermore, issues of distribution
will be tied up in the promotion of events. For instance, given
a limited budget how can event organizers best distribute promotional materials to the market that they have identified?

Packaging and programming

Packaging is the combination of related and complimentary
services in a single-price offering. For larger food and wine festivals packages may consist of a selection of sub-events being
sold together or the event plus transportation. Programming
is the variation of service or product in order to increase customer spending and/or satisfaction, or to give extra appeal to
an event or package. For example, many wine festivals have a
programme of different activities and tasting which are timed
to follow and interrelate with each other over the various days
on which the festival is held (Hall and Mitchell, 2008). Even
many farmers' markets also include other elements than just
stalls selling produce, such as music and entertainment or
face painting for children (see Chapter 13). The specific mix of
activities which are developed with the overall event framework may have the capacity to extend the interest of certain
markets and hence, potentially, increase their level of satisfaction. Programming should consider such factors as the event
venue and location, inclement weather options if part of the
event is to be staged outside, which is especially important in
the case of outdoor farmers' markets, and the needs of different target markets, and their relative availability to attend (e.g.
if a farmers' market is appealing to a domestic market and is
held during the week, some potential target markets may not
be able to attend during the day because of work commitments), and balance within the choice of activities.

Partnership

Collaboration is a very important part of food and wine event
marketing management, in community terms with a wide range
of institutions and stakeholders; and in commercial terms with

respect to bringing together the various sectors of the food sector as well as the needs of public and/or private sponsors. In their review of farmers' markets fail, Stephenson et al. (2006) noted the importance of ensuring that some smaller markets and those at the start-up phase had community financial support, noting that 'farmers' markets are an important part of a local economy and enhance the quality of community life. There is justification for government and economic development sector support.

Sponsorship and support may come in many forms: financial assistance, facilities, provision of event infrastructure or space, management skills, labour and, of course, donations of produce. Sponsors see events as a means of raising profile, promoting particular products through enhanced profile and image, obtaining lower costs per impression than those achieved by advertising, improve sales, and in being seen as good corporate citizens. Nevertheless, from the perspective of food event organization and the host community it is essential that the potential sponsor be appropriate to the objectives, needs and image of the event.

In many jurisdictions, government agencies and/or local government are significant sponsors of farmers' markets as well as other food events such as festivals. A number of different areas have been identified in the literature (e.g. Hilchey et al., 1995; Colihan and Chorney, 2004; Thilmany, 2005) where government agencies could provide support, especially with respect to farmers markets where particular planning and health regulations may need to be addressed (see also Chapter 13) (Table 2.2). Indeed, it is significant to note that Stephenson et al. (2006) concluded their report on why farmer's markets fail by noting:

Access to financial and other resources is a national policy-related issue with significant impacts on farmers' markets, particularly small markets. Small markets are expected to be self-sustaining, while other publicly delivered services do not have a similar expectation. Public funds support services that enhance the global trade of food products, but a similar level of support is not made available to support local agricultural markets. This is a political decision (Stephenson et al., 2006, p.20).

However, collaboration and the development of strong positive networks are not always easy and significant barriers may exist including:

- Absence of a champion or network leader(s).
- Physical distance between producers who may be potentially interested in working in a network thereby reducing communication.

Table 2.2 Areas of potential support and assistance for farmers' markets by government agencies

Area	Forms of potential support and assistance
Finance	• Raising funds for facilities and promotion. • Providing appropriate and adequate liability insurance coverage. • Establishing a revolving loan fund for vendors that can provide growers with seasonal start-up funds, or that can help a food processor by needed equipment. The fund could be capitalized with support from larger businesses, local financial institutions and the vendors themselves.
Education and training	• Linking educational and training opportunities in marketing, merchandising, market gardening, book-keeping, food processing, state and local regulations, personnel management, and labor regulations. Many educational agencies can provide training support for farmers' markets. • Training and professional development of market managers so they can further help the vendors as well as improve promotion and marketing. • Identifying possible clients for more intensive support. • Preparing manuals for new vendors.
Facilities/organizational development	• Helping to secure a permanent farmers' market location, or, if desired, a year-round facility. Dealing with planning and regulatory issues. • Helping to establish a certified inspected food processing centre where necessary for farmers' market vendors. • Helping to establish producer cooperatives as separate business entities that sell product surpluses wholesale to local restaurants, grocery stores and institutions.
Regulatory Assistance	• Helping market managers and vendors stay abreast of legislation affecting them. • Working with local code enforcement, zoning, and planning agencies to ensure a safe and prosperous market.
Public Relations and Networking	• Facilitating open and ongoing dialogues with local businesses to alleviate concerns about traffic congestion, parking problems, and competition. • Promoting inter-agency and governmental cooperation.

Source: Derived from Hilchey et al. (1995); Abel et al. (1999); Colihan and Chorney (2004); Thilmany (2005); Stephenson et al. (2006).

- Lack of a strong social network or sufficient social capital to underpin the business network.
- Insufficient meetings between stakeholders.

The further development of social capital through the creation of networks is extremely important in terms of its capacity to reduce the level of uncertainty for entrepreneurs in the creation of new businesses. Network-based relationships can provide entrepreneurs with critical information, knowledge and resources. Social and intellectual capital, including access to prior experience, can therefore be used to maximize the scarce capital available to some small food and wine businesses and associated events.

The long-term benefits of network relationships remain an interesting question for small wine and food tourism businesses. Venkataraman and Van de Ven (1998) argue that it only makes sense to leverage social capital in the early stages of a new venture. According to their research, as ventures progress businesses base their decisions on economic criteria, and social capital has less impact. Ironically, this means that the very network relationships that help to reduce risk and uncertainty in small business start-ups fade in importance when uncertainty becomes less. Such an interpretation may mean that the importance of social ties may therefore be a function of the level of uncertainty facing a small business entrepreneur. Yet, the application of this to the food and wine tourism sphere may be problematic, given the importance of regional brands as a means not only of destination promotion, but also of place and product differentiation (Hall, 2004).

Arguably, once the geographical designation is established and accepted in the market (e.g. appellations such as Champagne, Burgundy or Napa Valley), it then becomes extremely difficult for ventures to withdraw from networks which support the place–brand as it would potentially mean the loss of significant intangible capital and a direct economic resource. This observation may have substantial implications for the longevity and success of place and brand-oriented clusters and networks. Once place–brands have established their presence in the market, they not only contribute to the success of collective and individual businesses, but they also contribute to the development of further social capital because they become integral to the identity of place and the firms and individuals within it (Figure 2.3). This iterative and recursive process does not mean that such collaborative partnerships and networks as embodied in local food systems have an infinite lifespan, nor does it mean that wine and food regions and food systems

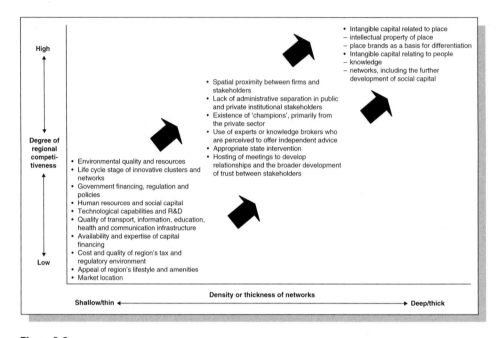

Figure 2.3
Ideal pathway for the increasing connectedness and competitiveness of local food networks and systems (after Hall, 2004)

automatically shift in building-block fashion and then form a dense network set of social, economic and intangible capital which comes to be deeply embedded in the sense of place and cultural capital. However, the particular congruence of intangible capital to be found within the food, wine and tourism industries and its maintenance through events, such as farmers' markets and food festivals, does potentially lead to longer business life cycles and the associated longer-term maintenance of social networks and capital (Hall, 2004).

Conclusions

This chapter has discussed event market and management within the context of local food systems or foodsheds. However, it has stressed that such systems do not just develop automatically, as an appropriate match, still has to be found between products and consumers, nor do they imply isolation from the broader marketplace. In fact, appropriate localization may well be an appropriate strategy with which to contend with some of the undesirable effects of globalization on place and on food systems in particular. Globalization is therefore a two-edged sword and can be recognized as potentially offering benefits for producers as well as the likelihood of increased competition.

The chapter has also highlighted, how local food systems and the food events within them still require good planning, marketing and management in order for them to thrive. Although often described as part of 'alternative' (e.g. Food System Economic Partnership, 2006) food systems, the business and organizational requirements of members of such systems are the same as those of any other system. For example, farmers' markets serve pivotal roles for small farmers and local food systems. However, 'the success of each is closely tied to the other. Knowledge of market failure and how it occurs is an important step in improving the viability of farmers' markets and therefore, maintaining and expanding a marketing channel for small farmers, and enhancing community food systems' (Stephenson et al., 2006, p. 2). This chapter has provided some initial insights into some of the ways that such market issues may be addressed and the need for clear planning strategies. Most important of which is to regard markets and other events as part of the overall strategy of a business or a community, rather than seeing them as ends in their own right.

References

Abel, J., Thomson, J. and Maretzki, A. (1999). Extension's role with farmers' markets: Working with farmers, consumers, and communities'. *Journal of Extension*, 37(5). http://joe.org/joe/1999october/a4.html

Anderson, M.D. and Cook, J.T. (2000). Does food security require local food systems?. In Harris, J.M. (ed.) *Rethinking Sustainability: Power, Knowledge and Institutions*. University of Michigan Press, Ann Arbor.

Blaauboer (2007a). Have a bite! Policy document produced to promote local food in the Yorkshire and North East region, National Trust.

Blaauboer (2007b). Personal discussion with Marianne Blaauboer, Policy Manager for Yorkshire and the North East, National Trust.

Brown, M.D., Var, T. and Lee, S. (2002). Messina Hof Wine and Jazz Festival: An economic impact analysis. *Tourism Economics*, 8(3), 273–279.

Brown, O. (2005). *Supermarket Buying Power, Global Commodity Chains and Smallholder Farmers in the Developing World*. United Nations, New York.

Buck, K., Kaminski, L.E., Stockmann, D.P. and Vail, A.J. (2007). *Investigating Opportunities to Strengthen the Local Food System in Southeastern Michigan, Executive Summary*. University of Michigan, School of Natural Resources and Environment.

Burns, A.F. and Johnson, D.N. (1996). *Farmers' Market Survey Report*. US Department of Agriculture, Agriculture Marketing Service, Transportation and Marketing Division, Wholesale and Alternative Markets Program, Washington, DC.

Clarke, I. (2000). Retail power, competition and local consumer choice in the UK grocery sector. *European Journal of Marketing*, 34(8), 975–1002.

Colihan, M.A. and Chorney, R.T. (2004). *Sharing the Harvest: How to Build Farmers' Markets and How Farmers' Markets Build Community!* Farmers' Markets Ontario, Brighton.

Coster, M. and Kennon, N. (2005). *'New Generation' Farmers' Markets in Rural Communities*. Rural Industries Research and Development Corporation, Barton.

Farmers' Markets Ontario (2007). About us, http://www.farmersmarketsontario.com/AboutUs.cfm

Farmers Market Ontario (undated). *Characteristics of a Community-Driven, Producer-Based Farmers' Market. "The Model Farmers' Market"* (poster). Farmers' Market Ontario, Brighton.

Feagan, R. Krug, K. (2004). Towards a sustainable Niagara foodshed: Learning from experience. In *Leading Edge 2004. The Working Biosphere*, March 3–5, Niagara Escarpment Commission.

Fearne, A., Duffy, R. and Hornibrook, S. (2005). Justice in UK supermarket buyer-supplier relationships: An empirical analysis. *International Journal of Retail and Distribution Management*, 33(8), 570–582.

Fisher, A. (1999). *Hot Peppers and Parking Lot Peaches: Evaluating Farmers' Markets in Low Income Communities*. Community Food Coalition, Venice, CA.

Food System Economic Partnership (2006). *Alternative Regional Food System Models: Successes and Lessons Learned: A Preliminary Literature Review*. Food System Economic Partnership, Michigan.

Friends of the Earth (2003). *Supermarkets or Corporate Bullies?* Friends of the Earth, London.

Gursoy, D., Kim, K.M. and Uysal, M. (2004). Perceived impacts of festivals and special events by organizers: An extension and validation. *Tourism Management*, 25(2), 171–181.

Guthrie, J., Guthrie, A., Lawson, R. and Cameron, A. (2006). Farmers' markets: The small business counter-revolution in food production and retailing. *British Food Journal*, 108(7), 560–573.

Hall, C.M. (2004). Small firms and wine and food tourism in New Zealand: Issues of, clusters and lifestyles collaboration. In Thomas, R. (ed.) *Small Firms in Tourism: International Perspective*. Elsevier, Oxford, pp. 167–181.

Hall, C.M. and Mitchell, R. (2001). Wine and food tourism. In Douglas, N., Douglas, N. and Derrett, R. (eds.) *Special Interest Tourism: Context and Cases*. John Wiley & Sons, Brisbane, Australia, pp. 307–329.

Hall, C.M. and Mitchell, R. (2008). *Wine Marketing: A Practical Approach*. Butterworth-Heinemann, Oxford.

Hall, C.M., Mitchell, R. and Sharples, E. (2003). Consuming places: The role of food, wine and tourism in regional development. In Hall, C.M., Sharples, E., Mitchell, R., Cambourne, B. and Macionis, N. (eds.) *Food Tourism Around the World: Development, Management and Markets*. Butterworth-Heinemann, Oxford, pp. 25–59.

Hall, C.M. and Williams, A. (2008). *Innovation and Tourism*. Routledge, London.

Hilchey, D., Lyson, T. and Gillespie, G. (1995). *Farmers' Markets and Rural Economic Development: Entrepreneurship, Small Business Creation and Job Creation in the Rural Northeast*. Farming Alternatives Program, Cornell University, Ithaca, NY.

Hughes, A., Buttle, M. and Wrigley, N. (2007). Organisational geographies of corporate responsibility: A UK–US comparison of retailers' ethical trading initiatives. *Journal of Economic Geography*, 7, 491–513.

Kloppenburg, J., Hendrickson, J. and Stevenson, G. (1996). Coming into the foodshed. *Agriculture and Human Values*, 13, 23–32.

Kotler, P. and Levy, S.J. (1969). Broadening the concept of marketing. *Journal of Marketing*, 33, 10–15.

Lyson, T.A. (2004). *Civic Agriculture: Reconnecting Farm, Food, and Community*. Tufts University Press, Medford, MA.

Made in Cumbria (2007) at http://madeincumbria.co.uk

Mowle, J. and Merrilees, B. (2005). A functional and symbolic perspective to branding Australian SME wineries. *Journal of Product and Brand Management*, 14(4), 220–227.

National Farmers' Retail and Markets Association (FARMA) (2006). Sector briefing: farmers markets in the UK; nine years and counting, Southampton (also downloadable from http://www.farma.org.uk/Docs/1/%20Sector/%20briefing/%20on/%20farmers'%20markets%20-%20.June06.%2006.pdf)

National Trust (2007a) at http://www.nationaltrust.org.uk/main/w-vh/w-visits/w-findaplace/w-wallington

National Trust (2007b) at http://www.nationaltrust.org.uk/main/w-cw/w-countryside_environment/w-food_farming.htm

Northumbria Larder (2007) at http://northumbria-larder.co.uk

Nicoll, P. (2007). *Personal discussion with Paul Nicholl.* Property Manager, Wallington.

Rayner, M. (2002). Product, price or principle? *Ethical Consumer,* 76, 32–34.

Retail World (2007). Consumers search for the 'fresh factor'. *Retail World Magazine,* 60(April 16–27), 38–39.

Stephenson, G., Lev, L. and Brewer, L. (2006). *When Things Don't Work: Some Insights into Why Farmers' Markets Close.* Special Report 1073. Oregon State University Extension Service.

Tasslopoulos, D. and Haydam, N. (2006). A study of adventure tourism attendees at a wine tourism event: A qualitative and quantitative study of the Breedekloof Outdoor Festival, South Africa. In Carlsen, J. (ed.) *World Wine and Travel Summit and Exhibition Academic Stream Proceedings,* 13–17 November 2006, pp. 53–71.

Thilmany, D. (2005). *Planning and Developing a Farmers Market: Marketing, Organizational and Regulatory Issues to Consider.* Agribusiness marketing report. Department of Agricultural and Resource Economics, Cooperative Extension, Colorado State University, Fort Collins.

United Nations Development Programme (2005). *International Cooperation at a Crossroads: Aid, Trade and Security in an Unequal World.* United Nations, New York.

Venkataraman, S. and Van de Ven, A.H. (1998). 'Hostile Environmental Jolts, Transaction set, and New Business', *Journal of Business Venturing,* 13, pp. 231–255.

CHAPTER 3

From haggis to high table: A selective history of festival and feast as mirrors of British landscape and culture

Ian D. Rotherham

Food, festival and feast emerge from communities and their landscapes. Be they ancient traditions or recent inventions? they resonate with culture and reflect environment. Festivals tend to emerge from local character, and often succeed in celebrating local foods, drinks and customs. All these will generally have origins in landscape and its history, and recent interest in promoting festivals and events, is often with a clear intent to support local economies. Festivals and events may be local cultural celebrations and even a re-birth of community awareness of itself, or they may be continuation of ancient traditions. In some cases they mix food, drink, crafts, arts and music, perhaps with distinctive or customary sports. In many cases, such as for example the *Highland Games* in Scotland, the history may be more myth than truth, and others such as the *Maldon Mud Race* (in Essex), or the many regional food festivals across Britain, they are recent inventions. Other events such as annual cheese rolling, or a *Burns Night Supper*, are steeped in history. As a celebration and as a spectacle, this needn't matter. So festivals and events vary in authenticity, scale, and they also range in size and frequency. Many are annual, others may be one-off happenings. Some occur in one location, other may occur anywhere and everywhere, such as the increasingly popular *St George's Day Dinners*.

The nature of the celebration or happening and the particular food, wine or other drinks consumed, reflect location and history. So in Somerset, we would expect a festival to have cider and perhaps local cheeses, in an upland region there might be goats' cheese and roast lamb, and in the highlands of Scotland there might be haggis, oatcakes and whisky. Furthermore, the style of cooking or preparation of food and drink also reflected landscape, climate and topography. So in poor, upland areas or in fenlands, foods were strong on oats, and often pot boiled over a turf fire. In well-wooded landscapes, roasts over a fire of wood faggots or wood charcoal would be the norm. These constrains have mostly gone from day-to-day lives in these regions, but they are carried on in major festivals and foods.

Also reflecting the landscape and its people were the annual cycles and seasonal highs and lows. It was these that generated many of the original festivals and events. So great feasts represented a key-time of year, and the food and drink consumed might be either that characteristic and abundant in a region, or perhaps a product most highly valued and saved for these special days. In medieval times, especially, many foods were highly significant and symbolic of social status and hierarchy, their public consumption, or event of giving to others, established status. The importance of venison and a food and as a gift is a good example of this. So what is on the plate or in the glass at an event says much about the area, the community, the landscape and the host. It may also say something about the individual who is consuming it.

As food and landscape are complex products of human and natural processes, interactions between landscape and society and with food in both staple diet and feast are of great interest. A simple consideration of Britain confirms that throughout history the production or harvesting of foods has dominated landscape character. Regional variations reflect underlying environmental parameters and food production; and though declining now, the latter often has distinctive regional distinctions (Rotherham, 2003). Some of the relationships are direct and obvious, others more oblique. The impacts of farming on ecology are increasingly recognized. Lovegrove (2007), for example, described in detail the impacts on wildlife of the obsessive eradication of 'vermin' from Tudor times onwards, in order to protect 'game' for sport and for the pot. Yet, whilst there is an extensive literature on food, feasts and festivals (e.g. Drummond and Wilbraham, 1939; Hartley, 1954; Hammond, 1993; Beardsworth and Keil, 1997; Strong, 2003; Fletcher, 2004), there is little that relates these to the landscapes (social and ecological) in which they are placed. This chapter begins to look at some key issues and ideas.

Consequent on this complexity is that food reflects landscape and culture, and both are affected by processes of food production. After period of distinct severance in food, culture and environment in the agro-industrial farming landscapes of late twentieth century Britain, there is a re-awakening in awareness of the importance of food and drink in local distinctiveness and associated tourism (Rotherham, 2003). Hospitality is an attractant to visitors. However, and important for rural economic renaissance, it is a means to convert visitors to economic impact. It helps local people take money off the tourists. This may be through distinctive local products marketed with a hint of historic authenticity in becoming a part of the everyday touristic experience; the Cornish pasty eaten on the seafront at St Ives in Cornwall for instance, or a malt whisky drunk in the Royal Highland Hotel in Inverness. Each imparts an essential touch of the culture and the landscape to the traveller, or it can be taken away to be consumed later and invoke the memories of a holiday, of a visit, of a landscape and of a culture. There is also the interesting concept of locally distinctive foods now available around the country or around the world, by mail-order.

The importance of such distinctive food and drink can be invoked and celebrated further through organized events: festivals, tastings and feasts. These can be within the region or locale, or often as a cultural promotion or community celebration, perhaps hundreds or even thousands of miles away. The bond between landscape, culture, food and drink is deeply ingrained and multi-faceted. It reflects a co-evolution of people and landscape, of food, drink, culture and community, though the linkage may change and the evolution can be oblique, as illustrated later by the haggis. The culture of food and festival goes back to the emergence of organized civilization and has been considered in detail (e.g. Hammond, 1993; Strong, 2003; Fletcher, 2004).

Food and culture interact and both relate to, and reflect landscape. The mechanisms for this include transportation and topography, culinary technology and available fuels, and local environmental influences over both domesticated and wild foods (Rotherham, 2003). In some cases the linkages are real and deep, in others they are emotional and to a degree mythical or even mystical. In terms of contemporary celebrations and food-related tourism, perhaps it doesn't matter. Food and its celebration can represent many things in society, and food-related tourism is increasingly important (see Hall et al., 2003). The red grouse or pheasant from moor or wood may represent both the culmination of one social system and at the same time, the suppression of another. Feasting subsequent to the 'Glorious Twelfth' is a symbolic representation of a social and landscape management system. Ironically of course, the birds would be best if hung a while rather than rushed to expensive restaurant tables as the finale of a race to conserve, shoot, bag, transport, prepare and eat as quickly as possible.

Food, feast, festival and landscape

Landscape through topography, geology and climate affects influence and sometimes determine the availability and quality of many foods and drinks. Until modern transport, refrigeration and technological growing systems, this was a defining influence. Through this close relationship evolved a close bond between local environment and distinctive foods. Furthermore, through the impacts on society and culture, landscape also affects festivals and feasts. Not only did the local environment provide the day-to-day sustenance, it also produced the special foods for celebration and festivities. In many cases such as the great medieval deer parks, the landscape setting also offered the pre-feast entertainment and sport.

In subsistence farming and in rural peasant societies, the annual cycle of nature and the seasonal changes in activities and in production are hugely important. In communities that are directly dependent on their own natural resources for food and drink, fertility and famine become big issues. The annual cycle is itself the subject of speculation and of symbolism. The spectre of a bad harvest, of drought and famine, are never far away. Indeed before the advent of modern scientific farming, much emphasis was placed on magic and ritual, and on religion, to appease the gods and to implore their support in a productive landscape. Through this complex interaction between people, food, landscape and nature, the annual cycle is woven through seasonally repeated activities, and their celebration in feasts and festivals. Festivals included food and drink, and these might reflect the area or region, perhaps along with some more exotic and rare items for the rich and powerful. Meats and certain fish might be consumed as special treats. For a farming community, an ox might be slaughtered and roasted whole, and for a family the annual slaughter of a pig was hugely important.

The food provided might be as a celebration by a community of a successful harvest, or perhaps as a gift to maintain status by the Lord of the Manor or by some other benefactor. What is special depends very much on who you are, where you are and when you are; once again a complex and dynamic situation. From menus and other sources, it is clear that from early times certain foods were restricted within the social hierarchy, peacocks, for example, often only for the immediate table of the King. In a similar vein certain species retain enhanced status, and this may have protected them from an even earlier demise than that which they eventually suffered. These important food species were often particularly associated with certain wildlife habitats, such as the Great Bustard of the plains and wolds. This species is one of the world's largest flying birds; males weighing up to 39 pounds (18 kg) (Cocker and Mabey, 2005). However, unfortunately for the Great Bustard, its combined size with a reputation for good eating: as something between turkey and goose, it was a *'rare union of gastronomic excellence'*. This was not necessarily the immediate cause of its demise. It ultimately succumbed to habitat loss as the open range grasslands were converted to modern fields and hedgerows. With the difficulty in catching the very wary Bustards, it was common practice to take the eggs to be hatched and reared in captivity. As the supreme gastronomic bird of Salisbury Plain, until the eighteenth century, the Great Bustard roasted was the centrepiece of the inaugural feasts for the Mayors of Salisbury.

Menus and memories

Feasting as a celebration takes many forms and has a range of origins. However, it was often an event for both commoner and ruler, but with a social hierarchy in terms of both menu and occasion. The trigger for a special food event might be an occasional happening such as a royal visit or a domestic celebration, or else a regular part of the annual cycle like harvest-time or mid-winter. The feast of the elite, or sometimes of the commoner, evolved to be a celebration in food and drink distinctive to the event and the locale. The dynamic relationships between landscape and community, and between environment and food mean that information can easily be lost, and linkages once deeply ingrained can be quickly forgotten. Insight into these interactions can be gleaned from the accounts and especially the menus of both rich and poor, and of everyday subsistence and of feast and festival. These sources also provide valuable and sometimes unique information on early landscapes and their uses. Indeed, some of the feast menus provide us with the earliest written information about medieval landscapes and areas now long-since destroyed by agricultural 'improvement' and by urbanization. One of the older feast recorded was that of King Offa on Boxing Day in 781 AD, at his royal court in Tamworth (Wood, 1981). As the King progressed on his itinerary towards Tamworth for the mid-winter, his staff went on ahead to make necessary preparations. Stocks needed to be plentiful, bread had to be baked, animals should be ready for slaughter and ale must be brewing. The list of food for just one night gives some idea of what the local area had to provide, and the productivity of the regional landscape: 10 jars of honey, 300 loaves, 12 casks of Welsh ale, 30 of clear ale, 2 old oxen, 10 geese, 20 hens, 10 cheeses, a cask full of butter, 5 salmon, 100 eels and 20 pounds weight of fodder. By medieval times, the 'Royal Larderer' might be sent in advance to stock the destination from whichever Royal Forest was close by. There was a complex system of rights, dues and obligations; so in exchange for gifts of land, for example, the King's followers would be obliged to feed and shelter the royal court if on its perambulations it arrived on their doorstep. This obligation to provide food was termed 'food render', and was established under the Anglo-Saxon Laws of Ide in the seventh century. When Offa passed an estate at Westbury-on-Trym (Gloucestershire) to the church at Worcester, he cancelled the expectation of military service, but maintained the food tax with an annual payment of '*two big casks of pure ale, a cask of mild ale, a cask of Welsh ale, seven oxen and six wethers, forty cheeses'* (Wood, 1981). Tamworth was a landscape that was well wooded to the north, with fertile meadows and fields on the valley flood-plains, and extensive areas of marsh and reed-bed; altogether a rich and productive region. As discussed by Hammond (1993); Strong (2003) and Fletcher (2004), a royal feast was a major undertaking and highly symbolic both politically and socially. Wealth and loyalty were displayed, power was on show, and gifts or favours were dispensed. However, they were also very expensive obligations. The preparations for a royal visit were huge undertakings, and cost in like measure. For lesser aristocrats, the threat of a royal stay could mean the spectre of near bankruptcy. For Lord Burghley in the sixteenth century, each of Queen Elizabeth I's 12 visits costs between £2,000 and £3,000, a small fortune (Rowse, 1950).

The memory of the long-lost South Yorkshire fenland has gone, but the menus from great households provide a fascinating insight into the once extensive landscape. For over 200 years, the pressure from farming was to tame the wilderness and 'improve' the land. The landscape and its wildlife, once so vital to local people, rich and poor, were inexorably obliterated. The social commentator Cobbett in 1830 described the land reclaimed from the Humber area of Lincolnshire and South Yorkshire, as (with the exception of the Cambridgeshire fenland) the richest and most fertile he had seen in the whole of England. The value of land at Hatfield Chase was raised from 6d per acre to 10s by the Dutch improvers. This was the value to the farmer and landowner, and does not reflect that to the community living and working in and around the wetlands. We get some idea of the native resources from household accounts and feast menus as noted below. For example, the accounts of Leland (1710–1712) (Henry 17 antiquary) describe the feast for the enthronement of George Neville as Archbishop of York in 1466. Although these may have a degree of exaggeration, much of the food would have been supplied from the region's wetlands, or else from the estates and farms of the region. The menu suggests the likely wildlife at the time in the South Yorkshire and Humber marshes and fens, the productivity of the region's farms, and their capability to supply both staple and feast. Around 41,833 items of meat and poultry are noted and as brother to the Earl of Warwick ('The Kingmaker'), this was in part a political gesture to the reigning monarch Edward IV (Fletcher, 2004):

400 swans, 5,000 geese, 3,000 mallards and teales, 204 cranes, 204 bitterns, 400 herons, 400 plover, 200 ruff, 400 woodcock, 100 curlew, 4,000 pigeons, 104 peacocks, 200 pheasants, 500 partridges, 100 dozen quail, and 1,000 egrittes.

suggested that in 1842, around 60 dozen were sent to London by coach in 1 day, and in the early 1800s just in the vicinity of Eastbourne, trappers brought in 1,840 dozen birds a year. These were migrating birds in numbers almost unthinkable now, and a reflection of the still-remaining habitat across the whole of Britain (Beckett, 1909).

Subsistence use of the landscape to provide essential food for the table is a different matter from that of the Lord's Table, or the feast menu. From commoners taking small game and other materials as of right, to poachers of the eighteenth, nineteenth and twentieth centuries taking for the pot from the landed estates what they to be their inheritance, at times risking life and limb in the process, this is a more pragmatic approach to feeding. This use was often by its very nature locally distinctive; the local community taking what it could find, and what was allowed, or perhaps what could easily be stolen. This varied with location and season, and might link to feasts or festivals based around locally available food and drink for celebration of saints days or other significant events. The autumnal carousing in oak forests and medieval parks as commoners went in search of hazel nuts is one such example that caused much consternation for landowners. Illicit distillation of strong alcoholic beverages in the wilds of a remote peat bog in the Scottish Highlands and its subsequent consumption in local festivities is another one.

Whilst the poor might feed on the abundant house sparrows that infested every farm, the rich dined on finer fare. Sparrow pie or pudding had a long tradition going back over 1,000 years, with a dark and flavoursome meat, and apparently endowed with powers of sexual arousal (Coker and Mabey, 2005). Perhaps this is the real reason why the House Sparrow is now a rare species. In southern England, however, the wealthy might dine on wheatears, but in Europe the prize was the Ortolan Bunting. Although this has always been a very rare vagrant to Britain, the Victorians ate birds imported from the Mediterranean. Oscar Wilde described the *'luscious ortolans wrapped in their crinkled Sicilian vine-leaves'*. Birds were caught and then specially fattened in captivity by feeding with millet or oats. This small bird can nearly quadruple its weight; becoming *'little more than a ball of fat'*. It is suggested by French exponents of the art of Ortolan eating, that the whole, very hot bird should be put in the mouth. It is then pressed up against the roof of the mouth with the tongue. The juice and fat explode into the mouth, the peak of the experience after which you are left with a mouthful of fine bones (Birkhead, 2003).

'Eating the view' or lunching on the landscape

In the hustle and bustle of the globalized modern world, we have often lost touch with nature and with regional character. With food and drink there has been an inexorable drift in homogenization, and in particular a loss of seasonality. Local provenance and especially seasonal local provenance have proved challenging for retailers and restaurateurs. The developed economies such as Britain, many of locally distinct aspects of food and hospitality of feast and festival, have diminished to a point of oblivion in the rush to intensify and to unify during the late twentieth century. Only now, in the early twenty-first century, these trends are beginning to reverse. Local and regional character and distinctiveness are again emerging as a new *cause celèbre*. This new fashionability may depend as much on myth as on historic reality. A brace of fresh mallard or pheasant handed deftly over a counter in a Derbyshire Inn has the appeal of linking rural heritage and the dinner plate. This gives added value to the urban dweller's tourist palate, and added income to the publican's purse. Pot roast pheasant or well-hung venison consumed at a hostelry on the edge of a Peak District moor suggest that the Duke of Devonshire himself was perhaps involved in bringing this delicacy to the table. As with the haggis, by association, the product of the landscape becomes symbolic of the land itself, and the history of the area.

The descriptions by visitors over the ages also give a vivid insight into local conditions, into hospitality and cuisine, and these in the context of the landscapes through which they travel. Alexandre de la Rochefoucauld and Maximilien de Lazowski were visitors from France to Britain during the late 1800s. Their last journey recorded in their diaries was to Scotland and then a return to south-east England (Scarfe, 2001). Their experience on leaving Inverness alongside Loch Ness is worth repeating. It might be wondered whether similar conditions could have been experienced in one of the remoter marshes or similar areas, perhaps in the mountains of rural France, and whether the tourists ever looked closer to home. Alexandre describes their inn on the south side of the Loch, in the middle of woods:

'Nothing would give you more of an idea of poverty, dirt and squalor than this place offers. The house was well enough built, but the kitchen, which is separate from the main part of the building, is at the same time the family's parlour and bedroom. The hearth is in the middle of the room and made with three or four stones without mortar. The whole family warms itself round a turf fire; the smoke finds its way out through the door. The beds are only rough bits of wood nailed together, with straw for warmth. Chairs are tree-stumps. The light gets in only through a door which serves as door, chimney and window. The straw roof-thatch is full of holes and used as a hen-roost.' But there was more and it obviously made a great impression on the French aristocrats: 'But this isn't all; our great horror was to find that the whole family has scabies. However, one has to eat; but we couldn't face the oatcake; after putting on a pair of gloves, I was ready to eat fresh eggs, which enabled me to feel rather less impatient for supper' (Scarfe, 2001).

Past feast menus can connect the reader with a forgotten landscape. However, it is also increasingly obvious that food today is a link to the countryside and to crises in the rural landscape and its economies. If nature conservationists want species-rich wildflower meadows, then they need traditional grazing management to produce and maintain them. This management of often difficult farming land for wildlife often involves sites on rough terrain, and is best accomplished by traditional breeds of livestock: highland cattle, for example. To achieve this economically, there must be a market for the product and this must have 'added value', if it is to be worthwhile. This may be in either or both price and desirability. Joined-up thinking to associate conservation, history, heritage, image and sustainability with hoteliers and restaurateurs, and encourage people to literally eat the view. This presents tremendous opportunities to move food production towards a more sustainable future; linking land use to nature conservation, to tourism and leisure and to local employment. There is the opportunity to develop much more vibrant links between economic sectors and stakeholders in rural communities. Many serious problems facing landscape managers and planners and countryside users in Britain are due to a lack of such joined-up thinking. The historic links between community and cuisine have been severed and therefore need to be re-established. In the past, sustainable farming and food processing as a way of life naturally joined land-use and process to ecology and economy. The closely woven relationships functioned sustainably to generate local and regional character of landscape and of cuisine. However, with an increasingly sophisticated society especially during the twentieth century, these links have been cut. Re-awakening awareness and rejuvenating synergies may be a first step towards relevant and sustainable food production, processing and presentation.

This is not just an issue for declining rural areas and an affluent, educated tourist market. Local and organic food production is being developed in economically deprived, urban centres such as the Manor estate in Sheffield. Local people are growing their own vegetables, and local, organic food markets are emerging. Similarly, in poorer, former coal-mining towns such as Askern near Doncaster, the local farmers' market became a regular feature, just as it is in the highly affluent town of Bakewell in the Peak District. One major initiative is from the former Countryside Agency's *'Eat the View'* campaign as evidenced by the regional project for Yorkshire and the Humber (Cookson and Pasley, 2001). This seeks to embed regional initiatives in a coherent national policy, to promote regional food production and to relate this to landscape value. First moves are to identify interested and active individuals, organizations, networks, initiatives and potential projects, and then develop themes related to regional environmental issues in the context of the food-producing rural landscape. The intention is to establish and understand local and regional identities and distinctiveness. These are related to efforts to grow economies and employment through local markets, farmers' markets and market towns initiatives, immersing the initiatives in sustainable rural regeneration.

This isn't new, but it has perhaps been undervalued. The relationship between people, food and the environment is intimate, long-term and on-going. Until relatively recently food production had by its very nature, to be sustainable and sustained. Communities required and therefore produced and processed local food and drink. At a certain level of society and this evolved over time, luxury items or seasonal foods would be imported over greater distances. However, problems of transport and of preservation made this both difficult and expensive. Modern transportation and technologies such as refrigeration changed all of these. Yet until recently, even major urban centres would have been closely linked to their farming hinterland; with two important impacts. Firstly, there was room for locally distinctive products. Secondly, almost all local people would be well-acquainted with the production, processing and supply of food. In the last half of a century in Britain these links have been almost totally severed, and the relationship is distant and the understanding diminished. Many environmental and economic problems in rural areas stem from this severance.

It is often assumed that ideas of local hospitality and locally produced foods are new, and that the problems of loss of regional distinction are somehow a modern phenomenon. Yet Thomas Burke writing in 1945 recounted a now familiar tale (Burke, 1945). He writes about inns and their hospitality, saying *'But with all this high feeding the inns of the past said little about their food. It seems to have been taken for granted that there would be a generous table, and thee was no need to talk, as our inns* of to-day do, of 'butter and cream from our own farm', or 'fruit from our own orchard', or 'home-made honey and preserves'. Nobody in those days expected the food to come from anywhere except the local fields'. Burke is writing about change over the preceding 70 years, so back to around 1880. Accordingly, a country dinner for two might consist of 'a turbot of four pounds weight, two roast ducks, an apple-pie, cheese and desert. Breakfast was cold ham and beef, Cambridgeshire sausages, fried eggs, followed by a roast mallard'. He then continues that 'By the end of the eighteenth century an inn dinner for one person (John Byng) was: spitch-cocked eels, roast pigeons, a loin of pork, tarts, jellies, custards and cheese. The dinners of the middle eighteenth century, if not of so many dishes, were even heavier in substance, and at the end of the seventeenth century eight or nine courses was usual'. And of course most of this was sourced or at least prepared locally or regionally.

There is a real danger today that we have lost touch with our farming landscapes and with the production and heritage of food and drink. If this is so, then it is to the detriment of the environment, the rural community and the experience of locally distinctive fare. Across Britain in the last 50 years, the demands for huge quantities of foods and at low process, often regardless of deep-rooted quality issues, have driven the final stage of this relationship. Fuelled by cheap energy, mechanization and technology, food and its production have erased ecology and culture from huge swathes of Britain's landscape. Locally distinctive cuisine and hospitality are now re-emerging to challenge these trends. The question remains as to whether it is possible to move the balance back and to restore the intimacy of the long-term interaction between genuinely sustainable and regional foods, and their celebration in feast and festival. This new approach is borrowing much from the past; indeed, until relatively recently most of it simply happened at a regional level out of necessity. So in many ways the idea is to celebrate the past and the regional or local, but to do so in a way which also looks forwards. This is heritage on the plate and history in a glass, but it is much more. The approach taken by organizations such as the National Trust in England, or the former Countryside Agency with its Eat the View campaign, is positive and pragmatic solutions to problems of both food quality and of rural renaissance. These initiatives are deeply grounded in ideas of community and education and in a long-term re-awakening and celebration of local distinction, but for a contemporary palate. By celebrating this distinction in feasts, festivals and events, some ancient and other newly created, there is a rich and emerging vibrancy that will have even greater impacts in the decades to come.

References

Beardsworth, A. and Keil, K. (1997). *Sociology on the Menu: An Invitation to the Study of Food and Society*. Routledge, London.

Beckett, A. (1909). *The Spirit of the Downs*. Mehtuen & Co., London.

Birkhead, T. (2003). *The Red Canary*. Weidenfeld and Nicolson, London.

Burke, T. (1945). *English inns*. In Turner, W.J. (ed.) *The Englishman's Country*. Collins, London.

Cocker, M. and Mabey, R. (2005). *Birds Britannica*. Chatto and Windus, London.

Cookson, P. and Pasley, S. (2001). *Eat the View Yorkshire and Humberside Action Plan*. Countryside Agency, Leeds.

Drummond, J.C. and Wilbraham, A. (1939). *The Englishman's Food: A History of Five Centuries of English Diet*. Jonathan Cape, London.

Fletcher, N. (2004). *Charlemagne's Tablecloth: A Piquant History of Feasting*. Weidenfeld and Nicolson, London.

Hall, C.M., Sharples, L., Mitchell, R., Macionis, N. and Cambourne, B. (2003). *Food Tourism Around the World: Development, Management and Markets*. Butterworth Heinemann, London.

Hammond, P.W. (1993). *Food and Feast in Medieval England*. Alan Sutton Publishing Ltd., Stroud, Gloucestershire.

Hartley, D. (1954). *Food in England*. Macdonald and Jane's, London and Sydney.

Hudson, W.H. (1900). *Nature in Downland*. J.M. Dent & Sons Ltd, London and Toronto.

Kiple, K.F. and Ornelas, K.C. (eds.) (2001) *The Cambridge World History of Food*. Cambridge University Press, Cambridge.

Lovegrove, R. (2007). *Silent Fields: The Long Decline of a Nation's Wildlife*. Oxford University Press, Oxford.

Rotherham, I.D. (2003). Lunching on landscapes of leisure, history and location: eating the view as an opportunity for sustainable hospitality. In Ball, S. (ed.) *Trends and Developments in Hospitality Research. Proceedings of the 12th Annual CHME Hospitality Research Conference*, 23–24 April 2003, Sheffield, pp. 332–341.

Rowse, A.L. (1950). *The England of Elizabeth*. Macmillan & Co. Ltd, London.

Scarfe, N. (2001). *To the Highlands in 1786*. The Boydell Press, Woodbridge, Suffolk, England.

Strong, R. (2003). *Feast: A History of Grand Eating*. Pimlico, London.

Wood, M. (1981). *In Search of the Dark Ages*. BBC Books, London.

Food events and festivals

PART II

Food events and
festivals

Conceptualizing festival-based culinary tourism in rural destinations

Carol Kalkstein-Silkes, Liping A. Cai
and Xinran Y. Lehto

Introduction

Destination branding is a powerful marketing resource used to differentiate one location from another (Cai, 2002; Kotler and Gertner, 2002). Successful destination branding must incorporate various elements of a destination to portray a unique and positive image to attract tourists. Festivals staged in rural areas can utilize a destination branding strategy to differentiate their location. Festivals often include food and food related elements as unique regional celebration of culture. Cultural significance combined with food at festivals and implemented as a branding strategy will form a powerful emotional connection with a destination. Experiencing food and food related elements at a destination can be defined as culinary tourism. It is known that the sharing of food also elicits an emotional response and a sense of an identity with place (Visser, 1991; Bessiere, 2001; Long, 2004). The use of food and food related elements in destination branding materials will not only evoke a positive response to a destination, but also invoke an emotional identification with the food image affirming a positive response to a destination.

Food is present at the majority of festivals, and is considered an essential service (Getz, 1991). In many cases, food is the primary reason for the festival celebration. For the tourists, it is a way to experience new cultures and flavours (Mitchell and Hall, 2003; Rusher, 2003; Long, 2004). The experience of the food exceeds mere sustenance. People consume food with others to form social relationships (Visser, 1991; Long, 2004). Experiencing local cuisine through demonstration or experiential interaction allows a tourist to take ownership in a destination (Bessiere, 2001; McKercher and du Cross, 2002). The personal nature of this interaction translates into a deeper appreciation for the culture (Long, 1998; McKercher and du Cross, 2002). This deep appreciation generates an emotional identification and connection with a destination. The affective component associated with the consumption of local food at a destination assimilates into the destination's image (Lewis, 1997; Felsenstein and Fleischer, 2003). The objective of the study was to develop a conceptual framework for the study of festival-based culinary tourism as a unique way to differentiate rural destinations through branding.

The framework

The synthesis of existing literature resulted in the conceptualization of a framework for festival-based culinary tourism in rural destinations (Figure 4.1). The foundation of this framework is

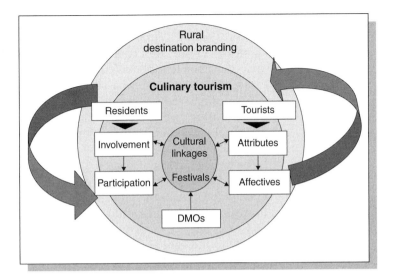

Figure 4.1
Conceptual
framework of
festival-based
culinary tourism

the model of destination branding proposed by Cai (2002) and its underlying theories. As defined by Cai (2002), destination branding is the selection of consistent elements to identify and distinguish a brand through positive image building. Image building is the core activity of destination branding. A key element of the destination branding model is the projection of positive images to the target market. These images would create an emotional response reminding a tourist of a destination. This emotional response would be the affective intangible component a person would associate with a destination.

Place is considered one of the greatest untapped resources for branding opportunities (Morgan et al., 2004). Culinary tourism as defined by Long (2004) is any experience of food or foodways other than one's own. Hall and Mitchell (2001, 2005) offer a comprehensive definition of culinary tourism including 'visitations to primary and secondary food producers, food festivals, restaurants and special locations for which food tasting and/or experiencing the attributes of specialist food production region are the primary motivation factor for travel'. For the purpose of this study, the definition is confined to food and food related elements associated with festivals. Hall and Mitchell (2005) identify 'experiencing the attributes' of food as an element of culinary tourism. It is this emotional identification intertwined with the symbolic interaction between a resident and tourist that makes culinary tourism a powerful factor in destination image development. Culinary tourism is a specific branding strategy suggested to differentiate one rural location from another. Food is considered an element of culture (Visser, 1991). Cultural assets involving food and food related elements (FFRE) from festivals that are indigenous to the rural area could be identified as culinary tourism. Rural destinations can capitalize on cultural assets and elements of culinary tourism unique to their community for branding. FFRE specific to a community and presented at festivals can contribute to the success of culinary tourism through destination branding. FFRE at festivals are the basis of the conceptual model.

The framework in Figure 4.1 considers all stakeholders in the process of developing successful culinary tourism through destination branding. The stakeholders are the residents and tourists. They are brought together by the festivals with food and food related elements. FFRE are defined as specific items related to indigenous plants, animals or food products, recipes, culinary preparation, cultural food rituals or ceremonies, culinary customs or cultural traditions, presentation, manufacture, restaurants and consumption of food or any other culinary item an area would consider proprietary. This framework focuses on the FFRE at festivals as the cultural linkage. For example, a festival centred on indigenous food or a food harvest would be a cultural link. Members of the rural community would identify the food as an element of the rural destination brand. These cultural linkages are resources that must be effectively branded and managed for short- and long-term planning of the community.

Successful staging of festivals and exhibition of food depends on the enthusiasm, involvement and passion of the residents. Local residents, as stakeholders, need to be involved from the planning stage through execution and evaluation (see left panel of Figure 4.1). The left panel represents the contributions of the resident stakeholders to portray the image of a destination. The residents work to form critical alliances with the area destination marketing organization to determine what FFRE from festivals they wish to showcase. Communication and involvement among local planners, destination marketing organizations and festival organizers that is vital to ensure the needs of all stakeholders are being considered. The marketing effort must be unified among the stakeholders to make sure the images and elements being portrayed are consistent.

The tourists as stakeholders (see right panel of Figure 4.1) experience the food or FFRE of a festival. A successful experience will lead to a deeper appreciation of the culture. The tourist will identify with the culinary experience and elicit positive feelings regarding the destination and FFRE shared. A positive attitude will remain with the tourist regarding the destination long after the tourist has returned home (Hall and Mitchell, 2005). This residual good will reinforces the image of the destination again in the visitor's mind long after the trip has ended (Lewis, 1997; Felsenstein and Fleischer, 2003). Using FFRE as a symbol for culture and festivals as a medium for cultural exchange, food can be used as a destination image builder (Lewis, 1997; Cai, 2002).

Much academic research has been done on the study of image as it relates to the tourist destination selection process (Gunn, 1988; Baloglu and McCleary, 1999; Tapachai and Waryszak, 2000; Cai, 2002; Anholt, 2004; Baloglu and Love, 2005; Connell, 2005; O'Leary and Deegan, 2005). The affective component of an image by a tourist is one of the most powerful determinants regarding destination selection (Cai, 2002). The image of FFRE creates an emotional identification enriched with symbolic meaning of culture, creating an affective association with FFRE at a destination.

Baloglu and McCleary (1999) discuss two components of images, the perception or cognitive portion, as well as the affective component. The cognitive component refers to the knowledge, or information one possesses. The affective component refers to how a person feels about the information. Their research concluded that image is more likely influenced by affective components than cognitive and affective components together. Essentially, an emotional attachment or feeling is more influential than direct knowledge and emotions. The destination branding model of Cai (2002) integrates organic and induced image concepts with attributes, attitudes and affective components of a destination. The images along with the emotional attachments made are integrated into the marketing components, contributing to the branding elements and strengthening the brand identity of a destination.

There are two types of images that exist in the mind of a tourist, organic and induced (Gunn, 1988; Cai, 2002; O'Leary and Deegan, 2005). Organic images are images that a person gathers throughout one's life. These images are unsolicited and occur randomly. Unsolicited images happen in everyday readings, newscasts, on the Internet, in the classroom, or anywhere a discussion about a specific location is taking place. These impressions can either be positive or negative (Gunn, 1988; Cai, 2002; O'Leary and Deegan, 2005). Induced images are images placed in the media consciously by advertisers, destination management organizations, travel organizations or any person wanting to market a specific location for future travel. People are constantly bombarded with induced images that attempt to claim product or destination loyalty. These images are designed to be favourable and are separate from organic images since they have an element of planning by designers (Gunn, 1988). Some examples of induced images would be destination brochures, travel posters, television commercials or advertisements in a magazine.

Food image as an element of a brand

Food and beverage expenditures make up the largest portion of a tourist's budget while at the destination (Mill and Morrison, 2002). The economic impact of food consumption is one of the most relevant considerations in how to increase consumer spending at a destination. By adding FFRE to the marketing materials, culinary tourism can enhance and strengthen the brand of a rural destination.

According to the American Marketing Association, 'A brand is defined as a name, a logo, symbol, package design or other attribute that identifies a product and distinguishes it from others'. A brand extends beyond traditional, tangible product features. It includes the intangible qualities assigned by a consumer that adds value to the product. At the base, it is a product along with its quality, function, attributes and usefulness. It also encompasses symbols, images, emotional attachments, organizational associations and relationships (Aaker and Joachimsthaler, 2000).

Aaker and Joachimsthaler (2000) identify four dimensions guiding brand development: brand awareness, perceived quality, brand associations and brand loyalty. These dimensions contribute to the equity or total value of a brand. Brand awareness is the familiarity a consumer has with a specific brand. Awareness is also associated with perception and attributes. Perceived quality is another dimension that can affect profitability by influencing brand associations. It is the perception of a location by a tourist that is the most critical. Positive attributes of an image translate into a favourable intangible identification with a destination. Also contributing to brand development are the associations made with the specific brand. Associations such as imagery, emotional attachments or symbols are key. However, any positive association a consumer makes with the brand contributes to the strength of the brand. The fourth dimension is brand loyalty. Loyalty is at the core of brand development and each contribution made by awareness, quality and associations will increase the loyalty. As the dimensions guiding brand development grow stronger, the value or the equity of the brand increases. By adding FFRE elements from festivals to a destination brand, the awareness, imagery and emotional connection increase. This increase in brand identity will strengthen the brand.

Community support

Support and involvement from the community is important for the success of any destination (Lewis, 2001; Fagence, 2003). With intense resident involvement comes integration into local economies and culture. All stakeholders must be involved from the inception and planning process, to ensure maximum acceptance and success. This theory holds especially true for fairs and festivals. Regional festivals often centre on a community culture or local specialty. Since the inception of the festival is local, the management of the event takes on a 'grassroots' effect, allowing the community integral control of the event. Participation in festival events allows residents an opportunity to socialize with tourists. This interaction allows for a cultural exchange and appreciation for 'other'.

A tourism initiative has a greater chance for success if it comes from within the community, assessing its own resources and assets. Since festivals occur annually and need to grow from year to year, stakeholders must consider that the local environment may experience changes and respond accordingly to ensure continued growth and success. Using local talent for leadership roles, it provides for future growth and use of proprietary assets, and maintains control from a local base of support. With residents of a community behind a tourism initiative, garnering support from local agencies, it has the greatest chance of success.

Continued festival success translates into an increase in food at festivals and a strengthening of the destination brand. This theory works well with fairs and festivals. A festival is a celebration of culture from a specific region, typically, but not exclusively, rural. The festival starts small with locals handling all aspects of the event. If a festival is perceived by organizers as an opportunity for tourism growth, it already has local support and inherently, cultural significance. These steps exemplify Twining-Ward's (1999) and Lewis's (2001) philosophy of identifying a community's strengths to be used for an economic advantage. The increase in FFRE means an increase in the images and attributes of a destination, creating a powerful branding strategy.

Cultural tourism is said to improve the quality of life for the residents (Bachleitner and Zins, 1999). There is much debate over this topic. Some people believe that by inviting rural tourism to an area it only leads to cultural exploitation and decline. The increase in vehicular traffic, demands of natural resources and pedestrian traffic take away from the leisure experience and leave the consumer and the resident with a feeling of being consumed and discarded. If the resident has little or no control over the tourism area, there may be negative attitudes towards visitors of any kind (Smith and Krannich, 1998; Russo, 2001; Davis and Morias, 2004). Regional festivals celebrate community, culture and heritage. One reason tourists visit destinations is to experience culture different than their own (Bessiere, 2001). This conceptual model of culinary tourism in rural destinations is community based. Festivals are an excellent way to incorporate community involvement with resident interest in tourism planning.

Residents' attitudes

In the last 20 years, tourism scientists have constantly examined social aspects of tourism, including the community issues as residents' attitudes towards tourism. It is widely believed that tourism must have support of the host community (Morrison et al., 1986; Murphy, 1986; Long, 1988; Hu and Ritchie, 1993; Lankford, 1994; Fagence, 2003). However, research work has unequivocally found that support is not always there. In fact, support only constitutes one pole on a continuum of host community's attitudes. The other pole is opposition. Depending on the stage of the destination life cycle, the distribution of residents on this 'love–hate' continuum varies. Tourism scientists agree on some factors that underlie different attitudes. These factors include attachment to the community (Mc Cool and Martin, 1994), level of knowledge about tourism and the local economy (Davis et al., 1988), level of contact with tourists (Akis et al., 1996), and perceived ability to influence tourism planning decisions (Lankford, 1994).

Bachleitner and Zins (1999) used a survey instrument developed by Lankford and Howard (1994) to measure the residents' perception of the impacts of tourism. The researchers uncovered a significant factor in the data that suggests that, the further away the residents live from the centre of tourism activity, the stronger they perceive negative impacts on the environment. Conversely, the more residents are involved in the process of change, the more favourably they perceive the process.

Role of destination marketing organizations

The underlying factors of community involvement, knowledge of tourism activities and host–guest interaction can be influenced to improve resident's attitudes, but tourism scientists have yet to offer solutions that are conceptually generalizable, and pragmatically adaptable to rural communities, where the task of tourism development is in the hands of either an ad hoc tourism council or in most cases, a convention and visitors bureau (CVB). The conceptual model proposed with its foundation of festivals being thoroughly embedded in the community, offers a pragmatic and adaptable solution to resident involvement and participation.

In the context of destination branding for rural tourism, the destination marketing organizations (DMOs) must work together in the community to enlist the full support of the residents. Destination branding is an arduous task that takes commitment and dedication from all of the stakeholders. All interested parties must have a unified branding strategy to make sure the consumer is receiving a consistent message about a destination. Destination branding is one of the most useful tools a destination management organization has available when trying to reach a consumer, creating an emotional attachment and identification with a location (Morgan et al., 2002; Morgan and Pritchard, 2004; O'Leary and Deegan, 2005). The planning and staging of festivals offer a great opportunity for a DMO to 'combine forces' with the community to maximize the branding opportunity of a rural area.

Conclusion

Many regions of the world celebrate their culture or heritage through festivals. Often, one of the themes highlighted in a cultural celebration is food. When tourists are attracted to a destination community by FFRE of the destination, culinary tourism takes place. The quality of this unique tourism experience on the part of tourists depends on the extent to which they (guests) can interact with the residents (hosts) over FFRE. The success of this unique tourism forms on the part of the destination depends on its ability to create an enriching tourist experience and to optimize the economic and socio-cultural impacts of tourism. Festivals provide an optimal opportunity for tourists and residents to interact and share each others experience; and FFRE are a fixture at almost all festivals or festive events. This chapter posits that the festivals staged by rural communities are de facto venues of culinary tourism, and as such their potential to rural destination branding remains untapped.

Brand-essence, a single thought that identifies the soul of a brand (Aaker and Joachimsthaler, 2000), is an expensive but powerful proposition for a brand owner. The word, 'essence' elicits a culinary sensory response – the sense of smell. It would be interesting for a destination to develop a 'branding essence' using a food item or product from a festival to assist in destination brand identification. A potential strategy to strengthen or contribute to a brand of a destination would be to incorporate the indigenous cuisine or food products of a regional festival and use them as an element of the brand. Food items should be unique to a place, region or area and hold social significance that allows differentiation from other destinations. By adding food into a brand element, the concept of brand essence takes on a whole fragrant or aromatic new meaning.

Successful culinary tourism must incorporate the needs of residents and tourist while considering the short- and long-term effects of area resources to sustain tourism development. Residents must be actively involved in the tourism planning process in order to facilitate acceptance of tourism activity within the rural community. Festivals provide an excellent way to integrate tourism and community support in rural areas. Branding is a way that rural areas can capitalize on their indigenous resources and market a destination. Using FFRE at festivals as an element of the branding mix can strengthen a brand and contribute to the uniqueness of place. This add-ition will make a rural destination more competitive in today's marketplace.

The contemporary notion of destination branding empha-sizes the personal experience of tourists at a destination (Morgan et al., 2004). Whether food consumption is for sus-tenance, epicurean adventure or an attempt to share the local culture, an exchange occurs. Research has shown that posi-tive host–guest interactions will leave lasting impressions of the destination on the tourist, long after the vacation is over. A positive experience of an enriching nature triggers repeat visitation, as well as positive word-of-mouth – the bench-marks of successful destination branding. When FFRE are branding themes, they become the benchmarks of successful culinary tourism. Rural destination branding would be signifi-cantly enhanced if FFRE from festivals were incorporated into the branding strategy of a rural destination. Further research will be needed to empirically test the model and the propositions.

References

Aaker, D. and Joachimsthaler, E. (2000). *Brand Leadership*. Free Press, New York.

Akis, S., Peristianis, N. and Warner, J. (1996). Residents' attitudes to tourism development: The case of Cyprus. *Tourism Management*, 17(7), 481–494.

Anholt, S. (2004). Nation-brands and the value of provenance. In Mogan, N., Pritchard, A. and Pride, R. (eds.) *Destination Branding: Creating the Unique Destination Proposition*, 2nd edition. Elsevier, London.

Bachleitner, R. and Zins, A. (1999). Cultural tourism in rural communities. *Journal of Business Research*, 44(3), 199–209.

Baloglu, S. and Love, C. (2005). Association meeting planners' perceptions and intentions for five major cities: The structured and unstructured images. *Tourism Management*, 20(5), 743–752.

Baloglu, S. and McCleary, K. (1999). A model of image destination. *Annals of Tourism Research*, 26(4), 868–897.

Bessiere, J. (2001). The role of rural gastronomy in tourism. In Roberts, L. and Hall, D. (eds.) *Rural Tourism and Recreation: Principles to Practices*. CABI, New York, pp. 115–118.

Cai, L.A. (2002). Cooperative branding for rural destinations. *Annals of Tourism Research*, 29(3), 720–742.

Connell, J. (2005). Toddlers, tourism and Tobermory: Destination marketing issues and television-induced tourism. *Tourism Management*, 26(5), 763–776.

Davis, D., Allen, J. and Consenza, R.M. (1988). Segmenting local residents by their attitudes, interests, and opinions towards tourism. *Journal of Travel Research*, 27(2), 2–8.

Davis, J.S. and Morias, D.B. (2004). Factions and enclaves: Small towns and socially unsustainable tourism development. *Journal of Travel Research*, 43, 3–10.

Fagence, M. (2003). Tourism and local society and culture. In Singh, S., Timothy, D.J. and Dowling, R.K. (eds.) *Tourism in Destination Communities*. CABI Publishing, USA.

Felsenstein, D. and Fleischer, A. (2003). Local festivals and tourism promotion: The role of public assistance and visitor expenditure. *Journal of Travel Research*, 41(May), 385–392.

Getz, D. (1991). *Festival, Special Events, and Tourism*. Van Nostrand Reinhold, New York.

Gunn, C. (1988). *Vacationscape: Designing Tourist Regions*, 2nd edition. Van Nostrand Reinhold, New York.

Hall, C.M. and Mitchell, R. (2001). Wine and food tourism. In Douglas, N., Douglas, N. and Derrett, R. (eds.) *Special Interest*

Tourism: Context and Cases. John Wiley & Sons, Australia, pp. 307–329.

Hall, C.M. and Mitchell, R. (2005). Gastronomic tourism: Comparing food and wine tourism experiences. In Novelli, M. (ed.) *Niche Tourism: Contemporary Issues, Trends and Cases.* Butterworth, Great Britain.

Hu, Y. and Ritchie, J.R.B. (1993). Measuring destination attractiveness: A contextual approach. *Journal of Travel Research,* 32(2), 25–34.

Kotler, P. and Gertner, D. (2002). Country as a brand, product, and beyond: A place marketing and brand management perspective. *Journal of Brand Management,* 9(4/5), 249–261.

Lankford, S.V. (1994). Attitudes and perceptions towards tourism in rural regional development. *Journal of Travel Research,* 32(3), 29–34.

Lankford, S.V. and Howard, D.R. (1994). Developing a tourism impact attitude scale. *Annals of Tourism Research,* 21: 829–31.

Lewis, G. (1997). Celebration asparagus: Community and the rationally constructed food festival. *Journal of American Culture,* 20(4), 73–78. Winter.

Lewis, J.B. (2001). Self-developed rural tourism. In McCool, S.F. and Moisey, R.N. (eds.) *Tourism, Recreation and Sustainability: Linking Culture and the Environment.* CABI, New York, pp. 177–194.

Long, L.M. (1998). Culinary tourism: A folkloristic perspective on eating and otherness. *Southern Folklore,* 55(3), 181–204.

Long, L.M. (2004). *Culinary Tourism.* University Press of Kentucky, Lexington.

McCool, S. and Martin, S.R. (1994). Developing a tourism impact attitude scale. *Annals of Tourism Research,* 21(1), 121–139.

McKercher, B. and du Cross, H. (2002). *Cultural Tourism: The Partnership Between Tourism and Cultural Heritage Management.* The Hawthorn Hospitality Press, New York.

Mill, R.C. and Morrison, A. (2002). *The Tourism System.* Kendall/Hunt Co, Iowa.

Mitchell, R. and Hall, C.M. (2003). Consuming tourism: Food tourism consumer behavior. In Hall, C.M., Sharples, L., Mitchell, R., Macions, N. and Cambourne, B. (eds.) *Food Tourism Around the World: Development, Management and Markets.* Butterworth-Heinemann, Boston.

Morgan, N. and Pritchard, A. (2004). Destination branding: Meeting the destination branding challenge. In Mogan, N., Pritchard, R. and Pride, (eds.) *Destination Branding: Creating the Unique Destination Proposition,* 2nd edition. Elsevier, London.

Morgan, N., Pritchard, A. and Piggott, R. (2002). New Zealand, 100% pure. The creation of a powerful niche destination brand. *Journal of Brand Management*, 9(4/5), 335–354.

Morgan, N., Pritchard, A. and Pride, R. (2004). Introduction. In Mogan, N., Pritchard, A. and Pride, R. (eds.) *Destination Branding: Creating the Unique Destination Proposition*, 2nd edition. Elsevier, London.

Morrison, A.M., Pearce, P.L., Moscardo, G., Nadkani, N. and O Leary, J.T. (1986). Specialist accommodation: Definition, market served, and roles in tourism development. *Journal of Travel Research*, 35(1), 18–27.

Murphy, P.E. (1996). Tourism as an agent for landscape conservation: An assessment. *The Science of the Total Environment*, 55(1), 387–395.

O'Leary, S. and Deegan, J. (2005). Ireland's image as a tourism destination in France: Attribute importance and performance. *Journal of Travel Research*, 43(2), 247–256.

Rusher, K. (2003). The bluff oyster festival and regional economic development: Festivals as culture commodified. In Hall, C.M., Sharples, L., Mitchell, R., Macions, N. and Cambourne, B. (eds.) *Food Tourism Around the World: Development, Management and Markets*. Butterworth-Heinemann, Boston, MA.

Russo, A.P. (2001). The 'vicious circle' of tourism development in heritage cities. *Annals of Tourism Research*, 29, 165–182.

Smith, M. and Krannich, R. (1998). Tourism dependence and resident attitudes. *Annals of Tourism Research*, 25(4), 783–802.

Tapachai, N. and Waryszak, R. (2000). An examination of the role of beneficial image in tourist destination selection. *Journal of Travel Research*, 39, 37–44.

Twining-Ward, L. (1999). Towards sustainable tourism development: Observations from a distance. *Tourism Management*, 20, 187–188.

Visser, M. (1991). *The Rituals of Dinner*. Penguin Group, New York.

CHAPTER 5

Case study on the use of Scottish food events in promoting Scottish tourism and food

Wendy Barrie

Thanks to cheap airfares, we can now travel almost to the ends of the earth, feasting our eyes on all the wonders of the world. Save enough Airmiles and Virgin Galactic will even shoot you into space. But if good food opportunities are scarce, all holiday memories will fade sooner, along with the ozone layer.

Fortunately, we have European neighbours a short hop from home, where we can indulge our passions to the full. What's more, by consuming the local food in its country of origin, we will be saving food miles and the planet! Ideally, and in the spirit of European unity, Scotland should be offering reciprocal excellence, but do we? There is no doubt that discerning travellers seeking exceptional food experiences in Scotland will find them, but are we perceived as a good food destination?

I am proud to be Scottish, and my home from home is Aberdour, in the Kingdom of Fife. We are in a seaside village, across the Forth estuary from Edinburgh, our capital city and round the coast from St. Andrews, the ancestral home of golf. Before we Scots discovered holiday hot-spots like Spain's Alicante, Aberdour was a favourite Victorian and Edwardian resort. The paddle steamers, works outings and miners galas are now long gone, but the railway still provides excellent communications with the city, award winning beaches are safe and pleasure sailing with a host of other leisure pursuits and a clutch of art studios are the popular attractions. Thankfully the river estuary is cleaner than before and the waters are home to fine crabs, lobsters, sea trout and a crustacean endearingly known as the Pittenweem Prawn.

As kingdoms go, Fife's footprint on the planet is not very large. Travelling its entire length or breadth is only an hour's drive, but here you will find a fertile landscape with mixed farming, large and small units, producing root vegetables and greens, prime beef and lamb with soft fruits, game and seafood worthy of any royal table. Organic producers are well represented and the best restaurants attract custom from all over the UK and beyond. Tourism is a thriving industry providing valuable employment in an area that, hitherto, has been too reliant on coal mining, aluminium processing and naval dockyard activities, all now defunct with scars removed.

All regions in Scotland can be justly proud that 'Produce of Scotland' is recognized the world over as a hallmark of quality, not least by internationally famous chefs. We can be equally proud of our own skilled and dedicated chefs and cooks, who use our local larder to great effect and acclaim, but alas they are the exception and not the rule. If only food on the plate, as served to the majority of our visitors, could be held, universally, in the same high regard as our produce. Fellow

Europeans must wonder how a country so well endowed in the larder department, can be a disappointment in the dining room. When millions come each year to enjoy the Scottish experience, how many more would come if indifferent food was off the menu?

Historians may argue whether it was the warring Picts or the voracious midges that sent the Romans packing, but perhaps the legionnaires just wanted home for Mamma's cooking. We can't do much about midges, but we can about food. What seems obvious to most of us, holidaying at home or abroad, is that eating contributes as much to our enjoyment as any other activity. For some destinations, good food is the attraction. In Scotland, we have relied successfully on our scenery, heritage, whiskies and tartans, to pull the visitors and too often allowed Big Macs and their ilk to feed them. Not surprising then if surveys reveal much of our served food to be the least attractive feature of a Scottish holiday. Increasing numbers of cultural tourists who appreciate our music, our history and our ways are also hungry for equally good food experiences. Too many are missing that added value and we are missing the very trick at which our European rivals excel.

What frustrates all our best efforts to feed our visitors well is, we no longer feed ourselves or our children well. Lifestyle changes and fast food have seen to that. A generalization of course, but we are in serious danger of losing the plot, especially in our own kitchens. Like so many others, I deplore the decline of family eating and taste education for youngsters and its consequences for food offered in Scotland. If the locals, who are eating out in greater numbers than ever before, are not demanding higher-quality food on the plate, what incentive is there for everyday caterers to raise their game?

We are not the only country to be in the thrall of fast food, but the UK is 'credited' with consuming half of all ready meals manufactured in Europe. Some EU countries saw the danger signs earlier and culturally were better disposed to resist it. In Italy, where familial eating is a way of life, Carlo Petrini went further and counterattacked with Slow Food, which is now an international movement with 80,000 members. There are seven Convivia so far in Scotland. Perth is our first city to be awarded 'Cittaslow' status and in 2005 the inaugural UK Slow Food Congress was held on the enchanted Isle of Skye, accompanied by much Highland dancing!

I attended the Salone del Gusto and Terra Madre in Turin (see Chapter 20), where Scottish Food Guide was selected as a Food Community and I was invited to speak on Food Tourism. I also revisited the local school lunch scene that had greatly impressed me at the previous Salone. Attendance ran to 8.5 thousand at the Congress in Turin and many thousands more at the Salone, all with support from an enlightened Government, alive to the rewards state-sponsored food tourism can bring. Research in other countries shows that customers can respond favourably, where seasonal fresh food is valued as part of the business matrix. Visitors have an increased awareness and appreciation of local food, and likewise interest in local culture with benefits for the economy through employment, trade and return visits.

Scotland has a strong culture of regional dishes and specialities but, sadly, it is more in evidence in glossy cookbooks than in contemporary family kitchens. Recent generations have drifted away from kitchen-lore, leaving our present youngsters, badly served with role models and with little understanding of basic cooking, provenance or seasonality to pass on to their families. Not a happy trend for a nation with good food destination aspirations. Even less so for the long-term health of the population. Fortunately the condition is reversible. Thanks to the media and the popularity of TV celebrity chefs, the subject of food, where it comes from and what to do with it, is ever topical, creating favourable conditions for many positive initiatives-individual, collective and Governmental, many of which I have had a hand in and which I am pleased to report, are showing promise. The following list shows some of these initiatives:

1. The **Food Standards Agency** (Food Standards Agency, 2007) maintains permanent watch on a sometimes fallible food industry and the nation's dietary excesses with new legislation to ban certain junk food advertising aimed at children.
2. The web, is a wonderful resource for all seekers and providers of good food, especially when information is free, constantly updated, personally vetted and recommended by a well informed and contactable 'face'. Such is the award winning www.*scottishfoodguide.com* launched in 2002, making the positive connection between good hotels and restaurants and good food producers and suppliers, including Farm Shops and the Scottish Food Trail.
3. Scotland's Tourist Board, **VisitScotland** (Visit Scotland, 2007) has recently introduced a national food appraisal scheme, which any food outlet from chip shops and ethnic restaurants to the grandest of fine dining establishments may join, subject to due payment and relevant criteria being met. This initiative aims to encourage everyone to raise their game.

4. As part of its education agenda **Slow Food Edinburgh** (Slow Food, Edinburgh, 2007) runs schools competitions and restaurant visits while encouraging chefs to work with their local schools to foster taste education and appreciation of seasonal produce.

5. Children at schools adopting the **Soil Association's 'Food for Life'** (Soil Association, 2007) scheme are experiencing real organic, local and unprocessed foods at their lunch table and are blazing a trail for others to follow.

6. **Healthy Living Award,** the initiative of the Scottish Consumer Council (Scottish Consumer Council, 2007) and the Scottish Executive is aimed at place of work restaurants and canteens.

7. Although some food providers still believe the road to riches is to give the easily pleased what they shouldn't have, others cook with their heart, are passionate about our produce and pragmatic enough to know that provenance lends quality to their brand. There is an ever-growing list of outstanding chefs, hotels and restaurants featuring local produce in cooperative, like-minded marketing, typically **'Loch Lomond and Beyond'**, in the West of Scotland and **'Scotland's Finest Flavours'** in the North-East, winning the coveted **Catering in Scotland Tourism Award**. (Catering in Scotland Tourism Award, 2007)

8. Scotland also now boasts an impressive collection of farmers' markets; and food and drink festivals which all help to add value to the Scottish Tourism experience, as well as playing an important role in supplying and educating about local food. There are over 40 certified farmers' markets, which belong to the Scottish Association of Farmers' markets (Scottish Farmers' Markets, 2007), spread throughout Scotland from Stornaway in the Isle of Lewis in the North to Ayr in the South.

The 'Eat Scotland' web site is a good source of information about other food and drink festivals in Scotland. (Eat Scotland, 2007). These range from traditional food events such as Burn's Night suppers and feasting associated with Hogmany (New Year) celebrations to newer, more commercial food shows such as 'Taste' of Edinburgh (Taste Edinburgh, 2007).

Food events, understandably, reflect the wealth of products which Scotland is proud to be associated with throughout the world. There are a number of Whisky events including Whisky Live which attracts up to 5,000 visitors (Whisky Live, 2007), the Speyside Whisky Festival and the Islay Malt and Music Festival (Islay Festival, 2007). Porridge is celebrated at the Golden Spurtle World Porridge making Championships (Golden Spurtle, 2007) and Arbroath Smokies (a unique 'name-protected' type of smoked fish) are promoted at the Arbroath Sea Fest which attracts up to 30,000 visitors. (Arbroath Smokie, 2007). Some of the old traditions associated with food production are remembered at the Celtic Food and Drink Festival (Celtic Food and Drink, 2007), and there is even a food show, Healthy Highland, which aims to promote a healthy lifestyle (Healthy Highland, 2007).

International events like the Royal Highland Show also now major on impressive food halls, bringing in 146,000 visitors and many travelling great distances to attend (Royal Highland Show, 2007).

So, is Scotland yet up there with Italy and France as a universally perceived great food destination? Not quite. But our produce is already superb and there's a new air of confidence about Scottish hospitality catering, if not yet our home cooking. There is a strong core of gifted chefs running established restaurants of distinction with new talent and new enterprises continually rising to the challenge. There are great smoke-free pubs serving great beer and great grub and who would have believed we could do pavement cafés like the continentals. Super delis in every town, farmers' markets, farm shops and food festivals are springing up all over the place. With the stirrings of a new food enlightenment in Scotland there is good reason to be optimistic for the future. Much has still to be done, but blessed with produce second to none and a passion for our task, how can we fail?

References

Arbroath Smokie (2007) at http://www.angusahead.com/VisitAngus/VisitEvents/SeaFestIntro.asp

Catering in Scotland Tourism Award (2007) at http://www.cateringinscotland.com/awards.html

Celtic Food and Drink (2007) at http://www.crannog.co.uk

Eat Scotland (2007) at http://www.eatscotland.com

Food Standards Agency (2007) at http://www.food.gov.uk

Golden Spurtle (2007) at http://www.goldenspurtle.com

Healthy Highland (2007) at http://www.healthyhighland.com

Islay Festival (2007) at http://www.islayfestival.org

Royal Highland Show (2007) at http://www.royalhighlandshow.org

Scottish Consumer Council (2007) at http://www.scotconsumer.org.uk

Scottish Farmers' Markets (2007) at http://www.scottishfarm-ersmarkets.co.uk

Slow Food, Edinburgh (2007) at http://www.slowfoodedin-burgh.co.uk/slow_food_edinburgh/Slow_Food_Edinburgh

Soil Association (2007) at http://www.soilassociation.org

Taste Edinburgh (2007) at http://www.channel4.com/life/microsites/T/taste/edinburgh.html

Whisky Live (2007) at http://www.whiskylive.com

Visit Scotland (2007) at http://www.visitscotland.com

Food and wine festivals: Stakeholders, long-term outcomes and strategies for success

Anne-Marie Hede

Let the progress of the meal be slow, for dinner is the last business of the day; and let the guests conduct themselves like travellers due to reach their destination together.

Jean-Anthelme Brillat-Savarin, *The Physiology of Taste*, 1825

Introduction

Destinations around the world have adopted an events strategy to assist in their economic and tourism development world (see, for example, Dubai (Anwar, 2004), Melbourne (Hede and Jago, 2005) or Edinburgh). As such, many events are at least in part financially supported by government funding, foregrounding the need to implement government policy. Under these circumstances, it can become a political imperative for events to deliver not only positive economic, but also positive social and environmental outcomes for their host communities. While such an imperative directly impacts those events that are financially supported by governments, it also places considerable demands on the rest of the event sector to enhance the outcomes of events for their host communities, both in the short and long term.

In the context of this trend, the management of events has become an increasingly complex task. The range of event stakeholders and the short- and long-term expectations they have of their associations with events are often diverse. Few events have escaped the impact of this trend; food and wine festivals, which are the focus of this chapter, are no exception. The primary aim of any food and wine festival is to enhance the sustainability of its key stakeholder industries, namely the hospitality, food and wine industries. As a minimum, a well-managed food and wine festival should be able to achieve a range of short-term outcomes for these stakeholders such as:

- Increased demand for the food and wine produce that is available at the festivals; increased trade at participating restaurants, hotels and cafés.
- Increased demand for other facilitating services such as accommodation and transport.

Promoters and managers of food and wine festivals should, however, be aiming to develop a number of longer-term benefits resulting from food and wine festivals, such as:

- Increased exportation of local food and wines, and/or reductions in the importation of food and wine.
- Improved skills in the hospitality, wine and food industries.
- Enhanced destination image and position in relation to competitors.
- Improved environmental conditions in the host community.
- Greater opportunities for community engagement and participation in cultural activities.

By achieving some of these longer-term outcomes, food and wine festivals thus enhance their own sustainability. Their achievement, however, is not an easy task; strategies need to be developed and implemented to achieve the desired outcomes. It becomes very important, therefore, that food and wine festivals work collaboratively with their extensive range of stakeholders – particularly the hospitality, food and wine industries – to identify what long-term benefits are desired and how they may be achieved through a food and wine festival.

This chapter examines the ways in which food and wine festivals can collaborate with their stakeholders to produce some long-term benefits. First, the chapter identifies the stakeholders of food and wine festivals and explores their expectations of their association with a food and wine festival. The chapter then focuses on the hospitality, food and wine industries, which are considered to be the key stakeholders for food and wine festivals, and examines the short- and long-term outcomes they desire from their association with a food and wine festival. The chapter explores the strategies that might be used to achieve those longer-term objectives which, as to be expected, are not as easy to implement or achieve as some of the shorter-term goals. Case study material of the Melbourne Food and Wine Festival in Australia is interspersed throughout the chapter to illuminate the ways in which stakeholder objectives might be achieved, and to highlight best practice in the burgeoning event sector.

Food and wine festivals: Stakeholders and their expectations

Stakeholders, or constituents, are defined as those groups or individuals who can affect, or are affected by, the achievement of the organization's objectives (Freeman, 1984). Clarkson (1995) stated that 'stakeholders are persons or groups that have claim or ownership rights, interests in a corporation and its activities, past present and future'. Food and wine festivals have many stakeholders. Figure 6.1 depicts a generic set of stakeholders for a food and wine festival, highlighting the diversity in the stakeholder network and showing that the stakeholders represent of wide cross-section of the host community. Not all food and wine festivals will have all the stakeholders included in Figure 6.1, but some may have a greater range of stakeholders, which may, for example, be a function of their location.

Undoubtedly, the primary objective of any food and wine festival is to increase the stakeholders' support (e.g. financial,

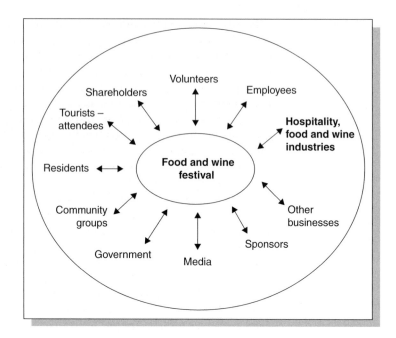

Figure 6.1
Stakeholder map for food and wine festivals

political, social) for the local hospitality, food and wine industries. By definition, the various stakeholders of a food and wine festival will also be interested in achieving this objective. In reality, however, stakeholders will have their own objectives in relation to their association with a food and wine festival. Indeed, stakeholders will very often have differing, sometimes competing, expectations of their association with a food and wine festival. One challenge for festival organizers is to identify and capitalize on the differences and synergies between the stakeholders, particularly of those of their sponsors, while also capitalizing on their commonalities. Understanding the various stakeholders' motivations and expectations for their association with the food and wine festival is imperative.

Differences between the various stakeholders' motivations and expectations are to be expected, but they do impose unique challenges for promoters and managers of food and wine festivals. For example, some sponsors are primarily focused on the exposure they will gain as a result of their association with a food and wine festival. The role and importance of sponsors in the event sector have grown markedly over the past few decades. Sponsors have been found to be concerned with the influence that their association with an event has on their brand equity, which encompasses the heritage of the brand, its logo, the people behind the brand, and the brand's values and priorities. Sponsors may also be interested in achieving maximum audience/consumer reach through the media exposure they might gain from their endorsement of a food and wine festival. As a stakeholder, the media has different priorities; the media is interested as to whether it will source a story in relation to the festival worthy of public interest, which will increase the readership of its publications (e.g. magazines, book and web sites). It is increasingly apparent, however, that the media and media organizations are sponsoring food and wine festivals themselves; blurring the lines between the role of the media as sponsor and the role of independent reporter.

Governments have become stakeholders of food and wine festivals. Each government's focus and expectations of a food and wine festival will vary, but will be contingent on the focus of the specific government department funding the food and wine festival. For example, a tourism department will be interested in the economic impacts that such a food and wine festival can produce, whereas an education department will be interested in the educational and training outcomes resulting from a food and wine festival.

On the individual level, attendees of food and wine festivals are motivated to attend food and wine festivals for a range of reasons. In a study exploring the motivations of attendees of a wine festival, Yuan et al., (2005) found that attendees were motivated by different elements of the event's theme – the synergy of wine, travel and special event. Special event research, across a range of events, indicates that attendees can be motivated to attend events for a number of reasons including novelty-seeking behaviour, curiosity, the need to socialize with family and friends, to be with people who are enjoying themselves, and relaxation (Mohr et al., 1993; Uysal et al., 1993). Charters and Ali-Knight (2002) suggested that the wine tourism experience, which they highlighted is linked with experiences related to food, is most noticeably accessed when wine tourists participate in events and festivals. Experiences at food and wine events and festivals can be highly satisfying for attendees. Indeed, Gorney and Busser (1996) found that attendance at special events generally improved attendees' satisfaction with life in general.

We tend to think of the individual at the food and wine festivals as the 'attendee', or as the 'consumer', but there are also volunteers and employees who, functioning as individuals, come to a food and wine festival for their own reasons. Their participation has a number of outcomes for them including the development of social networks and technical and life skills (Fairley et al., 2007). Although much research has focused on volunteers within the context of special events and festivals (see, for example, Elstad, 1996; Saleh and Wood, 1998; Davidson and Carlsen, 2002); little attention has been directed towards the paid employees of events and festivals. Walle (1996), however, noted that participation in some special events becomes a symbol of a performers' professional status. This notion certainly extends to food and wine festivals, as increasingly cooking demonstrations, expert panels of food and wine critics and public lectures are included on the festival programmes – resulting in industry professionals, including chefs, food and wine authors and critics, being elevated to performer, and sometimes even celebrity status. Indeed, this was the case at the Melbourne Food and Wine Festival in 2007 when a number of chefs, food and wine authors and critics were an integral part of the festival's programming.

The Melbourne food and wine festival: A network of stakeholders

The Melbourne Food and Wine Festival is incorporated as a not-for-profit organization, and derives its funding from both the public and private sectors. The 14-day event is held in March each year. In 2007, the festival celebrated its 15th festival, making it the 'longest running food and wine festival in the southern hemisphere' (Melbourne Food and Wine Festival, 2007a). In 2007, over 300,000 people attended 140 ticketed and non-ticketed events. The majority of the events were held in Melbourne, but some were held in regional destinations. Each year, a number of high profile international chefs are invited to attend the festival. One of these, Rose Gray of the River Café in London, stated that 'we just don't have festivals like this in London … Melbourne's food and wine culture, with festival events sprawling over the CBD, is unlike any other in the world' (Melbourne Food and Wine Festival, 2007b). The ticketed and non-ticketed programme provides an interesting context for analysis as case study, as it highlights how the long-term benefits of a food and wine festival can be enhanced for stakeholders through the active collaboration with the hospitality, food and wine industries.

The Melbourne Food and Wine Festival has been successful in recruiting a number of sponsors, that, despite having a diverse range of objectives in relation to their associations with the festival, appear to have some commonalities among them, particularly with regard to the commitment they have to the festival (Table 6.1) which details the sponsors and their various sectors that they represent. Like many other events and festivals, the

Table 6.1   2007 Melbourne Food and Wine Festival: hierarchy of sponsors

Type of sponsor	Sponsor	Industry/sector
Presenting sponsor	The Age	Media (print)
Government partners	State of Victoria Tourism Victoria City of Melbourne	State government
Major partners	Crown Casino Sanpelligrino	Gaming venue Soft drink importer
Major sponsors	Coffex Mièle	Coffee maker and distributor Kitchen appliance manufacturer
Official hotel	Langham Hotel	Accommodation
Media partner	ABC local radio RRR Radio	Media (broadcast)
	Morpheum Delicious: the food magazine	Media (print)
Venue partner	Arts centre Southgate	Government arts institution Commercial arts and dining precinct
	Federation Square Telstra Dome Delaware North Companies	Government leisure precinct Sporting attraction Corporate caterers
Product partner	Phase 5 Pura Equal All-Clad	Agriculture (organic tea oil) Agriculture (dairy) Artificial sweetener manufacturer Cookware manufacturer
Wine partner	Wines of Victoria Brown Brothers	Wine industry body Wine industry
Other sponsors	Melbourne Zoo William Angliss	Attractions Hospitality educators
	Voice of the Vine Coldstream Hills Yarraloch Matilda Bay Montalto Mirka at Tolarno	Wine industry

Melbourne Food and Wine Festival developed a hierarchy for its corporate stakeholders (i.e. sponsors). For example, in 2007 one of the two local newspapers, *The Age*, with an average daily readership of approximately 800,000 (The Age, 2007) was the festival's 'Presenting Sponsor'. Government partners for the festival were the State of Victoria, Tourism Victoria and the City of Melbourne (the municipality which is host to most of the festival's events).

As can be seen in Table 6.1, major partners for the festival were local hospitality and/or food organizations, namely Crown (Melbourne's casino) and Coffex (coffee-maker and distributor), and international hospitality and/or food organizations, namely Miele and Sanpelligrino. These organizations and their products/services were widely used in the festival. The official hotel for the festival was the Langham Hotel, where ticketed events such as a series of MasterClasses were held. Media partners included radio (local government sponsored radio stations on two frequencies, and a privately owned radio station); *Delicious: the food magazine* (government sponsored food magazine); and a web site design and hosting organization, Morpheum, that has been successful in targeting local government agencies. Four venue partners were the Arts Centre (a government-managed performing arts venue); Southgate (leisure precinct comprised privately owned businesses); Federation Square (Melbourne's central public space and leisure precinct, which is managed by a state government instrumentality); and the Telstra Dome (a professional sports and leisure venue with corporate facilities). Delaware North Companies, a major contract catering company in Australia and catering provider at the Telstra Dome, was the festival's venue partner.

The festival's 'product partners', originating from the hospitality and food industries were Phase 5, a supplier of organically produced camellia tea oil; Pura, Australia's major producer and supplier of dairy products; Equal; and All-Clad, a US-based company specializing in the production of professional-standard cookware. The festival's 'wine partners' were: Wines of Victoria, which operates as a industry body under the auspices of the Victorian Wine Industry Association; and the long-time established Victorian vineyard, Brown Brothers. William Angliss, the tertiary institution that has supplied education and training to the Victorian hospitality, food and wine industries since 1940, was also one of the festival's sponsors. In addition to the festivals' official sponsors, in 2007 the festival acknowledged the generosity of a number of hospitality, tourism and leisure organizations, including: the Melbourne Zoo and a number of regional wineries including Voice of the Vine, Coldstream Hills, Yarraloch, Matilda Bay, Montalto and Mirka at Tolarno. Overall, the festival developed a network of sponsors that were able to facilitate achieving the festival's vision.

The hospitality, food and wine industries: Key stakeholders for achieving long-term outcomes

Food and wine festivals are inextricably linked to the local, and increasingly it seems, to the international hospitality, food and wine industries. While stakeholder theory suggests that all stakeholders are equally important, the relationship a food and wine festival has with the hospitality, food and wine industries is paramount to its success. In an effective relationship, the association between the central organization (i.e. the food and wine festival) and its stakeholders is reciprocal. That is, while a food and wine festival is designed to sustain the hospitality, food and wine industries, it is dependent on them for its own sustainability. *But, what are the possible long-term outcomes of a food and wine festival? How does a food and wine festival collaborate with its key constituents to achieve desired long-term outcomes?*

Table 6.2 presents some of the potential long-term benefits resulting from a food and wine festival, and these are linked to the short-term benefits that a food and wine festival can produce. The outcomes of food and wine festivals have been categorized into those that are economic, social and environmental. Although the contents of Table 6.2 are not exhaustive, it highlights the links between the short and long-term outcomes of a food and wine festival. Furthermore, analysis of Table 6.2 illustrates the importance of capitalizing on short-term outcomes in order to develop longer-term outcomes through the implementation of strategy.

Producing long-term economic, social and environmental outcomes (e.g. those outlined in Table 6.2) resulting from a food and wine festival is best done in collaboration with all the festival stakeholders. Given that the primary aim of a food and wine festival is to enhance the sustainability of the hospitality, food and wine industries, their expectations and desired outcomes should, however, be given the most serious consideration. Breaking the outcomes down into those that are economic, social and environmental is useful, but noticeably these are invariably interrelated, and there are generally synergies between them. Once the long-term outcomes of the festival are decided upon, specific objectives and targets can be then set.

There is the expectation that most tourism events (e.g. food and wine festivals) will produce a positive economic impact for their host communities. The economic impact of a food and wine festival, like other types of events, is measured in terms of: the value-added contribution it makes to the host community's gross product; the employment it generates; and the level of tourist visitation to the host destination that it induces.

Table 6.2 Food and wine festivals: some short- and long-term outcomes, strategies for development, and stakeholder 'benefactors'

	Short-term outcomes	→	Strategies for development	→	Long-term outcomes	→	Stakeholder 'benefactors'
Economic	• Increased demand for local food and wine produce • Increased trade at participating restaurants, hotels and cafés • Positive economic impact		• Expos and exhibitions (commercial and public) of local produce • On-going loyalty programs for participating restaurants, hotels and cafés		• Increased consumer preference for locally produced food and wine comparable to imported produce • Increased investment in local food and wine industries • Increased opportunities for long-term employment in hospitality, food and wine industries • Increased exporting of local food and wine produce		• Residents • Hospitality, food and wine industries • Other businesses • Governments • Employees and volunteers • Sponsors • Shareholders (if relevant)

Social	• Improved opportunities for leisure • Improved opportunities for learning experiences • Improved opportunities for cultural exchanges through food and wine	• Ticketed and non-ticketed programming • Educational programs • Multicultural programming	• Improved social and intellectual capital in host community • Increased recognition and tolerance of cultural diversity in host community	• Residents • Tourists • Employees and volunteers • Hospitality, food and wine industries • Government • Media
Environmental	• Reduced food and wine miles travelled • Increased awareness of the Slow Food Movement • Improved awareness of environmental issues • Reduced diversion rates from landfill	• Promotion of local food and wine industry participation • Promotion and application of eco-friendly practices for festival and industry and public stakeholders	• Reduction in carbon footprint of festival and food and wine industries • Greater support for the Slow Food Movement and its philosophies	• Residents • Tourists • Employees and volunteers • Hospitality, food and wine industries • Government • Community groups

While bringing new income into the host economy by way of tourism is integral to producing a positive economic impact for the host economy, the long-term economic outcomes of food and wine festivals, such as industry infrastructure and employment, can be enhanced by maximizing the value-added contribution they make to the host communities' gross product. Thus, a food and wine festival can enhance its longer-term outcomes by adopting a strategy that promotes food and wine production, and value-adding practices related to the production of food and wine within the host community. Such a strategy requires not only the co-operation of the food and wine industries, but also that of other facilitating industries, including the agricultural and farming industries. In addition to this, the role of government in facilitating the implementation of such strategies is invariably integral to their success.

There has been a tendency for the events sector to justify the staging of events, which as mentioned are often funded by the 'public purse', by the level of economic impact that they produce. Currently, there is much discussion about the reliability of such analysis, and the techniques that have been used to determine the economic impact of event in the past (see, for example, Dwyer et al., 2003). Further to this discussion, there is an increasing acknowledgement that special events, including food and wine festivals can contribute to the development of social capital in their host communities (see, for example, Arcodia and Whitford, 2006). Food has long been understood as a symbol of personal and group identities, creating a sense of both individuality and group membership (Wilk, 1999). When food and wine festivals promote local and international foods, they facilitate social and cultural exchanges, which create new forms of social and intellectual capital within their host communities.

One of the most innovative developments in the events sector in recent years is the notion that events can be more environmentally friendly than they have been in the past. This has translated to the development of a range of initiatives, policies and tools to reduce the negative environmental impacts of special events, such as 'waste-wise' and recycling programmes. The fact that food and wine are the central theme of food and wine festivals provides them with a unique opportunity to produce positive environmental outcomes for their host communities. If food and wine festivals are able to increase the production of local food and wine, and its consumption, within the local community, both food and wine travelled miles are reduced. By reducing the number of miles that fresh produce travels from the 'farm to the plate', various factors which are detrimental to the environment are minimized. For example, fuel consumption is reduced, not only with regard to delivery of the produce to the consumer, but also with regard to the delivery of waste produce to landfill sites. Overall, if this strategy is successful, the ecological footprint of host communities can be reduced, which has the potential to produce substantial benefits for the local, and ultimately, global environment.

In addition to these initiatives, promoters and managers of food and wine festivals have enormous potential to produce a range of positive environmental, and economic and social, outcomes for their host communities by affiliating their festivals with the organizations that are committed to ethical consumption and biodiversity, such as the Slow Food movement or a Fair Trade organization (see Exhibit 20.1).

The synergies that exist and can be developed between the Slow Food movement and other similar organizations, and food and wine festivals are apparent, but require an understanding of their potential for them to be realized.

The Melbourne food and wine festival: Enhancing the long-term benefits through the hospitality, food and wine industries

In 2007, the Melbourne Food and Wine Festival employed a number of strategies to enhance the long-term economic, social and environmental outcomes of the festival. These were achieved in conjunction with the hospitality, food and wine industries through a range of events – each developed with specific outcomes.

Local food and wines were promoted through a number of initiatives. The menu for the 'Longest Lunch', for example, was developed around Victorian food produce and wines from the festival's wine partner Brown Brothers and by Melbourne's 2006 Caterer of the Year Delaware North Corporation. In Melbourne the event was host to over 1,400 guests. Regional Victoria hosted 20 'Longest Lunches'; for each of these the menus were developed around local food and wine, and produced by local chefs and winemakers. While the short-term outcomes of these events include an increased demand for local produce and services, and exposure of Victorian food and wine, it is envisaged that the long-term benefits will be a sustained demand for regional produce and services, e.g. tourism. A 'Longest Lunch' was also staged in Singapore as part of Australia's RSVP Program (Melbourne Food and Wine Festival, 2007a).

Both ticketed and non-ticketed events were incorporated into the festival program designed to educate festival participants about food and wine culture. The MasterClasses, a series of ticketed events, provided attendees with an opportunity to learn about food and wine culture from some of the world's master chefs and winemakers. The MasterClasses were held at the Langham Hotel (the festival's hotel partner). Out of the Frying Pan, another ticketed event was designed to respond to the ways in which the media is impacting the hospitality, food and wine industries. The all-day event was billed as a 'thought-provoking all-day conference for anyone interested in food, eating out and the food media; the future of food; and how the face of Australian food will be shaped in the coming years' (Melbourne Food and Wine Festival, 2007a).

The programming of non-ticketed events on the Melbourne Food and Wine Festival's programme increased the accessibility of the festival for the Melbourne and Victorian community. This is an important aspect of publicly funded event and festivals. Non-ticketed events were incorporated into the festival's programme at Federation Square in Melbourne, including cooking demonstrations and two newly created public events: The International Flour Festival and Wicked Sunday. The hospitality, food and wine industries were integral to the success of these events, as they provided their expertise as exhibitors, suppliers, and vendors at the events, and as ambassadors. The events were well attended by the public and highlighted to festival management the interest that Victorians, and visitors to Victoria, have in food and wine culture. The public events enable the Melbourne Food and Wine Festival to engage with a wide cross-section of attendees, thus enhancing the opportunities to create greater social outcomes in the host community.

Other initiatives and collaborations were also essential in realizing both the short and long-term benefits of the festival. For example, the Melbourne Food and Wine Festival is certified as a Waste Wise Event by the Victorian Government's Department of Sustainability and the Environment (DSE). As part of this certification, the festival has followed the five step approach recommended by the DSE to consider the environmental impact of the festival and develop strategies to neutralize them. For example, recycling and waste reduction systems are employed to avoid waste and litter where possible; the use of reusable packaging is promoted instead of disposable packaging; and sustainable waste management systems are promoted to attendees at the festival. Importantly, the Melbourne Food and Wine Festival works with its key stakeholders – the hospitality, food and wine industries – and encourages them to embrace the notion of sustainability, not only within the context of the festival, but also within their own operations.

Summary

In this chapter, the ways in which food and wine festivals collaborate with their stakeholders to produce a range of outcomes for their host communities were examined. These were categorized as being social, economic and environmental, and it was also noted that there are synergies between these outcomes. In an era of increasing competition in the event market place, the potential for food and wine festivals to contribute substantially to their host communities enhances both their own sustainability and success.

While the event sector has burgeoned in the past few decades, many events have found it difficult to survive. Food and wine festivals, however, are in the unique position of having two essential cultural symbols as their core attributes, and it is perhaps for this reason that they have become increasingly popular. Thus, the food and wine theme is a most valuable asset that can be used to enhance the economic, social and environmental outcomes of a food and wine festival – in the short term, and most definitely in the long term.

References

Anwar, S.A. (2004). Festival tourism in the United Arab Emirates: First-time versus repeat visitor perceptions. *Journal of Vacation Marketing*, 10(2), 161–170.

Arcodia, C.V. and Whitford, M. (2006). Festival attendance and the development of social capital. *Journal of Convention and Event Tourism*, 8, 1–18.

Charters, S. and Ali-Knight, J. (2002). Who is the wine tourist? *Tourism Management*, 2(3), 311–319.

Clarkson, M. (1995). A stakeholder framework for analyzing and evaluating corporate social performance. *Academy of Management Review*, 20(1), 92–117.

Davidson, C. and Carlsen, J. (2002). Event volunteer expectations and satisfaction: A study of protocol assistants at the Sydney 2000 Olympics. Paper presented at the *Annual Council of Australian Tourism and Hospitality Educators' Conference*, Edith Cowan University.

Dwyer, L., Forsyth, P., Spurr, R. and Ho, T.V. (2003). Computable generalised equilibrium modelling in tourism. Paper presented at *Cauthe*, Coffs Harbour.

Elstad, B. (1996). Volunteer perceptions of learning and satisfaction in a mega-event: The case of the XVII Olympic Winter Games in Lillehammer. *Festival Management and Event Tourism*, 4(3/4), 75–84.

Fairley, S., Kellett, P. and Green, B.C. (2007). Volunteering abroad: Motives for travel to volunteer at the Athens Olympic Games. *Journal of Sport Management*, 21(1), 41–57.

Freeman, E.R. (1984). *Strategic Management: A Stakeholder Approach*. Pitman, Boston, MA.

Gorney, S.M. and Busser, J.A. (1996). The effect of participation in a special event on importance and satisfaction with community life. *Festival Management and Event Tourism*, 3(3), 139–148.

Hede, A.-M. and Jago, L.K. (2005). Perceptions of the host destination as a result of attendance at a special event: A post-consumption analysis. *International Journal of Event Management Research*, 1(1), 1–11.

Melbourne Food and Wine Festival (2007a). 2007 Melbourne Food and Wine Festival Program. *The Age*, Melbourne.

Melbourne Food and Wine Festival (2007b). 2007 Melbourne Food and Wine Festival Web Site, http://www.melbournefoodandwine.com.au/ accessed 15.04.2007.

Mohr, K., Backman, K., Gahan, L. and Backman, S. (1993). An investigation of festival and event satisfaction by visitor type. *Festival Management and Event Tourism*, 1(3), 89–98.

Saleh, F. and Wood, C. (1998). Motives of volunteers in multi-cultural events: The case of the Saskatoon Festival. *Festival Management and Event Tourism*, 5(1/2), 59–70.

The Age (2007). The Age: Audience and circulation, http://ageadcentre.fairfax.com.au/adcentre/newspapers/age/audcirc.html accessed 0103.2007.

Uysal, M., Gahan, L. and Martin, B. (1993). An examination of event motivations: A case study. *Festival Management and Event Tourism*, 1(1), 5–10.

Walle, A.H. (1996). Festivals and mega-events: Varying roles and responsibilities. *Festival Management and Event Tourism*, 3(3), 115–120.

Wilk, R.R. (1999). 'Real Belizean food': Building local identity in the transnational Caribbean. *American Anthropologist*, 101(2), 244–255.

Yuan, J.J., Cai, L.A., Morrison, A.M. and Linton, S. (2005). An analysis of wine festival attendees' motivations: A synergy of wine, travel and special events? *Journal of Vacation Marketing*, 11(1), 41–58.

CHAPTER 7

Ludlow Marches Food and Drink Festival

Liz Sharples and Howard Lyons

Introduction

This chapter discusses the Ludlow Marches Food and Drink Festival, arguably the longest running and most popular food festival of its type in the UK.

In particular, the chapter argues the importance of appropriate research and evaluation as part of the event planning process, and then proposes several factors which have contributed to the event's current success. The chapter draws upon information, data and observations gathered over a 4-year period between 2004 and 2007.

Ludlow festival: setting the scene

Ludlow is a small rural town of just 10,000 inhabitants nestled close to the border which divides England and Wales. This town is a historic and architectural gem, and an examination of the local tourism web site (Ludlow Tourism, 2007) reveals the reasons behind Ludlow's success as a popular tourist destination.

A wealth of Tudor half-timbered and Georgian houses line the streets, a stunning castle dominates one end of the town and a range of interesting, independently owned shops encircle a traditional market square. Surrounded by wonderful rolling countryside, Ludlow is an attractive place for both day- and short-break visitors.

About 15 years ago, however, the economy of the town was not looking too healthy. The UK farming industry and associated sectors had seen a downturn and this, combined with a short British tourist season in that region, had left some local businesses struggling to survive. Consequently, the morale amongst the local business community and some of the residents was poor, and a strategy was needed to revive the town's fortunes. The decision to host an annual food and drink festival has proved to be an important step in the town's regeneration.

The concept for holding the food festival was originally conceived in 1995, during a meeting of the Ludlow and District Chamber of Trade and Commerce, when the event was proposed as a bold idea to boost the town's image and to encourage more visitors. The concept of organizing an event with a food focus was originally a 'stab in the dark', but in retrospect, it has turned out to be highly appropriate. As plans for the first food festival developed, and subsequently, the committee has come to appreciate the wealth of food producers who are operating within this rich agricultural area.

Local farms produce top-quality pork, lamb, mutton and beef, and the town boasts no less than four family owned independent butchers, all of whom are serviced by one of the last remaining regional abattoirs in the country. This area is also good for dairy cattle, and this has resulted in a number of small, specialist cheese makers operating within the region. Apples, pears and hops grow well here and the area is well known for its production of excellent cider, perry and traditional beers. Expertise about food is not in short supply, either as the town is home to a number of artisan food producers including a master baker whose family have run their bakery business in Ludlow for over 60 years (Prices, 2007).

The organizers had no concerns about the town's ability to stage such an event. Ludlow was already playing host to a popular Arts and Shakespearian festival, which had been held in Ludlow for a number of years, and therefore the infrastructure needed to cater for a large influx of visitors was already in place. As the Arts festival takes place each May, it was decided to stage the food festival in September spreading the demand for services, such as hotels and restaurants, throughout the summer season.

The Food and Drink Festival has come a long way over the last 12 years. In the first year the Festival took place in a hall in Ludlow College and was a small affair with just a handful of local food suppliers promoting their goods. Today the magnificent Ludlow Castle and its grounds provide the perfect setting for this event which is always held on the first weekend of September. In 2007, approximately 20,000 tickets were sold over the 3 day event.

What does the festival look like?

After organizing the festival for over a decade, the organizing committee now have a good idea of how to manage the marketing and management of the event. Some elements of the event are well 'tried and tested' and are therefore rolled out for the following year with minor adjustments. The committee is not frightened of change however and each year will make adjustments to the programme, site layout, timings, etc to make the operation run as smoothly as possible.

Marquees are erected in the Outer and Inner Baileys of the Castle, and these provide covered accommodation for over 120 local food producers who attend the event to promote their goods. Nearly all of the producers come from the surrounding region of about 30/40 miles radius of the town. It is tempting to allow good producers from further afield to exhibit, but the organizers have resisted this trend in favour of supporting local enterprise. The festival site also accommodates a number of 'talks' tents where cookery demonstrations and culinary talks are given throughout the weekend. A small charge is made to attend some of these talks, but visitors are happy to pay due to the quality of the lecturers and demonstrators. In 2007 these ranged from a talk about black pudding and perry to a bread-making class run by a master baker. These activities add value to the event in providing both entertainment and education and differentiate the festival from a regular farmers' market.

Visitors to the festival can sample many foods as they move around the site, but there are also a number of concessionary stands which provide all manner of snacks and meals from paella to hog roast. Whenever possible, local businesses are used to provide this catering service. For example, one of the catering businesses which was contracted to attend in 2007 was a local company who provided a great range of organic and fair trade food and who operated from an old repainted bus. This was located at the entrance to the festival ground allowing people to buy snacks and drinks on arrival or on departure.

In the centre of the festival ground, an open area provides space for competitions, such as the popular Waiters Obstacle Race to take place. This has been a regular event for the last few years and attracts many competitors from local hotels, restaurants and pubs. The dry moat of the castle is even used as a 'quiet' picnic area allowing people to escape the noise and bustle of the main thoroughfare. Picnic tables and chairs are provided in this area, and in 2007 a small folk music group entertained visitors as they relaxed.

The festival also extends its programme into the town centre. The market square is filled each day by additional food and craft stalls and street entertainers, acrobats and musicians perform around the town adding value and interest to the visitor's experience by creating a carnival atmosphere.

A number of food trails take place over the festival period including the famous 'Sausage Trail' which has become a popular 'high-spot' of the event. Over 1,500 tickets are sold in advance for this activity, which involves the participants embarking on an early morning sampling tour of the town's butchers in an attempt to name the 'festival sausage'. Other trails include a beer tour which takes the participants on a circuit of the town's hostelries.

Methodology: a 'hands-on' approach

Event evaluation and impact assessment are now an acknow-ledged part of the event planning process, and there are a number of authors (e.g. Hall, 1997; Getz, 1997; Shone and Parry, 2004; Bowdin, 2006) who have proposed evaluation methodologies that can be adopted by event organizers. Chapter 19 discusses various approaches and issues that researchers face at food and drink festivals and events.

The close link that has existed between the festival and researchers at Sheffield Hallam University has spanned 5 years to date. This relationship has developed following an interview in 2002 conducted by Liz Sharples with John Fleming, one of the original committee members responsible for the setting up of the festival.

Research has been carried out by Sharples and Lyons at the 2004, 2005, 2006 and 2007 festivals on a pro-bono basis. The focus of each year's research has been a joint decision made between the researchers and the festival committee, and has been primarily driven on a 'needs' basis, i.e. what information/ data was needed by the organizers to help the future planning of the event.

In 2004 the focus of the research was the festival visitor. In-depth questionnaires (administered by the researchers) were used to build up a detailed profile of the visitors/visitor groups who attended the event. Research also examined their accommodation and transport needs to see if these were being satisfactorily met. In 2005 this 'customer' research focus was repeated, but on this occasion, the researchers used focus groups to expand on some of the issues which had emerged in 2004.

In 2006 the research focused on the festival volunteers. The research involved the use of a postal questionnaire, which was distributed to all of the festival volunteers prior to the event, and then focus groups were conducted at the event to follow up 'key' issues. In 2007 the subject of accommodation provision was explored again to build on information gathered in 2004.

The methods and approach used by the researchers throughout their 4 years of study may be seen by some as being unusual. Sharples and Lyons have adopted, what they refer to as an 'Expert Interviewer' approach when conducting research at the festival.

The authors argue that due to the very special nature of food festivals and events, a highly structured and mechanistic approach to surveys is sometimes inappropriate. For example, the utilization of 'employees' (possibly undergraduates) to simply hand out large numbers of questionnaires on arrival at the festival gate and then collect them at the gate on departure may not necessarily result in useful, rich or even accurate data. Groups of visitors completing questionnaires over lunch, without guidance, following a 'heavy' morning of beer or wine sampling is clearly not productive.

Sharples and Lyons would argue, however, that a highly flexible research approach conducted in the context of a well specified brief can contribute to the production of fascinating and useful knowledge. This type of flexibility requires interviewers, who are experienced subject 'experts' and not just paid operatives or even skilled interviewers. At Ludlow, this has resulted in a totally hands-on approach, where Sharples and Lyons have been on site throughout the entire festival carrying out all of the data collection without the help of outside agencies.

This presence has even allowed the changing of data collection method, away from the planned methodology, when the conditions on site called for a change of tactics. Changing weather conditions, the fact that some festival-goers are time-poor and others time-rich and the fact that consumer segments can vary considerably over the duration of the festival are all factors which have called for the researchers to have a degree of flexibility in their approach. This has involved, on occasions, changing the location of the interviewing area, how respondents were approached, the speed of the interview and the language used. Lessons were constantly being learnt and the interviewers regularly 'de-briefed' each other to discuss progress.

This 'expert interviewer' approach is not new and can be seen in action in other disciplines. Most notably, it is associated with the medical profession and medical research which is intuitively appropriate as human health is a complex series of symptoms and medical conditions, and not very susceptible to a simplistic questionnaire.

In 2004, Sharples and Lyons collected a large quantity of consumer data, which was then passed on to two final year undergraduate students, who processed and analysed these data as part of their dissertations. Ironically, the opposite approach is adopted by some researchers, but the Ludlow researchers prefer to have the experts at 'the sharp end'.

This 'on-site' approach also brings other benefits. A close and comfortable relationship has been developed with regular stall holders, volunteers and committee members. The researchers are seen as 'critical friends' and this relationship solicits a wealth of feedback which is invaluable for the organizing committee. Comments, both positive and negative, are made in confidence, as the researchers move about the site, which are collated and fed back as part of the formal reporting process. The fact that the research team live outside Ludlow and are not formal members of the committee is useful as organizational 'politics' are not involved. Observation can also take place by the research team, and problems and issues that are identified on-site form a crucial part of the feedback process.

Following the event, a 'rapid response' summary report is sent to the committee within 1 to 2 weeks to help in their debriefing process. A meeting then takes place approximately 2 months later, at the start of the planning process for the following year, when a formal presentation is made by the research team outlining their detailed findings. If problems have been identified then solutions are discussed. The research focus for the following year is usually decided at this point.

Success factors

So what are the factors that have contributed to Ludlow's success and longevity? The following discussion is derived from the substantial findings that have emerged during the 4 year research process. The raw data belongs to Ludlow Food Festival, and it is not appropriate to publish it as part of this chapter; however, the following pointers should be of help to anyone interested in organizing a food event in the future.

Fixing the event within the local food system: clear objectives

According to Bowdin (2006), the development of SMART (specific, measurable, achievable/agreeable, realistic and time-specific) objectives are an important stage in the planning of any major event. This is echoed by several authors (e.g. Shone and Parry, 2004). Ludlow has stayed true to its original aims and objectives throughout its life. The homepage for the festival includes the following information:

Our objective has remained the same: we are celebrating the quality and diversity of the superb independent food and drink producers and suppliers that abound in Ludlow and the Marches. You won't find us promoting the globalized, standardized, industrially produced products that you can find in every supermarket. What you will find here is an abundance of **REAL food and drink**: from rare breeds of meat to real ale, cider and perry, produced and sold by people who really care about what they are doing.

And you'll also find that our festival is **great fun**. There's a brilliant atmosphere throughout the weekend that you won't forget. There is really something for everyone, from gourmet to sausage fan to beer lover. Once you've tried it, you'll come to Ludlow again and again! (Ludlow Food Festival, 2007).

The objective is totally relevant to the environment of Ludlow. This is a town which is passionate about supporting and celebrating its local food producers and therefore it is only fitting that the food festival aims should be consistent with the available resources.

Local approach to funding

The festival is unusual in that it does not rely purely on long-term formal funding from government agencies to stage the event. Financial support is provided by a number of regular sponsors, including Tyrell's Potato Crisps of Leominster, who have been the main sponsor for several years, and accountants from Tenbury Wells and Bewdley. Much of the funding, however, is generated by ticket sales and donations from local businesses and food companies such as Hobson's Brewery of Cleobury Mortimer and the Radnor Hills Mineral Water Company of Knighton.

The event also receives some funding from the European Regional Development Fund of the European Union, Advantage West Midlands and other local government departments, but this is secondary to other forms of funding. The organizers try wherever possible to engage support from organizations which operate locally. In this way, there is a stronger connection and level of understanding built between the two parties.

As a general principle the festival avoids the use of paid 'celebrities', such as television chefs, as this could be a burden on the budget. Instead, the event fosters local celebrities from restaurants, cookery schools, colleges and food suppliers to carry out demonstrations, etc.

Making the most of volunteers

The staffing arrangements for the festival are also noteworthy. There is one paid employee, who is charged with the overall operational aspects of the event, but for the remainder of the work the festival relies almost entirely on a host of local volunteers. In total, there are over a 100 volunteers from all age groups, but the majority are of retirement age. There are even whole families who volunteer. Collectively they are a great skills base and the group includes engineers, educators, linguists, electricians, drivers and joiners amongst others. Many of these volunteers are involved in a number of volunteering activities in the Ludlow community and are totally committed to ensuring that the festival is a success for the town. These willing co-workers tackle all manner of jobs from the selling of tickets at the gate to the emptying of refuse bins, and the management of audiences in the tasting tents. The Mayor of Ludlow even rolls up his sleeves to help clear up the site at the end of the festival! The event is also supported by an active 'Friends' group, some of whom are local and some live at a distance. Their annual subscription allows them to enjoy certain privileges at the event, such as the provision of lunches and refreshments, but in return many of the Friends undertake duties over the weekend.

The festival is now registered as a company and as such has a board of directors who meet regularly to plan and co-ordinate the event. The organization and management of the volunteer workforce is an important part of their discussions. The board works hard to ensure that volunteers are well looked after, throughout the festival itself, but also maintain good communication channels throughout the rest of the year by the sending of regular bulletins and Christmas cards, etc. Informal events such as barbecues are sometimes organized by the committee to get the volunteers together socially as a thank you for all their hard work. Some of the volunteers have been committed to the event for over 10 years and are recognized as being key members of the Ludlow food festival family.

Formation/development of partnerships

The Food Festival organizing committee has worked hard to build a number of strong and enduring relationships which have made significant contributions to the success of the festival. A list of these partners is included on the festival web site and includes local shops, food producers, restaurants, estate agents, hotels, farmers and local government departments.

The town of Ludlow is also fortunate in becoming something of a culinary phenomenon in recent years due to the arrival of a significant number of excellent chefs who have established businesses in or around the town. As the local tourism states on its web site:

It's not just Michelin – other independent restaurant guides come to the same conclusion in and around Ludlow, there are more top quality restaurants than anywhere else in Britain except for London. Most of the chefs who started these restaurants chose the location at least partly because of the proximity of local food supplies of the highest quality produced by people who really care (Ludlow Tourism, 2007).

The first chef to set up an up-market restaurant in the town was Shaun Hill who established the world famous Merchant

House, now sadly closed. He has now moved on to develop other food ventures, but has paved the way for chefs, such as Alan Murchison at La Becasse (La Becasse, 2007) and Chris Bradley at Mr Underhills (Mr Underhills, 2005) amongst others. Anyone wanting to book a meal at any of the Michelin listed restaurants can often expect a wait of several months before securing a table.

The presence of these restaurants in and around the town is hugely beneficial to the food festival. These chefs will often become involved with the judging of cookery and food competitions at the event and will carry out demonstrations and master classes, which are hugely popular with visitors. There is obviously a payback for the restaurants which are booked to capacity during the festival week.

The town has also built on this culinary success in becoming a 'flag ship' for the International Slow Food Movement (Slow Food, 2007). In 2004 it became the first town in the UK to be awarded the title of 'Citta Slow' (Slow Food Ludlow, 2007). This is a rare honour only bestowed on those communities who demonstrate a lasting commitment to the supply of good regional food and a good quality lifestyle for their citizens. In 2006 the town became home to the Slow Food UK office. The partnership which has been established between the Food Festival and the Slow Food Movement brings benefits for both parties.

Strategy for the future

The organizers of any event should have a clear idea of future policy. How big do we want to become? Are we too big already? How do maintain our leading position?

The Ludlow Food Festival organizers are no exception to this and recognize the need to concern themselves with the long-term sustainability of the Festival, now that the event product is at such a mature stage. The questions which are topical to the discussion at the present time are:

- Can the Festival maintain the size of its audience or are the numbers likely to drop as other events/attractions/activities become popular?
- Would the organizers like the Festival to grow further and if so, does the town have the space and infrastructure that will accommodate this growth?
- Is it wise to keep the castle as the main venue for the event or would it be more advisable to move the event to a green-field site outside the town where transport and parking may be easier?

- How can the organizers best promote the festival and to whom?
- Can they improve their communication with visitors or potential visitors to the event regarding the festival pro-gramme, accommodation in and around Ludlow, transport arrangements, dining opportunities in the town and other associated activities?
- What impacts has the festival already had upon the town; economically, politically, socially and environmentally and what are the likely impacts for the future?
- What aspects of the event need improvement or fine-tuning?

The Food and Drink Festival committee are constantly look-ing for ways to improve the organization of the event and one recent success has been the introduction of a 'Park and Ride' system which buses visitors from a number of fields on the outskirts of Ludlow into the town centre. This has eased the traffic congestion in the town centre considerably and has been well received by many of the festival-goers.

Conclusion

It is not easy to fully understand the complex set of reasons for the development of the town, as such an important culin-ary centre in the UK, and why the Ludlow Food Festival has become so important in the town's revival. However, it is probably fair to assume that the combination of an attractive historic town, a stunning rural setting and an abundance of top-class local ingredients has helped to seal its success.

More importantly the festival has been allowed to emerge naturally from its locality, and the local food system surround-ing Ludlow, rather than being manufactured in a place that it does not belong. The organizers have played a careful hand in taking fully into account the economic and social dynamics of the town before planning each move and as such the event has a very good chance of surviving for years to come.

References

Bowdin, G. et al. (2006). *Events Management*. Elsevier, Oxford.

Ludlow Food and Drink Festival (2007) at www.foodfestival. co.uk

Getz, D. (1997). *Event Management and Event Tourism*. Congnizant Communication Corporation, Canada.

Hall, C.M. (1997). *Hallmark Tourist Events: Impacts, Management and Planning*. Wiley, Chichester.

La Becasse (2007) at http://www.labecasse.co.uk

Ludlow Tourism (2007) at http://www.ludlow.org.uk

Mr Underhills (2005) at http://www.Mr-Underhills.co.uk

Prices (2007) at http://www.pricesthebakers.co.uk/index. php?Pid1=1@PLv=1

Shone, A. and Parry, B. (2004). *Successful Event Management*. Thomson, London.

Slow Food (2007) at www.slowfood.com

Slow Food Ludlow (2007) at www.slowfoodludlow.org.uk

Food and wine events in Tasmania, Australia

Stuart Crispin and Dirk Reiser

Tasmania is a gourmet paradise, where people live close to the land and the sea and there is an easy flow from harvest to plate. (*Tourism Tasmania*, 2007b)

Introduction: Event tourism in Australia and Tasmania

Tourism is now an important part of the Australian economy. In 2005–2006, it provided 4.6 per cent of the total employment and the tourism Gross Value Added is worth A$31.3 billion to the Australian economy – higher than agriculture, fishing and forestry (A$27.3 billion), electricity, gas and water (A$22.2 billion) and communication services (A$22.3 billion) (Australian Government, 2007). Tourism Gross Value Added grew by 19 per cent in the period 1997/1998 to 2003/2004, with tourism exports increasing by 35 per cent. The industry is dominated by small- to medium-sized businesses, with 91 per cent of tourism businesses in Australia being small businesses. Tourism is also a vital part of the economy of most Australian states, and is an important tool in diversifying the economy of regional areas.

Special events have been a significant component of Australia's tourism development since the 1980s (Hall, 2007). Events have helped to broaden the appeal of Australia as a destination, and represent an important attractant for domestic and international tourists. Reflecting the importance of events, the Australian Government has enacted legislation (the *Tourism Australia Act 2004*) requiring Tourism Australia, the national tourism organization, 'to establish a division to concentrate on the business and major events sectors' (Tourism Australia, 2005). Called *Events Australia*, the purpose of this division is to promote Australia to the meetings, incentives and events (MICE) sector of the tourism industry. Many Australian states have also established their own events organization. For example, in 1991 the Victorian Government established the Victorian Major Events Company with the aim of attracting international cultural and sporting events to the state (The Victorian Major Events Company, 2007).

In Tasmania, the State Government has also sought to make events a major part of the local tourism industry. There are around 4,000 events held annually in Tasmania. These range in size from international sporting events – such as the Sydney to Hobart Yacht Race and test match cricket – to small community events (Events Tasmania, 2007c). Events Tasmania, part of the Tasmanian Department of Tourism, Arts and the Environment, is charged with stimulating event growth in Tasmania across five key areas: the attraction and retention of events to the state, growth and development of events and the event industry by providing access to updated event research and information (Events Tasmania, 2007c). Events Tasmania helps to develop and support three tiers of events: Events of State Significance (ESS), Events of Regional Significance (ERS) and Local, Community and Special Interest events (Events Tasmania, 2006b).

In 2007, Events Tasmania is expecting up to 31,000 interstate and international visitors to participate in Tasmanian events (slightly down on the previous year), staying an average of seven nights and spending A$200 per day. This will inject more than A$40 million into the Tasmanian economy (Events Tasmania, 2007d). In addition to interstate and international visitors, events are also popular with the Tasmanian community. Events Tasmania does much to support events within the state. In conjunction with regional organizations such as Totally South Tourism, Cradle Coast Authority and Northern Tasmanian Development, Events Tasmania has developed a Tasmanian Event Management Guide (TEMG). This guide provided guidance and information for people looking to hold events in Tasmania (Events Tasmania, 2007b). The Tasmanian Government also operates a Regional Event Assistance Program (REAP) which provides financial support for those developing or holding events in Tasmania (Events Tasmania, 2007). The Tasmanian Minister of Tourism, Arts and the Environment Paula Wriedt stated at the launch of the program that events help to:

- built stronger, more vibrant communities,
- instil a real sense of pride in local communities,
- showcase the values and attributes of Tasmanian communities,
- illustrate a living expression of the Tasmanian experience,
- generate travel by Tasmanians (in Events Tasmania, 2007a).

Events showcasing local cultures are particularly important in achieving these goals. The celebration of local culture in Tasmania is often connected with local food and wine products, and food- and wine-based events have become an important part of the Tasmanian events calendar. Some of the notable food and wine-based events held in Tasmania include:

- Taste of Tasmania, held in Hobart over the Christmas/New Year period.
- Festivale, held in Launceston's City Park during the second weekend in February.
- Taste of the Huon, held in Ranelagh during the second weekend in March.
- The Great Tasmanian Oyster Riot, held at Barilla Bay every October.
- Salamanca Market, every Saturday in Hobart.

Food-and wine-based event tourism is an important part of the tourism industry in many regions. Despite the fact that the market of tourists travelling with the primary motivation of consuming special foods and food events and festivals is small (Hall and Sharples, 2003), their benefits for rural regions may be great. They include economic benefits such as the reduction in economic leakage, attraction of external resources and the adding of value to local produce, socio-cultural benefits such as the development of new relationship between producers, the facilitation of a local identity (Hall, 2005) and employment for local residents. Many tourists may continue to purchase these products upon their return home, furthering the economic benefit of food and wine tourism events. For the consumer, it helps to create an authentic tourism experience through the consumption of quality products within or close to the place of production. These potential benefits of food tourism events are recognized by Tourism Australia. Food tourism and events are therefore an integral part of domestic and international Australian tourism marketing campaigns.

Food and wine tourism to Australia

In Australia, the 'development of wine and food tourism is closely related to the growth of small-scale and specialist wine and food producers' (Hall and Mitchell, 2001, p. 309). The production includes specialist wines, cheeses, chocolates, oils, fruit and vegetable. It has been fostered in great part by Australian's migrant population and has made Australia a culinary destination (Rath, 2002) with an international profile.

Tourism Australia (2005) defined a culinary domestic visitor as 'domestic visitors who travel for holiday/leisure purposes and one of the reasons for their trip is to experience Australia's food or wine'. International culinary visitors are international visitors who state that one of their reasons for visiting Australia is to experience Australia's food, wines and wineries' (Tourism Australia, 2005). In 2004, 40 per cent of all domestic culinary tourists originated from Melbourne and Sydney, while 57 per cent of all international visitors were from Europe, USA, Canada and New Zealand. Their motivations include escape and unwind, and luxury and indulgence purposes, and they therefore spend more on average per day and visit than other visitors (Tourism Australia, 2005).

In addition, Tourism Australia has identified food and wine tourism as one of seven key experiences it can use to target the Experience Seekers segment of the international tourist market. Experience seekers are tourists looking for an unique, involving and personal experiences while holidaying (Tourism Australia, 2007). Food and wine tourism, especially in the form of local food and wine events, can arguably cater for the needs and wants of this lucrative segment. It can also facilitate the establishment of a strong regional identity while at the same time conveying the message of authentic experiences for tourists (Hall and Mitchell, 2001).

Countries that market themselves with clean, green and healthy lifestyle images, such as Australia and New Zealand, can benefit from place promotion synergies between food production, local events and tourism. Within Australia, Tasmania is a state with a very strong focus on those images. In comparison to other Australian states and territories, with the exception of Western Australia, domestic tourists have 'the highest propensity to be culinary visitors' (Tourism Australia, 2005).

Food and wine tourism events in Tasmania

Tasmania – the island host of dynamic and engaging events. (Vision statement Strategic Plan 2006–2010; Events Tasmania, 2006, p.5)

Tasmania is the southernmost state of Australia, located at latitude 40° south and longitude 144° east. It is a group of 300 islands separated from the Australian mainland by Bass Strait, more than 200 km south of the eastern side of continental Australia (Brand Tasmania, 2007). Temperate in climate the main Tasmanian land mass covers 68,332 square kilometre with many mountains, forests, lakes and streams.

In the year ending March 2007, Tasmania received 812,200 visitors staying an average of 8.7 nights and spending A$1.301 billion. Of those tourists visiting the state, 144,300 were international (up 9 per cent from the previous year) and 697,900 were domestic (unchanged) (Tourism Tasmania, 2007). Tourism is one of the top export industries in the state along with food and agricultural production. Food and agricultural products have been an important part of the Tasmanian economy since the start of European settlement. Apples for example played a pivotal role, giving Tasmania the name 'Apple Isle' (Servant, 2005). The importance of tourism and agricultural production is reflected in the various local food and wine events in Tasmania. A visit to one of those food and wine events can be seen as complementary to the connection of local food and wine with tourism.

Recognizing the growing importance of food and wine tourism and events to the state economy, Tourism Tasmania has increasingly included them in their promotional and planning activities. In November 2002, Tourism Tasmania published the Tasmanian Wine and Food Tourism Strategy to underpin the broader Tasmanian Experience Strategy. The state government believes that Tasmania has a sustainable competitive advantage in food and wine tourism, especially given 'the mix of wine and food with the appeal of natural beauty and history' (Tourism Tasmania, 2002). In 2004, Tourism Tasmania published a brochure (online and printed) called 'Tasmanian Journeys. Cool Wine & Food and Cool Wilderness' outlining a number of food and wine tourism tours across Tasmania (Tourism Tasmania, 2004). The food and wine segment is described as being in its early stages of development with growth potential with interstate and international visitors (Tourism Tasmania, 2002).

In 2007, Tourism Tasmania connected food and tourism with its broader promotional efforts such as the 'Tasmania Island of Inspiration' campaign, describing Tasmania as the 'perfect getaway combination of fine wines, fantastic cuisine, cultural heritage and breathtaking wilderness and scenery' (Tourism Tasmania, 2007a). Additionally, as part of the Government-funded Tourism Promotion Plan double-page advertising campaigns were undertaken in travel, food and lifestyle publications including *Australian Gourmet Traveller*, *Wish Magazine* (*The Australian*), *Explore Magazine* (*Sun Herald* and *Sunday Age*), *ABC Life Etc* and *Australian Travel and Leisure* in Spring 2007 (Tourism Promotion Plan Working Group, 2007). It also reflects the research results that the key experiences sought by visitors to Tasmania include browsing a market (48 per cent), drinking Tasmanian wine (56 per cent) and tasting Tasmanian specialty food (47 per cent) (Tourism Tasmania, 2006). There is a clear link between local food and wine, tourism, local events such as markets and the key experiences that visitors to Tasmania look for. Consequently, wine and food tourism is now one of the three key attributes of Tourism Tasmania's brand (the other two being nature and wilderness and cultural heritage) (Walch, 2005). Food tourism events fit very well into the Tourism Brand Tasmania, as they offer personality in the sense of being perceived as friendly, genuine and fresh, express the core values of warmth authenticity and originality as well as being located in the key attribute wine and food.

The connection between the creation of value, the evolution of the Tasmanian brand and the creation of event experiences through tourism is outlined by Events Tasmania in its *Strategic*

Plan 2006–2010 (Events Tasmania, 2006b). It clearly states the mission of the unit:

- Enhance event visitors experiences.
- Stimulate the development of industry capacity.
- Grow the 10 year event calendar.
- Enrich the lifestyles of Tasmanian communities (Events Tasmania, 2006b, p.5).

The combination of food, tourism and events is seen as vital to fulfil the mission. This is also expressed by the increasing importance of food and wine-based events within regional Tasmania. Food markets help for example to reduce seasonality, create local and regional seasonal distinctiveness, strengthen local food produce experiences (Tourism Tasmania, 2002) and establish employment and income opportunities. Taste of Tasmania and Festivale are two examples.

Food and wine events in Tasmania

Events are an important part of the Tasmanian lifestyle that enriches the fabric of our society. Whether a local or a visitor, a large event or local festival generates interest and excitement and a sense of being part of what's happening in Tasmania. (Events Tasmania, 2006b, p.3)

In recent years Tasmania has developed a number of annual events dedicated to showcasing the quality of the states' food and wine. These events include Taste of Tasmania (in Hobart between Christmas and New Years), Festivale (in Launceston in mid-February) and Taste of the Huon (held in early March). These events have proved popular with both locals and visitors to Tasmania, and are timed to coincide with peak season in the State's tourism industry. The following is a discussion of two of the state's premier annual food and wine events – Festivale and the Taste of Tasmania.

Case study 1: Festivale

Celebrate Tasmania's enviable life style with gourmet food and wine all the colour and fun of family entertainment, provided by both local and interstate artists. (Events Tasmania, 2006a: online)

Festivale is a 3-day food and wine event held in the Northern Tasmanian city of Launceston. The city of Launceston is one of Tasmania's major tourist gateways, and is the hub destination for the Tamar Valley Wine Route. Festivale is an annual event, held on the second weekend in February (late summer in Tasmania and a time of peak tourist demand). The timing of Festivale coincides with a number of other major events in Launceston, such as Australian Football League (AFL) pre-season matches at Aurora Stadium (an event that attracts between 16,000 and 20,000 patrons) and the Launceston Cup Carnival. Many tourists try and incorporate a number of these events into their visit to the area.

Festivale was first held in 1988 as part of Launceston's celebrations of the Australian Bicentennial. The event was originally intended as a showcase of the city's multicultural heritage and was held in the car park of the local Italian Club. The event featured food stall, music and dance representative of the different cultural groups living in Launceston. In the following year Festivale was moved into the city streets, with the Launceston CBD being divided into Northern European, British, Asian and Australian precincts.

Festivale remained primarily a multicultural festival until around 1995 when the logistics of managing the event was taken over by the Launceston City Council. At this time Festivale was moved to its current location in the historic City Park, and the focus shifted away from multiculturalism and towards showcasing Tasmanian food and wine. Since this time the event has grown considerably. In 2007 there were 73 stalls at Festivale – 27 selling wine, 30 selling food and 6 dedicated coffee stalls (Midgley, 2007b).

Stalls are operated either by producers (primarily the case with the wine-based stalls) or local restaurants. For producers, Festivale represents an opportunity to showcase their products to end consumers. The emphasis for stallholders is on featuring Tasmanian food and wine, with a heavy emphasis on food and wine from Northern Tasmania. Festivale also features over 40 musical acts and street performers over the 3 days (Midgley, 2007a). Musical acts perform on one of the two main stages, while street performers are free to roam the park and entertain patrons (Price and Bryan, 2007). Festivale has proved popular with visitors and local's alike, attracting between 32,000 and 35,000 patrons over the 3 days of the event (Price and Daniels, 2007).

Holding Festivale in City Park has been seen as an advantage – it enables the organizers to hold an open-air event with the feel of a village picnic. People are able to set up blankets on the grass and enjoy the food, wine and entertainment. This central location makes easy access for locals and visitors alike. The park environment is also very inviting, with large expanses of grassed areas for patrons to spread out and enjoy the food and sunshine. The site is intended to make patrons feel like they are attending a big family or community picnic.

Planning is a vital part of the success of the event. An 11-member volunteer committee oversees the organization of Festivale, with two people employed on a permanent part-time basis to organize event sponsorship and coordinate the running of the event (Blewett and Midgley, 2007). Planning for Festivale commences as soon as the last event is completed. Maintaining quality standards is an important issue for the event organizers. All menus and prices must be submitted and approved before stallholders are given a space in the event. Stallholders are also encouraged to offer customers a range of meal and drink sizes – range from taster size, to small plate, and platter (Blewett and Midgley, 2007). This enables the event to cater to different market segments and allows patrons to try a wider range of Tasmanian produce. Some of the dishes served at Festivale included The Basin Café's Duck and Citrus Salad, Rossilli Café Salt and Pepper Squid, Amulet's Cured Ocean Trout with Chine Crème Fraiche, and Mount Roland Goats Cheese Tart with Tomatoes and Pesto (Osborne, 2007). There is an annual award for the best stall at Festivale – the Julian Bamping Glass Platter (Midgley, 2007b). All staff selling wine are expected to have completed a responsible service of alcohol course.

Event organizers also try to keep Festivale fresh by varying the mix of new and old stalls. For example, there were 10 new stalls at Festivale in 2007. In recent years event organizers have included a cooking master class – Tasmania on a Plate – and this has proved popular with patrons of the event. During 2007 there were over 100 spectators at each of the Tasmania on a Plate sessions (Price and Bryan, 2006). The master class taps people's desires to get to know their food and how it is prepared.

Events such as Festivale have been critical for gaining acceptance of Tasmanian foods and wines amongst consumers. According to Dr Andrew Pirie, a prominent local winemaker, local wines only began to be served in Tasmanian restaurants after 1994, and events such as Festivale have been critical to gaining acceptance of these products amongst visitors to Tasmania and locals (Midgley, 2006). By attending events such as Festivale, Tasmanians have begun to appreciate the high quality of food and wine produced in their state. In addition, many interstate and international visitors continue to seek out these Tasmanian products when they return home, helping to build demand in key markets such as Melbourne, Sydney and Brisbane.

Funding for Festivale comes from a number of sources. Firstly, patrons are charged a fee for entering the event site (in 2007 the fee was $10 per person). Secondly, stallholders pay a site fee for having a stall at Festivale. Thirdly, money is generated from sponsorship and in-kind support from local businesses. Finally, the Launceston City Council provides the event organising committee with about $25,000 and another $7,750 in-kind support (Waterhouse, 2007b). For both Festivale and the Taste of Tasmania the support of volunteers and community groups is very important. For example, many local community groups help out with cleaning at these events in return for donations from the event organizers to their charity or cause. This helps event organizers keep down the cost of running these events.

Case study 2: Taste of Tasmania

'For locals and lovers of food and drink everywhere, summer in Hobart means one thing – it's time for the Taste of Tasmania.' (Hobart Summer Festival, 2007)

Taste of Tasmania is a 7-day food and wine event held at Princess Wharf in the state capital Hobart, in Southern Tasmania. The event is held in an old warehouse on Prices Wharf, which is located between the harbour and the historic Salamanca Place. Hobart is the main tourism gateway for interstate and international visitors to Tasmania. Now in its 18th year, Taste of Tasmania is held every year at the end of December to the start of January (Hobart Summer Festival, 2007). As with Festivale, the event coincides with the peak in tourist numbers for the State. In particular, it coincides with the end of the Sydney to Hobart Yacht Race – Australia's premier blue-water yacht race. The combination of yachts arriving and the Taste of Tasmania makes the Hobart waterfront the centre of entertainment over the New Years period. The Taste of Tasmania is organized and managed by the Hobart City Council (HCC).

The focus of the Taste of Tasmania is showcasing Tasmanian food and wine. There are currently 71 stalls at the Taste of Tasmania, with stallholders representing a mix of both food producers and restaurant owners (Taste of Tasmania, 2007). Some of the stalls in last year's event included:

- Island Berries Tasmania
- Salt Miners of Tasmania and Delemere Vineyards
- Huon Valley Mushrooms
- Fritto Mitto and Bishops Vineyard
- Taste of Persia
- Valhalla Ice Cream
- Inn Cider and Mussel Bar
- Tasmanian Game and Gourmet
- Stefano Lubiana Wines.

Since 2006, the organizers have included a Gourmet Taste as part of the overall Taste of Tasmania event. Stalls that are part of the Gourmet Taste showcase innovative combinations of fresh Tasmanian ingredients (Taste of Tasmania, 2007). The Taste of Tasmania attracts between 240,000 and 260,000 patrons each year, with approximately 35,000 people attending each day (Waterhouse, 2007). This makes it the largest single event held in Tasmania each year.

The venue and its location are an important part of the Taste of Tasmania's success. As mentioned previously, the Taste of Tasmania is held in an old shipping warehouse on Princes Wharf Number One on the Hobart water front. The open space of the warehouse is an ideal location for an event such as the Taste of Tasmania. Food stalls are arranged around the inside walls of the warehouse enabling patrons to move around the venue in a circular movement. Patrons can stop and taste the offerings of a stall before moving on to the next stall. The large space in the middle of the warehouse is filled with tables and chairs where patrons can sit while enjoying their food and wine. Tables and chairs are also provided on the outside apron of the warehouse, which looks over the Hobart waterfront. Being able to hold the event in a warehouse affords the event some protection against the weather – both rain and the intense summer sun can be issues at this time of the year in Tasmania. Patrons seated outside also have the opportunity to see yachts finishing the Sydney to Hobart race.

The surrounding area also helps make the event a success. Princes Wharf is part of the Sullivan's Cove Historic Precinct (which includes Salamanca Place). Sullivan's Cove and Salamanca Place Area are historically and culturally significant in Tasmania. The Sullivan's Cove area was where the township of Hobart was first established in 1804 (Ellis and Clark, 1985), making it the second oldest site of European settlement in Australia. Consequently, Sullivan's Cove is home to some of the Australia's oldest buildings. Since the 1970s, Salamanca Place and the surrounding area has become a centre for the Tasmanian arts community, with many galleries and shops being located in the old sandstone buildings along Salamanca Place. In recent years Salamanca Place has also become a popular entertainment venue with locals, with many cafes, restaurants, bars and clubs located in the vicinity of Sullivan's Cove. Many patrons use these entertainment facilities after they leave the Taste of Tasmania. Locating the Taste of Tasmania in this area has been part of the HCC's overall strategy to make Sullivan's Cove and Salamanca the entertainment centre for Hobart.

The area is also popular with tourists. Salamanca Place is a major tourist attraction in its own right, and a number of Hobart's major hotels are located within easy walking distance of the event site (including the Hotel Grand Chancellor, The Old Woolstore Apartments Hotel, The Henry Jones Art Hotel, Zero Davey, The Salamanca Inn and The Lenna). Every Saturday Salamanca Market is held along Salamanca Place, and is popular with tourists and locals alike.

While location has been an important part of the event's success, it is also the event's Achilles heel. The Princes Wharf site is owned by the State government and managed by Hobart Ports and the Sullivan's Cove Waterfront Authority. Therefore, the HCC must lease the site to hold the event. In recent years the State government has been openly exploring opportunities to redevelop the Princes Wharf site (the primary use for the site outside of the event is as a car park). Currently, no guarantees have been given to the HCC that they will be able to use the Princes Wharf beyond the 2007/2008 event, and the state government is on record as saying that Princes Wharf is a prime site for redevelopment as a hotel and retail precinct (Neals, 2005).

If the site is redeveloped then the event will need to be moved to an alternate location, however many are concerned that such a move would be detrimental to the event's continued success (Waterhouse, 2005).

Entertainment is also a major part of the Taste of Tasmania. There are a number of stages at the event and there are regular performances by local and interstate artists. In addition, the International Buskers Festival is held in conjunction with the Taste of Tasmania (Taste of Tasmania, 2007). This Buskers Festival attracts artists from around the world, and continues to prove very popular with visitors – in particular those with a family.

Given the size of the event, waste management is a major issue at the Taste of Tasmania. The event organizers have taken a number of steps to help reduce the amount of waste generated on the site. To begin with, visitors to the event are encouraged to purchase their own Taste of Tasmania wine glass (either in glass or plastic). This helps to reduce the amount of disposable cups used, and also provides visitors with a tangible souvenir of the event. Secondly, all stallholders are required to use biodegradable cardboard plates and wooden cutlery on their stalls. Finally, separate rubbish bins are provided on site for biodegradable waste (such as food scraps paper plates and wooden cutlery), glass, and plastic. This has enabled the event organizers to better manage the flow of waste and reduce the amount of waste going to the rubbish dump.

Entry to the Taste of Tasmania is free (except for a special event on New Year's Eve), with funding for the event coming from sponsorship, fees charged to stallholders, and financial support from the HCC. Council funding of the event has become an issue in recent years. In 2006–2007 the HCC budgeted around $300,000 for the event, or around $6.20 per resident of the Hobart municipal area (Waterhouse, 2007a). Some believe that this is an unfair bourdon to place on Hobart residents, and that financial support should be sought from other councils, the State government, or from an entry fee (Waterhouse, 2007a, b). To date council has rejected calls for an entry fee.

Conclusion

Tourism is an important part of the Australian economy, especially in rural regional regions like Tasmania. It provides a variety of socio-economic benefits such as employment opportunities, foreign exchange earnings, showcasing local produce and increased local appreciation for their community. Increasingly, special events are used to achieve these goals. Tasmania provides a good example for this development, especially through its food and wine festivals.

The two cases outlined, Festivale and the Taste of Tasmania offer valuable insights into some of the issues with such events. Both food and wine festivals are now running for over 15 years with increasing participation numbers. This is in itself significant as it demonstrates the attractiveness of these events to locals and visitors. This success is determined by the timing of the event during the summer holiday period, the location and accessibility of the events close to the city centres of the two major tourism hubs in Tasmania, Launceston and Hobart, their acceptance by the local communities and the continuing support by the local, regional and state administrations.

Additionally, the events foster local pride in their communities, generate local travel by Tasmanians and visitors, add attractions to the Tasmanian tourism products, can be used for marketing purposes and showcase Tasmanian produce to local, national and international audiences. They also help to reduce the impact of the seasonality of the Tasmanian tourism industry and stimulate its development.

Due to the cost of staging events, sponsoring is emerging as an important issue. For example, issues have been raised about sponsorship of the Taste of Tasmania. In 2006–2007 one of the event's major sponsors was Tamar Ridge Estate, a division of the timber company Gunns Limited. Many claimed that this association was inappropriate given the damaging impact that logging has on the Tasmanian environment, and the clean, green image of Tasmania (Paine, 2007). This is especially true, given the national attention that has been given to the plan by Gunns Limited to build a pulp and paper mill in the Tamar Valley, one of the State's premier wine regions. Many food and wine producers in the region have therefore been opposed to the mills development given the potential impact it may have on their crops.

Overall, it can be said that special events play an important role in the Australian and the Tasmanian tourism industry. They are particularly relevant for rural regions, their industries and their communities. Food and wine events are thereby increasingly used to showcase and sell local produce, to attract tourists and enhance their local cultural experiences, and to increase community pride. The two case studies, Festivale and Taste of Tasmania, confirm these points as well as making suggestion how to retain the longevity of such events.

Web site addresses for further information

Events tourism:
Events Australia: http://www.events.australia.com
Events Tasmania: http://www.eventstasmania.com

Food and Wine tourism in Australia:

Restaurant and Catering Australia: http://www.restaurantcater.asn.au

Winemaker Federation of Australia (WFA): http://www.wfa.org.au

Australia Wine Export Council (AWEC): http://www.wineaustralia.com

Tourism Australia: http://www.tourism.australia.com

Food and Wine Atlas: http://www.foodandwineatlas.com

References

Australian Government (2007). Department of Industry, Tourism and Resources 2007, Australia's tourism industry fact sheet, http://industry.gov.au/content/itrinternet/cmscontent.cfm?objectid=86562E5E-65BF-4956-BD7541205A8ED978&indexPages=/content/itrinternet/cmsindexpage.cfm?objectid=48A5DFEA-20E0-68D8-EDB550B8BD2CB714&indexType=crossindustry accessed 03.09.2007.

Blewett, D. and Midgley, E. (2007). Festivale's secret is keeping it fresh. The Examiner, 05.02.2007: online, http://northern-tasmania.yourguide.com.au/home.asp?ix=2&mast_id=134 accessed 30.09.2007.

Brand Tasmania (2007). Facts about Tasmania, http://www.about-australia.com/facts/tasmania/accessed 03.07.2007.

Dimmock, K. and Tiyce, M. (2001). Festivale and events: celebrating special interest tourism. In Douglas, N., Douglas, N. and Derret, R. (eds.) *Special Interest Tourism*. John Wiley & Sons Australia Ltd, Milton.

Ellis, D. and Clark, J. (1985). *Sullivans Cove. Birthplace of a Nation*. Tasmanian Museum and Art Gallery, Hobart.

Events Tasmania (2006a). Tasmanian Events Calendar: Festivale, http://events.dtpha.tas.gov.au/Events/Controller/view_event.asp?id= 337 accessed 03.09.2007.

Events Tasmania (2006b). Events Tasmania Strategic Plan 2006–2010, Events Tasmania: Hobart, http://events.tas.gov.au/StrategicPlan2006-10.pdf accessed 03.09.2007.

Events Tasmania (2007a). $30,000 grants for regional events and festivals, Events Tasmania: Hobart, http://www.eventstasmania.com/subpage.cgi?pageID=19&subsectionID=94&task=DISPLAY&id=317384 accessed 16.08.2007.

Events Tasmania (2007b). Tasmanian Event Management Guide, Events Tasmania: Hobart, http://www.eventstasmania.com/

subpage.cgi?pageID=19&subsectionID=91&task=DISPLAY &id=317356 accessed 16.08.2007.

Events Tasmania (2007c). About us, Our role, Events Tasmania: Hobart, http://www.eventstasmania.com/subpage.cgi?pageID=2&subsectionID=21 accessed 01.09.2007.

Events Tasmania (2007d). Event Tourism on the increase, Events Tasmania: Hobart, http://www.eventstasmania.com/subpage.cgi?pageID=19&subsectionID=91&task=DISPLAY&id=317375 accessed 16.08.2007.

Hall, C.M. (2005). Rural wine and food tourism cluster and network development. In Hall, D., Kirkpatrick, I. and Mitchell, M. (eds.) *Rural Tourism and Sustainable Business*. Channel View Publications, Clevedon.

Hall, C.M. (2007). *Tourism in Australia. Development, Issues and Change*, 5th edition. Pearson Education Australia, Frenchs Forest.

Hall, C.M. and Mitchell, R. (2001). Wine and food tourism. In Douglas, N., Douglas, N. and Derrett, R. (eds.) *Special Interest Tourism*. John Wiley & Sons Australia, Milton.

Hall, C.M. and Mitchell, R. (2006). Gastronomy, food and wine tourism. In Buhalis, D. and Costa, C. (eds.) *Tourism Business Frontiers. Consumers, Products and Industry*. Elsevier Butterworth-Heinemann, Oxford.

Hall, C.M. and Page, S.J. (2006). *The Geography of Tourism & Recreation. Environment, Place and Space*, 3rd edition. Routledge, Abingdon.

Hall, C.M. and Sharples, E. (2003). The consumption of experiences or the experience of consumption: An introduction to the tourism of taste. In Hall, C.M., Sharples, E., Mitchell, R., Cambourne, B. and Macionis, N. (eds.) *Food Tourism Around the World: Development, Management and Markets*. Butterworth-Heinemann, Oxford, pp. 1–24.

Hobart Summer Festival (2007). The Taste, http://www.hobartsummerfestival.com.au/event.php?id=8 accessed 03.09.2007.

Midgley, E. (2006). Celebration of life in wine region, The Examiner: online, 02.05.2007, http://northerntasmania.yourguide.com.au/home.asp?ix=2&mast_id=134 accessed 29.09.2007.

Midgley, E. (2007a). Festivale to show variety with 40 acts, The Examiner: online 02.02.2007, http://northerntasmania.yourguide.com.au/home.asp?ix=2&mast_id=134 accessed 29.09.2007.

Midgley, E. (2007b). States produce takes on the world, The Examiner: online, 06.02.2007, http://northerntasmania.

yourguide.com.au/home.asp?ix=2&mast_id=134 accessed 30.09.2007.

Osborne, N. (2007). A festival of flavours to savour, The Examiner: online, 07.02.2007, http://northerntasmania. yourguide.com.au/home.asp?ix=2&mast_id=134 accessed 29.09.2007.

Paine, M. (2007). Taste loses Gunns backing, The Mercury: online, 09.08.2007; http://themercury.news.com.au/?from=ni_story accessed 30.09.2007.

Price, N. and Daniels, G. (2007). Event's success has organizers delighted, The Examiner: online, 13.02.2007, http://north-erntasmania.yourguide.com.au/home.asp?ix=2&mast_id=134 accessed 30.09.2007.

Rath, J. (2002). Immigrants and the tourist industry. The commodification of cultural resources, XVth World Congress of Sociology, Brisbane (07.07.-13.07.2002), http://bibemp2. us.es/turismo/turismonet1/economia%20del%20turismo/ turismo%20y%20antropologia%20social/inmigrants%20and %20tourism%20industry.pdf accessed 24.10.2007.

Servant, N. (2005). *Apple Industry, in Alexander, A., The Companion to Tasmanian History, Centre for Tasmanian Historical Studies.* University of Tasmania, Hobart.

Taste of Tasmania (2007). The Taste Navigator, http://www. hobartsummerfestival.com.au/Taste_Navigator.pdf accessed 01.10.2007.

The Victorian Major Events Company (2007). VMEC Mission, http://www.vmec.com.au/mission.html accessed 01.10.2007.

Tourism Australia (2005). Snapshots: culinary tourism in Australia, Tourism Australia: online, http://www.tourism. australia.com/content/Niche/niche_snapshot_culinary.pdf accessed 22.06.2007.

Tourism Australia (2007). Tourism info: Food & Wine, Tourism Australia: online, http://www.tra.australia.com/niche. asp?lang=EN&sub=0128 accessed 01.10.2007.

Tourism Australia (2007). Visitor Arrival Data, http://tourism. australia.com/Research.asp?sub=0318&al=2602 accessed 21.06.2007.

Tourism Promotion Plan Working Group (2007). Programme Two- Spring Campaigns http://www.tpptasmania.com/sub-prog2.html accessed 28.06.2007.

Tourism Tasmania (2002). Tasmanian Wine and Food Tourism Strategy, Tourism Tasmania: Hobart, http://www.tourismtas-mania.com.au/pdf/food&wine_strategy2002.pdf accessed 28.06.2007.

Tourism Tasmania (2004). Tasmanian Journeys. Cool Wine & Food, Cool Wilderness, Tourism Tasmania: Hobart, http://

www.tourismtasmania.com.au/pdf/2004_mktg_winefood. pdf accessed 27.06.2007.

Tourism Tasmania (2006). Short Breaks Market Profile, Tourism Tasmania: Hobart, http://www.tourismtasmania. com.au/pdf/2006_shortbreaks_marketprofile.pdf accessed 27.07.2007.

Tourism Tasmania (2007). Wine & Food. Feeding the World Tasmanian Style, Tourism Tasmania: Hobart, http://travel-media.tourismtasmania.com.au/inspired/cellardoor/feed_world.html accessed 29.06.2007.

Tourism Tasmania (2007a). Food & Wine a Way of Life, Tourism Tasmania: Hobart, http://travelmedia.tourismtasmania.com. au/inspired/cellardoor/way_life.html accessed 29.06.2007.

Van der Wagen, L. (2005). *Event Management for Tourism, Cultural, Business and Sporting Events,* 2nd edition. Pearson Education Australia, Frenchs Forest.

Walch, B. (2005). Making Your Business Even More Successful, Tourism Tasmania: Hobart, http://www.cradlecoast.com/ Files/00858_BridgetWalch-TourismTasmania.pdf accessed 26.06.2007.

Waterhouse, C. (2005). Taste Future Fears Over Location Woe, The Mercury: online, 25.08.2007, http://themercury.news. com.au/?from = ni_story accessed 29.09.2007.

Waterhouse, C. (2007a). Ratepayers foot Taste bill, The Mercury: online, 03.11.2006, http://themercury.news.com. au/?from = ni_story accessed 29.09.2007.

Waterhouse, C. (2007b). Ratepayers foot Taste bill, The Mercury: online, 5.11.2006, http://themercury.news.com. au/?from = ni_story accessed 29.09.2007.

PART III

Wine and drink festivals

CHAPTER 9

Apples, cider and celebration

Liz Sharples

Introduction

Wherever, and whenever, there is a harvest, there is a cause for celebration. The autumnal gathering of apples from orchards and groves around the world is no exception. This is a crop which is consumed, appreciated and savoured by millions of people, young and old, and apple juice and cider, made from the pressing of this precious commodity, is also widely revered.

Apples and cider have been at the heart of many communities for hundreds of years. In certain regions, for example in Somerset, England, the story of apples and cider is part of their rich social history. Cider was even used as currency between the seventeenth and late nineteenth centuries when farm labourers in the region received an allowance of cider as part of their daily wages (Crowden, 1999; Evans, 2002). In other countries today, for example in China, apples have become a valuable export crop and are an important part of their economic well-being.

Apple producing areas are also interesting and attractive places for tourists to visit. A walk around a local orchard in spring, when the apple blossom is out, or a tour of a cider works in autumn, when apples are being pressed, can be an evocative, memorable, experience for a visitor. These landscapes are great backdrops for some of the ceremonies, festivals and events, which take place in honour of apples and cider.

This chapter explores the themes behind several apple and cider festivals and their role and relevance to modern society. The chapter primarily focuses on the UK, but information from around the world is used to support the discussion.

Firstly, to develop an understanding of the basis on which apple and cider celebration is built, the following section explores the commodity's international historic and current significance and identifies trends in the market.

Apples and cider: history and markets

Apples are the fruit of one of the most widely cultivated trees in the world. Its true origin is a subject of healthy debate, but it is possible to trace the current species *Malus domestica*, back to its wild ancestor, *Malus sieversii*. This species, still native in the Tien Shan mountain range of Central Asia in Kazakhstan, is known as 'alma' and the region where it is thought to originate is called 'Alma-Ata' or 'Father of Apples'. Traces of apple found at historic sites provide evidence that apples were in existence more than 4,000 years ago (Institute of Food Research, 2007).

Apple trees were some of the earliest trees to be cultivated and there are now more than 7,000 cultivars of apples worldwide (Food Reference, 2007). The world's largest collection of apple cultivars is kept in England at the National Fruit Collection at Brogdale, where 2,300 varieties are housed (Brogdale, 2007). Apples have become an important commodity across many cool climate countries of Asia, Europe, the USA, South Africa and Australasia.

Over 80 countries around the globe grow apples commercially and together they produce in the region of 58 million metric tons each year with a value of about $10 billion (USDA, 2005). More than half of this total is produced by the top five apple producing countries, China (which grows two-fifths of the total) the USA, Turkey, France and Iran (USDA, 2005).

The UK apple market is worth about £320 million, but only 30–35 per cent of eating apples in the UK are grown there, despite there being a wealth of traditional varieties in existence. The majority of apple sales occur in the supermarkets (70 per cent) and many of these stores carry only about eight varieties, although on a positive note, this is double the number of varieties that they held 5 years ago (Institute of Food Research, 2007). In the USA, it is a similar picture with eight varieties accounting for about 80 per cent of all the US production, although new varieties are now being introduced (Food Reference, 2007).

Wherever apples are grown, apple juice and cider become part of that culture. Cider can be made from the pressing and fermentation of juice from any species of apple, but in many regions certain cultivar are favoured and may be known as 'cider apples'. One point that must be remembered, however, is that in the USA the term 'apple cider' is often used to describe non-alcoholic apple juice, rather than the fermented version. This fact can be confusing when accurately trying to establish the size of markets (Browning, 1998).

Many European and Scandinavian countries have long cider traditions, including France (particularly in Normandy and Brittany) Spain, the Channel Islands, Germany, Finland, Sweden and Denmark. The USA, Canada, Australia, New Zealand, Argentina, Chile, Mexico and South Africa also have well established cider industries.

Cider is very popular in the UK, especially in the South-West, where its history and traditions can be traced back for many centuries.

Folklore would suggest that cider apples, like vines, were introduced to England by the Romans in 55 BC, however; some would argue that wild crab apples and other indigenous apple species were part of English landscape for many years prior to the Roman occupation. For example, the town of Glastonbury in the Northern part of Somerset (one of the major cider producing regions) was also called Avallon or Ynys Avallac, The Isle of Apples by the Iron age tribes who dwelled there (Copas, 2002). There are many early references to cider production in the county, which are nicely discussed by Crowden (1999).

Since its early beginnings, the UK cider industry has seen its good times and bad with regards to its popularity and market size, which have been well documented by a number of authors (Crowden, 1999; Copas, 2002). The late seventeenth century and early eighteenth century were the 'heyday' of UK cider production, but unfortunately by the end of the nineteenth century the industry was in decline being squeezed by 'wine from above and beer from below' (Crowden, 1999). Over the last century, there has been a substantial loss of traditional orchards in Somerset and other counties such as Kent and Hereford, as farmers have ripped out trees in favour of more profitable crops. This has led to an overall decline in area of up to 70 per cent, over the last 50 years (DEFRA, 2004a). Despite a number of schemes that have been introduced to replant traditional orchards, the latest report by the Department of the Environment, Food and Rural Affairs (DEFRA, 2007b) still shows a small decline of 3 per cent in total orchard area in England and Wales between 2004 and 2007.

Organizations such as Common Ground (Common Ground, 2007a) have been influential in trying to halt this trend by helping to preserve orchards, the range of apple varieties which grow there, and the rituals and ceremonies associated with apple growing. This is discussed later in the chapter in Exhibit 9.2.

At the present time, the market is enjoying a modest revival with total cider production having doubled in the last 20 years (National Association of Cider Makers (NACM), 2007). Obtaining accurate data regarding the size and nature of the market is not easily accessible however. Members of the NACM make approximately 90–95 per cent of the UK cider, but this data does not include information from some of the smaller cider makers who operate independently and who sell much of their cider locally or from the farm-gate.

Figures from the NACM report that the UK currently has the highest per capita consumption of cider in the world (NACM, 2007) as well as the world's largest cider producing company, H.P. Bulmer, who produce 65 per cent of the 5 million hectolitres of cider sold annually in the UK (Bulmers, 2007).

There are marked differences between cider varieties on offer, ranging from modern pale 'designer' ciders made using mass produced techniques to the traditional farmhouse ciders made using techniques which have not changed for centuries.

Over the last decade, there has been a gradual decline in the sale of farmhouse cider, but there has been a growing interest in the production of specialist ciders, such as sparkling ciders, single varietal ciders (made using one variety of apples) and cider brandy.

Pomaceous celebration

So how are apples and cider celebrated? What are the drivers that create an interest in apple and cider festivals and what significance do these events have for the communities and localities in which they take place?

Finding accurate information about the number and nature of apple/cider events that take place globally is challenging as there is no definitive database. An examination of several key web sites, however, provides a snapshot across the sector and is a useful indicator of the *nature* of this phenomenon.

The National Apple Museum in Pennsylvania, USA, lists over 40 apple festivals which are held annually across the states (National Apple Museum, 2007) and the 'Pick Your Own' web site lists over 70 festivals which are held in the USA. (Pick Your Own, 2007). It is likely that these sources are a mere 'glimpse' of the actual level of activity that takes place. It is possible to see, however, that the majority of these are community seasonal events held at harvest time (September/October) and about a third of these are devoted to the manufacture and adoration of 'Apple Butter' which is discussed later in Exhibit 9.3.

Apple events are also well established across Canada. A theme which appears to be popular amongst many of the Canadian events is the combination of apples with crafts, as at the Apple Harvest Hoedown and Quilt Show held in Vernon, British Columbia and the Meaford Apple Harvest Craft Show held in Ontario (Pick Your Own, 2007).

In the UK, the preservation of heritage associated with apples and orchards appears to be a key message (Pick Your Own, 2007). Exhibits 9.1 and 9.2 demonstrate this commitment. The UK cider web site (UK Cider, 2007) is also useful in providing information about cider festivals and lists over 50 events, where cider is a key component. Some of these festivals are combined beer/cider celebrations and many incorporate food, for example, cheese, as part of their offering.

Apple festivals are also popular in Scandinavia. In Sweden, for example, the fishing town of Kivk hosts an annual apple market each autumn. The original aim of the event was to ensure the survival of apple varieties and the apple industry in Sweden, and now in its 20th year, it usually attracts about 20,000 visitors. An important element of the event is Apple Art and in 1998 the painting of Swedish botanist Carl Linnaeus entered the Guinness book of World Records as the world's largest apple artwork ever (The Local, 2007).

Each apple or cider festival or event which takes place has its own aims, objectives, markets and style of management. It is possible, however, to identify certain key attributes within these events which suggest their importance and relevance to their host communities. Getz (1997) identifies eight attributes which are inherent within many special events that 'create and define the sense of "specialness" and make the event memorable'. These include: festive spirit, uniqueness, quality, authenticity, tradition, hospitality, theming and symbolism. These attributes are echoed throughout the exhibits in this chapter.

Within the remit of this chapter, it is only possible to examine a small sample of these events, but the following exhibits serve to provide us with some level of insight and understanding. Two of the festivals are based in the UK, the other exhibit describes USA festivals.

Apples, fertility and symbolism

For thousands of years, apples have been associated with legends, stories and myths of love, sensuality, fertility and temptation. Apples appear in many religious traditions, often being portrayed as a forbidden or mystical fruit.

In the Garden of Eden popular Christian tradition holds that it was an apple that was used by Eve to coax Adam and in Greek mythology we read how Gaia (Mother Earth) presented a tree with golden apples to Zeus and his bride Hera on their wedding day. In the European fairy tale, Snow White, the beautiful young heroine is tempted and poisoned by her wicked stepmother with a delicious ripe red apple.

This first exhibit (Exhibit 9.1) tells the story of wassailing, a tradition which also has its roots in the distant past. This is usually a small-scale event which has no financial motive and is as important for the local community as it is for the visitors.

The abundance of the orchard is the main focus of the event and the symbolic ceremony which is performed there has a fixed pattern and elements which make it almost religious in nature. It is part of the ancient English agricultural calendar and folk lore, and the up-keep of this local tradition is a driving force behind its survival.

The apple as a symbol of fertility nicely demonstrated.

Exhibit 9.1   Wassailing

Wassailing is an ancient custom associated with cider apple trees. It is a tradition that is still kept in the South-West counties of England, such as Herefordshire and Somerset. The word itself comes from the Anglo-Saxon 'Waes Hael', and it is a toast which means 'good health to you' or 'be whole'. The earliest records of wassailing taking place date from the late seventeenth century (NACM, 2007) although it is likely that this type of ceremony took place in earlier times. The idea of carrying out a wassailing ceremony is to protect apple trees from bad spirits and to ensure a good crop for the following year. There are variations on how the ceremony is carried out at different orchards and in different regions, but they all contain several key elements.

The event starts by a group of people gathering in the orchard around an apple tree. A master of ceremonies, often known as the Butler, is appointed to lead the festivities. Sometimes this person will black his face in disguise. The youngest person in attendance is sometimes asked to place pieces of toast soaked in cider in the forked branches of the oldest tree to attract good spirits, and then a bucket of spiced cider is poured over the roots of the tree.

A wassailing song is then sung. This is an extract from the one that is sung at the Butcher's Arms in Carhampton in Somerset and is recorded in a book by Evans (2002):

> Oh apple tree we wassail thee
> And happily will thou bear
> For the Lord doth know where we shall be
> Till apples another year
>
> Old apple tree! We wassail thee!
> And hoping thou will bear
> Hatsful, capsful, three bushel bagsful
> And a little heap under the stair

This is followed immediately by shouting, cheering, banging on pots and pans, and guns are fired into the tress to drive away evil spirits and to ensure a bountiful crop for the following year. The health of the tree is then drunk using cider sometimes using a wassailing cup. This communal cup derives from the Tudor custom of passing round a cup at Christmas time. Eventually the spicy punch itself became known as the wassail.

(*Continued*)

The wassailing custom is still an important part of the festive calendar at English farms and orchards. The event usually takes place on the 'old' or the 'new' 12th night, in other words the 6th or the 17th January. We now normally consider the 6th January to be the 12th night, but back in 1752, the calendar was adjusted which resulted in an 11 day shift. The wassailing tradition was so firmly rooted in some local cultures that the original date is upheld. For example, in Somerset most orchards work to the old calendar (Evans, 2002).

The most reliable source of finding out about when, and where, the wassailing ceremonies will take place is the Common Ground web site (Common Ground, 2007a). It currently lists about 30 individual events which are taking place in 2008 at country houses, community orchards, pubs and farms.

For example, at Broome farm in Ross on Wye in Herefordshire, the ceremony is followed by music from a live band and guests enjoy hot soup and mulled cider (Broome Farm, 2007). The Butcher's Arms in Carhampton, Somerset, claims to have the longest unbroken wassailing tradition in England (Common Ground, 2007a).

Apples, heritage and local distinctiveness

As discussed earlier in this chapter, apples are an important crop, at an economic level, for many countries around the world. Due to their long history of cultivation, certain apple varieties also have strong linkages to specific geographic regions and, as such, apples and cider have importance and value as part of our culinary heritage. Changes in agricultural practice, and the globalization of the food chain over recent years, has led to a decline in the range of apples now available to the consumer, and there is now a drive to conserve, promote and educate the public about this key commodity. A number of organizations have shown their commitment to this campaign including the international Slow Food Movement who has an Ark of Taste project to protect certain species (Slow Food, 2007 and see Exhibit 20.1).

Common Ground is another UK based organization who have taken up this challenge, and the following exhibit demonstrates the way in which a food 'event' can play its part in raising public awareness about a foodstuff and its links to the locality in which it is produced. This is a major event, in that it is organized and administered at a national level, but due to the strong political and environmental debate that this event evokes, it could be argued that the impacts can be felt at a local, national and even international level.

The themes of tradition, authenticity and heritage are well demonstrated.

Exhibit 9.2   Apple Day

Apple Day was initiated in the UK by the organization Common Ground in 1990. It is an annual celebration of 'apples, orchards and local distinctiveness' (Common Ground, 2007a), and each year hundreds of local events take place on or around the 21st October.

It has two main aims. Firstly, Apple Day is in an attempt to raise awareness of the incredible knowledge base and heritage associated with both apple growing and apple juice/cider production, held within the UK and secondly, there is the aim of protecting both orchards and the wealth of apple varieties that grow within them.

The event supports Common Ground's 'Save the Orchard' campaign, launched in 1988, which has an aim to:

Reverse the loss of beautiful and productive orchards and once common local varieties of fruit, and to reassert their place in landscape and culture, their potential for active community involvement and their genetic importance (Common Ground, 2007a).

The festival is actually a series of events held throughout the country around harvest time in October and is 'locally driven', i.e. all of the events are individual 'happenings' organized by a number of different organizations throughout the country. Common Ground, however, promote the events centrally via their web site encouraging organizers to inform them of events so that they can advertise them on their 'Apple Map'.

The launch of Apple Day took place in 1990 at Covent Garden in London and 'rolled out' in 1991 with 50 events around the country. By 2000, there were more then 600 events taking place and in 2007 over 400 events were advertised on the Common Ground web site (Common Ground, 2007b).

The participants include individual apple growers, garden centres, apple juice and cider makers, schools and colleges, local authorities, farmers' markets, allotment associations and wildlife trusts. National organizations such as The National Trust, English Heritage, the Royal Horticultural Society, CAMRA and Brogdale Horticultural Trust also get involved. For example, see the National Trust web site (National Trust, 2007).

The types of events taking place are diverse including: orchard planting, horticultural lectures, guided tours of orchards, cookery demonstrations, apple juice and cider tasting, apple displays, and plays, poetry and storytelling about apples and cider. Apple Day even has its own resident poet, James Crowden.

Identification sessions take place where visitors are encouraged to bring along unusual apples, which they may have growing in their own garden or orchard, for apple experts to identify. In this way, certain varieties, which were thought to have become extinct, are rediscovered. Certain games, such as the 'longest apple peel competition' have become popular at a number of events.

Apples, community and hospitality

Apples and cider are an important part of American culinary heritage, particularly in the mid-West states. As in many other countries, the Americans have a number of popular apple stories of personal endeavour which are a rich part of their oral and written history. One story tells of how an apple farmer called John Chapman from Massachusetts became famous in the 1800s when he travelled the states of Indiana, Illinois and Ohio distributing apple tress and seeds to the settlers. Johnny Appleseed, as he became known, is celebrated in America as a symbol of expansion and development. This figure of Johnny Appleseed is a well-known symbol, which is used at many orchards and apple festivals as a key part of their visitor interpretation.

Virginia State is a well established apple producer which has an impressive number of apple festivals advertised as a key part of their tourist product. The longevity of many of these festivals suggests that these events have a strong local significance and importance for the communities in which they are staged. Their collective marketing approach, however, also demonstrates a desire to extend their hospitality by the sharing of this experience with visitors.

Exhibit 9.3   Virginia State Apple Harvest and Apple Butter Festivals

---

The State of Virginia adopts an organized and professional approach to the marketing of their apple festivals.

The Virginia Apple Growers Association (VAGA, 2007a), which is an official commodity board of the Virginia Department of Agriculture and Consumer Services (VDACS, 2007) produces a comprehensive list of all the apple events which take place in the state during the year.

Their web page (VAGA, 2007b) lists about 20 apple events, which are staged annually during the months of September, October and November. Apples are important to the state's economy contributing an estimated $235 million annually through the sales of apples, apple juice, cider, processed apple slices and apple butter (VAGA, 2007c). Apple butter is a sweet jam-like product which is made through the boiling of apples, sugar, cinnamon and other spices such as cloves.

(Continued)

The state also acknowledges the money that is brought into the region through attendance at the festivals by tourists. Although the majority of these festivals are local or regional in nature, collectively they make a contribution through visitor spending at the event itself and at businesses nearby.

Many of these festivals are long-standing community events, many of which have been in existence for 20 to 30 years. For example, the Annual Boones Mill Apple Festival has been in existence for 31 years and is a family event which includes entertainment, an Apple Queen Parade as well as an art show and apple based crafts. The event is sponsored by the local Lions Club (Boones Mill, 2007). Another long-standing festival is held at Flippin-Seaman Inc.; an apple grower, packer and shipper, who have held an Apple Butter Making festival for over 30 years on the first and third Saturdays in October. Apple butter is made in the traditional way over open fires using large copper kettles. Live music is provided by local groups and there are apples, cider, pumpkins and crafts for sale (Flippin Seaman, 2007). At the Graves Mountain orchards the owners open their doors to visitors at their annual Apple Harvest festival, which has been running for 39 years. This event includes a lunch with an apple theme, bluegrass music, cloggers, arts and crafts and horseback rides. The orchards are open for visitors to 'pick their own' or apples can be purchased from the farm shop area (Graves Mountain, 2007).

Conclusions

So apples and cider have obviously been, and continue to be, important commodities at a local, regional, national and international level.

They have a long and distinctive history, are part of man's heritage and culture and make an important contribution to the health of economies around the world. They are also a great subject of celebration and festivity at many levels. The exhibits displayed in the chapter provide just a flavour of the diverse nature of these events which take place around the globe.

References

Boones Mill (2007) at http://boonesmillapplefestival.com
Brogdale (2007) at http://www.brogdale.org/nfc_home.php

Broome Farm (2007) at http://www.rosscider.com/wassailing.htm

Browning (1998). *Apples: The Story of the Fruit of Temptation*. Penguin Books, London.

Bulmers (2007) at http://www.bulmer.com

Common Ground (2007a) at http://www.commonground.org.uk

Common Ground (2007b) at http://www.commonground.org.uk/appleday/a-events.html

Copas, L. (2002). *A Somerset Pomona. The Cider Apples of Somerset*. The Dovecote Press, Dorset.

Crowden, J. (1999). *Cider: The Forgotten Miracle*. Cyder Press, Somerset.

DEFRA (2004a). *Basic Horticultural Statistics for the UK*. Department of Environment, Food and Rural Affairs, London.

DEFRA (2007b). *Orchard Fruit Survey-Feb 2007, National Statistics*. Department of Food and Rural Affairs, London.

Evans, R. (2002). *Blame It on the Cider: Scrumpy Tales from Somerset*. Countryside Books, Berkshire.

Flippin Seaman (2007) at http://www.flippin-seaman.com/ABFest.htm

Food Reference (2007) at http://www.foodreference.com/html/fapples.html

Getz, D. (1997). *Event Management and Event Tourism*. Cognizant Communication Corporation, Canada.

Graves Mountain (2007) at http://www.gravesmountain.com/appleharvest.htm

Institute of Food Research (2007) at http://www.ifr.ac.uk/Public/FoodInfoSheets/applefacts.html

National Apple Museum (2007) at http://nationalapplemuseum.com/festivals.html

National Association of Cider Makers (NACM) (2007) at http://www.cideruk.com/index.htm

National Trust (2007) at http://nationaltrust.org.uk/main/w-vh/w-visits/w-events/w-corporate_partners-copella-2.htm

Pick Your Own (2007) at http://www.pickyourown.org/index.htm

Slow Food (2007) at http://www.slowfoodfoundation.org/eng/arca/lista.lasso

The Local (2007) at http://www.thelocal.se/8593/20070924

UK Cider (2007) at http://www.ukcider.co.uk

USDA (2005). Fruit and Tree Nuts Outlook/FTS-315/March 31, 2005. Economic Research Service, USDA.

VAGA (2007a) at http://www.virginiaapples.org

VAGA (2007b) at http://www.virginiaapples.org/events/index.html

VAGA (2007c) at http://www.virginiaapples.org/facts/index.html

VDACS (2007) at http://www.vdacs.virginia.gov/

CHAPTER **10**

Segmenting wine festival visitors using their personal involvement with wine

Jingxue (Jessica) Yuan, Alastair M. Morrison, Liping A. Cai, Tim H. Dodd and Sally Linton

Introduction

In recent years, wine festivals have become popular in many regions. Wine festivals present a unique synergy between wine, special events, and travel activities, adding value to the tourism development of a wine region (Salter, 1998; Yuan et al., 2005). Wine-related events attract visitors and give opportunities for wineries and wine regions to promote the destination and products (Getz, 2000; Hoffman et al., 2001; Houghton, 2001). Having a good time at a wine festival, visitors leave with a positive image of the wine and/or the wine tourism region. This image may then lead to future purchase of the product and re-visitation. Wine festivals have increasingly become an effective promotional strategy for wine regions, attracting a wider audience than wineries alone (Collins, 1996).

Visiting wine festivals is one activity encompassed within wine tourism, which incorporates service provision and destination marketing (Getz and Brown, 2005). In this process, wineries and winegrowing regions provide the core products, namely the wine and the tourist attractions, whereas wine festivals are developed to promote and to enhance the awareness of these products. By partnering together to stage a regional event, wineries develop a high profile opportunity to market their products to the wider community (Beverland et al., 2001). Wine festivals therefore play an important role in selling wine brands, promoting the attractiveness of winegrowing regions, and helping build customer loyalty towards individual wineries. It is then important to understand the nature of wine festival visitors and their segmentation in order to develop appropriate promotional strategies. Wine festivals, if taking place at convenient locations, may attract attendees who do not intend to visit any winery or winegrowing region and thereby would never be ascribed to the category of wine tourists.

The current research was conducted to develop a typology of visitors attending a regional wine festival. The purposes of the research were as follows:

1. To segment visitors at a wine festival based on their personal involvement with wine.
2. To profile the segments based on visitors' motivations to attend the wine festival, their evaluation of the festival quality, their satisfaction, value perception, behavioural intentions, and demographic characteristic.

Literature review

Personal involvement with wine as a segmentation tool

The concept of involvement has been identified as an important factor in explaining consumer behaviour since Krugman (1965) introduced the term to consumer psychology. Numerous studies have since then been produced in a wide variety of consumer-related research. Yet one underlying theme appears to remain constant. Involvement is postulated as the consumer's perceived importance or relevance for an object, such as a product, based on inherent needs, value, and interest. For example, Antil (1986), on the basis of the inherent interrelationship of involvement components, defined involvement as the level of perceived personal importance and/or interest evoked by a stimulus (or stimuli). The stimulus may refer to a product class. Involvement is then conceptualized as interest in or perception of importance of a particular product category (Zaichkowsky, 1985), such as wine.

The level of personal involvement with wine demonstrates a wine consumer's generic feelings of importance and relevance with the product class. It also reflects his or her genuine level of interest in wine on a daily basis. The concept captures a wine consumer's feelings of interest, enthusiasm, and excitement about the product category. Personal involvement with wine reflects an underlying aspect of a wine consumer's lifestyle. It is determined by an individual's inherent value system as well as his or her unique experiences.

Lockshin et al. (1997) asserted that wine consumers could be ascribed into two different groups: those involved in wine and those not involved in wine. Highly involved wine consumers are wine enthusiasts. These individuals relate to wine as part of their lifestyle where it holds an important place in their daily lives. According to Lockshin (2001), these individuals often spend considerable time reading specialty magazines, lingering in the retail stores, talking to sales people and discussing their hobby with friends. Wine becomes a pursuit of pleasure for an individual. Wine enthusiasts take approximately one-third of wine consumers, but buy more wine and spend more per bottle than low involvement buyers. When visiting wineries, a study by Dodd and Gustafson (1997) found that there was a positive relationship between product and purchase involvement and wine purchase. In addition, there was a positive relationship between product involvement and purchase of souvenirs.

Meanwhile, in the wine tourism research area, it has also been realized that wine tourists are not alike in terms of their needs, wants, and personal characteristics. They should be treated as heterogeneous groups. There have been attempts to classify wine tourists and a variety of segments have been produced in different parts of the world:

Western Australia – Ali-Knight and Charters (1999)
British Columbia – Williams and Dossa (2003)
Italy – Movimento del Turismo del Vino study, 1996 (cited in
      Cambourne and Macionis, 2000)
New Zealand – Hall (1996)
Texas – Dodd and Bigotte (1997)

Charters and Ali-Knight (2002) continued with the research effort. They asked respondents in two wine regions of Western Australia to self-classify on the basis of their interest in and knowledge of wine. This classification produced four groups – the wine lover (the 'highly interested'), the wine interested (the 'interested'), the wine novice (those with limited interest), and the 'hangers on,' a marginal group who went to wineries with no apparent interest in wine, but as a part of a group. The previous educational experience of different segments varied, with the wine lovers having a more comprehensive grounding in wine.

A more recent and comprehensive review of the post-visit consumer behaviour of New Zealand winery visitors by Mitchell and Hall (2004) also identified a number of segments. In their study, a higher propensity for brand loyalty (i.e. post-visit purchase and repeat visitation) was found among those with intermediate or advanced wine knowledge, and those drinking wine more frequently and purchasing more wine. More importantly, brand loyal behaviour was found in repeat visitors to wineries and those who purchased wine during the visit. The findings suggest that routine wine consumption is part of a wider relationship with winery and its wine.

Can wine festival visitors be segmented on the basis of their personal involvement with (i.e. their interest level in) wine? If so, will there be any differences exhibited between the market niches related to their socio-demographic characteristics, travel motivations, and other trip behaviours related to the festival?

Previous examinations of wine event goers suggest that wine festivals largely attract wine enthusiasts who would pay repeat visits to the event (Weiler et al., 2004). It is therefore noteworthy to investigate the motivation and satisfaction characteristics of different segments among the festival goers. This exploration would help wine destination marketing and management to develop a more comprehensive understanding of wine festivals and their catalyst effect on repeat wine tourism (Taylor, 2006).

Promoting wine tourism with wine festivals

By fully understanding what their customers want, wine regions can provide the total wine tourism experience in a number of ways, the most notable being cultural heritage, hospitality, education, and festivals and events (Charters and Ali-Knight, 2002). Wine festivals are the cultural resources of an area and also create a one-stop shopping opportunity to sample wines from a particular region (Hoffman et al., 2001). Attending festivals is recognized as the main reason and specific motivation for visiting wineries or wine regions (Hall and Macionis, 1998). Yuan et al. (2005) defined a wine festival, from the consumer's perspective, as a special occasion that attendees 'actively engage in for the satisfaction of their interest in wine and/or for the entertainment made available by other leisure activities' (p. 39).

According to Arnold (1999), there are six reasons for staging festivals: revenue generation, community spirit, recreation/entertainment, social interaction, culture/education, and tourism. As opposed to site or permanent attractions, festivals can be developed at places convenient to the market. Hosting festivals to encourage tourist visitation is an increasingly common phenomenon (Derrett, 2004). Because of their intrinsic uniqueness, festivals often create an image that will help attract tourists to a destination (Getz, 1997). The image associated with the event is transferred to the destination, thereby strengthening, enhancing, or changing the destination's brand (Jago et al., 2003). In recent years, festivals have become a viable component of both the wine and wine tourism industries. When marketing a winegrowing region as tourist destination, festivals offer an extremely good tool for stimulating and increasing awareness and interest in the area (Getz, 2000; Getz and Brown, 2005).

Similarly, wine festival visitors are not alike in terms of their needs, wants, and personal characteristics. They should not be considered as being a homogenous group. It is important for festival organizers and wine marketers to recognize these different groups in order to implement appropriate promotional strategies. Yuan et al. (2005) made an initial attempt in their study to segment wine festival visitors on the basis of attendance motivations. They identified three different types of wine festival attendees, namely 'wine focusers', 'festivity seekers', and 'hangers-on'. The wine focusers was the wine-intensive group, whose members seemed the most highly interested in wine. They were purpose driven and pursued the wine theme when attending the festival. Their motivations were very much focused on the wine. The hangers-on had limited interest in wine and this was not the reason for attending the festival. This group had no particular goals in seeking the festival's leisure experience. The festivity seekers searched for a more diversified or integrated experience incorporating wine, food, environment, setting, learning, and cultural aspects. The festivity seekers may have an interest in wine, but their participation also involved savouring the total experience with wine at the festival.

The purpose of this study was to explore the segmentation of wine festival visitors using their personal involvement with wine and to examine their demographics and some festival-related characteristics of each segment, such as their motivations to attend the wine festival, their evaluation of the festival quality, their satisfaction, value perception, and behavioural intentions.

Research method

Data collection

A visitor survey was conducted at the 2003 Vintage Indiana Wine and Food Festival, a 1-day event organized by the Indiana Wine Grape Council which took place in downtown Indianapolis. It is Indiana's only statewide wine and food festival and was initiated in June 2000. The 2003 event featured live music, a variety of foods presented by local restaurants, wine and food educational sessions. More than 6,000 visitors attended the event in 2003. Ten trained field workers intercepted the attendees on the site of the festival with the survey. Only visitors above 21 years old were approached and a total of 501 useable questionnaires were collected.

Involvement and its measurement

The core variable in this study was personal involvement with wine. Research on involvement has long been conducted in the field of consumer studies, among which a five-item measurement scale, the Personal Involvement Inventory (PII), was developed and validated (Zaichkowsky, 1985; Mittal, 1995). PII has become one of the more widely used self-report measures in marketing research on involvement. It is effective in identifying product enthusiasts and provides direction to marketing strategy aimed at involved customers.

When being applied to classifying wine consumers, this multi-item scale incorporated five pairs of seven-point bipolar descriptive expressions: wine (to the subject) is (1) important/unimportant, (2) of concern/of no concern at all, (3) means a lot/means nothing, (4) significant/insignificant, and (5) matters/does not

151

matter at all. The total score on the five items was secured to denote the overall degree of personal involvement with wine. Wine festival visitors were subsequently segmented into the high wine involvement, medium wine involvement, and low wine involvement groups. Differences between the involvement groups were then examined. These differences pertained to the visitors' motivations to attend the festival, their quality perception of the event, their satisfaction and value perception as well as their behavioural intentions. Demographic characteristics of each segment, including age, gender, marital status, income, and education, were also checked.

Other variables and their measurements

A total of 25 elements were generated to measure motivations to visit the wine festival. Respondents were asked to indicate the importance of the reasons on a seven-point scale where 1 = *not at all important* and 7 = *extremely important*. The 25 motivational elements were further factor analysed and the analysis produced a four-factor solution. The four dimensions were named as: (1) *festival and escape*, (2) *wine*, (3) *socialization*, and (4) *family togetherness*. Nineteen motivational items were retained in this process.

Twelve items were used to assess perceived quality of the wine festival on a seven-point scale, where 1 = *strongly disagree* and 7 = *strongly agree*. A factor analysis was performed to reduce the 12 variables to three perceived quality dimensions labelled as (1) *facility*, (2) *wine*, and (3) *organization*. One quality perception item was deleted in the analysis.

Seven-point scales were employed to evaluate festival attendees' overall satisfaction with the visit (1 = *very dissatisfied*; 7 = *very satisfied*) and their experience at the festival in terms of value for money (1 = *very poor*; 7 = *very good*). Three behavioural intentions were examined: (1) intention to return to the festival next year (1 = *very unlikely*; 7 = *very likely*), (2) likelihood of buying local wines after the wine festival (1 = *very unlikely*; 7 = *very likely*), and (3) possibility of future visitation to a local winery after the wine festival (1 = *very unlikely*; 7 = *very likely*).

The analysis

The summed scores on the five-item PII ranged from 5 to 35 with an overall average of 14.52 (SD = 6.83). In order to assess the dimensionality of the involvement scale applied in this study, an exploratory factor analysis was performed. A single factor solution was reached, explaining 73.92 per cent of the total variance. Coefficient alpha in the reliability test was 0.906. The Kaiser–Meyer–Olkin measure of sampling adequacy was 0.853. It was therefore justified to combine the five PII items to form a total involvement score. In her research, Zaichkowsky (1985) used the overall distribution derived from data collected from 751 subjects to classify the scorers into either low-, medium-, or high-involvement subgroups. Her approach was chosen by the current study as the baseline for the segmentation of the festival visitors. Analysis of variance (ANOVA) tests followed to detect possible differences between the involvement groups in regard with their motivations, quality perceptions, overall satisfaction, value perception, and behavioural intentions. Finally, χ^2 tests were conducted to trace the demographic differences between the involvement groups.

Results and discussion

Sample description

About 76 per cent of the respondents at the festival had college or above degrees. Nearly 69 per cent had annual household incomes of more than $40,000. The respondents were younger than the average wine consumers, as 29.5 per cent of them were in the 21–29 age group and another 22.6 per cent in 30–39 category; and a total of 74.1 per cent were less than 50 years old. The percentages of male and female respondents were 35.9 and 63.7, respectively. Married (53.3 per cent) and not married (46.5 per cent) respondents were nearly evenly split.

Involvement segments

The low involvement cluster was defined as those scoring in the first quartile of the distribution; they had scores ranging from 5 to 10. The medium involvement group was made up of those scoring in the middle 50 per cent of the distribution; they had scores from 11 to 19. High involvement segment consisted of those in the upper quartile of the distribution; they had scores from 20 to 35. Of the 480 valid subjects, 158 (32.9 per cent) had low involvement, 194 (40.4 per cent) displayed medium involvement, and 128 (26.7 per cent) showed high involvement. The mean scores of the five PII items all differed significantly between the three involvement groups (see Table 10.1).

Table 10.1 Level of personal involvement with wine

	Mean of each involvement level			
Involvement item	High involvement	Medium involvement	Low involvement	*F*-value
Wine is important to me	4.3984[a]	2.6701[b]	1.2785[c]	328.787***
Wine is of concern to me	4.1406[a]	3.1443[b]	1.3861[c]	183.490***
Wine means a lot to me	4.8125[a]	3.2680[b]	1.4557[c]	405.870***
Wine is significant to me	4.7109[a]	3.0928[b]	1.4494[c]	446.682***
Wine matters to me	4.7813[a]	2.9948[b]	1.4114[c]	477.840***
N	128.00	194.00	158.00	
%	26.70	40.40	32.90	
Mean of total score	22.8438	15.1701	6.9810	

***Significance level at $p < 0.001$ level.
[a,b,c]The mean difference is significant at the 0.05 level in post hoc test.

Involvement and motivations

Of the four motivational factors, three showcased significant differences (see Table 10.2). The high involvement segment differed from the other two groups in terms of 'festival and escape' and 'wine'. The difference was particularly evident in the dimension of wine. The high involvement segment also had different mean value on 'socialization' from the low involvement group. No difference was revealed on 'family togetherness'.

In order to present a better picture of the differences, items within each motivational dimension were compared, with the exception of those factored in 'family togetherness'. Table 10.3 displayed the results concerning the 'festival & escape' items. The high involvement group was found to give substantially lower scores than the other two involvement groups to five out of the nine items. The low and medium involvement groups

Table 10.2 Wine involvement level and motivational factors to attend the wine festival

| Motivational factor | Mean of each involvement level | | | F-value |
	High involvement	Medium involvement	Low involvement	
Festival and escape	4.7126[a]	5.1622[b]	5.1333[b]	5.554**
Wine	4.7033[a]	5.3059[b]	5.6160[b]	19.607***
Socialization	2.6913[a]	3.0357	3.1645[b]	3.395*
Family togetherness	3.2583	3.5769	3.1892	1.861

*Significance at the $p < 0.05$ level.
**Significance at $p < 0.005$ level.
***Significance level at $p < 0.001$ level.
[a,b]The mean difference is significant at the 0.05 level in post hoc test.

Table 10.3 Wine involvement level and motivational items on 'festival and escape'

| Motivational item | Mean of each involvement level | | | F-value |
	High involvement	Medium involvement	Low involvement	
Because I enjoy special events	5.0472[a]	5.4896[b]	5.5192[b]	4.128*
For the festive atmosphere	4.3016[a]	4.8860[b]	5.1484[b]	7.607**
So I could enjoy a festival crowd	4.2016	4.5579	4.5350	1.407
So that I could enjoy a day out	5.4961	5.8073	5.8280	2.332
For a change of pace from everyday life	4.7619	5.1675	5.0968	2.046
To enjoy the entertainment	4.9760[a]	5.4819[b]	5.4395[b]	4.376*

(Continued)

Table 10.3 Continued

Motivational item	Mean of each involvement level			F-value
	High involvement	Medium involvement	Low involvement	
The Festival is unique	4.5645[a]	5.0729[b]	5.1538[b]	4.163*
To get away on weekend	4.1532[a]	4.8168[b]	4.4038	3.839*
To try something new	4.8346	5.1554	5.1019	1.326

*Significance at the $p < 0.05$ level.
**Significance at $p < 0.005$ level.
[a,b]The mean difference is significant at the 0.05 level in post hoc test.

wanted more than these high scorers to enjoy the special event, the festive atmosphere, the entertainment, and the uniqueness of the festival. In addition, the medium involvement segment desired a weekend getaway at the festival more than did the high involvement group.

The most noticeable differences occurred in the motivation dimension of 'wine' (see Table 10.4). The mean scores varied on each of the five items included in this factor. The high involvement group showed lower level of desire than others to experience local wineries, to get familiar with local wines, and to buy wines. The high involvement group also wanted less than their low involvement counterparts to use the festival as a venue to increase their wine knowledge. The three segments differed from each other on their motivation for wine tasting, in which the low involvement group demonstrated the highest mean score and was followed by the medium involvement group.

No differences, however, were detected in the *post hoc* tests upon the three items included in 'socialization', even though the F value was significant in the ANOVA test. Apparently the difference was minor and therefore no further information was provided in this regard. It was then deemed necessary to examine the six motivational items which were dropped in the factor analysis process. Three of the relationships were found to be significant (see Table 10.5). Compared to the high and low involvement segments, the low involvement group more

Table 10.4 Wine involvement level and motivational items on 'wine'

Motivational item	Mean of each involvement level			F-value
	High involvement	Medium involvement	Low involvement	
To experience local wineries	5.2188^a	5.9016^b	6.1338^b	17.215^{***}
For wine tasting	5.4800^a	6.0262^b	6.4713^c	19.863^{***}
To get familiar with Indiana wines	4.7857^a	5.5288^b	5.8462^b	18.044^{***}
To increase my wine knowledge	4.0968^a	4.5855	4.8701^b	5.818^{**}
To buy wines	4.0160^a	4.5291^b	4.8344^b	6.642^{**}

**Significance at $p < 0.005$ level.
***Significance level at $p < 0.001$ level.
^{a,b,c}The mean difference is significant at the 0.05 level in post hoc test.

Table 10.5 Wine involvement level and other motivational items

Motivational item	Mean of each involvement level			F-value
	High involvement	Medium involvement	Low involvement	
Always wanted to attend this festival	3.5203^a	4.3298^b	4.6846^b	11.399^{***}
I could be with friends	4.9040^a	5.4432^b	5.4581^b	3.974^*
For food tasting	3.5806	3.8624	3.6513	1.024
Find thrills and excitement	3.2419	3.5106	3.6795	1.686

(Continued)

Table 10.5 Continued

Motivational item	Mean of each involvement level			F-value
	High involvement	Medium involvement	Low involvement	
To relieve tension	3.8699	4.4084	4.3226	2.520
I have been here before and had a good time	3.0957[a]	3.0888[a]	3.7391[b]	3.091[*]

[*]Significance at the $p < 0.05$ level.
[***]Significance level at $p < 0.001$ level.
[a,b]The mean difference is significant at the 0.05 level in post hoc test.

likely had been to the festival before and had a good time. This may explain why they always wanted to attend the festival where they could spend some time with their friends.

Involvement and quality perceptions

Quality perceptions encapsulated three dimensions, namely 'facility', 'wine', and 'organization'. Only 'facility' showed significant mean differences in the ANOVA test (see Table 10.6). A closer look at the five 'facility' items found three to be different between the involvement groups. The low involvement group gave a better score than did the high involvement segment to music and parking facility. They also tended to consider the festival more ideally located than the other two groups, who had very similar opinions in this aspect (See Table 10.7). All three groups thought of 'wine' as exceptional, a dimension including such items as a variety of wines and multiple wineries.

Involvement and satisfaction, value perception, and behavioural intentions

Finally, it was found that the low and medium involvement groups displayed a better perception of the festival in terms of value for money. They also would more likely return to the

Table 10.6 Wine involvement level and quality perception factors of the wine festival

| Quality perception factor | Mean of each involvement level | | | F-value |
	High involvement	Medium involvement	Low involvement	
Facility	5.1443[a]	5.3866	5.5436[b]	5.670[**]
Wine	6.0352	6.1218	6.2120	0.968
Organization	4.4226	4.6882	4.6968	2.552

[**]Significance at $p < 0.005$ level.
[a,b]The mean difference is significant at the 0.05 level in post hoc test.

Table 10.7 Wine involvement level and quality perception items on 'facility'

| Quality perception item | Mean of each involvement level | | | F-value |
	High involvement	Medium involvement	Low involvement	
Entertaining live music	5.5938[a]	5.8342	6.0382[b]	4.029[*]
Arts/crafts: good addition to the festival	4.4262	4.7749	4.5677	1.698
Ideal location	5.6406[a]	5.7789[a]	6.0949[b]	6.103[**]
Knowledgeable staff	5.2131	5.4973	5.5066	2.026
Convenient parking	4.9106[a]	5.0585	5.4323[b]	4.082[*]

[*]Significance at the $p < 0.05$ level.
[**]Significance at $p < 0.005$ level.
[a,b]The mean difference is significant at the 0.05 level in post hoc test.

Table 10.8 Wine involvement level and satisfaction, value and behavioural intentions

| Satisfaction, value and intentions | Mean of each involvement level | | | |
	High involvement	Medium involvement	Low involvement	*F*-value
Overall satisfaction with the visit	5.5512	5.7784	5.8544	2.478
Perception of value for money	4.9921[a]	5.4456[b]	5.6139[b]	7.410[**]
Intention to revisit	5.3906[a]	5.9588[b]	6.0190[b]	7.154[**]
Intention to buy local wines	5.2344	5.5440	5.6456	2.378
Intention to visit local wineries	5.1680[a]	5.4227	5.7452[b]	4.496[*]

[*]Significance at the $p < 0.05$ level.
[**]Significance at $p < 0.005$ level.
[a,b]The mean difference is significant at the 0.05 level in post hoc test.

festival in the future. The low involvement group was also more inclined than the high involvement segment to visit local wineries after the festival (see Table 10.8). No differences were shown between the groups on overall satisfaction with the visit or the intention to buy local wines after the festival.

Finally, no significant differences were found concerning the demographic variables.

Conclusion

Wine is a beverage associated with relaxation, communicating with others, or hospitality (Bruwer, 2003). The extant literature has argued that wine consumers or wine tourists are not homogenous. In particular, wine tourists look for different types of experiences in their travel and great diversity exists among them. There is no single, stereotypical wine tourist (Mitchell and Hall, 2004). A mass-market approach therefore appears highly unrealistic. Wine tourists need to be segmented so that appropriate marketing strategies can be applied. A proper segmentation

of wine tourists enables a better understanding of the characteristics and needs of the particular groups, increases the effectiveness of advertising and promotional efforts, and enables wine
tourism marketers to better target customers (Dodd and Bigotte,
1997; Getz, 2000).

When examining wine consumer/tourist segmentation, researchers sometimes measure personal involvement with wine as this
concept leads to a systematic analysis of consumption/travel
patterns for product development and service quality evaluation.
Personal involvement with wine refers to a perceived importance or relevance for and feelings of interest and enthusiasm
about wine. Lockshin (1997, 2001) recommended two groups
(high vs. low involvement) of wine consumers and discussed
their major characteristics. Charters and Ali-Knight (2002) identified four groups of winery visitors on the basis of their interest in wine. The current study explored wine festival visitors'
segmentation using their personal involvement with wine. The
findings of this study lend further support to integrate the concept of personal involvement in developing segmentation strategies aimed at high-yield wine festival visitors.

The construct was measured by a multi-item scale used in the
overall consumer research realm on involvement. Visitors at a
regional wine festival were clustered into three groups, those
with high involvement, those with medium level involvement,
and those with low involvement. Relationships to other tourist
activities and behaviours at the festival were incorporated in the
analysis of the segmentation of the market. Differences between
the groups were subsequently found with regard to their motivations to attend the festival, their quality perceptions of the festival, their perception of the festival in terms of value for money,
and their intention to visit local wineries after the festival.

The low involvement group showed constantly higher ratings
on all the festival-related items included in this study. Apparently
this group of visitors was less critical and attempted to enjoy the
festival more as a special event. They were pleased that they did
not have to travel far. The wine festival allowed an ideal venue
for them, alongside their friends in a fun and relaxing setting,
to do wine tasting, to come into contact with local wineries, and
to increase wine knowledge, a unique experience in which their
curiosity with wine could be satisfied. Therefore, they saw the
festival as good value for money and would want to visit again.
The experience also made them want to visit local wineries. The
medium involvement group's ratings showed similar differ-
ential patterns. The most visible difference between these two
groups lied in the latter's higher level of desire to use the festival as a venue to get away on weekend.

The low and medium involvement groups were similar to the wine novices (those with limited interest in wine) as described by Charters and Ali-Knight (2002). Their interest in wine was limited and perhaps it was not the major reason for them to attend the festival. Instead, they searched for a more diversified experience incorporating wine, food, environment, setting, learning, and cultural aspects (i.e. the appeal of a festival). It is then evident that wine festivals, if taking place at convenient locations, may attract visitors who do not intend to visit any winery or winegrowing region and thereby would never be ascribed to the category of wine tourists. This group may have limited interest in wine, but the exposure at the event had very much probably opened up the world of wine to them. Their readiness to participate in such type of festivals and their highly positive perception of the event shed light on future marketing efforts for the pursuit of new markets. The festivities put these visitors at ease and thus appealed successfully to a large group of attendees. This is where the event organizers and wine marketers may accentuate the unique 'wine plus fun' theme and the total wine tourism experience to help create interest in regional wines and local wineries among this group.

The high involvement group showed lower ratings on all the items. Nevertheless their high scores on certain items ($\overline{X} > 5.0$) warrant some discussions. Apparently, the high involvement attended the wine festival because, overall speaking, they enjoy special events and more specifically they wanted to have a day out at the event. They were interested in wine tasting and an experience with local wineries without having to travel far. Besides live music and knowledge level of the staff, they also appreciated the wine variety and the large array of wineries available at the festival. They were satisfied with the visit and would like to return next year. They intended to buy local wines and to visit local wineries after the festival.

The high involvement segment seemed somewhat close to the 'wine lovers' group identified by Charters and Ali-Knight (2002). This was the wine-intensive group, whose members were the most highly interested in wine and saw wine as personally important to them. When attending the festival, this group could be more purpose driven, that is, to do wine tasting and experience local wineries. They were hungry for information on wine. They may have been pursuing 'novelty' experiences. Festival organizers and wine marketers may provide more learning opportunities (e.g. wine and food parings, seminars on healthy drinking, contests on wine tasting) for these highly involved visitors.

References

Ali-Knight, J. and Charters, S. (1999). The business of tourism and hospitality: The attraction and benefits of wine education to the wine tourist and Western Australian wineries. *Proceedings of the Ninth Australian Tourism Hospitality and Tourism Research Conference.*

Antil, J.H. (1986). Conceptualization and operationalization of involvement. *Journal of Marketing Research*, 22, 388–396.

Arnold, N. (1999). Marketing and development models for regional communities: A Queensland experience. *Proceedings of the 9th Australian Tourism and Research Hospitality Conference*, CAUTHE 1999, Adelaide, South Australia, Bureau of Tourism Research, Canberra.

Beverland, M., Hoffman, D. and Rasmussen, M. (2001). The evolution of events in the Australasian wine sector. *Tourism Recreation Research*, 26(2), 35–44.

Bruwer, J. (2003). South African wine routes: Some perspectives on the wine tourism industry's structural dimensions and wine tourism product. *Tourism Management*, 24, 423–435.

Cambourne, B. and Macionis, N. (2000). Meeting the winemaker: Wine tourism product development in an emerging wine region. In Hall, C.M., Sharples, L., Cambourne, B. and Macionis, N. (eds) *Wine Tourism Around the World: Development, Management and Markets*. Butterworth-Heinemann, pp. 81–101.

Charters, S. and Ali-Knight, J. (2002). Who is the wine tourist? *Tourism Management*, 23(3), 311–319.

Collins, C. (1996). Drop in for more than just a drop. *Weekend Australian*, 9(March), p.3.

Derrett, R. (2004). Festivals, events and the destination. In Yeoman, I., Robertson, M., Ali-Knight, J., Drummond, S. and McMahon-Beattie, U. (eds.) *Festival and Events Management: An International Arts and Culture Perspective*. Elsevier Butterworth-Heinemann, pp. 32–50.

Dodd, T. and Bigotte, V. (1997). Perceptual differences among visitor groups to wineries. *Journal of Travel Research*, 35(3), 46–51.

Dodd, T. and Gustafson, W. (1997). Product, environmental, and service attributes that influence consumer attitudes and purchases at wineries. *Journal of Food Products Marketing*, 4(3), 41–59.

Getz, D. (1997). *Event Management and Event Tourism*. Cognizant Communication Corporation.

Getz, D. (2000). *Explore Wine Tourism: Management, Development and Destinations*. Cognizant Communication Corporation.

Getz, D. and Brown, G. (2006). Critical success factors for wine tourism regions: A demand analysis. *Tourism Management*, 27, 146–158.

Hall, C.M. (1996). Wine tourism in New Zealand. In *Proceedings of Tourism Down Under II: Towards a More Sustainable Tourism*. Centre for Tourism, University of Otago, Dunedin.

Hall, C.M. and Macionis, N. (1998). Wine tourism in Australia and New Zealand. In Butler, R., Hall, C.M. and Jenkins, J. (eds.) *Tourism and Recreation in Rural Areas*. John Wiley & Sons Ltd., pp. 197–224.

Hoffman, D., Beverland, M.B. and Rasmussen, M. (2001). The evolution of wine events in Australia and New Zealand: A proposed model. *International Journal of Wine Marketing*, 13(1), 54–71.

Houghton, M. (2001). The propensity of wine festival to encourage subsequent winery visitation. *International Journal of Wine Marketing*, 13(3), 32–41.

Jago, L., Chalip, L., Brown, G., Mules, T. and Ali, S. (2003). Building events into destination branding: Insights from experts. *Event Management*, 8, 3–14.

Krugman, H.E. (1965). The impact of television advertising: Learning without involvement. *Public Opinion Quarterly*, 29, 349–356.

Lockshin, L. (2001). Using involvement and brand equity to develop a wine tourism strategy. *International Journal of Wine Marketing*, 13(1), 72–81.

Lockshin, L., Spawton, A.L. and Macintosh, G. (1997). Using product, brand, and purchasing involvement for retail segmentation. *Journal of Retailing and Consumer Services*, 4(3), 171–183.

Mitchell, R. and Hall, C.M. (2004). The post-visit consumer behavior of New Zealand winery visitors. *International Wine Tourism Research: Proceedings of the International Wine Tourism Conference*. Margaret River, Western Australia.

Mittal, B. (1995). A comparative analysis of four scales of consumer involvement. *Psychology and Marketing*, 12(7), 663–682.

Salter, B. (1998). The synergy of wine, tourism and events. *Wine Tourism: Perfect Partners: Proceedings of the 1st Australian Wine Tourism Conference*. Margaret River, Western Australia.

Taylor, R. (2006). Wine festivals and tourism: Developing a longitudinal approach to festival evaluation. In Carlsen, J. and Charters, S. (eds.) *Global Wine Tourism: Research, Management and Marketing*. CAB International, Oxon, UK, pp. 175–195.

Williams, P.W. and Dossa, K.B. (2003). Non-resident wine tourist markets: Implications for British Columbia's emerging wine tourism industry. *Journal of Travel and Tourism Marketing*, 14(3/4), 1–34.

Yuan, J., Cai, L.A., Morrison, A.M. and Linton, S. (2005). An analysis of wine festival attendees' motivations: A synergy of wine, travel, and special events? *Journal of Vacation Marketing*, 11(1), 37–54.

Zaichkowsky, J.L. (1985). Measuring the involvement construct. *Journal of Consumer Research*, 12, 341–352.

CHAPTER 11

Beer festivals: A case study approach

Howard Lyons and Liz Sharples

This chapter looks at the types of beer festivals that exist, the seasonality of these festivals, how branding is being developed, and the chapter concludes with some short case studies on a range of beer festivals.

Why the study of beer festivals is interesting is that they are about an intangible service that focuses on a single tangible product, beer. Although beer comes in many varieties and may be accompanied with food, entertainment and paraphernalia, those beers associated with festivals typically have distinctive local character. Beer festivals are associated with the intangibles of hedonism, celebration and ritual rooted in local community. International and global beer brands may feature in some beer festivals, but normally local brews dominate.

How and what to study at beer festivals is closely linked to a consideration of the research methods that are available. The tools available to the student of beer festivals include those of marketing research, sociology, the behavioural sciences and anthropology. In this chapter, the research method used is a study of published data as the purpose of the research is to study the factual descriptors of the festivals with a view to identifying major characteristics, whereas the other research methods identified are more useful when trying to study a festival in depth.

What that means in practical terms is that when undertaking in-depth study, students of beer festivals can ask questions about attitudes and behaviours, may observe behaviours, and may even live with the stakeholders as a participant observer. An interesting discussion of a modern interpretation of participant observation is provided by Hein and Austin (2001).

Gaining access to a beer festival as a research site may be a challenge, but the potential to deliver value to the organizers for future years is a case worth making.

Beer festivals come in all shapes and sizes

The variety of styles in beer festivals is initially staggering. The largest is Munich's Oktoberfest with an estimated six and a half million visitors over several days. The estimation of the number of visitors varies, often by a factor of plus or minus half a million, probably because of the variety of tickets that are available. For example, does a person visiting a festival on 2 days count as two visitors, etc?

At the other extreme, some festivals boast of numbers in the mid-hundreds and last perhaps a day. Some beer festivals are cultural foci for drinking, eating, music and other local activities, whereas others are primarily concerned with competition; judging and drinking beers without too many distractions.

The beer festivals reported in the journals and media are largely in English speaking countries and Germany, with some in Central Europe particularly the Czech Republic. Other such festivals do exist elsewhere from Greece to Japan and China (technically saki is said to be a rice beer not a wine because of the method of production).

In preparing this case study chapter on beer festivals, we anticipate that beer festival activities are more widespread than suggested here, because many may be 'genuine' local festivals and celebrations rather than tourist activities which are actively marketed. However, it is likely that some organizers will become more concerned with tourism as the economic advantages of staging such events become more widely appreciated.

Although the UK beer festivals are not typically large, by some North American and German standards, the organizing influence of Campaign for Real Ale (CAMRA) is of key importance, and ensures that there is both a central body to promote festivals and also to provide a level of quality kite-marking, although this is based more on the provenance of beers than festivals. What CAMRA (2007a) says of itself is:

CAMRA campaigns for real ale, real pubs and consumer rights. We are an independent, voluntary organization with over 85,000 members and have been described as the most successful consumer group in Europe. CAMRA promotes good-quality real ale and pubs, as well as acting as the consumer's champion in relation to the UK and European beer and drinks industry. We aim to:

Protect and improve consumer rights.
Promote quality, choice and value for money.
Support the public house as a focus of community life.
Campaign for greater appreciation of traditional beers, ciders and perries as part of our national heritage and culture.
Seek improvements in all licensed premises and throughout the brewing industry.

The level and nature of organization of beer festivals varies greatly. Some festivals are highly organized with co-ordinated activities and talks, whereas others are really 'free for alls' where autonomous behaviour is central. Belgium has a varied tradition of street or free entry beer festivals in which beer is purchased from street vendors or vendors on a festival showground. During a festival in Bouillon, for example, each shopkeeper puts up a stand and tries to sell their products. However, Belgium has other festivals, some with a greater degree of structure. Also featuring local producers of special beers, but with organized tasting sessions, the general style of the large Zythos festival is similar to Bouillon although the venue is more formal (Visit Belgium, 2007).

In the UK, the festival is more typically on a closed show-ground or venue where a fixed payment is made for entry and further purchase of beer is expected. The USA has a wide variety of festival styles, but some shows in the USA charge a much higher entry price, with beer sampling being free.

The creation or capture of beer festivals by capitalists, from enthusiasts who are beer lovers, typically marks an attempt to expand the scale of a festival, and to turn it from a visitor's experience into a profit-making venture for the organizers. To a greater or lesser extent a beer festival is always going to be a profit-making event for exhibitors who seek to sell their beers on the day. However, the festivals also create customers who search for the beers after the festival, and become brand customers with some level of loyalty.

Seasonality of beer festivals: the theory has some basis in fact

The seasonality of beer festivals linked to harvest time is apparent after an inspection of many web sites; some of which assert this. A quotation that may well underline this linkage is:

Great quantities of ale were consumed and the wages, which were often very small, would be handed out. It was likely that the harvest-ers would be less likely to grumble about their low wages if their stomachs were full and their heads muddled by ale! (The British Food Trust, 2007).

Circumstantial evidence to support this assertion of season-ality for UK beer festivals is available and is demonstrated in Table 11.1 which looks at the timings of the UK CAMRA festi-vals. In Germany, the Oktoberfest (discussed later in the chap-ter) is a harvest beer festival, whereas in the USA Oktoberfests are widely spread across the calendar.

The UK data on CAMRA (ibid) is very concise in cover-ing festivals and is a useful measure of seasonality, and the number and percentage of festivals is in Table 11.1 by month. The Table provides circumstantial evidence of several forms of seasonality. Low numbers of festivals may be accounted for by school holidays particularly in August and December and possibly January. During these periods many people are away

Table 11.1   Seasonality of beer festivals

2008	Number of festivals	Per cent of festivals
January	7	4.2
February	17	10.2
March	12	7.2
April	12	7.2
May	12	7.2
June	15	9.0
July	12	7.2
August	8	4.8
September	30	18.1
October	25	15.1
November	14	8.4
December	2	1.2

Source: CAMRA, 2007b

from home and beer festivals are fewer. This may also high-light the voluntary nature of festival organizing. The greatest number of CAMRA recorded beer festivals in 2008 are in the autumn months of September and October, and account for a third of all festivals; these occur in the harvest festival season. As students of beer festivals, it is important that we do not assume that the reasons inferred for seasonality are not truth. We are just inferring, and the use of language must reflect this.

The branding of beer festivals: a lost opportunity?

The major name that is recognized in the beer festival sector is the Oktoberfest, which began in Munich. However, Janiskee (2003), identified at least 430 Oktoberfest celebrations in America each year. Hence the name Oktoberfest would appear to the casual Anglo-Saxon observer to be a brand name. However, whilst Oktoberfest has a brand image, it is not a registered brand name of the Munich festival. This is different from the problem of say, 'Hoover', which is a registered brand name yet is permitted to be used as a generic description of vacuum cleaner because it has not been effectively protected by the brand owner.

Official German Government web sites in the USA and elsewhere (primarily post-colonial 'new' nations) promote the German antecedents of citizens. In the USA, German stock is said to have provided the largest proportion of Northern European Americans. Oktoberfest is a national identifier in this context and seems to be a welcome method of emphasizing German-ness. This presumably has both a political dimension as they could be the basis of a lobby, and an economic dimension as they may be pre-disposed to 'buy German'. Hence the Oktoberfests in the USA provide a tool for promoting German identity and business.

However, as the Germany Oktoberfest is not a registered trademark, and the brand has been so widely copied, the organizers of the Munich Oktoberfest sought to identify symbols and names that could be the subject of intellectual copyrighting. In 1995 a logo was developed containing two laughing beer mugs and this became the registered brand for the Munich Oktoberfest. In addition in 2000 the Oktoberfest was promoted by a 'canine mascot', a bright pink wire-haired daschund dressed in lederhosen, Tylorean hat and traditional shirt. Clearly, the overarching Oktoberfest name could not be readily registered as a trademark as it has become a generic identifier. However, whether these rather populist brand identifiers fully exploit the Munich Oktoberfest potential is unclear.

In the USA, the use of law differs, and may be predatory when considered in an international context. In 1962, the State of Wisconsin registered the name 'Oktoberfest, USA' which became a federally recognized brand name in 1963. This name is held by the La Crosse Chamber of Commerce. The local or regional nature of American Oktoberfests means that a local Oktoberfest may wish to retain its local monopoly, and as such a defence is clearly desirable.

Having discussed the variety found in the form, style, structure and scale of beer festivals and their branding, we will now look at some festivals and what their official publicity claims are to make them distinctive.

In the remainder of this chapter we will look more closely at a small, but diverse selection of beer festivals. We do not even attempt to cover all possible types of beer festival, but rather we give a flavour of what is out there, leaving it to other students of beer festivals to write more about them.

The first case study is distinctive because it is small, takes place on school premises in South Yorkshire, England, as is not an untypical example of a community-based local CAMRA festival.

Exhibit 11.1 Rotherham's Oakwood Beer Festival

This beer festival is based in a suburb of Rotherham, a largely post-industrial South Yorkshire town in England that was based on heavy manufacturing and coal mining. It is located in a school called Oakwood Technology College. As such it is not the romantic rural setting that some would expect of a beer festival.

The purpose of the festival may also raise some questions as it is to raise funds for the school, and it is run with the assistance of the Rotherham branch of the Campaign for Real Ale. The festival takes place in the actual school, which makes for an interesting venue, where you wander into classrooms and find another bar! They also put entertainment on the stages in the school halls and in a marquee!

Oakwood features over 200 real ales, all on hand pump, from Yorkshire, Lancashire, East Anglia, Cumbria, the South Midlands and Scotland, with each bar dedicated to a specific region. There will also be foreign beers, cider, wines and food available.

In 2008 the festival ran from Wednesday 15th February to Saturday 18th February and was open from 6 p.m. to 11 p.m. each day, plus 12 p.m. to 5 p.m. on Saturday. However, note that Wednesday and Thursday is limited to sponsors and CAMRA members only. CAMRA members can get in free on these 2 days.

On Friday and Saturday, admission is £8, however you can save money by buying an advance ticket for just £6. A list of outlets can be found on the festival web site: www.realale.oakwood.yorks.com.

Holders of advance tickets can enjoy free travel to the festival with 'First Bus', and all visitors benefit from free travel home, from the festival with 'First Bus' to anywhere in South Yorkshire. The free bus service is clearly a great benefit as it is a way of persuading people not to drink and drive; however, it may also indicate something about the local geographical segmentation and socio-economic group of visitors.

Derived from:

http://www.sheffieldcamra.co.uk/articlefeb06_oakwoodpreview.htm

http://www.realale.oakwood.yorks.com

The next case study is also small scale and local in focus, but this time it is American. It is distinctive because the focus in the official materials is on competition between beers, so although it is quite similar to its UK equivalent, its stance is at least superficially very different.

Exhibit 11.2 Illinois Craft Brewers Guild Annual Festival of Wood and Barrel-aged Beer

---

This festival takes place in Goose Island Wrigleyville in Chicago, USA, a rather more prosperous post-urban, largely post-industrial location than South Yorkshire, but an area nonetheless with patchy economic success and an industrial history. The event has been running for 5 years.

This beer festival also has beers from a wide geographical area. In 2007, the festival presented over 80 beers from 29 different breweries, representing 10 states.

From their web site it claims to be the USA's first and largest beer festival dedicated to the art of wood and barrel aging, and it occurs in November. Their sell-out visitors are limited to 500 people. The festival contains a competitive element with judging in eight categories which dominate their official materials (listed below) together with a best of show listing:

Category 1: Classic porter/stout (Brown, Robust Porter; Dry, Oatmeal, Sweet Stout).
Category 2: Strong porter/stout (Foreign, Imperial).
Category 3: Barleywine (English, American).
Category 4: Classic style (other styles not higher than 16° Plato SG).
Category 5: Strong pale beers (IPA, American Strong, Amber, Red, etc. >16° Plato SG).
Category 6: Strong dark beers (Brown, Scottish, Old Ale, etc. >16° Plato SG).
Category 7: Experimental beers (any beer that employs unusual ingredients and/or techniques, i.e. fruits, spices, blends of different beer styles, etc.).
Category 8: Wild beers (any beer fermented or aged with micro-organisms other than *Saccharomyces cerevisiae*).

Derived from: http://www.illinoisbeer.com

Having looked at some small events in the UK and USA, we move on to the 'grand daddy of all beer festivals', the hallmark event that is the Munich Oktoberfest. However, a close analysis will still demonstrate strong community roots (nearly three-quarters of visitors are from the home state of Bavaria), and an element of competition between beers.

Exhibit 11.3 The Munich Oktoberfest

The Munich Oktoberfest is the largest German 'Volksfest' (local festival) and the only one bearing the name 'Oktoberfest' which functions somewhat like a trademark. It is said to promise:

the world's biggest good-time affair, attended by millions of thirsty souls from all over the globe, and takes place on the 'Theresienwiese' with its giant beer tents, where buxom beer maidens serve the precious brew by the litre in large steins, where 30 piece Bavarian bands rock the thick air, and where there's no end to singing them old-time drinking songs.

The first Oktoberfest was actually part of a marriage celebration, when in 1810 October, Bavarian King Max Joseph gave a large wedding for Crown Prince Ludwig, later to become King Ludwig I, with the Princess Therese von Sachsen-Hildburghausen. It culminated with a series of horse races and gave rise to the tradition of the October festival. In the following year it became an annual affair commemorating this grand wedding forevermore. The Oktoberfest we know today evolved over time and incorporated a number of different traditions.

The Oktoberfest is now celebrated in September, because the chilly Bavarian October winds blowing from the Alps can surprise with early cold and snow. The 16-day Fest always starts on a Saturday in September and ends on the 1st Sunday in October. The dates of the festival for some forthcoming years are:

2008: September 20 to October 5
2009: September 19 to October 4
2010: September 18 to October 3
2011: September 17 to October 3

http://www.oktoberfest.de/en/02/content/faq1/

Over time certain rituals evolved which are followed from year to year.

For the opening day ceremonies, promptly at 11 a.m., a parade enters the grounds on the Wies'n headed by the Münchner Kindl – the little Munich city's coat of arms. The mayor arrives in a festive coach followed by civic dignitaries and horse-drawn brewer's carts decorated with flowers. This colourful ceremony with elaborate floats, beer bands and men, women and children wearing traditional costumes (lederhosen and dirndls) dates back to 1887. More than 70,000 people participate in the four-mile long parade.

At noon the parade winds its way to the 'Schottenhammel' tent which is the oldest private tent at 'Oktoberfest'. It is here that the mayor will tap the first keg of beer and declare, 'o'zapft is'! (The keg is tapped.)

In the evening, the 'Zirkus Krone' may give a 2-hour performance. Munich's six major breweries, brewers of the Oktoberfest Märzen beer (Hacker-pschorr,

(Continued)

Lowenbrau, Spaten, Hofbrauhaus, Augustiner, Paulaner) are represented in seven festive halls and usually have live music throughout the day and evening.

On the second Sunday of Oktoberfest all of the bands performing during the 16 days may gather at the main entrance and give a 1-hour concert, and there is dancing and plenty of sideshows, booths, and rides.

Food is clearly important. 'If you're hungry, you can stop in at "Schottenhammel" or "Käfers Wies'nschänke" and try the "Brathendl" (the grilled chicken) or "a Münchner Weisse", the veal sausage only found in Bavaria. For fish lovers, there is trout and eel grilled outdoors on long sticks and sausages galore abound for the festival-goers'.

Derived from: http://www.oktoberfest.de/en/

Having looked at the original Oktoberfest in Munich, we will now look briefly at the American Oktoberfest. The resonance in style and cuisine is strong although the scale is clearly different.

Exhibit 11.4 La Crosse Oktoberfest (USA)

Most Oktoberfests in the USA try to emulate, or at least to cash in on, the name of the most famous Oktoberfest in the world.

The festival in the USA which comes closest to the Munich Oktoberfest is the German Fest in Milwaukee. Started in 1846 by German settlers, it celebrates its 150th anniversary this year. It takes place over 3 days in late July, and typically draws about 100,000 visitors.

La Crosse is another long-standing Oktoberfest this time in Wisconsin USA. The festival incorporates three parades currently: Opening Day Parade, Maple Leaf Parade, and the Torchlight Parade. Parades, pageantry, royalty, bratwurst, beer and world famous entertainment have made La Crosse's Oktoberfest one of the finest in the nation. 'It's great down there, the ambiance is spectacular and the beer is cheap too', says UW-L Senior Angela Riedel. There is always plenty to do at Oktoberfest, but let's take a look at how it all started.

The first La Crosse Oktoberfest was held in 1961. Officials for the La Crosse-based G. Heileman Brewing Company, now known as City Brewery, were discussing a way to promote their product. It was two German employees who suggested the festival could be held in autumn similar to the one held in Munich. The others liked the idea of having a fall festival because the scenery at this time of year in La Crosse is spectacular.

(Continued)

The idea was then passed to the La Crosse Chamber of Commerce and they agreed to sponsor the event. In 1962, the State of Wisconsin registered the name 'Oktoberfest'. In 1963, 'Oktoberfest, USA' was listed as a trademark with the federal government. Ever since, the event has gained in popularity. In 1965, La Crosse Festivals, Inc. took over the event and became the sponsor.

The purpose of the festival is to promote local pride, national publicity and tourism to the Coulee region. Oktoberfest is one of the few Old World local events held annually in the USA, La Crosse won the All-American City Award in 1961. The Oktoberfest Grenadiers consist of a group of 35 active couples that are dressed in authentic costumes and act as ambassadors for the festival. They escort the Festmasters, Fraus, along with Miss La Crosse and Mrs Oktoberfest to various events during the fest and throughout the year. They also care for the floats used in the Oktoberfest parades.

City Brewery released a new beer for the festival called Oktoberfest USA Amber Ale craft beer.

Derived from: www.oktoberfestusa.com

Before completing the chapter we will look at a very different and very new beer festival in China. Although the folk roots in local beer of this festival have much in common with those festivals in Europe and America, the festival dimension is new. Festivals in China typically relate to other sorts of folk and local culture.

Exhibit 11.5   Qingdao City Beer Festival

Qingdao is situated at the Southern tip of the Shangdong Peninsula. Nothing more than a fishing village until the early 1900s. Qingdao has gone through an amazing period of investment and development, and has now become a modern and vibrant city and trading port. South Korea and Japan, in particular, have invested heavily in the city. The majority of residents are immigrants, for example at least 30,000 South Koreans reside there, who have moved to take advantage of the opportunities that Qingdao offers. The city attracts many tourists due to its seaside setting and excellent weather and in 2008 will be the host city for the Beijing Olympics sailing regatta.

Qingdao is also the home of the world famous Tsingtao Brewery, which German settlers founded in 1903. It is the earliest brewery to be founded in China.

(Continued)

The first Qingdao Beer Festival took place in 1991 and now runs annually opening on the second weekend every August for 16 days. This is the largest beer festival in Asia attracting over 3 million visitors each year. There are more than 240,000 square metres of attraction space, dedicated to staging the event, which includes an opening ceremony, beer drinking areas, a carnival, fairground rides, fireworks, beach competitions and arts performances. More than 20 internationally known beer manufacturers take part in the event. The event also incorporates a major beer trade exhibition. Wen Yuansheng, Vice Director of the beer festival said, it's a Citizens Festival, a Carnival Festival and an International Festival. Our first and main objective in hosting the festival is to 'he pijiu' (drink beer!). Here we say 'Qingdao ganbei (cheers!) the world!!'

Derived from: The Development of the Festival Industry in China, Unpublished Masters thesis written by Na Jiang, formerly of Sheffield Hallam University. and ... http://www.qdbeer.cn

Conclusions

This chapter demonstrates the diverse range of beer associated festivals which are being staged around the world, from the local community event, such as the one at Oakwood College, to hallmark events such as the Oktoberfest. Each in its own way has an impact on the community in which it is hosted and provides a link between the brewing industry and its consumers. As tastes, fashions and markets in beer consumption change so too will the nature and shape of beer festivals. This is an exciting developing area with many opportunities for further research.

References

CAMRA (2007a) at http://www.camra.org.uk/page.aspx?o =about

CAMRA (2007b) at http://www.camra.org.uk/page.aspx?0 =181254

Hein, S. and Austin, W. (2001). Empirical and hermeneutic approaches to phenomenological research in psychology. A Comparison. Psychological Methods, vol. 6; no. 1, pp. 3–17

Janiskee, R. (2003) 'Oktoberfest in America'. In *Food Tourism around the World, Development, Management and Markets*. C.M. Hall, Sharples, E, Cambourne, B, Macionis, N, Mitchell, R. (eds). Butterworth Heinemann, Oxford. 331–335

The British Food Trust (2007) at http://www.greatbritishkitchen. co.uk/ff_harvest.htm

Visit Belgium (2007) at http://www.visitbelgium.com/beer.htm.

Wine connoisseurs or curious tourists? The participants in wine festivals

Meg Houghton

Introduction

Creating and staging wine festivals has become an important promotional component of winery visitation (National Wine Tourism Strategy, 1999), and it could be argued that festivals have the unique position of being able to combine sales promotion, consumer promotion and relationship marketing to achieve the promoter's (the winery operator's) goals. According to Ivers (1999, p.36) 'effective marketing is about spending less to achieve more'; this, he suggests, includes segmenting the target audience and isolating behaviour patterns. Kohli and Jaworski (1990) stress the importance of information gathering about customers and incorporating it in planning, while Snepenger, (1987) and Dodd and Bigotte (1997) propose that socio-demographic variables can be useful tools for identifying and segmenting a market, predicting behaviour and developing marketing strategies to target the groups of interest. In relation to the wine industry, Fry (1999, p.11) concurs stating that wine tourism providers need to 'know their customers', and Dodd (1995) offers, as an example of the effectiveness of this strategy, the fact that an individual's income has been shown to be a mostly reliable predictor of wine consumption (Houghton, 2007 in press).

However, while undeniably a successful consciousness raising exercise, some winery operators view wine festivals with reservation; a condition that is magnified by the very large numbers who can attend these events. Hall and Macionis (1998, p.218) suggest that the 'image of a large drunken party' may not provide the required promotional image (e.g. quality) that the stakeholders seek while noting that the opportunity to build a relationship is also diminished. Wine festivals, while recognized as having a role in attracting a wide range of people to wineries (Rasterhoff in Collins, 1996), can overwhelm the individual wineries and they are therefore approached by some winery operators with ambivalence. This suggests that although wine festivals are successful mediums for attracting large numbers, their very popularity makes quality interaction difficult; organizers query whether 'serious wine drinkers' are kept away by the event, while others (perhaps new conumers) are attracted. This makes it important to understand the characteristics of wine festival attendees in order to ascertain who comes, the level of their interest in wine and the influence festival participation has on their ongoing involvement with the industry. This chapter will explore the characteristics of wine festival patrons and try to identify the 'types' of people who attend these events and if consequently wine festivals are an effective promotional tool for wineries.

Profiling wine Festival Patrons

A marketing orientation means improving your understanding of your customers and their needs (Uncles, 2000) and, as Getz (1991) suggests, while there are commonalties of type in festival attendees in general, there are variations dependent upon the theme of the event. Many studies of wine festivals patrons have been conducted since the mid-1990s. Examples include Victorian Wineries Tourism Council (VWTC) 1996, 1998, Ritchie and Houghton (1997), Houghton (2001), Beeton and Pinge (2001), Weiler, Truong and Griffiths (2004), Yuan et al., (2005) and Taylor (2006).

One of these research projects involving over 1,000 participants was conducted in the Rutherglen winegrowing region of south eastern Australia (Table 12.1) (Houghton, 2001, 2005, 2007 in press). This region is well known for a variety of tourist attractions, including skiing, national parks, heritage attractions (notably the outlaw Ned Kelly and old gold mining sites), water sports, and food and wine production. Rutherglen is typical of many wine regions in Australia in that it consists of many small, independently owned wineries that cooperate to conduct annual wine events.

The development of the wine industry in Rutherglen is in many ways similar to other 'New World' wine regions. The town of Rutherglen, began life in the 1850s, as a gold rush town and within 3 months the town was considered a well established and settled community (Mortensen, 1990). At this time, Lindsay Brown of Gooramadda planted the district's first vines. By 1862, the demand for his wine exceeded the supply of 'Colonial' wine which was sold at hotels for one shilling a tumbler. In 1863, he commenced a campaign to persuade gold miners that if they were unsuccessful in that industry they should turn to winegrowing – 'they would only have to dig down a foot!'(Mortensen, 1990). Within a few years, thousand of gallons of Rutherglen wine (both red and white) were being shipped from Melbourne to the world. By 1892, there were 350 vignerons within 56 kilometres of the town but, in 1899, phylloxera (a root-attacking aphid) was discovered and many wineries failed or turned to other crops. It was not until 1925 that the district was judged free of the pest and by this time the Rutherglen wine industry had changed substantially.

In addition to shipping wine to Melbourne distributors, from the early days until the end of the 1940s there was a steady trade in jar and small barrel sales. Vignerons traded directly, either via mail order, small licensed groceries or cellar door sales. This bulk wine was then sold and shipped in returnable,

Table 12.1 Table of participating Rutherglen wineries listing distinguishing features

Key	Winery	Original Established	Additional distinguishing attractions
1	All Saints Estate	1864	Castle, Hall of Fame, Restaurant
2	Anderson Winery	1992	'Above ground cellar'
3	Bullers Caliope	1921	Bird Park
4	Campbells Winery	1870	Winemaking memorabilia
5	Chambers Rosewood	1870	The 'king of fortified wines'
6	Cofield Wines	1990	BBQ-Picnic Facilities
7	Fairfield Vineyard	1880	Historic Mansion – 1889
8	Gehrig Estate	1858	Historic House and Bell Tower
9	Jones Winery	1860	Original structures
10	Lake Moodemere	1886	Lake Moodemere
11	Morris Wines	1864	Glass walled tasting pavilion
12	Mount Prior Vineyard	1860	Underground cellars/Heritage accommodation and meals
13	Pfeiffer Wines	1984	Sunday Creek and gardens: Picnic hampers
14	Stanton and Killeen	1864	BBQ, picnic area
15	Sutherland Smith	1880s	Old cellars, area history
16	Warrabilla Wines		
17	St Leonards	1860s	Murray River billabong

refundable one, two, three and five-gallon stone jars or octave, quarter casks and hogshead barrels. The growing popularity of flagon sales (no need to return or decant), the introduction of bottle shops and the closing of wine saloons ended this trade and this, combined with cheaper production elsewhere, saw the local industry struggle for some years; by 1960 only a dozen wineries remained in Rutherglen (Mortensen, 1990).

This all began to change in the 1970s. European (especially Italian) migrants discovered the wines, roads improved, cars were more comfortable and cellar door trade as it is known today began to grow. Single bottle licenses were obtained and winemakers set about offering tasting and wine education to these early cellar door patrons (wine tourists) who were eager to learn about these unfamiliar beverages. As an outlet for wine product it is for both large and small wineries an important part of their marketing mix. Today Rutherglen vineyards are some of the oldest vinegrowing and winemaking centres in Australia. The fortified wines, (muscats and Tokays) produced in this region are unique and are produced by winemaking families which have, in many cases, been there for generations. Each winery offers, in addition to wine tasting and sales, various exhibitions and displays, and most open to cellar door visitors seven days a week.

Autumn 1968 marked the commencement of Rutherglen district wine festivals. The inaugural festival grew and became very popular during the 1970's. Initially this festival was held in Rutherglen township precincts, but the increasingly boisterous crowds created many problems of drunkenness, vandalism and hooliganism and the town festival was abandoned (and this perhaps is the historical background of the organizer's scepticism as to the type of patrons these events attract). It was replaced by the 'Winery Walkabout Weekend' which is still held in winter, at the property of each of the participating wineries (19 in 2007), over a long weekend. In 1990 the 'Tastes of Rutherglen' festival commenced. The wineries felt that the autumn period was of special significance to winegrowers, 'harvest time', and as the weather was generally reliable at that time, an additional, alternative festival was arranged.

Today the region hosts four major festivals per year (Table 12.2). These festivals, each with a different theme and significance, are managed by festival specific sub-committees. The two most popular festivals attended by the general public are the 'Tastes of Rutherglen' and 'Winery Walkabout' and it is these events that form the basis of this case study.

The major focus of the study was to evaluate the effectiveness of wine festivals as a promotional activity for wineries. Festival participants were interviewed at the two wine festivals and further responses were collected from the cellar door visitors to the area's 17 participating wineries. These respondents completed voluntary questionnaires over a 12-month period. A sample group of 800 plus people who had at some point attended a wine festival was identified and it is these respondents who are used to illustrate the types of people who attend wine festivals.

Generally, establishing the profile of individuals in touristic studies commences with an examination of the basic

Table 12.2   Major wine festivals conducted by winemakers of Rutherglen (2007/2008)

Name	Date and season	Duration	Focus or theme	Main patrons
Tastes of Rutherglen	March Autumn	8 days	Regional food and wine	General public
Winery Walkabout	June Winter	3 days	Wine tasting and releases of new wines	General public
Rutherglen Wine Show	September Early spring	8 days	Judging of national wines	Wine producers – industry
Young Bloods and Bloody Legends Weekend	October Spring	2 days	The younger generation of winemakers continuing the family tradition	General public

demographic variables which may include combinations of age, gender, income, origin and education standard; these provide a functional insight into participants. From this perspective, not surprisingly, wine festival participants and wine tourists share many common characteristics. Wine tourists have been found to be more often female than male, predominately from the local area, generally aged between 30 and 50 years, have a moderate to high income, and a university or tertiary qualification, is more prevalent in these groups (Macionis and Camborne, 1998; Mitchell et al., 2000). Wine festival participants also exhibit these traits with the one exception, being that of age (Table 12.3).

There is evidence that particularly the young are more inclined to attend festivals than the middle age and older groups. A number of studies give some indication of this phenomenon. For example, in a 1997 Australian (Yarra Valley) wine festival survey they represented 32 per cent; in the 2000 Rutherglen survey (a self-selecting, convenience sample) the 18 to 30 olds were the noticeably largest group. Taylor (2006) also observed this in a longitudinal study (conducted in Western Australia between 1999 and 2003). This study revealed that not only are these events popular but that the rate of participation by the young is increasing. In the Rutherglen study many first-time visitors to wine festivals responded very positively to the idea of a return visit to a winery or festival as a consequence of their initial

Table 12.3 Comparison of demographic variables of visitors to Rutherglen wine festivals as a percentage of the total sample

Variable	Percentage of attendees	Variable	Percentage of attendees
Age		Education	
18–30	25.8	Secondary	25.8
31–40	25.7	Technical College	20.1
41–50	25.7	University Degree	35.6
51+	22.8	Higher Degree	18.5
Income			
<20,000	5.1		
20,001–35,000	10.6		
35,001–50,000	22.6		
50,001–70,000	23.4		
70,001–100,000	22		
>100,001	19.1		

experience. Given that the preponderance of these first-time festival visitors are in the 18–30 age group this would appear to translate into ongoing benefits for the wineries and in fact may be proof of Rasterhoff (in Collins, 1996) suggestion that wine festivals play a key role in demystifying the wine industry.

Delving Deeper

In the introduction to this discussion of wine festival patrons, mention was made of the reservations held by winery operators as to the motivations of people who attend wine festivals. Winery operators question whether many people who attend these events come only for the party atmosphere and social outing and that the wine is almost an incidental element of the event (Houghton, 2007 in press). Additionally there is some anecdotal evidence, gleaned in the form of discussion with winery operators, to suggest that some 'serious' wine tourists have the same ambivalent attitude towards wine festivals and the large crowds of 'non-serious' wine tourists they attract. This leads some wine festival promoters to feel that these particular (and in many cases, 'preferred') wine consumers would rather visit wineries outside of festivals, regardless of the 'special attractions' that are developed and aimed at them, the committed wine consumer (Houghton, 2007, in press).

In 1996, Hall published a study of New Zealand wine tourists and suggested, based on their demographic and behavioural characteristics and the varying strengths of these traits, that wine tourists could be categorized into three segments which he labelled 'wine lovers', 'wine interested' and 'curious tourists' (Table 12.4). If wine festival attendees could be similarly gauged (e.g. identify the characteristics of the participants) then the disquiet and uncertainness experienced by winery operators may be allayed by a better knowledge and understanding of who these events attracted. In Hall's study, seven characteristics (education, family income, age of respondents plus the propensity to purchase wine at winery, to join a mailing list, their familiarity with the winemaking process and whether visiting wineries was the sole reason for their visit to the destination) were present to a greater or lesser degree in each of the wine tourism 'types' (Houghton, 2007, in press).

Using the Rutherglen sample group, all of whom had at some point attended a wine festival, these seven characteristics were isolated and form the basis of an analysis and comparison with Hall's (1996) wine tourist segments.

The first three characteristics age, income and education are discussed earlier in this chapter (for full details see Table 12.3). Four behavioural or attitudinal statements designed to measure the strength of consensus or disagreement expressed by the respondents to certain propositions make up the balance. These statements took the form of Likert statements where the most appropriate response could be circled (Table 12.5).

Table 12.5 demonstrates that overall more than half (57.3 per cent) of festival participants concurred with the suggestion that visiting a winery was the prime motivator for visiting the region. Of fundamental interest to the wineries is the possibility that visitors will purchase wine when they visit the winery; this question elicited a very positive response with 80 per cent stating that they expected to purchase wine. Hall (1996) suggests that the propensity to subscribe to an individual winery's mailing list is a distinguishing characteristic between wine tourists groups. The table indicates that approximately 40 per cent of festival attendees would add their name to mailing lists, although more (39.9 per cent) disagreed with the statement. The final question was to assess the respondent's perceptions of their familiarity with the process of making wine. Fifty three per cent of festival patrons attested to being confident that they understood the winemaking process.

Table 12.4   Wine tourism market segments

Market segment	Characteristics
Wine lovers	Extremely interested in wines and wine making. Wineries may be sole purpose of visit to destination. May be employed in wine and food industry. Likely to be mature with high income and education levels. Likely to be a regular purchaser of wine and food magazines. Will have visited other wine regions. Highly likely to purchase at winery and add name to mailing list.
Wine interested	High interest in wine but not sole purpose of visit to destination. Likely to have visited other wine regions. Familiar with winemaking procedures. Moderate to high income bracket, tend to be university educated. 'Word of mouth' and wine columns in newspapers may be important for arousing interest in region. Occasional purchaser of wine and food magazines, regular purchaser of 'lifestyle' magazines. Likely to purchase at winery and add name to mailing list. Potential for repeat purchase of wine through having visited winery.
Curious tourist	Moderately interested in wine but not familiar with wine making procedures. Winery tour a by product of visit to region as visiting was for unrelated purposes. Wineries may be 'just another attraction'. May have visited other wine regions. Curiosity aroused by drinking or seeing winery product or general tourism promotion or pamphlets. Moderate income and education. Opportunity for social occasion with friends and/or family. May purchase at winery but will not join mailing list.

Source: Interviews with wineries, tour operators, regional tourism organizations and Macionis and Cambourne, 1994. Adapted from: Hall, C.M., 1996. Wine tourism in New Zealand. In *Tourism Down Under II, Towards a more Sustainable Tourism*, Conference Proceedings, G. Kearsley ed., pp. 109–119, Centre for Tourism, University of Otago, Dunedin, New Zealand.

Two techniques were employed to gather, compare and move respondents into the three groups or cluster centers. K-means clustering which allows the movement of respondents into a user specified number of clusters based on their possessed

Table 12.5 Comparison of wine festival participants by attitudes and behaviours as a percentage of the overall sample

Statement put to the respondent	Agree	Neither agree/ disagree	Disagree
'The opportunity to visit the wineries was the sole purpose of my trip to this region'	57.3	11.4	31.3
'When I visit a winery I am very likely to purchase wine'	80	11	9
'When I visit a winery, if the opportunity arises, I add my name to the winery's mailing list'	38.4	21.7	39.9
'I am quite familiar with the wine making process'	53	25.2	21.8

characteristics and Pattern Analysis (using PATN software) enables the analysis, summarization and display of patterns in the data. The use of multiple techniques (triangulation) offered the opportunity to verify the reliability and accuracy of the data. These two analytical techniques generated similar responses although in some instances the values differed (Houghton, 2007 in press).

What became apparent was that there were three definable groups who exhibited many of the characteristics that correspond to the groupings observed by Hall (1996) in wine tourists. Table 12.6 illustrates that while it seems possible to distinguish the 'Wine Lovers' the other two groups, 'Wine Interested' and 'Curious Tourist' are apparent but less conclusively defined.

Analysing each cluster further reveals some interesting variations but variations for which a possible explanation can be advanced. For example, the 'Wine Lovers' cluster closely aligns with the attributes expected of this group. However, the two areas where they register a lower score than may have been expected are in the responses to the 'mailing list' and 'winemaking process' questions. It is possible that the explanations for not subscribing to a mailing list might include either their lack of interest in that form of marketing or perhaps a

Table 12.6 Cluster centers for festival attendees ($n = 753$)

	Cluster		
	1 Wine lovers	**2 Wine interested**	**3 Curious tourist**
Level of Education var5	3.91	3.50	2.87
Age var6	2.79	2.53	2.00
Family Income var7	4.94	4.09	2.71
Sole purpose of trip var1	4.36	1.72	4.29
Purchase Wine var2	4.52	3.66	3.92
Mailing List var3	3.80	2.47	2.56
Wine making process var4	3.80	3.21	3.12
Mean Score	4.02	3.03	3.07

desire to source their own purchases independent of external influences. The members of this group, who are considered the most knowledgeable about wine, could be expected to have high levels of confidence in their ability to make selections from a variety of sources. The other area in which they registered a low score was that of knowledge of the winemaking process. This is perhaps more explainable. The researcher, while not able to comment on those who filled in the self completion cellar door surveys, did note that many of those who professed a deep interest in wine also acknowledged the complexity of the winemaking process and indicated that they had 'a lot to learn'. There was a feeling that they more they understood about winemaking the less sure they were that they understood the process and all its variables. Less experienced patrons were more prone to assert that they understood the winemaking process (Houghton, 2007 in press).

Cluster 2 ('Wine Interested') and Cluster 3 ('Curious Tourist') are distinctively different in some facets, however overall they are similar and close in score. Most noticeable is the difference in responses to the 'sole purpose' question. Hall (1996) suggests that for the 'Wine Interested' the trip to the region is part of the appeal but not the sole motivator, while for the 'Curious Tourist' it was at best a secondary attraction. The group that exhibited the characteristics closest to the 'wine interested' type scored low when asked if the opportunity to visit the wineries was the sole reason for their visit to the region whereas the 'curious tourist' group registered a high score (higher in fact that the 'wine lovers'). This may reflect an inclination by the 'curious tourist' to make a special trip to satisfy their curiosity in contrast to the other two groups who are aware of what is on offer in various regions and avail themselves of an opportunity as it arises. The higher score recorded for purchasing wine and joining a mailing list may also be a sign of this curiosity and be an indication of less selective behaviour (Houghton, 2007, in press).

The results indicate that wine festival attendees can be classified into relatively homogeneous groups but suggest that these categories are not as decisively different as those attributed by Hall to wine tourists. The 'serious wine drinker' along with the novice would appear to be attracted by these wine events.

Crowds and crowds of Participants

Many winery operators, the promoters of these events, were unsure whether the size of these events discouraged others (particularly 'serious wine drinkers') from visiting the wineries. On the one hand they felt that the festive crowds made patrons more comfortable (e.g. they liked the company of others), but they also said that they thought many customers preferred to visit when there were no festivals (Houghton, 2004). What became apparent when analysing the data was that though some patrons were in agreement, overall their opinions were not nearly as strong on this subject as the winery operators feared and it could be concluded that while there are some cellar door patrons that festivals may deter the majority are not concerned. There appears to be some justification for this thinking but whether it is to the degree the wineries fear is unlikely for two reasons.

First, as mentioned earlier in this chapter, the mix of patrons who are attracted to festivals is fairly evenly distributed over the categorized wine tourist 'types', that is all sorts of visitors are represented including the informed wine tourist. Secondly, in respect of the cellar door respondents, only one-fifth agreed that they preferred to visit wineries outside festival periods. Further, even of those who had never attended a festival (one can only speculate as to whether this non-attendance was as a result of inclination or lack of opportunity) only 44 per cent concurred with the statement that they preferred non-festival visits. These outcomes indicate that while there may be some who avoid festivals, the gains from holding these events outweigh any potential loses and as such they are successful promotional tools.

When the festival is over, what next?

The literature on wine festivals as a promotional strategy reveals that for the promotion to be declared successful it should result in increased sales, visitation, brand recognition and enhanced reputation for the staging winery (Dodd, 1995; Cambourne, 1998; Hall et al., 2000). Table 12.7 summarizes the responses to a series of questions as to the intentions of participants in regard to future wine festivals and future visits to wineries. The table defines two major groups, (a) those who had attended a Rutherglen festival and (b) those who attended a wine festival in another region. In the Rutherglen group, patrons attending their first festival in particular, responded very positively to the question of return visitation. Repeat festival patrons were almost as positive about future visits, the exception being that they were not as interested in festivals in other areas. Similarly respondents who had attended a festival

Table 12.7 Summarized outcomes of responses to winery visitation questions

Question 'Will you......'	(a) Rutherglen Festival Attendees		(b) Attendees of other Festivals (%)
	First festival (%)	Repeat patron (%)	
Visit another Rutherglen Festival?	>80	≤80	
Visit Rutherglen winery when no festival?	≤80	≤80	
Visit Festival other region?	≤80	≤40	≤60
Visit winery other region?	≤80	≤80	≤80
Visit wineries when no festival?			≤80

in another region also appeared less inclined to travel (≤60 per cent). These findings show that these events are valued by the public and suggest that for wineries they provide many ongoing benefits both on the day of the event and later.

A wine festival model

Wine festivals are created to attract the public to a specific wine product or region. But, as Taylor (2006, p.180) asks, 'why [do] people attend wine festivals amongst the congestion, queues and confusion of a wine festival when they can obtain many of the tangible tourism products ... during the other 51 weeks of the year'. There must be other benefits. What are the patrons of these events looking for? As a direct outcome of the information gathered in the Rutherglen study (reported in this chapter and other articles) a model was devised to conceptualize the melding of the aspirations of both the wine festival promoter and the wine festival patron (Figure 12.1). This model illustrates how a wine festival can become the catalyst for developing a mutually beneficial interaction between both parties.

The model acknowledges that initially the two parties have similar but differing aspirations, namely the desire to attract winery visitation by the promoters and a wine-based touristic experience by the visitor. On an individual basis, to achieve benefit for a specific winery that winery needs to promote recognition of its products and the wine festival and by providing an attractive wine-based experience, has the ability to accomplish this by drawing people to the region. The visitor is seeking knowledge of both the existence of quality wineries and the opportunity to trial the products. This trial stage provides the winery promoter with the opportunity to provide insights into winemaking promote an image of quality and develop a relationship while at the same time gaining market intelligence and feedback. These steps if accomplished satisfactorily for the patron may then work as a stimulus to purchase the individual winery's product. This process has then fulfilled the goals of both promoter and patron. That is, the winery promoter has made a sale plus ensured the possibility of maintaining ongoing contact through other festivals, mailing lists and brand recognition. The satisfied wine festival patron has acquired knowledge, product and will in all probability (as demonstrated earlier in Table 12.7) return to the winery both during normal trading hours and for other events and in so doing demonstrate a loyalty to both the wine and the wine region.

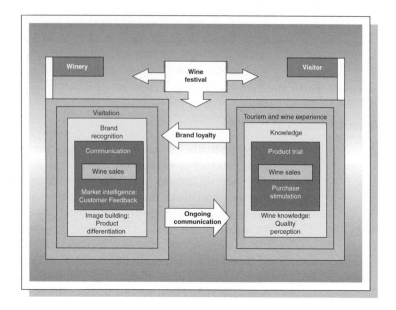

Figure 12.1
Wine festival
model illustrating
synergies between
winery operators
and wine festival
visitors

Conclusion

Wineries have wondered whether the benefits required (purchases, visitation and brand recognition) are being realized. They have wondered whether the 'right type' of person is being attracted to these highly successful and well-patronized events. Studies indicate that this promotional strategy is effective. Wine festival patrons represent a wide range of types (from connoisseur to curious tourist) and arrive with varying levels of interest in, and experiences of, wine. What they have in common and is conclusively demonstrated in the Rutherglen case, is that whatever their background and their level of interest, the wine festival has the ability to attract them and they have the potential to become continuing consumers of the wine festival promoters product.

References

Beeton, S. and Pinge, I. (2001). *Bendigo Heritage Uncorked: Festival Report*. La Trobe University, Bendigo, Australia.

Cambourne, B. (1998). Wine tourism in the Canberra District In Dowling, R. and Carlsen, J. (eds.), *Wine Tourism Perfect Partners, Proceedings of the 1st Australian Wine Tourism Conference*, Margaret River, Western Australia. Australia: Bureau of Tourism Research, ACT.

Carlsen, J. (1999). A profile of visitors to the Sunday Times Margaret River Wine Region Festival 1999. In *Proceedings of The First New Zealand Wine Tourism Conference*. New Zealand: Blenheim.

Collins, C. (1996). Drop in for more than just a drop. *Weekend Australian*, 9 March, p. 3.

Dodd, T. (1995). Opportunities and pitfalls of tourism in a developing wine industry. *International Journal of Wine Marketing*, 7(1), 5–16.

Dodd, T. and Bigotte, V. (1997). Perceptual differences among visitor groups to wineries. *Journal of Travel Research*, 35(3), 46–51.

Fry, C. (1999). Key drivers in cellar door sales. *Second Australian Wine Tourism Conference: Book of Abstracts*. Bureau of Tourism Research, ACT, Australia.

Getz, D. (1991). *Festivals, Special Events and Tourism*. Van Nostrand Reinhold, New York, USA.

Hall, C.M. (1996). Wine tourism in New Zealand. In Kearsley, G. (ed.) *Tourism Down Under II, Towards a More Sustainable Tourism*. Centre for Tourism, University of Otago, New Zealand.

Hall, C.M. and Macionis, N. (1998). Wine tourism in Australia and New Zealand. In Hall, C. and Jenkins, J. (eds.) *Tourism and Recreation in Rural Areas*. John Wiley & Sons, New York, USA.

Hall, C.M., Johnson, G., Cambourne, B., Macionis, N., Mitchell, R. and Sharples, L. (2000). Wine tourism: An introduction. In Hall, C., Sharples, L., Cambourne, B. and Macionis, N. (eds.) *Wine Tourism Around the World: Development, Management and Markets*. Butterworth Heineman, Oxford, UK.

Houghton, M. (2001). The propensity of wine festivals to encourage subsequent winery visitation. *International Journal of Wine Marketing*, 13(3), 32–41.

Houghton, M. (2005). Wine festivals: the promoters perspective. In Boyle, A. and Tremblay, P. (eds.) *Sharing Tourism Knowledge, CAUTHE 2005*. Charles Darwin University, Alice Springs, Australia.

Houghton, M. (2007) in press. Classifying wine festival customers: Comparing an inductive typology with Hall's wine tourist classification. *International Journal of Culture, Tourism and Hospitality Research*, (accepted April, 2007).

Ivers, T. (1999). Breaking into new markets – spending less to get more. In *Second Australian Wine Tourism Conference: Book of Abstracts*, Bureau of Tourism Research, ACT, Australia.

Kohli, A. and Jaworski, B. (1990). Market orientation: the construct, research propositions and managerial implications. *Journal of Marketing*, 54 April, 1–18.

Mitchell, R., Hall, M. and McIntosh, A. (2000). Wine tourism and consumer behaviour. In Hall, C., Sharples, L., Cambourne, B. and Macionis, N. (eds.) *Wine Tourism Around the World: Development, Management and Markets*. Butterworth Heinemann, Oxford, UK.

Mortensen, H. (1990). *The Winemakers of Rutherglen*. Mortensen, H. Albury, NSW, Australia.

National Wine Tourism Strategy (1999). *National Wine Tourism Strategy Working Party*. Winemaker's Federation of Australia, August.

Snepenger, D. (1987). Segmenting the vacation market by novelty seeking role. *Journal of Travel Research*, 26(2), 8–14.

Taylor, R. (2006). Wine festivals and tourism: Developing a longitudinal approach to festival evaluation. In Carlsen, J. and Charters, S. (eds.) *Global Wine Tourism: Research, Management and Marketing*. CAB International, Oxford, UK.

Uncles, M. (2000). Defining market orientation. *Australian Journal of Management*, 25(2), 1–9.

Victorian Wineries Tourism Council (1996). *A Survey of Tourism Activity at Victorian Wineries 1996*. Victorian Wineries Tourism Council, Melbourne, Australia.

Victorian Wineries Tourism Council (1998). *A Survey of Tourism Activity at Victorian Wineries 1998*. Victorian Wineries Tourism Council, Melbourne, Australia.

Weiler, B., Truong, M., and Griffiths, M. (2004). Visitor profiles and motivations for visiting an Australian wine festival. In *Proceedings of the International Wine Tourism Conference*, Margaret River, Australia.

Yuan, J., Cai, L., Morrison, A. and Linton, S. (2005). An analysis of wine festival attendees' motivations: a synergy of wine, travel and special events. *Journal of Vacation Marketing*, 11(1), 37–54.

PART IV

Farmers' markets

PART IX

Farmers' markets

The authentic market experience of farmers' markets

C. Michael Hall, Richard Mitchell,
David Scott and Liz Sharples

Introduction

In a trend towards more ethical or morally acceptable consumption, consumers are increasingly demanding foods that are healthy, spray-free, organic, biodynamic, non-genetically modified organisms (GMO), have low food miles, are eth-ically produced, and/or fair-trade (McEachern and Willock, 2004; Padel and Foster, 2005). As Holloway and Kneafsey (2000, p.290) put it, this '... is leading to an interest in foods which are not only felt to be safe, but which are traceable, and associated with ideas of sustainability and ecological-friendliness'. Meanwhile Sassatelli and Scott (2001) suggest that in responding to food crises, such as Genetically Modified foods or Bovine Spongiform Encephalopathy (BSE) outbreaks, 'consumer-citizens' may exercise their political muscle by changing their purchasing behaviour to distribution channels that they place more trust in. These constructs all require the consumer to be aware of the conditions under which food has been produced, who produced it and the trustworthiness of that producer. While Sassatelli and Scott (2001) suggest that the use of farmers' markets as a source of 'embodied trust' is more likely to occur in traditional agricultural economies such as Italy, they acknowledge that this is increasingly the case in the industrialized corporate production systems like the UK, manifested in highly sophisticated agri-food systems. In fact, Holloway and Kneafsey (2000) suggest that farmers' markets are a logical outcome of these trends as they represent the local and allow the consumer to connect directly with the producer of the food. This is reflected in definitions of several national and regional farmers' market organizations (Table 13.1), where terms such as 'local', 'fresh' (which implies that food has only travelled a short distance from its origin), and 'direct to consumer' or terms that imply that the goods are vendor produced are frequently used.

However, the definition of a farmers' market has long been regarded as problematic. As Pyle (1971, p.167) recognized, '... everything that is called a farmers' market may not be one, and other names are given to meeting that have the form and function of a farmers' market'. Other names for similar types of markets in the North American context include farm shops, swap meets, flea markets, tailgate markets and farm stands (Brown, 2001). As she explained this is a major problem in farmers' market studies as many markets will advertise that they are a so-called farmers' market when in fact they are technically not in the true sense of the term with respect to direct purchase in a market context of the grower of the produce

Table 13.1 Definitions of farmers' market

Country	Organization	Definition
Australia	Australian Farmers' Market Association	'… a predominantly fresh food market that operates regularly within a community, at a focal public location that provides a suitable environment for farmers and food producers to sell farm-origin and associated value-added processed food products directly to customers.'
Canada, Ontario	Farmers' Markets Ontario	'… is a seasonal, multi-vendor, community-driven (not private) organization selling agricultural, food, art and craft products including home-grown produce, home-made crafts and value-added products where the vendors are primary producers (including preserves, baked goods, meat, fish, dairy products, etc.)'
New Zealand	New Zealand Farmers' Market Association	'… a food market where local growers, farmers and artisan food producers sell their wares directly to consumers. Vendors may only sell what they grow, farm, pickle, preserve, bake, smoke or catch themselves from within a defined local area. The market takes place at a public location on a regular basis.'
UK	National Farmers' Retail and Markets Association (FARMA)	'…… a market in which farmers, growers or producers from a defined local area are present in person to sell their own produce, direct to the public. All products sold should have been grown, reared, caught, brewed, pickled, baked, smoked or processed by the stallholder.'

(Continued)

199

Table 13.1 Continued

Country	Organization	Definition
USA, California	California Farmers' Markets Association	'The certified farmers' markets (CFM) are diversified markets offering both certifiable and non-certifiable goods for sale. The CFM provides producers with the opportunity to sell their fresh, local products directly to the consumers without the intervention of a middleman. Each CFM is operated in accordance with regulations established in the *California Administrative Code* (Title 3, Chapter 3, Group 4, Article 6.5, Section 1392) pertaining to Direct Marketing. Each market is certified by the County Agricultural Commissioner as a direct marketing outlet for producers to sell their crops directly to consumers without meeting the usual size, standard pack and container requirements for such products. However, all produce must meet minimum quality standards. The non-certifiable goods add variety and enhance the festive ambiance of the farmers' market. Although the State Direct Marketing regulations require the producers of fresh fruit, nuts, vegetables, flowers, honey, eggs, nursery stock and plants be required to be certified, the same producer-to-consumer philosophy applies for all items sold at the Market. The resale of products is prohibited' (CFMA 2006, p. 1).
USA	United States Department of Agriculture	'... a common facility or area where multiple farmers/growers gather on a regular recurring basis to sell a variety of fresh fruits, vegetables, and other farm products directly to customers' (in Payne 2002, p. 1).

Source: Australian Farmers' Market Association, http://www.farmersmarkets.org.au/about. jsp; California Farmers' Markets Association (2006, p. 1); Farmers' Markets Ontario (2007a); National Farmers' Retail and Markets Association, http://www.farmersmarkets.net/; New Zealand Farmers' Market Association, http://www.farmersmarket.org.nz/home.htm; Payne (2002, p.1).

purchased. Although to an extent the different terms used for farmers' markets reflect retail change over time, the focus of 'official' definitions of farmers' markets reflects the notion that farmers' markets are 'recurrent markets at fixed locations where farm products are sold by farmers themselves ... at a true farmers' market some, if not all, of the vendors must be producers who sell their own products' (Brown, 2001, p.658). The issue of definition is not just academic but, as discussed throughout this chapter, reflects broader concerns of consumers and producers that the farmers' market and its produce be regarded as a space in which consumers can trust the 'authentic' qualities of what is being offered. We begin the chapter with a discussion of the antecedents of the modern farmers' market movement as well as contemporary growth and development before introducing some recent conceptualizations of the markets from around the world.

The fall and rise of farmers' markets

Markets of various kinds have been a part of most cultures for as long as trading economies have existed. Entire towns and cities grew to support the trading of food products, especially in strategic locations, such as at major sea ports, at the cross-roads of major trading routes or in areas with specialized production. Additionally markets have influenced both the growth and decline of urban areas throughout the ages. Devizes, a market town in Wiltshire, England, was developed as a direct result of the 'hundreds' market granted in the twelfth century to Potterne, approximately two miles away (Britnell, 1978). However, a degeneration of urban centres was seen between the fourteenth and sixteenth centuries with the removal of royal charters from market towns, subsequently resulting in a migration to rural areas to enable access to sufficient foodstuffs (Dyer, 1991). During the industrial revolution the mass-urbanization of many western countries saw the development of urban markets that brought food from the rural hinterland to the population, while rural service towns also continued to hold regular markets. In America Hamilton (2002, p.73–74) suggests that:

... in the mid-1700s, came a crucial shift. As urban areas flourished, consumer power grew exponentially, tipping the delicate balance of interdependence between customers and suppliers. Growth did cause an increased demand for food, creating more selling opportunities, but in these changing versions of the old markets, the customer became top priority.

Exhibit 13.1 Newcastle upon Tyne Farmers' and Country Market

Newcastle is situated in the North East of England on the northern bank of the River Tyne and is England's most northerly city, situated just 60 miles south of the Scottish border. This vibrant city has a history spanning back to Roman Times when the city was founded under the name Pons Aelius. The city itself is the 20th most populous in England with a population of 259,536 but it is part of the Tyne and Wear conurbation which is the fifth largest conurbation in England (British History Online, 2007).

By the Middle Ages Newcastle had become England's northern fortress and was an important trading community and as early as Elizabethan times Newcastle was exporting coal. The tax from this trade brought great wealth to the city and by the nineteenth century Newcastle had also developed other industries such as shipbuilding and heavy engineering. During the Industrial Revolution the city was seen as a powerhouse of innovation and excellence.

Markets have always played an important part of Newcastle life and continue to do so. Records show that when King John made Newcastle a borough in 1216 there were already markets thriving in the town. Several historic maps, James Corbridge's map of 1723, Charles Hutton's map of 1770 and John Wood's map of 1827 are helpful in recording the rise of fall of food markets in the city. We know, for example, that in 1723 a fish market, herb market, flesh market, milk and poultry market, groat market, wheat market and butcher bank were in existence (Newcastle upon Tyne City Council, 2007).

In the 1830s the heart of the city centre was developed in a neoclassical style largely by architects Richard Grainger and John Dobson. Many of these fine buildings and frontages have recently been restored and in 2005 Grey Street was voted to be England's finest street in a survey of Radio 4 listeners.

A small portion of this area of the city, locally known as 'Grainger Town', was demolished in the 1960s to make way for a new shopping centre but many key buildings remain including the magnificent Grade 1 listed Grainger Market. This indoor market, which has a lettable area of 38,000 square feet, makes it one of the largest market halls in the country. At the time of its opening it was considered to be one of the most spacious and elegant markets in Europe and to mark its opening a grand dinner was held complete with an orchestra and attended by 2,000 guests (Newcastle upon Tyne City Council, 2007).

It was therefore fitting that Grainger Town, at the heart of Newcastle's trading and commercial activity for many centuries, was chosen as the location for the development of Newcastle upon Tyne Farmers' and Country Market. The market is held next to the 134 feet Roman Doric Column, Greys Monument, at the top of Grey Street, and a few steps away from the Grainger Market. This is an ideal location to catch passing trade as it is in the heart of the city centre and adjacent to a busy 'metro' station.

The market is promoted and organized by two full time employees who work for the markets team of the city council, who pay careful attention to maintaining the quality of the delivery. All potential stallholders are carefully vetted to ensure that they comply with the market's high standards. This market is certified by National Farmers' Retail and Markets Association (FARMA) and therefore all food products sold on the market must be raised, grown or produced within a 50 mile radius of the market site. Occasionally producers from up to a 100 mile radius may be considered if there is no suitable application from a local producer of a given product. This allowance away from the usual '30 mile' rule is due to the fact that Newcastle is a major city and the number of producers within the locality of the city is limited.

The number of stalls is strictly limited to 24 at the present time and there are no plans to grow the market as the council feel that this is an ideal size at this location. On one level the market team are in an enviable situation of being over-subscribed, with more producers wanting to take part than there are places available, but this does mean that sometimes hard decisions have to take place about stall allocation. The market team work hard to ensure that there is a balance of stalls on offer to customers and will actively seek out producers if they feel that the market would be enriched by their products (Blakemore, 2007). The market sometimes includes craft products which are produced locally but the main focus of the market is food.

The event is usually held on the first Friday of each month and at the current time there are no plans to hold the market more frequently. The team does however organize special market days, for example at Christmas, when the farmers' market becomes part of a 4-day long Christmas market. This event will attract visitors from around the region including coach parties (Blakemore, 2007).

The future development of markets in and around Newcastle is still strictly governed by the city council who grants licences under the city's historic charter regulations.

Liz Sharples

This shift in the nature of the relationship between consumer and producers was ultimately good for sales of produce, but bad for individual producer and this, plus the development of centralized market halls, made markets more profitable for middlemen than for producers of the goods (Hamilton, 2002). Over the ensuing 150 to 200 years, the development of mass communication, more efficient nationwide and global transport systems (e.g. rail, road, sea and air freight) and advances in the preservation of foodstuffs (e.g. canning, refrigeration, freezing, etc.) saw the development of state or regional distribution networks, then national markets in sprawling urban centres (Hamilton, 2002) and ultimately a global food market (Hall and Mitchell, 2001). According to Hamilton (2002, p.74), despite some farmers' markets in the USA continuing to be successful, 'by the turn of the twentieth century ... the bond between farmer and consumer had been replaced by the desire for almighty Convenience (sic.). The heyday was over'.

The advent of the supermarket during the twentieth century saw direct-to-consumer markets all but disappear. This was especially so in places such as the UK and USA, where the retail supermarket developed alongside the *mallification* of urban areas (Ghent Urban Studies Team, 1999), changes in agricultural production and distribution (Brown, 2001), the advent of the private motor vehicle (Hamilton, 2002) and extensive advertising and marketing of processed foods (Hamilton, 2002). It is interesting to note, however, that in Europe and many Asian countries, where large scale retail also developed throughout the twentieth century, food markets (admittedly many of which are not always purely direct-to-consumer markets) have managed to survive. France alone is estimated to have around 36,000 markets some of which do not fit the UK, US or Canadian definition of farmers' markets but which nevertheless do contain local farmers and producers selling their own produce (FARMA, 2006).

As the twentieth century began to draw to a close, however, something triggered a resurgence of interest in farmers' markets in the Anglophone world. It has been suggested this can be considered a response to what Beck (1992) considers 'risk society', that being the risks individuals perceive in contemporary society, including those discussed above. The (re)introduction of farmers' markets was initially witnessed in the USA, then Canada, the UK and finally Australia and New Zealand. In the USA it has been suggested that the main growth period of modern farmers' market came during the 1970s after 25 years of very low activity and this came on the back of changing attitudes by farmers to direct marketing and legislation that encouraged and enabled direct-to-consumer sales (i.e. Public Law 94-463, the *Farmer-to-Consumer Direct Marketing Act* of 1976) (Brown, 2001). Between 1970 and 1986 the number of US farmers' markets is reported to have increased fivefold (Brown, 2001). According to Hamilton (2002, p.77) 'by 1994 there were 1,755 farmers' markets nationwide, by 2000 there were 2,863', while more recent figures also show rapid growth between 1994 and 2006 (United States Department of Agriculture, 2006) (Figure 13.1) and, if it were not for a lull in growth as a result of decreased funding for

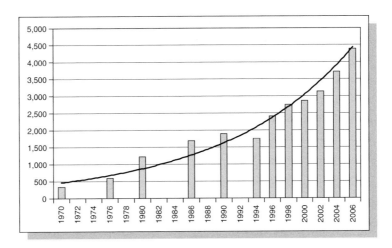

Figure 13.1
Growth in American farmers' markets (1970–2006) *Note*: No data is available for 1972, 1974, 1978, 1982, 1984, 1988 and 1992, but these years are included in order to show the exponential nature of the growth (*Source*: Brown, 2001; United States Department of Agriculture, 2006)

community initiatives during the Reagan administration (Brown, 2001), growth may well have been higher. However, the spatial distribution of farmers' markets is not consistent as it should be noted that there are nearly 500 certified farmers' markets (CFMs) in California alone (California Federation of Certified Farmers' Markets, 2003).

The Canadian experience generally mirrors that of the USA (see Jolliffe, Chapter 14). The farmers' market revival began in the 1970s and 1980s. The number of markets in Ontario increased from a low of 60 in the 1980s to more than double that number in 2007. Farmers' Markets Ontario (FMO), the umbrella organization for farmers' markets in that province, was established in 1991 and in 2007 had 115 member markets.

In the UK the first of the modern farmers' markets was (re)established in 1997 as a pilot project in Bath, which followed many of the elements of the most successful US markets (Holloway and Kneafsey, 2000; Kneafsey et al., 2001). In 2002 there were 240 (Purvis, 2002) and by 2006 the number had risen to more than 550 markets and there were estimates that up to 800 markets would be sustainable throughout the UK (FARMA, 2006). Similarly, Australian and New Zealand markets were first established in the late 1990s and have grown to around 93 and 36 respectively in recent years (Melsen, 2004; Coster and Kennon, 2005; Guthrie et al., 2006; New Zealand Farmers' Market Association (NZFMA), 2007; Regional Food Australia, 2007; see also Hede, Chapter, 16).

However, the definition of 'farmers' market' also goes hand-in-hand with regulatory and environmental factors. For example, in California farmers' markets are certified under state legislation. According to the California Federation of Certified Farmers' Markets (2003) CFMs operated in accordance with regulations established in 1977 by the California Department of Food and Agriculture 'are "the real thing", places where genuine farmers sell their crops directly to the public' and are regarded as having multiple benefits for small farmers, consumers and the community. Table 13.2 provides an outline of such benefits from the perspectives of CFM.

A CFM is a location approved by the county agricultural commissioner where certified farmers offer for sale only those agricultural products they grow themselves. Not only does such

Table 13.2 Benefits of CFMs in California

Stakeholder	Benefits
Communities	• Non-profit community service organizations which contribute to the social and economic welfare of the town or city they operate in. • Produce a strong sense of community identity, bringing people from diverse ethnic and other backgrounds together. • Serve to unite the urban and rural segments of the population. • The meeting of farmers and consumers serves as an educational experience whereby customers learn about their food sources have access to nutritional information, engage in a multi-cultural experience and become aware of agricultural issues.
Consumers	• Fresh picked, vine and tree ripened quality. • Cost savings that are possible because the direct sales by farmers to the consumer eliminate the cost of middleman marketing and other intermediaries.
Farmers	• Provide an outlet especially suited to moving smaller volumes of produce, thus creating a marketing channel outside of the traditional large volume distribution systems. • Allows farmers to sell field run produce not restricted to pack and grade standards. This enables the farmer to sell tree ripened fruit which is too delicate for standard packing and shipping processes. • Increases profits for farmers because of cost savings.

Source: Derived from CFM (2003).

an approach reinforce the local nature of what is available at a farmers' market but it also provides a guarantee to customers that the food is direct from the producer rather than being repackaged. The concept of certifying farmers' markets was also introduced in Ontario, Canada, in 2006 although through a process of self-regulation rather than government regulation.

The Ontario concept was developed by farmers in the Ontario Greenbelt and Greater Toronto area through the support of Farmers' Markets Ontario (FMO), Friends of the Greenbelt Foundation (FGF) and Weston Farmers' Market. The reason for the introduction of the scheme was that many farmers' markets included non-farmers who resell produce bought at food terminals. The new CFM is instead dedicated to farmers selling locally grown products and excludes non-farmers reselling imports or produce bought from the Ontario Food Terminal. According to Laura Alderson, Manager of Weston Farmers' Market in Toronto,

There is a growing sense among farmers that present-day Farmers' Markets are a distortion of their origins … Many markets utilize public space, such as civic squares, and therefore should benefit the public interest. They can do this by delivering fresh, nutritious foods, building a sense of community between rural and urban neighbours, and investing in the local economy (FGF, 2006).

Similarly, Robert Chorney, Executive Director of FMO stated,

Farmers' markets should benefit the farmer by selling the freshest food in return for taking home a greater share of the dollar for what they grow. Instead, there are resellers at many Ontario farmers' markets with some simply mimicking large grocery retailers… This will be the first market in Canada that gives consumers a guarantee that the vendors are farmers and the food is fresh (FGF, 2006).

Such a perspective was also forcibly pushed by FMO in their set of rules and regulations for CFMs in Ontario.

During the summer of 2006, it became very clear to …FMO … that something needed to be done to combat the growing number of resellers or hucksters that had infiltrated and in some cases, were dominating, some of the markets in the Greater Toronto area. Farmers were being literally squeezed out of existing markets by resellers who continued to glut the market with food terminal sell-offs and in some cases, told there was no room for them to sell at market. Recognizing that most market operators would not soon purge their markets of resellers, hucksters and 'produce-jockeys', FMO studied the Greenmarket program in New York City and the State of California Certification program where all farmers are certified and where all vendors at market are 'the real thing' (FMO, 2007a,b, p.1).

Under the project certification includes, but is not limited to, each farmer undergoing a third-party certification inspection, showing proof of a farm business registration number, and posting a sign at each market stall to identify the location of their farm and what they grow (FMO, 2007a,b). The FMO have a zero tolerance for the reselling of products that have not been grown by the vendor.

All Ontario bona fide, conventional and organic growers and producers may apply for certification and, as part of the initial application, all prospective vendors are required to submit a full list of the produce/products to be sold and indicate when these items will be available for market. Table 13.3 outlines the various product categories of Ontario CFMs. The FMO (2007a,b, p.3) notes that 'as a general rule, a first-come-first-served process will apply; however, preference will be given to those farmers residing and operating within the Greenbelt'. In addition, the FMO also reserve the right to choose market vendors based on the

Table 13.3 Product categories of the Ontario CFMs

Primary products	Fresh/unprocessed fruit, vegetables, cut flowers, plants and nuts; honey and maple syrup; shell eggs; meat (fresh and frozen); fish (fresh and frozen); herbs; mushrooms.
Secondary products must meet three conditions	• The 'defining ingredient' must be from (produced on) the farmer's own farm • The value must be added from the farm (meat products may be an exception as the value might be added at an off-farm site) • The product must be in compliance with all regulations and there must be evidence of appropriate inspection (by health and/or other authorities)
Ready-to-eat 'fast food'; Permissible depending on agreement with host partners	• Coffee and tea sold by the market or a concession for community fund-raising obtained on a wholesale basis from an established business • Unique sandwiches such as venison on a bun provided that the principal ingredient (i.e. the venison) conforms to the requirements of secondary products

Source: Derived from CFM (2007, p. 4).

overall product mix available at the market and note that not all applicants are necessarily accepted. The first two Ontario CFMs opened in May and June 2007 respectively at Toronto's Liberty Village and Woodbine Centre using the label of 'MyMarket Certified Local Farmers' Market' (MyMarket, 2007):

In the UK three core principles have been developed with respect to farmers' markets which have been enshrined in a certification scheme administered by the FARMA and independently inspected.

(a) The stallholder comes from an area defined as local, 30 miles is suggested as the first mark, extending to 50 miles for urban and coastal locations.
(b) The stallholder has grown, reared, baked, brewed, caught, pickled or preserved the foods he/she is selling.
(c) The stall is staffed by the farmer or members of his/her team that knows about the production process.

The different sets of regulations highlights the difficulties in making international comparisons between farmers' markets although the California, Ontario and UK approach towards certification highlights the significance of being able to ensure, from the perspective of consumer confidence, that a farmers' market is actually a market in which produce is made available from those who actually farmed it. Indeed, if the UK approach was applied to Australian or New Zealand farmers' markets then at many markets there would be stallholders who would not qualify and for whom the market is an alternative retail channel, albeit often of high-quality produce, rather than an example of 'local food'. For example, in New Zealand Havoc Farm Pork from Waimate in South Canterbury was at one time simultaneously available at farmers' markets in Dunedin and Christchurch – both well over 100 miles from the farm.

However, in some locations, including Ontario, it can be extremely difficult for a stallholder to be able to provide farm grown produce all year round as well as providing an environment that is comfortable for consumers. For example, the farmers' market in Umeå in northern Sweden can only operate from late August to early October at the very latest because of weather restrictions on product availability and consumer comfort. Therefore, many farmers' markets are quite seasonal, typically the harvest months of summer and autumn, not only with respect to the range of produce that is available, but also the number of stallholders. Although from some perspectives this may be regarded as a source of delight with respect to the authenticity of seasonal local food it can also pose significant business challenges for individual stallholders as well as the market as a whole.

One solution to the problem of seasonality is to have a permanent market, often indoors or at least sheltered, that combines elements of a farmers' market as well as reselling. Such a category is recognized by the FMO under the category of a 'Public Market', defined as 'usually a municipally owned/operated (not private) year-round operation consisting of unique, specialty food and crafts merchants who sell some products they produce or grow themselves but who often sell items they buy from local producers or wholesalers. Public Markets usually include local producers during the growing season' (FMO, 2007a). Nevertheless, the lack of year-round availability may mean that other food retailers, such as supermarkets, may seek to provide substitutes for consumer demand for ethically or sustainably produced food, while in some cases – as in high latitude or altitude locations – to limit to fresh and locally farmed produce at some times of year would not only be almost impossible may be substantially restrict consumers' diets.

The farmers' market

Despite their growing significance as a retail outlet and visitor attraction there is relatively little knowledge of the market for farmers' markets, with research dominated by North American studies. In the USA, demographic surveys at farmers' markets have historically indicated that patrons are predominantly white females with above average incomes, age and education (Connell et al., 1986; Rhodus et al., 1994; Eastwood et al., 1995; Hughes and Mattson, 1995; Leones, 1995; Leones et al., 1995; Abel et al., 1999; Govindasamy et al., 2002; Conrey et al., 2003). That the majority of patrons to American farmers' markets are women should not be surprising. Women still make the bulk of all food purchases in the USA. 'A full 86% of the produce buyers surveyed for The Packer Fresh Trends edition were women. Women are more sensitive to price than men and are more likely to try new or unusual fruits and vegetables. The percentage of women making purchasing decisions in households with children under 18 is a whopping 99%' (Leones, 1995, p. 1). However, interestingly, she went on to note that because visits to farmers' markets tend to be more family oriented so other members of the family tend to take a more active role in purchasing decisions.

In their study of the Orono farmers' market, Kezis et al. (1998) found that quality, support for local farmers, and atmosphere were very significant to consumers. Nearly half of weekly patrons reported spending upwards of US$10.00 per visit. Consumers also indicated a willingness to pay more for produce at the farmers' market than for similar produce at a supermarket, with 72 per cent indicating a willingness to pay an average of 17 per cent more for farmers' market produce. Similar data regarding consumer perceptions of farmers' markets was also identified in a study conducted of farmer markets in San Diego California (Jolly, 1999). In the same study approximately equal proportions of the sample perceived prices to be higher or lower than supermarket prices. However, 73 per cent perceived quality at the farmers' markets to be superior to supermarket produce. Two-thirds of the respondents also indicated a preference to have items indicate a San Diego grown label and a half stated a willingness to pay more for San Diego grown products (Jolly, 1999).

As in California, the state of Oregon has also embraced the farmers' markets concept. A study of 2,714 consumers at the Albany and Corvallis Saturday farmers' markets and the Wednesday farmers' market in Corvallis indicated the significant economic impacts that farmers' markets may have on a community (Novak, 1998):

- Consumers at the markets bought goods from three to six vendors.
- Consumers spent an average of US$12 to US$15 a visit, with the amount increasing as more seasonal produce became available.
- Shoppers to the Wednesday market spent 30 per cent more than Saturday shoppers, with women and retired people forming a significant portion of the visitors.
- 88 per cent of the visitors to the Albany Saturday market and 78 per cent of the visitors to the Saturday market in Corvallis said their main reason for going downtown that morning was the farmers' market.
- 63 per cent of the Corvallis shoppers and 35 per cent of the Albany shoppers said they also planned to spend money at other downtown shops or restaurants after their market visit.
- 10 per cent of those who responded said they stopped shopping because they could not carry any more goods.
- The three markets attracted about 4,500 adults during an average week, even though they were open for only 13 hours during that time.

Given the growth of farmers' markets in the USA, particularly in urban districts, there is also increased interest in making fresh farmers' market produce available to working class and low-income neighbourhoods (Balsam et al., 1994; Brown, 2002; United States Department of Agriculture, 2002; Conrey et al., 2003) (see also Chapters 1 and 2). Suarez-Balcazar et al. (2006) undertook a study of a farmers' market run in a low-income neighbourhood of Chicago that primarily had an Afro-American population. At the time of the study it was reported that there were more liquor stores than supermarkets available in this area while the available food in the community was sold, for the most part, at high prices by small stores with a limited selection of poor-quality food with low nutritional content. According to the majority of shoppers, the top three things that they liked best about the farmers' market were the fresh produce, the reasonable prices and the cleanliness of the market. Most shoppers attending the farmers' market were looking for vegetables (e.g. greens and okra) and fruits (e.g. apples, peaches and plums). Respondents reported that, in order to improve the farmers' market, they would like to see more vendors and a greater variety of produce and other food products. Almost 100 per cent of the respondents would recommend the farmers' market to a friend, and 95 per cent would return to the market again (Suarez-Balcazar et al., 2006). The research found that

- Residents were more satisfied, overall, with the access to fresh fruits and vegetables provided by the summer farmers' market than they were with the access, quality, variety and prices of products available to them year round through local stores. The same results were replicated at a nearby community.
- Consumers at the market spent about $10 to $20 each week.
- The majority of consumers at the farmers' market consisted of females between the ages of 40 and 75 years (Suarez-Balcazar et al., 2006).

Canada

The positioning of Canada's farmers' markets means that consumers have many of the same characteristics of those in the USA and the UK (see Jolliffe, Chapter 14). Feagan et al.'s (2004) study of Niagara region farmers' markets reported that the modes of the ages for markets in St. Catharines and Port Colborne, and the overall survey were in the 60 to 69 years old age category while the less pronounced modal age for the Welland farmers' market was in the 50 to 59 years old category. This same age trend has been noted in the UK by Holloway and Kneafsey (2000), and by Griffin and Frongillo (2003) in upper New York State farmers' markets. Feagan et al. (2004) note that the age profile of their market respondents may be reflective of the proximity of the markets to areas that have a disproportionate number of older residents, and/or the greater availability of free time for this cohort or differences in this group's underlying attitudes. However, they also acknowledge, along with Griffin and Frongillo (2003), that the age of the primary cohort of consumers may affect the long-term prospects of some markets.

A telephone survey of the shopping behaviour of 1,000 Ontario households undertaken by the FGF in 2007 gives a valuable profile of the Ontario market. Although supermarkets dominate 17 per cent of those surveyed shop weekly at farmers' markets, with a further 57 per cent shopping there at least periodically. Two-thirds (65 per cent) of those who buy locally grown foods say they buy them supermarkets with a further 42 per cent buying them from farmers' markets. Women are more likely to purchase from farmers' markets than men (46 per cent of female respondents against 36 per cent of male) and are more likely to say it is very important to them that all of the food at farmers' markets are locally grown (60 per cent). In terms of level of education those with post-graduate qualifications are more likely to purchase from farmers' markets (FGF, 2007). The local food and experiential dimensions of farmers' markets are also significant:

- More than half (55 per cent) of respondents stated that it is very important to them that at farmers' markets, all of the food sold is locally grown. A further 31 per cent say it is somewhat important.
- Getting to meet and talk with the farmers is very important to 25 per cent, and somewhat important to 38 per cent.
- The opportunity to enjoy the social experience of chatting with neighbours while shopping at farmers' markets is very important to 23 per cent, and somewhat important to 34 per cent.
- 18 per cent of respondents felt that it was very important that the farmers' market was an interesting place with activities such as music and children's events and 31 per cent felt that it was somewhat important.
- Smaller proportions of respondents state that it is very important that there are prepared foods available and ready to eat (16 per cent) and that there is a variety of products, including fruits and vegetables not grown in Ontario (18 per cent). Those aged 18–29 years are less likely to say it is very important that all of the food is locally grown (48 per cent),

that they get a chance to meet and talk with the farmers (15 per cent), or that there are prepared foods available and ready to eat (12 per cent). Those aged fifty plus years give a higher level of importance to the produce being locally grown and the prospects of meeting the farmers (FGF, 2007).

The UK

Research by then UK National Association of Farmers' Markets suggested that the typical farmers' market customer falls into the AB (upper/middle class) or C1 (lower middle class) socio-economic group – working people with high disposable incomes, 'the kind who know a good cut of Dexter beef when they see one' (Purvis, 2002). Research by Archer et al. (2003) on latent consumers' attitudes to farmers' markets in North West England suggested that the majority of consumers were female (69 per cent), over 55 and retired. However, the age range was significantly lower in city centres (36–45). The majority travelled up to 10 miles and spent an average of £3 to £10. Consumers' perception of farmers' markets was that they 'sell fresh, quality, tasty, local produce, but that the food would not necessarily be cheaper. Consumers also enjoyed the atmosphere of the farmers' markets, supporting local producers and sampling food before purchasing' (Archer et al., 2003, p.488). An indication of the positive reaction to the farmers' markets was that 93 per cent of those who had been to a market stated that they would return again.

A national survey of 2,025 adult consumers in the UK undertaken in June 2004 on behalf of FARMA also indicated a positive attitude towards farmers' markets. Although supermarkets dominate food shopping, results indicated that 12 per cent of households shop from farmers' markets. If this was translated to the national population this would represent a figure of 2.5 million households. Overall, 71 per cent of respondents stated they would buy from farmers' markets if they could. More than half (54 per cent) also indicated that they were aware of farmers' markets in their area with women slightly more aware than men. Thirty per cent of households indicated that they had visited or bought from farmers' markets in the previous 12 months although by region this figure was lowest in Scotland where 26 per cent had visited or bought from a farmers' market. Coincidentally this was also the region with the lowest interest in farmers' markets (63 per cent). In comparison the South of England region had the highest level of interest at 76 per cent (FARMA, 2004).

Farmers' markets in New Zealand

Despite there being no tradition of farmers' markets in New Zealand (although there were markets of sorts in the early days of the colony, as is evident by the number of dormant 'market reserves' still present in many New Zealand towns and cities), the rapid recent growth and establishment of a farmers' markets association in New Zealand indicates the potential for farmers' markets in what is still primarily an agricultural economy. The first modern market was established at Whangarei in 1998 (Guthrie et al., 2006). As of late 2007 there were 36 farmers' markets listed by the Farmers' Market New Zealand Association (FMNZA), itself established in 2005, as either being open or about to open (Table 13.4).

The FMNZA has the following aims:

- To facilitate the formation of a network of authentic farmers' markets throughout New Zealand.
- To clearly define the concept of an authentic farmers' market and facilitate the development of this model in the cities and provinces of New Zealand.
- To support the viable and self-sufficient operation of existing and future farmers' markets by sharing information and providing appropriate resources.
- To protect brand 'farmers' market', clearly distinguishing the concept of a farmers' market from other markets, both retail and wholesale.
- To advocate on behalf of members at a national level. http://www.farmersmarket.org.nz/home.htm

An authentic farmers' market is defined by the FMNZA as a market that has at least 80 per cent local produce stalls. Local means from within the regional boundaries established by individual farmers' markets. Produce stalls can refer to farmer/grower stalls or ones that have a value-added product. Individual farmers' markets also decide whether other stalls that sell food or farm origin products, e.g. coffee and bread, should be allowed a place in the market.

The relative maturity of the farmers' market scene in New Zealand is also evident in growing cooperation between markets thanks to the networking opportunities provided by the NZFMA and around 100 people attended the first national conference for farmers' markets held in 2006. However, the growth of farmers' markets and the increasing appropriation of the concept by more traditional commercial models is not without its stress and has even become the focus of media debate.

Table 13.4 Farmers' markets in New Zealand

Area	Number	Members of NZFMA	Opening days and seasonality					
			Friday	Saturday	Sunday	Weekly	All year	
Northland	3	3	–	2	1	2	3	
Greater Auckland	7	6	–	4	3	6	6	
Waikato/Bay of Plenty	5	3	–	3	2	5	5	
East Coast	4	3	–	3	1	4	3	
Taranaki	1	1		–	1	1	1	
Lower North Island	4	2	2	2	–	4	4	
Marlborough/Nelson	2	1	–	–	1	2	1	
Canterbury	7	5	1	6	1	3	3	
Otago/Southland	3	2	–	1	2	2	2	
Total	36	26	3	21	12	29	28	

Source: http://www.farmersmarket.org.nz (accessed October 2007).

One of New Zealand's leading current affair television programmes, the Campbell Live show on TV3, ran a feature on the resurgence of farmers' markets around New Zealand in September 2007. In this feature they identified the resurgence as a response to consumers dislike of what goes into the production of their food. They pointed out that people are now more concerned about their health and nutrition and so they are looking to buy fresher produce that is grown locally. The reporter for this feature also focused on the controversy surrounding the opening of a new 'farmers' market' in Auckland named 'Farmers Market Plus' (see http://www.aucklandfarmersmarket.co.nz). The controversy was that other farmers' markets around the country (particularly Whangarei farmers' market) felt that the new Auckland market was not a farmers' market at all. The reporter defined a farmers' market as selling primary produce sold by the producer. Customers that were interviewed at the Whangarei farmers' market said that the sense of community and that fact that it was 'slow shopping' was what really defined a farmers' market. The NZFMA opposed the name of the Auckland market incorporating the term 'farmers' into it, because they felt the market was not a non-profit, community-based project but a commercially orientated business. The response of the organizers of the Auckland market was that they were simply extending the farmers' market model to work for urban Auckland (TV3, 2007).

Issues over the notion of what constitutes a farmers' market in New Zealand closer reflect the concerns expressed in Ontario noted above. According to Chris Fortune, a chef who began the Marlborough farmers' market, in an interview on the growth markets in New Zealand (Chalmers, 2006), the biggest plus is making sure that the farmers' market is brand-protected. The primary producer has to be the stallholder selling the product to ensure there are no middlemen or on-selling of goods. 'So when the public buy the product they are talking directly to the grower' (Chalmers, 2006). In addition, it also has to be produce from the local region and the produce has to be edible, with a few exceptions such as flowers, so there are no arts and crafts-type products.

The sustainable community focus of many New Zealand markets is well illustrated by Fortune.

'It is the first building block of sustainability within a community. It can be used by backyard growers, someone who enjoys growing vegetables, or has an excess of potatoes they can take to the market and sell. It also suits bigger, more commercially orientated growers'. The philosophy of farmers' markets is supporting local producers and selling direct to the public with no middleman. It also eliminates food miles – how far food travels to get to the table. 'It's about talking to the producer and finding out whether it's spray-free or organic, how it's been grown and how best to cook it' (in Chalmers, 2006).

Exhibit 13.2   Comparing the Canterbury and Lyttelton farmers' markets in Christchurch, New Zealand

---

These two farmers' markets are located within roughly 20 minutes drive of each other in Christchurch, New Zealand. The Lyttelton farmers' market is situated in the primary school grounds of the port town of Lyttelton whereas the Canterbury farmers' market is situated in the suburban location of the gardens of the historic Riccarton House in Christchurch. The servicescapes of the two markets are also noticeably different with respect to music with customers at the Canterbury farmers' market usually being accompanied by a jazz band while the Lyttelton markets has a changing selection of what would often be described as folk music every week. Although these different settings do give quite a different ambience to the markets, there are a number of similarities between the two farmers' markets.

Analysis of the two markets was conducted in September 2007. At the time of analysis there were 24 stalls at the Canterbury farmers' market and 30 at Lyttelton, which is the longest established farmers' market in the Christchurch region. The markets have relatively similar offerings of produce with the most common stall type being vegetable and/or fruit stalls, both had six such stalls at the time of survey although this number does fluctuate depending on the growing season. Figure 13.2 shows the range of stall categories for each of the respective markets.

One interesting issue is the way that the two markets handle the presence of stalls selling non-food-related items. At the Canterbury farmers' market there was a lavender stall selling lavender-based beauty products that was clearly part of the market. However, in Lyttelton an area in which people sell non-food items is kept purposefully separate from the farmers' market. The non-food items area is beside the farmers' market but is clearly distinguished. Such a separation reinforces the NZFMA definition of a farmers' market (see Table 13.1) which clearly indicates that is a food market. However, if we are to look at what Brown (2001) identifies a farmers' market to be, then the lavender stall would be included as she states that what is sold must just simply be produced by the seller and does not define that it should be an edible product. Such issues of course are not merely definitional but may affect the positioning of a farmers' market and how it is perceived by consumers and differentiated from other types of markets.

(Continued)

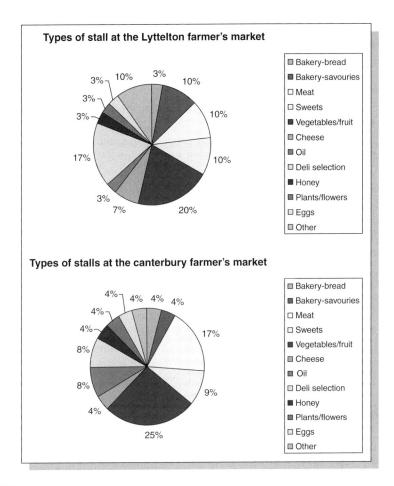

Figure 13.2
Types of stall at the Lyttelton and Canterbury farmers' market

Other observations on the marketing techniques of the two farmers' markets include that 27 per cent of the stalls at the Lyttelton market and 48 per cent of the Canterbury market did not have an obvious name for their stall. This is quite high, especially for the Canterbury market. Having a banner or sign that clearly states the stall's name is one of the simplest but yet most effective promotional practices and it is surprising that such a simple thing could be disregarded by so many stalls even when they are listed by name on the market's web site. One of the problems with some of the stalls was that although their products had a specific name, they did not have a banner above the stall identifying who they were. So unless you are up close to the stall, it is sometimes hard to determine who they were and what they

(Continued)

were selling particularly when visiting at a time when the market is relatively crowded.

The number of stalls that used pictures to promote their products ranged from 13 per cent at the Canterbury market to 30 per cent at Lyttelton. However, some vendors at each of the markets did use pictures to support the products being sold and provide information to the consumer. For example, the RaDiSo a sauce and dressings stall and the Canterbury Biltong stall at the Lyttelton market had laminated pictures of their products available for their customers to see. At the Canterbury farmers' market the two Ansley farm stalls which sold fresh eggs and meat both had pictures of the farm and animals. Having clear pictures and well-made signs can help in conveying product reliability and quality, particularly when in the majority of places it is clearly impractical for consumers to visit the farms that where production occurs.

A marketing technique the vendors at each market were doing slightly better was offering samples of their products for potential customers to try; 25 per cent of the stalls at the Canterbury market were offering samples and 30 per cent at the Lyttelton market. Many of the Lyttelton stallholders had recipes available for their product and, in some cases, pictures of the finished product whereas none of the Canterbury stalls did.

More Lyttelton vendors also displayed supporting advertising than did those at the Canterbury farmers' market. Only two vendors at the Canterbury market displayed supporting advertising. This included a web address on the banner of a French foods stall, and a written description of the making of the artisan breads which were sold by the Nikau Bakery. At the Lyttelton farmers' market, eight stall holders offered supporting advertising for the business. This ranged from newspaper articles published on the product being sold, promotional posters and brochures. For example, the Lovat deer farm stall at the Lyttelton market sold venison products but also had brochures of their bed and breakfast accommodation; thereby showing the potential of a presence at a farmers' market to extend the reach of their brand and products through cross-promotion. Interestingly, there was also a greater overt promotion of organic and spray-free products at the Lyttelton market even though discussions with stallholders at both markets suggest that there is likely little actual difference between the overall range of production methods used by producers selling at the two markets. However, this may also reflect the stages in organic certification that producers have reached rather than any differences in market strategy. Nevertheless, what the study of the two markets indicates is that there are clear differences in the market orientation of farmers' markets even though they may be selling similar produce in the same region and, as in the case of these two markets, even have some of the same producers selling at them.

Fiona Crawford and C. Michael Hall

The social construction of the 'modern' farmers' market

According to Hamilton (2002, p. 73):

> By definition, the modern American farmers market is not much different from its ancestor: a place where farmers sell the food they've grown and consumers buy it. Today, though, markets exist for more than just commerce. That they ride the social fence with my grandmother – somewhere between pure, raw agriculture and something earnest, *intentional* – seems contrary to their nature.
>
> (emphasis in original)

This suggests that the modern manifestation of the farmers' market serves some other purpose than simply the sale and purchase of goods. It is apparent that they have a social function that is meeting a need beyond sustenance. Indeed, Holloway and Kneafsey (2000, p. 292) suggest that the UK farmers' market can be considered as a '... liminal space in the sense that it subverts the conventional space of food shopping (i.e. the supermarket) but also reinforces free market entrepreneurialism and celebrates particular reactionary values'. They continue that there are '... sets of meanings revolving around contested and emotive terms such as 'quality', 'community', 'natural' and 'identity'' (Holloway and Kneafsey, 2000, p. 293). Meanwhile, McGrath et al. (1993, p. 283) argue that 'farmers' markets belong to a class of marketplaces experienced by consumers in a very particular way. The structure of such markets unfolds along the dimension of a formal–informal dialectic, and the function along that of an economic-festive dialect'. In a report published by the UK Institute of Grocery Distribution (IGD), Groves (2005) further extends the concept of a socially constructed meaning for fresh foods by suggesting that the purchase drivers for local and regional food products at various outlets not only include the 'freshness' of the food, but issues of 'sustainability', 'product trial', 'territory and identity', 'attention to detail' (or the care and effort taken in the growing and or preparation of the food) and 'everyday indulgence'.

The notion of territory and identity associated with the consumption of local foods is also explored by several authors (e.g. Bessière, 1998; Holloway and Kneafsey, 2000; Hall and Mitchell, 2001) both from the perspective of farmers' markets and tourism. Holloway and Kneafsey (2000), for example, suggest that UK farmers' markets can be conceived as both an 'alternative' space and a 'reactionary/nostalgic space'. As an 'alternative' space the farmers' market is used '... as a space in which producers and consumers can circumvent the consumption spaces constructed by powerful actors in the food chain [namely, supermarkets] – an ephemeral space 'in between' the dominant production–consumption networks' (Holloway and Kneafsey, 2000, p. 293). Meanwhile the 'reactionary/nostalgic' space of the farmers' market

... can simultaneously, and perhaps more convincingly, be read as a re-entrenchment of nostalgic and soci-politically conservative notions of place and identity. Their re-emergence during a period of 'millenial reflection' could be read as an element of nostalgia for a 'golden age' when food was supposedly more nutritious and life in general more wholesome (Holloway and Kneafsey, 2000, p. 294).

Holloway and Kneafsey (2000) use evidence from the Stratford farmers' market in the UK to demonstrate how this 'reactionary/nostalgic' space is expressed. This includes the use of local place names and descriptors such as 'fresh' or 'natural' which imply something that has not travelled far and is derived directly from the countryside. Elements of festival or country fair (e.g. flags) are also present and there are several expressions of heritage, including a logo that is reminiscent of an antique wood cut and the 'costumes' of vendors which have a strong nostalgic presence.

Such representations of local identity are also likely to be attractive to tourists. (Holloway and Kneafsey, 2000; Hall et al., 2003). Bessière (1998, p. 25) suggests that '... eating farm fresh products, for example, may represent for the urban tourist not only a biological quality, but also a short-lived appropriation of a rural identity. He (sic.) symbolically integrates a forgotten culture.' She further suggests that such symbolism surrounding food can take several forms: 'food as a symbol' (e.g. red wine as the blood of Christ); 'food as a sign of communion' (i.e. food to be shared); 'food as a class marker' (e.g. champagne or caviar) and 'food as an emblem' (i.e. a food that is representative of a place or a people such as Roquefort cheese). Of tourists Bessière (1998, p. 24) suggests: 'Today's city dweller escapes in a real or imagined manner from his (sic.) daily routine and ordinary fare to find solace in regional and so called 'traditional' food.'

Holloway and Kneafsey's (2000) analysis of the Stratford farmers' market provides an important framework for the understanding of the nature of the farmers' market space, while the work of others like Bessière (1998) have discussed the development of a strong desire for that which fresh (direct-to-consumer) food represents for the everyday consumer and tourist. Both studies suggest that the yearning for the nostalgic is important and that food can be the material focal point for the emergence of re-enactments of this enigmatic bygone era by the consumer and the producer. These re-enactments can be conscious and material (e.g. the use of costumes or the production and sale of 'heritage' or 'heirloom' breeds or varieties) or spontaneous, unconscious and experiential (e.g. the development of relationships between the consumer and producer), but either way they result in a space that is constructed from attempts '… to fix identity or build a sense of community' (Holloway and Kneafsey, 2000, p. 295) and therefore have an inherent sense of the authentic which is highly desirable for tourists.

Somewhere between artificiality and authenticity

The search for authentic experience is a core component of the postmodern condition and this is especially significant in discussions of tourism and food (McGrath et al., 1993). Hall and Mitchell (2008) suggest that, when it comes to the authenticity of wine, the consumer not only wants to be assured of the authenticity of the production process, but also of the symbolic value of the wine. In many circumstances, especially those that are festive in nature or which involve travel, this may also hold true for food (Bessière, 1998; Holloway and Kneafsey, 2000; Hall et al., 2003). Farmers' markets, by their very nature, also have a sense of authenticity which, as we have seen above, farmers' market organizations seek to protect. Authenticity is one of four themes identified by McGrath et al. (1993) that reflect the nature of the experience of one US farmers' market. These themes are:

1. *Activism*: This is the grassroots response to the dominant distribution channels of industrialized agricultural systems that is also discussed by others (e.g. Holloway and Kneafsey, 2000; Feagan et al., 2004; Groves, 2005).
2. *Authenticity*: This notion is similar to Holloway and Kneafsey's (2001)'reactionary/nostalgic space' and '… is a collective attempt to recapture or recreate an authentic, unmediated experience of a simpler, more wholesome era … [that] … is staged, or more properly, mythopoeic' (McGrath et al., 1993, p. 309). In this place …

Sellers enable buyers to enact a small scene in a larger agrarian myth. In foraging across the stalls for produce so fresh the dirt in which it was grown still clings to it in validation of its authenticity, in pursuing the small talk with the bearers of an idyllic culture which both enlightens and ennobles, and in enduring the physical rigors that an open air market demands, consumers invest the … experience with the kinds of symbolic and use values unattainable in more obviously contrived theme park-like retail settings' (p. 310).

3. *Artificiality*: McGrath et al. (1993, p. 310) contrast this with authenticity, suggesting that the experience of the farmers' market is, ironically, '... an almost unattainable idealism' where consumers attempt to '... buy a lifestyle from which they block the darker side'. This utopian idealism denies the fact that this is a vertically integrated retail environment like any other (e.g. *Crate and Barrel* and *Banana Republic*) and as such they are 'retail theme parks' that '... feign authenticity while surrounding the consumer with a myriad of items which are both props essential to the set and items available for purchase' (p. 311). They construct an outdoor rural environment in an urban setting (while other such theme park retail construct 'prototypes of home') that are '... larger than life, but more importantly, [they] must be nicer than life' (p. 311). Even the possessive nature of the term 'farmers' market' is seen by McGrath et al. (1993) as evidence of this artificiality as the farmers infrequently own the market, rather they belong to the city. Indeed, the structure of many farmers' markets are such that it is possible that some potential stallholders may be excluded by existing members because they may replicate the products offered by existing stalls or not 'fit' into the image or collectivity that existing members may be seeking to promote.

4. *Ambience*: McGrath et al. (1993, p. 312) liken the market ambience to 'retail theatre' that '... engages every sensory modality, sometimes to the point of synaesthetic over-stimulation'. They also posit that the 'disinhibiting ambience' of the open air market means consumers get 'carried away', swept up in the pleasure of it all. Such a place, they suggest, is a 'third place' where 'informal public life' takes place in a realm beyond home and work.

Conclusions

There are some interesting paradoxes in the themes identified above, not least of which is the apparent juxtaposition of the (staged) authenticity and artificiality of the farmers' market. Such staged authenticity (MacCannell, 1976) is often referred to in tourism terms as the ugly step-sister of true authenticity (whatever that might mean). While on the face of it this seems to be problematic, Hall (2007) suggests that authenticity need not relate to something that is in its pure original form and that 'replications' may, over time, become authentic. In this way, while the farmers' market may be perceived to have an element of the staged and artificiality, it may attain an element of the authentic over time as it allows for what Hall calls 'connectedness' – a condition that many farmers' markets seek to promote through their emphasis on being grounded in communities.

The notion of authenticity should not be used with respect to things or places. Authenticity is instead derived from the property of connectedness of the individual to the perceived, everyday world and environment, and the processes that created it and the consequences of one's engagement with it (Dovey, 1985). ... Authenticity is born from everyday experiences and connections which are often serendipitous not from things 'out there'. ... Connectedness that leads to authenticity can be provided anywhere as authenticity is not intrinsically dependent on location although place, in the sense of everyday lived experiences and relations, does matter (Hall, 2007, p.1140).

Such feelings of connectedness – as well as elements of activism, ambience and authenticity are often used in the promotion of farmers' markets. For example, Ian Thomas, Chairman of Farmers' Markets New Zealand in the *Guide to Farmers' Markets in New Zealand and Australia* (FMNZ 2007), states with reference to farmers' markets:

It's a special time when the pride and passion of farmers and artisans shines through. When lovingly grown fresh fruit and vegetables are eagerly snapped up. A time and place that is a firm and regular appointment for growing numbers of folk who relish the intimacy, the friendship and the excitement of discovery ... shoppers ... come back for either better tasting nutrition, the most enjoyable shopping environment, riper flavours, the ability to 'buy local' or as an antidote to the dominating 'more is more' philosophy ... A visit to a farmers' market will be a memorable and delicious experience. You'll engage in chat and often laughter. You'll learn about how and where the food was grown or produced, how to cook it, how and where to keep it, how long it will keep and usually some good recipes to boot. Most markets have hot coffee and a good selection of local delicacies to go with it, as well as freshly squeezed juice and live music. All in all, a wonderful place to shop and get involved in a local community (FMNZ, 2007, p.13).

Undoubtedly the farmers' market can be engaging and can connect with the consumer in very personal ways (Tiemann, 2004a,b). The experience is one that is often dialogic, where the actors are in constant communication with each other, rather than monologic as is the case with other forms of retail experience. So, irrespective of whether they are staged, mythopoeic or artificial, farmers' markets, as a manifestation of everyday lived experiences, are a site of authentic performance. Unlike the local consumer, who might be experiencing a mythical (romantic) place, the tourist outsider who visits the farmers' market is in fact, perhaps even paradoxically, experiencing it as an everyday (mundane) performance of local food culture, which, by virtue of its (local) cultural embeddedness, becomes the exotic, the other and therefore attractive to the tourist. For the tourist a farmers' market's artificiality is a component of its authenticity, it is a representation of the culture within which they are operated. It is this which the tourist can most readily and 'authentically' connect with. As Sassatelli and Scott (2001, p. 214) suggest 'it is not the exceptional event (be it war or ritual) alone which imbues us with our subjective sense of belonging, but the 'banal' practices of everyday life; what we habitually do and in whom and what we habitually trust'.

As such tourism potentially (re)constructs the farmers' market as an exotic (re)presentation of culture through the use of material objects (food) and an ephemeral (public) space. The space and the food brings the local culture into being, it constructs the local culture for consumption. This is not to deny that the mythopoeic element or the 'theatre' of the market, as the performance of these is as much an attraction as the market itself. Indeed McGrath et al. (1993, p. 307) suggest of their own case study

The Midville Market emerges as a periodic community with its own ecology, boundaries, periphery, development, members, social relationships and relationships with other communities. Participants derive pleasure from the relational aspects of this retailing institution. The personal interactions with vendors and consumers develop a loyal clientele that generates sales and sustains the institution. Here 'human institution' has successfully shed any oxymoronic notion and has developed to attract a growing and loyal clientele. It is relationship and perceived quality, not price, that guides their interactions and choices. Vendors guide and control this motivating force, in which consumers serve as willing partners.

This description could easily apply to many modern markets. Indeed a simple substitution of, for example, 'Otago farmers' Market' for 'Midville Market' (see Mitchell and Scott, Chapter 17), as well as other markets discussed in the following chapters would be possible and all would hold true. This is not to deny the merits or attractiveness of the farmers' market experience which is provided and promoted to local and visitor alike, but it is to recognize that authenticity is not something that can be easily regulated and that it is a product of social construction much more than it is a certification.

References

Abel, J., Thomson, J. and Maretzki, A. (1999). Extension's role with farmers' markets: Working with farmers, consumers, and communities. *Journal of Extension*, 37(5). http://joe.org/joe/1999october/a4.html

Archer, G.P., Sánchez, J.C., Vignali, G. and Chaillot, A. (2003). Latent consumers' attitude to farmers' markets in North West England. *British Food Journal*, 105(8), 487–497.

Balsam, A., Webber, D. and Oehlke, B. (1994). The farmers' market coupon program for low-income elders. *Journal of Nutrition for the Elderly*, 13(4), 35–41.

Beck, U. (1992). *Risk Society: Towards a New Modernity*. Sage Publications, London.

Bessière, J. (1998). Local development and heritage: Traditional food and cuisine as tourist attractions in rural areas. *Sociologica Ruralis*, 38(1), 21–34.

Blakemore, D. (2007). Personal conversation with Doreen Blakemore, Markets Team, Newcastle upon Tyne City Council.

British History Online (2007) at http://www.british-history.ac.uk. Visited October 2007.

Britnell, R.H. (1978). English Markets and Royal Administration Before 1200. *Economic History Review*, 31(2), 183–196.

Brown, A. (2001). Counting farmers markets. *Geographical Review*, 91(4), 655–674.

Brown, A. (2002). Farmers' market research 1940–2000: An inventory and review. *American Journal of Alternative Agriculture*, 17(4), 167–176.

California Farmers' Markets Association (2006). *California Farmers' Markets Association Rules and Regulations for Certified Farmers' Markets*. California Farmers' Markets Association, Walnut Creek.

California Federation of Certified Farmers' Markets (2003). What is a certified farmers' market? http://www.cafarmers-markets.com/about/

Chalmers, H. (2006). Farmers' markets are taking off. *Rural News*, August 6, http://www.ruralnews.co.nz/Default.asp?task=article&subtask=show&item=9575&pageno=1

Connell, C.M., Beierlein, J.G. and Vroomen, H.L. (1986). *Consumer Preferences and Attitudes Regarding Fruit and Vegetable Purchases from Direct Market Outlets*. Report 185. The Pennsylvania State University, Department of Agricultural Economics and Rural Sociology, Agricultural Experiment Station, University Park.

Conrey, E.J., Frongillo, E.A., Dollahite, J.S. and Griffin, M.R. (2003). Integrated program enhancements increased utilization of farmers' market nutrition program. *The Journal of Nutrition*, 133(6), 1841–1844.

Coster, M. and Kennon, N. (2005). *'New Generation' Farmers' Markets in Rural Communities*. Rural Industries Research and Development Corporation, Barton.

Dovey, K. (1985). The quest for authenticity and the replication of environmental meaning. In Seamon, D., and Mugerauer, R. (eds.) *Dwelling, Place and Environment: Towards a Phenomenology of Person and Word*. Martinus Nijhoff Publishers, Dordrecht, pp. 33–50.

Dyer, A. (1991). *Decline and Growth in English Towns, 1400–1640*. Cambridge University Press, Cambridge.

Eastwood, D.B., Brooker, J.R. and Gray, M.D. (1995). *An Intrastate Comparison of Consumers' Patronage of Farmers' Markets in Knox, Madison and Shelby Counties*. Research Report 95-03. The University of Tennessee, Department of Agricultural Economics and Rural Sociology, Institute of Agriculture, Agricultural Experiment Station, Knoxville.

Farmers' Markets Ontario (FMO) (2007a). Membership information, http://www.farmersmarketsontario.com/MembershipInfo.cfm

Farmers' Markets Ontario (FMO) (2007b). *'Real Farmers, Real Local' Certified Farmers' Market Rules and Regulations*. Farmers' Markets Ontario, Brighton.

Farmers' Markets New Zealand (2007). *Guide to Farmers' Markets in New Zealand and Australia*. R.M. Williams Classic Publications, Mosman.

Feagan, R., Morris, D. and Krug, K. (2004). Niagara Region Farmers' Markets: Local food systems and sustainability considerations. *Local Environment*, 9(3), 235–254.

Friends of the Greenbelt Foundation (FGF) (2006). *Canada's First Certified Farmers' Market: Greenbelt Farmers and Toronto Residents to Benefit from the First Certified Farmers' Market in Canada*. Friends of the Greenbelt Foundation and Farmers' Markets Ontario, Toronto. Press Release, November 22.

Friends of the Greenbelt Foundation (2007). *Greenbelt Foundation 2007 Awareness Research. Summary prepared by Environics Research Group*. Friends of the Greenbelt Foundation, Toronto. July.

Ghent Urban Studies Team (1999). *The Urban Condition: Space, Community, and Self in the Contemporary Metropolis*. Uitgeverij 010 Publishers: Rotterdam, The Netherlands.

Govindasamy, R., Italia, J. and Adelaja, A. (2002). Farmers' markets: Consumer trends, preferences and characteristics. *Journal of Extension*, 40(1). http://joe.org/joe/2002february/rb6.html

Griffin, M.R. and Frongillo, E.A. (2003). Experiences and perspectives of farmers from upstate New York farmers' markets. *Agriculture and Human Values*, 20, 189–203.

Groves, A. (2005). *The Local and Regional Food Opportunity*. Institute of Grocery Distribution, Watford.

Guthrie, J., Guthrie, A., Lawson, R. and Cameron, A. (2006). Farmers' markets: The small business counter-revolution in food production and retailing. *British Food Journal*, 108(7), 560–573.

Hall, C.M. (2007). Response to Yeoman et al.: The fakery of 'The authentic tourist'. *Tourism Management*, 28(4), 1139–1140.

Hall, C.M. and Mitchell, R.D. (2001). We are what we eat: Tourism, culture and the globalisation and localisation of cuisine. *Tourism Culture and Communication*, 2(1), 29–37.

Hall, C.M. and Mitchell, R.D. (2008). *Wine Marketing: A Practical Approach*. Butterworth-Heinemann, Oxford.

Hall, C.M., Mitchell, R. and Sharples, E. (2003). Consuming places: The role of food, wine and tourism in regional development. In Hall, C.M., Sharples, E., Mitchell, R., Cambourne, B. and Macionis, N. (eds.) *Food Tourism Around the World: Development, Management and Markets*. Butterworth-Heinemann, Oxford, pp. 25–59.

Hamilton, L.M. (2002). The American Farmers Market. *Gastronomica*, 2(3), 73–77.

Holloway, L. and Kneafsey, M. (2000). Reading the space of the farmers' market: A preliminary investigation from the UK. *Sociologia Ruralis*, 40(3), 285–299.

Hughes, M.E. and Mattson, R.H. (1995). *Farmers markets in Kansas: A profile of vendors and market organization*. Kansas State University, Agricultural Experiment Station, Manhattan, NY. Report of Progress 658

Jolly, D.A. (1999). 'Home made' – The paradigms and paradoxes of changing consumer preferences: Implications for direct marketing, paper presented at *Agricultural Outlook Forum 1999*, Monday, February 22, 1999, http://www.usda.gov/agency/oce/waob/outlook99/speeches/025/JOLLY.TXT

Kezis, A., Gwebu, T., Peavey, S. and Cheng, H. (1998). A study of consumers at a small farmers' market in Maine: Results from a 1995 survey. *Journal of Food Distribution Research*, February, 91–98.

Kneafsey, M., Ilbery, B. and Ricketts Hein, J. (2001). *Local Food Activity in the West Midlands*. Rural Restructuring Research Group, Geography Department, Coventry University, Coventry.

Leones, J. (1995). Farm outlet customer profiles. *Direct Farm Marketing and Tourism Handbook*. The University of

Arizona College of Agriculture, Cooperative Extension, Tucson, AZ.

Leones, J., Dunn, D., Worden, M. and Call, R. (1995). A profile of visitors to fresh farm produce outlets in Cochise County, AZ. *Direct Farm Marketing and Tourism Handbook*. The University of Arizona College of Agriculture, Cooperative Extension, Tucson, AZ.

MacCannell, D. (1976). *The tourist: A new theory of the leisure class*. Schocken, New York.

McEachern, M.G. and Willock, J. (2004). Producers and consumers of organic meat: A focus on attitudes and motivations. *British Food Journal*, 106(7), 534–562.

McGrath, M.A., Sherry Jr., J.F. and Heisley, D.D. (1993). An Ethnographic Study of an Urban Periodic Marketplace: Lessons from the Midville Farmers' Market. *Journal of Retailing*, 69(3), 280–319.

Melsen, L. (2004). *Identifying the potential tourism benefits of farmers' market visitation: An analysis of the Gippsland farmers' market visitor*. Unpublished Honours Sissertation, La Trobe University, Melbourne.

MyMarket (2007). Grand opening in 2 new locations, http://www.my-market.ca/

National Farmers' Retail and Markets Association (FARMA) (2004). *FARMA Consumer Survey June 2004: Nine Out of Ten Households Would Buy from a Farmshopping Outlet if They Could*. National Farmers' Retail and Markets Association, Southampton.

National Farmers' Retail and Markets Association (FARMA) (2006). *Sector Briefing: Farmers Markets in the UK; Nine Years and Counting*. National Farmers' Retail and Markets Association, Southampton. (also downloadable from http://www.farma.org.uk/Docs/1%20Sector%20briefing%20on%20farmers'%20markets%20-%20June%202006.pdf).

Newcastle upon Tyne City Council (2007) at http://www.Newcastle.gov.uk visited October.

New Zealand Farmers' Market Association (2007). Fresh market locations, http://www.farmersmarket.org.nz/locations.htm

Novak, T. (1998). A fresh Place. *Oregon's Agricultural Progress*, Fall/Winter (http://eesc.orst.edu/agcomwebfile/Magazine/98Fall/OAP98%20text/OAPFall9802.html#anchor1926968).

Padel, S. and Foster, C. (2005). Exploring the gap between attitudes and behaviour: Understanding why consumers buy or do not buy organic food. *British Food Journal*, 107(8), 606–625.

Payne, T. (2002). *US Farmers Markets – 2000: A Study of Emerging Trends*. Agricultural Marketing Service, United States Department of Agriculture, Washington, DC.

Purvis, A. (2002). So what's your beef. *The Observer*, 14 April. (http://www.observer.co.uk/foodmonthly/story/0,9950,681828,00.html)

Pyle, J. (1971). Farmers' markets in United States: Functional anachronisms. *Geographical Review*, 61(2), 167–197.

Regional Food Australia (2007). Australian farmers' markets Listings, http://www.farmersmarkets.com.au/

Rhodus, T., Schwartz, J. and Haskins, J. (1994). *Ohio Consumers Opinions of Roadside and Farmers' Markets*. Ohio State University, Department of Horticulture, OH.

Sassatelli, R. and Scott, A. (2001). Novel food, new markets and trust regimes: Responses to the erosion of consumers' confidence in Austria, Italy and the UK. *European Societies*, 3(2), 213–244.

Suarez-Balcazar, Y., Martinez, L.I., Cox, G. and Jayraj, A. (2006). African Americans' views on access to healthy foods: What a farmers' market provides. *Journal of Extension*, 44(2). Article Number 2FEA2, http://www.joe.org/joe/2006april/a2p.shtml

Tiemann, T.K. (2004a). American farmers' markets: Two types of informality. *International Journal of Sociology and Social Policy*, 24(6), 44–57.

Tiemann, T.K. (2004b). *'Experience' Farmers' Markets: Conduct Determines Performance*. Eastern Economic Association Meeting, Washington, DC.

TV3 (2007) Campbell Live, aired 7 pm, September 9.

United States Department of Agriculture (2002). *Improving and Facilitating a Farmers Market in a Low-Income Urban Neighborhood: A Washington, DC, Case Study*. Agricultural Marketing Service Transportation and Marketing Programs, Wholesale and Alternative Markets, United States Department of Agriculture, Washington, DC.

United States Department of Agriculture (2006). Farmers' market growth. http://www.ams.usda.gov/farmersmarkets/FarmersMarketGrowth.htm

Connecting farmers' markets and tourists in New Brunswick, Canada

Lee Jolliffe

Introduction

The farmers' market links the farmer producer with the consumer. The markets, most usually held weekly during the growing season, have the attraction of special events, focusing on seasonal produce and cuisine, and often featuring local entertainment. There is evidence that heritage tourists in Canada are interested in visiting and experiencing these markets (Canadian Tourism Commission (CTC), 2003). As tourism in rural areas grows it has been seen as an agent for rural regeneration and economic development (Lane, 2005). It is thought that rural tourism generates secondary income for agricultural and other rural households (Opperman, 1996). The farmers' market plays a role in this phenomenon, it provides a tourism product that links locals with visitors and has potential for positive economic impact in rural communities.

This chapter examines how farmers' markets and tourists are linked in the province of New Brunswick, Canada. This rural agricultural province features the community farmers' markets on the provincial tourism web site (Tourism New Brunswick, 2007). A number of regional tourism plans have recognized the potential of farmers' markets in relation to tourism. Some have suggested, for example in the case of the Upper Saint John River Valley Tourism Development Plan (Tourism Synergy, 2004), that the markets have potential to be linked to other food experiences or culinary trails or routes. Others have noted that the farmers' markets have a role as potential demand drivers for regional tourism and that they can be linked to tourism (Jolliffe, 2006). Using the province of New Brunswick, Canada as a case study location this chapter poses several questions about the relation of the markets to tourism and examines these through case studies of markets and in reference to the tourism marketing information on markets:

- Can the farmers' markets be developed and promoted through tourism?
- How can the farmers' markets be promoted as local festivals and events?
- Is it possible for the markets as a whole to be promoted as a tourism attraction for the province?

Field research uses various methods to obtain information and in this case the researcher was a participant observer at several of the markets profiled. The context for analysing farmers' markets and tourism here thus combines an outsider view (tourism and recreation) and an insider view (farmers and other locals in agricultural regions) as discussed by Daugstad, Ronningen and Skar (2006). A case study method was used to profile both a group of markets and an individual market that have potential for developing tourism. Secondary information was garnered from other relevant reports, such as local and regional tourism development plans.

The attraction of farmers' markets in Canada

'Buying direct from farmers can be seen as a wonderfully sta- bilizing ritual in this fast-changing world' (Hunt and Hunt, 1992, p. 4). The quote from Michigan demonstrates that North American visitors are attracted to farmers' markets where they are able to buy fresh produce and to interact with the farmer producers and other vendors. At farmers' markets in Canada the atmosphere of the markets is also appealing to visitors looking for authentic food experiences. The markets reflect local lives and livelihoods and many offer a festive environ- ment in which tourists may experience authentic local culture.

In Canada the popularity of these markets is growing, as reported by the Canadian Tourist Commission (2003). The activities that heritage tourists are interested in. Farmers' mar- kets can add to the appeal of a tourism destination, as noted by Timothy (2004) in the case of St. Jacobs, Ontario. This is a classic case of the influence of farm markets and traditions in creating a tourism destination. Here a number of farmers' markets operate weekly on a year round basis. The Canadian Broadcasting Corporation has reported (2006) that according to Farmers' Markets Canada, a newly formed national organ- ization, there are roughly 500 markets across the country. As part of this growing trend in Canada it furthermore reported that 'The demand for food, fresh from the farm, is growing in the Maritimes. There are almost 40 farmers' markets in Nova Scotia, PEI (Prince Edward Island) and New Brunswick ... and that number is expanding. New Brunswick and Nova Scotia are even having trouble keeping up with the demand and both PEI and New Brunswick have waiting lists for vendors want- ing to sell' (CBC, 2006). This chapter focuses on this growing farmers' market trend in New Brunswick.

Farmers' markets take place within a rural context contribut- ing to rural tourism, or they bring the rural to the urban setting. When held in urban settings it is typical for the produce to come from the rural areas that surround urban locales. Some research- ers have noted that the farmers' markets are more beneficial to farmers located in proximity to urban farmers' markets. In the case of the country farmers' markets these markets can be seen as part of the countryside capital (Garrod et al., 2006) that can contribute to the emergence of rural tourism. This 'capital' is viewed as including not only the landscape and historical features but also distinctive local customs, languages, foods, crafts, festivals, traditions and ways of life. Garrod et al. argue that investment in countryside capital should include food and tourism.

Part of the appeal of Canadian farmers' markets is their connection with local agriculture. Several authors connect agriculture and food with cultural heritage. Daugstad et al. (2006) argue that cultural heritage is closely connected to agricultural practice and management. In addition, a number of authors portray farmers' markets as being part of the developing food tourism niche area (Boniface, 2003). The encounter between the farmer producer and the tourist consumer is portrayed as the hallmark of the relationship between the farmers' market and tourism. The market experience can contribute substantially to

Table 14.1 Typology of farm markets

Types	Benefits for farmers	Benefits for tourists
Pick your own or u-pick	Located on site, can promote branding of their product, incorporates activity for visitors, value added product	Authenticity and experience of visiting the farm
Farm gate stands	Located on site at the farm, connects the visitor with the farm, encourages branding of the farm product	Purchasing directly from the farmer operators, experience of visiting the stand
Roadside stands	Located not far from the farm, allows farmers to connect with customers	More removed from the farm and the authentic experience depending on location
Farmers' markets	Community operated through cooperatives; additional outlet for goods; interaction with consumers, visitors, tourists	Festival atmosphere, direct contact with farmer producers and other locals

Adapted in part from Gale, 1997.

what Williams (1998) refers to as the experience at the destination. Direct contact with the farmer producer can therefore be seen as an experience imbued with the local authenticity that many tourists seek.

There are a number of types of markets where farmers can market their produce directly to consumers (Table 14.1). LaTrobe (2001, p. 182) states 'Farmers' markets are characterized by the selling of foods and other items directly to the customer by the person who grew, reared or produced the goods'. Farmers' markets of all types are recognized as the oldest and most common type of direct marketing by farmers. This direct selling from farmer to consumer is seen as a rural development tool (Gale, 1997). Farmers' markets include direct farm markets and community markets where farmers and others can bring their local produce and goods to be sold. In some cases the nature of 'local', the distance from which the local produce can come is defined and in Canada the local source of food is one of the criteria laid out by the National Association of Farmers' Markets (CBC, 2006), the organization which governs the processes behind the markets. This chapter has a focus on these latter community farmers' markets. Scheduled on a regular basis and having some local festival and event like qualities, these are the markets that appeal to both tourists and tourism marketing agencies.

Agriculture, farmers' markets and tourism in New Brunswick, Canada

The rural agricultural province of New Brunswick (Figure 14.1), almost bounded on three sides by the Atlantic Ocean and on the northwest by the US border with Maine, has been referred to geographically as a country by itself (Maxwell, 1951). With many rivers, lakes and islands it has rich agriculture lands as well as fishery resources that can contribute to the food tourism experience. The rich lands of the Saint John River Valley and its tributaries form one of the main agricultural areas of the Maritime region (that also includes Prince Edward Island and Nova Scotia). The Saint John River Valley contains the best farmland in the province (Bone, 2002). With a population of around 730,000 (Government of Canada, 2001), many locations in the province are associated with agriculture or fishery and their products are known beyond New Brunswick. For example, Hartland is home base for McCain's Foods, a multinational food corporation known initially for processing potatoes. The province exhibits rich culinary traditions of the aboriginal

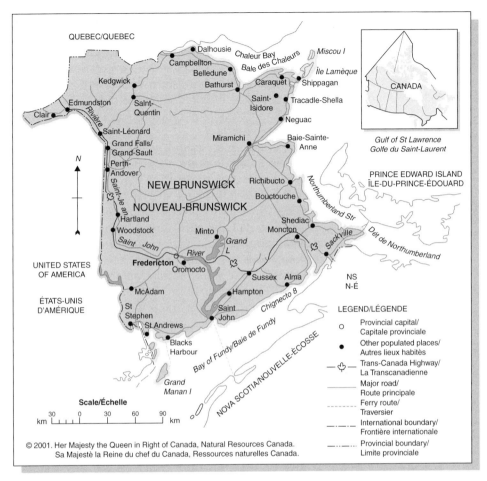

Figure 14.1
New Brunswick, Canada

people and those brought in by Acadian, Irish, English, French settlers and others.

Agriculture, forestry and tourism plays a strong role in the economy of the province (Bone, 2002) and it is logical that agriculture should be linked into the tourism offerings. It is reported that 1.86 million people visited New Brunswick in 2003 (Tourism New Brunswick). They also indicate that the performance of tourism in generating revenues of $1.1 billion and 31,000 jobs make tourism one of the leading economic generators in the province. A similar number of jobs are created by agriculture (food production and processing), mostly in rural areas. The agricultural sector is described as diverse, combining 3,034 farms with 100 processing plants to produce

$1.37 billion worth of agri-food and beverage products in 2004 (Government of New Brunswick). Examining these two major industries it is evident that there may be potential to combine and utilize the two resources together. Farmers' markets are one location where farmers and tourists and agriculture and tourism meet. However, the predominance of large-scale agriculture in the province may limit the number of farmers available to participate in markets.

Research on heritage tourists in Canada (Canadian Tourism Commission (CTC), 2003) notes their interest in museums, farmers' markets and historic sites. Culinary tourism activities can include visits to farmers' markets. In the province of New Brunswick in eastern Canada opportunities for tourists to experience food include visits to restaurants; agricultural fairs; museums; food festivals and farmers' markets. Research on tourist motivations for visiting the province within the category of festivals and events indicate an interest in visiting and shopping at farmers' markets (Tourism New Brunswick, 2001). These latter community markets within the province are of interest to tourists since besides offering produce they also sell prepared local and ethnic food and crafts. At the markets it is possible to find products that are place specific, such as the maple syrup that is characteristic of Northeastern North America (Buszek, 1982). In a study of visitor motivations in New Brunswick (LeBlanc, 2004), it was noted that francophone visitors showed a slightly higher motivation for visiting and shopping at farmers' markets than did the Anglophone visitors.

The farmers' markets of New Brunswick reflect the agricultural nature of the province. While 18 farmers' markets were identified in the province this chapter concentrates on the markets associated with the vicinity of the rich farming lands along the Saint John River that forms the main farming area of the province. This narrows the study to eight markets that are geographically clustered with proximity to the Saint John River. One of these, the WW Boyce Farmers Market in Fredericton, operates once a week year round and another, the Saint John City Market, operates 6 days a week year round, while the others are seasonal. In the province there are also a number of farm gate markets and roadside stalls where farmers sell directly to consumers, which are not examined here. For example, the Economic Planning Group (2006) reports that in the South-Central region of the province there are six community markets as well as a number of commercial farm market stalls.

The community farmers' markets of New Brunswick provide a venue for interaction between the farmer venders and the tourist visitors for an authentic tourist experience. The markets usually only open once a week or once every other week during the late spring, summer and early fall often taking on a festival-like atmosphere, in incorporating venders selling other locally produced products (e.g., soap, candles, hand made jewellery, woodworking, baskets, home baking, ethnic foods) and local musical entertainment. The farmers' market product mix in New Brunswick is demonstrated by the Bouctouche Farmers Market, listing a variety of products on their web site (Table 14.2).

The most historic farmers' market in the province is the Saint John City Market which is managed by the City of Saint John. It dates back to the 1800s and was the result of an amalgamation of a number of fresh produce markets in the city. The current building was opened in 1876 and renovated in the 1980s. The market is open year round from Monday to Saturday. While the web site of the City Market promotes a traditional 'farmers' market' experience few current vendors are farmers (Saint John City Market, 2007). However, the current market has an active schedule of events designed to attract visitors. For example, a Wool Fondlers weekend event held in January of 2007 featured spinning, weaving and dying demonstrations as well as introductory knitting classes. The market is one of the main tourism attractions for visitors to the city. In particular, the cruise ship visitors on cruises from Boston and New York are an important visitor segment for the market. Shopping such as that provided by the City Market in the form of arts, crafts and local food products, is recognized as a major shore-side activity for these passengers (Chesworth, 2006). In 2006, 30 ships called at Saint John with an approximate total of 88,000 passengers (Cruise Saint John, 2006).

The farmers' markets in the province are seen by Tourism New Brunswick (2007) as linked to tourism and this is reflected

---

Table 14.2   Product offerings at Bouctouche Farmers' Market, New Brunswick, Canada

Fresh vegetables grown by local farmers	Stained glass
Lots of fresh baked goods	Handcrafted jewellery
Shrubs, bushes and trees	Jams, jelly, pickles – all homemade
Fresh cut flowers	Quilts
Plants grown by local gardeners	Locally made soaps and oils
Paintings by local artists	Beach glass items from local area
Wood products made by local craftsmen	Ceramics
One of a kind pottery	Knitted products

Source: Bouctouche Farmers Market, 2007.

by their listing on the web site promoting tourism to New Brunswick. Farmers' markets are listed in the heritage, culture and arts section of the site with the descriptor 'Farm-fresh produce, artisan treasures, delicious local fare and so much more in that ever lively market atmosphere'. In their 2003 (Tourism New Brunswick, 2003) survey of consumer intentions, activities and interests farmers' markets scored 6.5 out of 10 as a mean score for interest. Using this data to examine visitor motivations in New Brunswick (LeBlanc, 2004), it was noted that Francophone visitors showed a slightly higher motivation for visiting and shopping at farmers' markets than did the Anglophone visitors.

However, the listing of markets for tourism is broader than just farmers' markets, including for example the Saint John City Market (which has few farmer vendors but is nonetheless one of the top tourism attractions in the city) suggesting that the provincial tourism officials are keen to trade on the appeal of farmers' markets. Recent tourism planning studies, such as that done for South Central New Brunswick (Economic Planning Group of Canada, 2006) and for the Kingston Peninsula (Reid and Stewart, 2004) in New Brunswick note the role of farmers' markets in providing activities for tourists. The farmers' market cooperative is a typical organizational framework for the emergence of farmers' markets in the province. A cluster of farmers' markets and an individual market are profiled in the following case studies.

Case study: Saint John River Valley farmers' markets

The Saint John River Valley, an area that extends from Edmundston in the north to Saint John in the south is known as a rich farming area. It is also recognized as a developing tourism destination. A number of markets parallel the River Valley route. This includes markets at Grand Falls; Perth Andover; Hartland, Woodstock, Fredericton and Grand Bay (Table 14.3). A recent tourism development plan for the upper portion of this region noted the markets as being part of the resource that could be grouped with other culinary products for regional crops or specialty food tours (Tourism Synergy, 2004).

Visitors to this tourism area (River Valley Scenic Drive) are characterized by Tourism New Brunswick research as 'Upscale visitors on long touring trips … they like being outdoors and close to nature, they often do things on the spur of the moment while on vacation and customer service and quality are essential' (Tourism New Brunswick, 2005, p.2). The farmers' markets of the valley would appeal to this demographic profile.

That several of the farmers' markets on the route are new (Grand Falls and Woodstock) could be noted as a potential sign of interest in developing this

(*Continued*)

Table 14.3 Saint John River Valley farmers' markets in New Brunswick, Canada

Location	Market Name
Grand Falls	Grand Falls District Farmers Market
Perth-Andover	Perth Andover Farmers Market
Hartland	Hartland Farmers Market
Woodstock	Woodstock Farm Market
Fredericton	WW Boyce Farmers Market
Grand Bay/Saint John/Kingston	Grand Bay Farmers Market
Kingston	Kingston Farmers Market
Saint John	Saint John City Market

Source: Adapted from Tourism New Brunswick, 2007.

product. The fact the markets in most cases are only open once a week in season limits their access to tourists and for tourism. However, when combined with other food experiences, such as visits to farms, historic villages (such as Kings Landing Historical Settlement) and production facilities, the farmers' markets have the potential to contribute to day touring products. These components could be developed for tour companies to offer, or self-guided itineraries or routes could be designated.

The case of the Saint John River Valley farmers' markets highlights the role that the markets might play, along with other food products and venues, in developing food tourism within the province. The geographical proximity of these markets suggests the potential for linkages, either through developing the markets into a 'farmers' market route' or by linking the markets with other providers (restaurants, festivals, museums, etc.) to form a food tourism route. An example of the assets for such a route is sketched out in (Table 14.4). A distinctive feature of this route is the variety of food traditions to be experienced, from the cuisine of the Acadians to that of the aboriginal peoples.

Partnerships towards this cause of developing a food tourism route will be essential if products are to be developed for interested tourists. Generic research on farmers' markets has indicated that consumers are interested in travelling further to attend markets if a number are clustered or scattered in a rural area (Brown, 2002). It could therefore be beneficial for the communities clustered along the River Valley to encourage the linked development of such markets, either as a stand alone food tourism product or as suggested above linked with other food and food interpretation providers, to form a dedicated route.

(Continued)

Table 14.4 A food tourism route for the Saint John River Valley, New Brunswick, Canada

Themes	Experiences	Locations and Establishment Examples
Local farmers markets	Saturday morning visits to markets to meet the farmer/producers and experience the local culture	Grand Falls Perth Andover Hartland Woodstock Fredericton Grand Bay Saint John Kingston
Museums and interpretive centres	Daily, in season visit the regions museums and sites that feature local food history	N.B. Potato Museum/Potato World Kings Landing Historical Settlement New Brunswick Botanical Garden Madawaska Maliseet First Nation Day Adventure
Restaurants and Cafes	Daily, year round experience the regions varied culinary traditions	Restaurant de l'Auberge Les Jardins Inn

Case study: Kingston Farmers' Market Cooperative Ltd

The rural Kingston Peninsula located in the south west of the province, once largely agricultural, is transitioning to more of a service-based economy. Located near the urban area of Saint John the peninsula is accessible both by road and by cable ferry. In their study of the emergence of cultural rural tourism here Gosse and Jolliffe (2006, p.5) indicate 'Now discovered by tourists an infrastructure of small tourism enterprises such as bed and breakfasts, inns, marinas, u-pick farms and farmers' markets are emerging to cater to visitors'. The study also found that over 75 per cent of tourism stakeholders interviewed agreed that tourism development is essential to the well-being of the community. This case profiles the larger of the two Saturday markets located in the small rural community of Kingston, The Kingston Farmers Market Cooperative Ltd.

With origins in a small community market that is still operational as The Original Kingston Farmers Market this cooperative was incorporated in 1997

(Continued)

and subsequently opened at its present location in 1998. Currently there are over 60 vendors on the roster for this weekly market which is attracting around 30,000 customers a year. The market is directed by a board of directors and is managed by a part-time Market Manager.

A significant part of the Kingston Farmers Market experience is the traditional breakfast that is served. Breakfasts are prepared by part-time staff and served at long tables by volunteers. This food tourism experience contributes to the market being a destination for visitors from the city of Saint John as well as tourists who are staying in cottages or camping on the peninsula. They come not only for the breakfast but also to socialize with friends and neighbours and to meet new people. While only a few of the vendors at this market are farmers it has been observed that both the farmer vendors and the customers at this market value the interaction in the selling and purchasing process. Many of the people who participate in this market have dual roles. For example, the part-time Manager of the market is also a farm vendor. One of the craft vendors at the market is the part-time market cleaner.

A recent report on tourism in the area recognized the Kingston Farmers Market as a demand supporter for tourism (Reid and Stewart, 2004). However, the report also identified the market buildings as being underused and the lack of sustained funding as a weakness. A visitor survey conducted by the market in the summer of 2004 had indicated an attendance from surrounding localities. It is not known how many tourists visit the market, although educational tourists taking photography courses in the area, from nature photographer Freeman Patterson, and friends and relatives of those who have cottages in the area are frequent visitors. The recommended improvements to market infrastructure are finally being implemented. In the summer of 2006 the Kingston Farmers Market received $187,000 in federal funding and $45,000 in provincial funding from the Provincial Government towards improvements including increased parking facilities, shelter constructed for outdoor vendors and improved kitchen facilities. Tourism stakeholders on the Kingston Peninsula surveyed recently noted the benefit of the market development to tourism on the peninsula (Gosse and Jolliffe, 2006).

This case of the Kingston Farmers Market shows investment in countryside capital advocated by Garrod et al. (2006) reflecting both direct investment through government agencies and indirect investment through the community shareholders of the Kingston Farmers Market Cooperative. As is seen by the 2006 government funding direct investment has a more immediate and tangible effect, however indirect investment is still significant. This market has therefore successfully addressed some of the challenges faced by farmers' markets. This includes maintaining the farm market mix; creating activities for locals and tourists and finding infrastructure funding. It has also contributed to the tourism product of the rural peninsula by complimenting other small-scale tourism offerings, such as inns and cottages.

Analysis: Farmers' markets and tourists in New Brunswick, Canada

A number of observations can be derived from both the survey of the farmers' market situation in relation to agriculture and tourism in New Brunswick and from the case studies presented above:

- The markets provide a venue for farmers to diversify their farm incomes. However, for the farmers it is likely that the markets play a small role in the potential diversification of farm revenues.
- The farmers' markets and tourists in the province are connected in the vender and consumer relationship.
- Some of the tourists coming to the province are interested in visiting and shopping at the farmers' markets. Francophone visitors have a higher motivation to participate in these markets than do Anglophone visitors.
- The markets have some of the characteristics of festivals and events, occurring at a dedicated time and often having elements of entertainment in the form of music or demonstrations.
- Tourism New Brunswick promotes the markets as part of the tourism product of the province.
- There is potential for the markets to join with other establishments (restaurants, museums, etc.) in creating composite food tourism products, such as food trails.
- The markets are at the beginning stage of their relationship to tourism and cooperative action will be required in the form of partnerships (of markets and with other stakeholders) if they are to be further developed for and linked in with tourism.
- It is possible to use local improvement grants, as with the case of the Kingston Farmers Market to improve market infrastructure, both for the benefit of locals and tourists.

Do these conclusions address the questions posed at the beginning of the chapter? The first question asked was can the farmers' markets be developed and promoted through tourism? The case studies demonstrate that the farmers' markets of the province are a component that could be used to develop the food tourism product. Because of the limited availability of the markets they will need to be combined with other products to become viable tourism products. While the markets are only informally linked with tourism they do have potential, along with other food tourism elements, such as restaurants, food festivals, food production facilities and farm gate stalls, to contribute to tourism development in the province. Tourism is therefore at a beginning stage of being harnessed as a vehicle for the development and promotion of the farmers' markets in the province. The markets are independently operated and do not at this stage have any kind of affiliation or association that would encourage joint marketing.

The second question asked how the farmers' markets can be promoted as local festivals and events. The farmers' markets of the province are considered by Tourism New Brunswick to be a form of local festivals and events. There is probably some potential for joint promotion of the markets with other regional tourism products. There may be potential for promoting the entertainment aspect of the markets through event listings at the accommodations in the vicinity of the market locations. For the tourists seeking an authentic local experience there is some benefit to be gained from attending farmers' markets. However, the fact that the markets are for the most part held once a week season-ally gives them a festival like quality but limits their availability to tourists. The one exception in the case of New Brunswick is the Saint John City Market which simulates a farmers' market experience, however with little involvement from farmers.

The third question queried the possibility for the markets as a whole to be promoted as a tourism attraction for the province. This focused review of farmers' markets in New Brunswick has demonstrated that they are definitely a resource that can be used in developing the food tourism product of the province. Being reflective of local culture and held on specific days and times the farmers' markets also have a role to play as festivals. This role will most likely be played out along with other culinary attractions, such as historic sites, museums and food establish-ments. As demonstrated by the literature and by the case of the Kingston Farmers Market both farmers and market organizers appreciate the genuine and authentic interaction afforded by the farmers' market setting. It is known that tourists often seek out this type of authentic interaction (Williams, 1998).

Conclusion

Using the case of New Brunswick it is recognized that farmers' markets serve to connect agriculture with tourism, and farm-ers with tourists. It is possible that the farmers' markets may evolve as tourist events and destinations but this evolution should be planned to safeguard local market needs and protect the authenticity that is valued by tourists. Cooperative action will be necessary if the markets are to contribute to the food tourism product of the province. As is reflected by the case of the Kingston Market these farmers' markets have the potential to be incorporated into local improvement projects that will benefit both locals and tourists. In addition, in the case of New Brunswick the clustering of markets along the Saint John River Valley suggests the potential for a 'Food Tour Route' in which farmers' markets have a role. Further research is needed in order to fully understand the nature of tourist motivations for visiting farmers' markets, as well as to understand their role in developing food tourism at destinations with rich agricultural resources such as the Saint John River Valley.

Acknowledgments

Chris Gosse, University of New Brunswick assisted with the literature review through Community University Research Alliance (CURA) funding from the Social Sciences and Humanities Research Council, Government of Canada. An earlier version of this paper was presented at the GEOTOUR 2006 conference held in Kosice, Slovakia.

References

Bone, R.M. (2002). *The Regional Geography of Canada*. Oxford University Press, Don Mills.

Boniface, P. (2003). *Tasting Tourism: Travelling for Food and Drink*. Ashgate, Aldershot.

Bouctouche Farmers' Market (2007). http://www.bouctouche-farmersmarket.com/, accessed February 11, 2007.

Brown, A. (2002). Farmers' market research 1940–2000: An inventory and review. *American Journal of Alternative Agriculture*, 4(17), 167–169.

Buszek, B.R. (1982). *The Sugar Bush Connection*. Cranberrie Cottage, Granville Centre, Nova Scotia.

Canadian Tourism Commission (CTC) (2003). *Canada's Heritage Tourism Enthusiasts: A Special Analysis of the Travel Activities and Motivations Survey*. CTC, Ottawa.

Canadian Broadcasting Corporation (CBC) (2006). CBC Maritime Magazine, Farmers' Markets, October 8, 2006.

Chesworth, N. (2006). The Cruise Industry and Atlantic Canada. In Dowling, R. (ed.) *Cruise Ship Tourism*. CABI, Wallingford, pp. 160–169.

Saint John City Market (2007). Web site at http://www.sjcity-market.ca, accessed May 21, 2007.

Cruise Saint John (2006). Cruise Saint John New Brunswick Canada. Web site at http://www.cruisesaintjohn.com, accessed February 11, 2007.

Daugstad, K., Ronningen, K. and Skar, B. (2006). Agriculture as an upholder of cultural heritage? Conceptualizations and value judgements – A Norwegian perspective in international context. *Journal of Rural Studies*, 22, 67–81.

Eastwood, D. (1996). Using customer survey's to promote farmers' markets: A case study. *Journal of Food Distribution Research*, 23–30.

Economic Planning Group of Canada (2006). *Strategic Directions for Tourism in South Central New Brunswick*. Prepared for Fundy Enterprise. Sussex, New Brunswick.

Gale, F. (1997). Direct farm marketing as a rural development tool. *Rural Development Perspectives*, 12(2), 19–25.

Garrod, B., Wornell, R. and Youell, R. (2006). Re-conceptualising rural resources as countryside capital: The case of rural tourism. *Journal of Rural Studies*, 22, 117–128.

Gosse, C. and Jolliffe, J. (2006). *Cultural Rural Tourism on the Kingston Peninsula*. Presentation to CURA Mini Conference, University of New Brunswick Saint John.

Government of Canada (2001). *Census Data*. Statistics Canada, Ottawa.

Government of New Brunswick (2006). Web Site at http://www.gnb.ca, accessed September 1, 2006.

Hunt, D. and Hunt, M. (1992). *Michigan Fresh*. Midwestern Guides, Albion Michigan.

Jolliffe, L. (2006). *Linking Farmers' Markets and Tourism*. Presented at Geotour 2006, Perspectives of Rural Tourism in the New Europe, Kosice, Slovakia, October 5–7, 2006.

Lane, B. (2005). Sustainable rural tourism strategies: A tool for development and conservation. *Interamerican Journal of Environment and Tourism*, 1(1), 12–18.

LaTrobe, H. (2001). Farmers' markets and local rural produce. *International Journal of Consumer Studies*, 25(3), 181–192.

LeBlanc, M. (2004). Tourist characteristics and their interest in attending festivals and events: An Anglophone/francophone case study of New Brunswick, Canada. *Event Management*, 8, 203–212.

Maxwell, G. (1951). *Round New Brunswick Roads*. The Ryerson Press, Toronto.

Oppermann, M. (1995). Rural tourism in Southern Germany. *Annals of Tourism Research*, 23(1), 86–102.

Reid, L. and Stewart, L. (2004). *A Case for Sensitive and Sensible Tourism Development – A Sustainable Tourism Plan for the Kingston Peninsula*. Tourism Synergy Ltd. and BDA Ltd. for Kingston Peninsula Chamber of Commerce, Saint John, New Brunswick.

Timothy, D.J. (2004). *Shopping Tourism, Retailing and Leisure*. Channel View Publications, Clevedon, UK.

Tourism New Brunswick (2003). *Consumer Interests, Motivators and Attitudes, Province of New Brunswick*. Fredericton, New Brunswick.

Tourism New Brunswick (2005). *River Valley Scenic Drive 2005 Consumer Profile. Province of New Brunswick*. Fredericton, New Brunswick.

Tourism New Brunswick (2001). *Tourism Survey, Province of New Brunswick*. Fredericton, New Brunswick.

Tourism New Brunswick (2007). *Tourism New Brunswick*. Web site at http://www.tourismnewbrunswick.ca, accessed May 21, 2007.

Tourism Synergy (2004). *Upper Saint John River Valley Tourism Development Initiative – A Product and Market Development Strategy*. Prepared for the Department of Tourism and Parks, Saint John, New Brunswick.

Williams, S. (1998). *Tourism Geography*. Routledge, London.

From saké to sea urchin: Food and drink festivals and regional identity in Japan

Atsuko Hashimoto and David J. Telfer

Introduction

The geographical and historic foundations of Japan have imprinted regional distinctions on food and drink products, and these have become part of the basis of cultural traditions, identity and festivals. Although parts of Japan such as Tokyo and Kobe are taking on more of a cosmopolitan feeling to them, there is still a very strong link to local communities all over Japan through traditional festivals and events that occur throughout the year. Regions have become known for specific food and drink products with regions claiming ownership over these products and celebrating them through festivals. The national government has set up a series of community development projects and implemented new laws setting the foundation for festivals and events celebrating the harvest or production. Examples include the Sea Urchin festival in Haboro in northern Japan to *Doburoku* (unrefined saké) festivals in Ota, Kyushu in southern Japan. Although Japanese festivals that accompany food and/or wine usually have a long history, many festivals that *'feature'* food and drink are rather new. Some of the festivals have been created or re-created in order to rejuvenate declining rural communities and it is believed that the success of these festivals will enhance the local people's regional identity, self-efficacy, and pride.

Many foreigners visiting Japan immediately notice the Japanese people's love for food and drink. Food and delicatessen sections in grocery stores and department stores are well stocked with artistic nouvelle cuisine as well as various side dishes that accompany meals. Many food festivals linked to the harvest have long traditions and are celebrated across Japan throughout the year. There are plentiful magazines featuring food and drink. On TV, there are numerous shows highlighting local cuisine, nouvelle cuisine, and international cuisine. Travel brochures and web sites have event databases and one can search by the category 'Food and Drink'. Although the day-to-day food consumption of the average Japanese household is modest, regional 'food and drink' components have become an important entertainment element for any festive occasion.

The Japanese are also known for their obsession with fresh ingredients. The TV show 'Iron Chef' (invited guest chef challenges resident master chef in a 1 hour cooking battle with a selected theme ingredient) was well received both inside and outside of Japan and emphasized the Japanese chef's obsession with fresh, high-quality ingredients along with artistic presentations of the final product (Fuji Television, 2000). The

Japanese idea of the 'best' food is fresh, preferably alive, and the ingredients are to be consumed as it is being cooked, with little intervention of condiments. Based on this belief, Japanese festivals and events that feature food and/or drink focus on 'in season', 'freshness', or 'just taken out of (water or field)'. Food festivals and events emphasize the 'localness', 'uniqueness to the area', and that the 'product is available only for a short period of time'.

This chapter will explore the evolutionary nature of Japanese food and drink festivals. The chapter begins by examining the relationship between regional identity and regional food ways in order to understand current trends in food festivals. It is argued that it is vital to understand the historical, geographical, and socio-political factors that have contributed to create the Japanese passion for regional food and food festivals. With the background set, the chapter turns to examine the changing nature of food festivals and the political, socio-cultural, and economic motivators behind the shift towards non-traditional, event-style food festivals. The chapter concludes by highlighting some of the challenges food festivals and events face now and will face in the future. This chapter emphasizes the importance of understanding the evolution of regional food and unique food ways, and how they have been adopted to create new 'food and drink' festivals in Japan.

Regional identity and food ways

Japan today is often considered a culturally homogenous nation because only 1.5 per cent of population is registered as non-Japanese nationals. The evidence shows that various ethnic groups including the indigenous 'Wa' (or 'Yamato', the ancient Japanese ethnic group) along with others from the Asian mainland as well as from northern and southern islands settled in the Japanese archipelago over thousands of years and formed a culture known as 'Japanese' culture. However the distinct cultural characteristics of northern Ainu and southern Okinawan are still visible.

Nevertheless the internal geography of Japan (high mountains and islands with limited links) isolated many settlements, resulting in clear regional distinctions in dialects and food ways. Such regional differences were identified in the early part of history. By the time the first constitution was established (702 AD) the imperial court were enjoying regional delicacies and unique food ingredients as part of the levy paid to it. There is a record showing how Lord Masamuné Daté of

Sendai, who was a known gourmand, entertained the Shogun with delicacies from all around Japan, prepared by Lord Daté himself in 1630. Another menu for Lord Daté's New Year's meals shows that they were made only from ingredients from his feudal territory (Food Kingdom Miyagi, 2007).

Although Japan is geographically small, various microclimates and geographical features contribute to the development of regional dishes and known food products (Figure 15.1 provides a map of Japan). Regional dishes may also be created to boost local morale or distinguish a community from others. Yet, the regional food is a powerful way to express territories and identities (Bell and Valentine, 1997; Avieli, 2005). Prof. Emeritus Yamano is warning about the loss of national identity among Japanese as

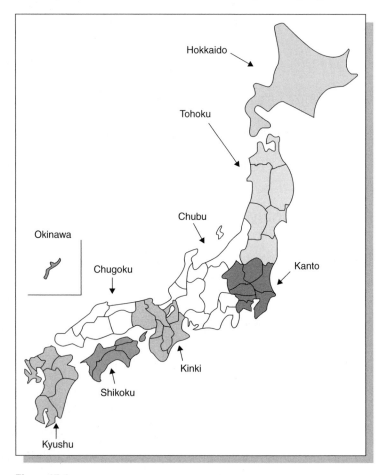

Figure 15.1
Map of Japan by regions (*Source*: Inoue, 2007, http://www.freemap.jp/php/japan_nurinuri_1_1/japan_nurinuri.html)

the Japanese diet is progressively being westernized (Shigeto, 2005). The foundation of the Slow Food Japan network empha-sizes the protection of regional dishes and foodstuff, and the diversification of diet among Japanese population (http://www.slowfoodjapan.net/index.html). The *Chisan Chisho* (locally pro-duced, locally consumed) movement is also contributing to the protection of traditional regional food and to regional festivals.

Political and social climate influences on food festivals

As mentioned in the introduction, it is not only the geographical foundations which have imprinted their mark on food festivals, it is also the historical development in food ways which have greatly influenced food festivals. Historical and social changes present the framework for understanding food consumption patterns. As will be illustrated below, the government has taken recent legal action to strengthen and celebrate traditional food products which have become the basis for many food festivals.

In 3 BC rice farming came from Mainland China. When trade with China was established in 7 AD, different kinds of vegetables and fruits were introduced; a new way of cooking with oil, drinking cow's milk, and consuming dairy products became fashionable among aristocrats. Meanwhile, the intro-duction of Buddhism forbade the consumption of meat. The Meiji era (1868–1912) was a pivotal point in Japanese history and the Japanese diet and food ways also changed. Meat con-sumption became fashionable among the aristocrats (Zenkoku Joho Gakushu Shinko Kyokai, n.d.). However consumption of meat, poultry, eggs, and dairy products was extremely rare among the lower classes (Dokkyo University, 1998; Onshindo Pharmacy, 2007). The post-World War II period was another pivotal point in terms of Japanese diets. During the recovery period, the American Government's 'PL 480: Food for Peace' supplies from the USA nearly replaced the traditional Japanese diet with wheat products (bread, baked goods) and highly con-centrated milk powder (Suzuki, 2003; Makino, 2007). Excessive amount of protein and fats were introduced through the con-sumption of meat/poultry, eggs, and dairy products. The Japanese began to eat less and less rice and consumed more and more fish, meat, and dairy products. Recently the Ministry of Agriculture Fisheries and Forestry (MAFF, 2005a) identi-fied an increase in diabetes and osteoporoses which can be attributed to an unbalanced diet. MAFF warns that the trend of increasing bad eating habits, unbalanced diet, complacency, and laziness drawn from a convenient life style are becoming a threat to Japanese food ways (MAFF, n.d.).

Today's Japan is an ageing nation. By 2050, the population is projected to decrease to 100 million people, and by 2100 it will be around 67 million (one-half of the 2007 population) (Ministry of Education, Culture, Sports, Science and Technology, 2000). Globalization brings fusion of culture and values, and the blurring of distinctions between traditions and cultural practices. In addition to the rise of globalization, the older generations who can teach traditions and customs are disappearing. Globalization in food culture also affects food safety and the health of Japanese.

With such a background, four government-initiated laws and movements have supported the increasing focus on food and the rise of food festivals in Japan. These are (1) Basic Law on *Shokuiku* [Food Education], enacted in June 2005 (MAFF, n.d.); (2) *Omatsuri hou*: Law Concerning the Promotion of Sightseeing and Commerce and Industry in Designated Areas by Organizing Events Taking Advantage of Traditional Music, Arts and Other Local Cultures (Haitani, 1996), began in 1992; (3) *Chisan Chisho* [locally grown, locally consumed] movement started in the 1980s, in conjunction with the Slow Food movement, which started in 2000 in Japan (Slow Food Japan, 2007); and (4) One Village One Product movement started in 1979 (OVOP, n.d.). These are described below in more detail as well as how they have influenced festival development.

The *Shokuiku* basic law was to promote a healthier body and mind through increasing Japanese people's knowledge to nutrition and a balanced diet. The specific aim is to raise 'awareness and appreciation of traditional Japanese food culture as well as educate people about food supply/demand networks as part of these opportunities of interaction between food producers and consumers were created. This was done in order to revitalize rural farming and fishing regions and to boost food self-sufficiency in Japan' (MAFF, n.d., p. 3). The law promotes education and awareness through school and with the knowledge people seek out food festivals.

The *Omatsuri* Law came in to practice after a Japanese site was recently designated as a UNESCO Cultural Heritage Site and the national interest in culture and heritage was heightened. Local community revitalization projects utilizing traditional events and cultural, including regional cuisine, were encouraged under this law. Many peripheral communities took advantage of this law and started food events/festivals to promote tourism revenues.

The *Chisan Chisho*, Slow Food and OVOP movements were originally meant to improve farming communities' well-being and ensure food safety. The focus was increasing self-sufficiency in agriculture and aquaculture products, bringing producers and the consumers together. The movement was seen as way to combat over-reliance on imported food, ensuring superior food safety of local produce over imported food, nurturing pride in local produce, and giving the depopulating and slowly dying rural communities opportunities to revitalize (MAFF, 2005b,c; Slow Food Japan, 2007; OVOP, n.d.). The OVOP programme links participating villages to one product, which they become known for and this is used in tourism marketing. At railway stations, for example, signs are posted alerting the travellers which product each village is known for. These products have been incorporated into food festivals attracting tourists.

With government campaigns such as those above, it is no wonder that numerous food festivals have been encouraged and have materialized in recent years. Many of these are modified versions of existing or traditional festivals and events. Reflecting the Japanese love for food and drink as part of entertainment, most of the festivals focus on food and drink; even if they are not the main attraction. The festival/event cannot survive without food and drink as added value. In most cases, the food and drink provided at festivals are unique to the area. Moreover, this uniqueness of dishes or the ingredients are the products of Japanese geography and climate.

History of festivals and speciality food

Although traditional Japanese meals today are drawing attention worldwide as often 'diet food', contemporary Japanese meals contains more protein and fat than meals several decades ago. With the influence from the western world, Japanese meals are resembling festival meals of old which tend to emphasize more fish, meat, and poultry side dishes than rice, cereals, and vegetables.

In an agrarian society, festivals and events gave purpose and expectations in repetitive and laborious ordinary workdays. Special events such as wedding and funerals, religious events, national/regional events were classified as *Haré* (non-ordinary or festive) while daily labour and rest are classified as *Ké* (ordinary) (Machida, 2002; Fujigoko, 2007; Makino, 2007). The time and space for *Haré* were set aside so that the 'festivity' was a totally different event from day-to-day activities. New Year's Day, weddings and funerals, religious rituals and performances, and *Noh* and *Kyogen* Dance Performances were some examples. Many *Haré* events are also linked to religious/spiritual events, focusing on prayers for healthy growth of crops and plentiful harvests, blessing on children's growth, warding off illness, injuries and bad luck, and for business prosperity (Fujigoko, 2007; Toshi Noson Gyoson Koryu Kasseika Kikou, 2007).

On *Haré* occasions, everyone dresses up in his or her best outfits and eats special meals. Valuable foodstuff such as refined white rice (Machida, 2002), rice cakes made from glutinous rice (Makino, 2007), and saké (Segawa, 2001) were only consumed at *Haré* occasions. Festive meals often reflects seasons – e.g. fish in season, seasonal vegetables, seasonal rice cakes, noodles of the season, and so on (Makino, 2007). Traditional *Haré* cuisine also bore symbolic meanings through word punning and the nature of the food. For instance, a kelp (*kobu*) dish was prepared to receive happiness (*yorokobu*); Red snapper (*tai*) is also for being festive and happy (*medetai*); salt-cured herring roe was for abundant offspring.

One example of festive food is Sushi. Up until the 1970s, Sushi was a special occasion food. Originating from *Naré* Sushi or *Naré* Zushi, it was invented in the fourth century AD in Asia. *Naré* zushi was believed to have reached Japan from southern China in the eighth century (Sushi Master, 2000). *Naré* zushi is the term used for fermented fish and rice was used to accelerate fermentation. The rice breaks down in the fermentation process and is discarded. However, Japanese turned it into a semi-fermented food so that rice can be consumed as well. This version of '*Naré* zushi' spread all over Japan and different kinds of fish available in the regions were used. It is commonly believed that the word Sushi means 'sour' rice, though contemporary characters for the word 'sushi' denotes happiness. The etymology reveals that the old characters for the word described marinated or fermented fish and fish source (Wikipedia, 2007a). In the nineteenth century, in the Tokyo area sushi chefs began to use fresh fish from Tokyo Bay. Rice was cooked and vinegar was added instead of waiting for natural fermentation (Sushi Master, 2000). This became the predecessor of today's *Nigiri* zushi. After the Kanto Earthquake in 1923, sushi chefs left devastated Tokyo and returned to their home regions to spread this form of sushi nationwide (Sushi Master, 2000; Wikipedia, 2007a). However, other than Tokyo-style *Nigiri* zushi, there are regional versions of sushi independently developed from *Naré* zushi. In Wakayama prefecture, local *ayu* (sweetfish) is used; in Akita prefecture, *hata-hata* (sandfish) is used. To illustrate regional development of sushi, in Kansai (Kyoto-Osaka area), there are *Futomaki* (various ingredients and rice rolled up in sea weed), *Battera* (vinegar-cured Mackerel box sushi), *Kaki-no-ha* zushi (salt-cured Mackerel sushi wrapped in persimmon leaves), just to name a few. However, the common homemade sushi is *Chirashi* (or *Bara*) zushi. Preserved or fresh vegetables are prepared and finely chopped and mixed with vinegar-added rice. This kind of sushi is not shaped and simply covered with local seafood, eggs, fresh greens, or even local fruit for decoration (Wikipedia, 2007a).

Beside sushi, people tend to eat more elaborate 'side dishes' than rice and cereal at festive occasions, i.e. more fish, shell fish, and recently more meat and poultry. Even the rice eaten is refined white rice. Unlike *Ké* (ordinary) occasions, the amount of fat and animal protein intake has become quite high (Onshindo Pharmacy, 2007). When recent festive meals were examined, Makino (2007) found that more westernized food (e.g. steak, Salisbury steak, BBQ meat, French fries/pommes frit, deep fried chicken) was preferred. She also found that the traditional festive food varieties were consumed more in southwestern parts of Japan.

Changing concept of haré (non-ordinary) and festivals and events today

Pagan animism, which developed into the Shinto religion, demanded an intimate relationship between nature and human life. Spring and autumn are the seasonal turning points when appeasing the deities and spirits will ensure health and growth in harsh seasons (summer and winter). Origuchi (2004) notes that ancient festivals in Japan were conducted only in autumn and spring. There was also a winter festival, which was often performed as a preparation for the spring festival, then later it became a festival on its own right. There was no summer festival yet the summer purification ritual (*hojo-é*) was combined with music and dance entertainment and transformed into a summer festival. This custom of adding entertainment to rit-uals can be observed from the beginning of Heian Period (794–1185 AD) (Origuchi, 2004).

These festivals are purely for the blessing of the crops, warding off disease, appeasing deities and lesser evils, and giving thanks for a bountiful harvest. *Doburoku* (unrefined saké) has been used as part of Shinto rituals in autumn festivals. The *Doburoku* festival of Shirahige Shrine in Oita prefecture has a recorded history since 710 AD. The Omori Shrine in Mié prefecture started its *Doburoku* festival in 1213 AD. *Doburoku* is, by law, illegal if brewed and consumed outside the 'designated areas'. The strict 2002 law was modified in 2004 and the number of the designated areas is increasing. When the law was relaxed in 2004, various villages applied for permission to brew *Doburoku* as part of a community development project. Today, 16 prefectures have designated areas (43 shrines, some designated *Doburoku* breweries, and inn/restaurants) (Satomi, 2005).

It has been observed that traditional festivals in the remote areas of Japan have begun to disappear mainly due to lack of resources. On the other hand, there is a phenomenon that 'organizers' create new festivals. The removal of authority or spirituality of traditional festivals is apparent in the new festivals. Hasegawa (2002) summarizes two types of contemporary festivals (Figure 15.2):

(a) *Traditional festival*: 'Emic' (insider) conceptualization by participants. Festivals are the spatial and temporal crossroads of social and historical identity of the participants.
(b) *Event-type festival*: 'Etic' (outsider) conceptualization by organizers. There is a clear purpose and objectives (i.e. number of participants, revenue/sales from the event, whether the sense of solidarity was shared by participants) of the event.

Hasegawa (2002) further identified from his research results that the above two types exist on two continua. The first is

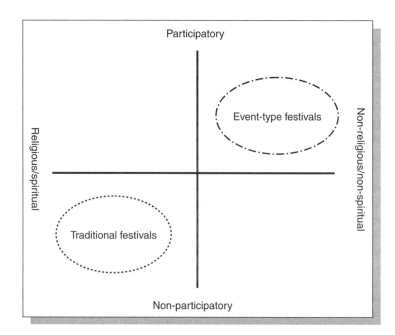

Figure 15.2
Two types of festivals (adapted from Hasegawa, 2002)

religious to non-religious continuum and the second is on the level of participation of visitors in the festivals.

The traditional festivals were meant for temporal and spatial purification and energizing events by inviting the *Haré* (non-ordinary) power of spirits and deities. However, contemporary events only pursue *Haré* occasions, at a time and place where people can leave the ordinary life behind and enjoy themselves in a non-ordinary environment. Hirai (2002) emphasizes the recent rapid emergence and growth in event-style festivals. Some of these event-style festivals already have a history of 50 or more years. The initial motivation to start the event varies. The *Tanabata* Festival in Shigehara city, Chiba-prefecture, was started as a street event in the shopping area to attract more visitors during the low business season. *Yosakoi* Festivals across Japan were instigated by the success of the Kochi-city *Yosakoi* Festival, started in 1953. The *Yosakoi* Festival has a carnival-like atmosphere with parades of dancers. The festival was organized by the Kochi Chamber of Commerce to beat the post-war recession and depression, and raise the morale of people (Mori, 1998). Inspired by Kochi *Yosakoi*'s success, one university student in Sapporo with volunteer students started *Yosakoi Soran* Festival in Sapporo in 1991. Their own festival committees, comprised of volunteers, run both festivals today in Kochi and Sapporo. The *Yosakoi* Festival is spreading across Japan (Yonehara, 2002; Yosanet, 2007). Another example is the Inagé *Kumin Matsuri* (Inagé Ward Festival) started in 1993 when the City of Chiba was divided into six wards. In order to raise solidarity among community members in the ward, the Inagé ward started a festival. This festival was initiated by government offices (city and the ward) (Hasegawa, 2002). Many peripheral towns are applying for a license to brew *Doburoku* and organize *Doburoku* festivals as part of community development projects. The total number of designated *Doburoku* special areas is 69, and these require extensive government intervention and regional initiatives for differentiation as a tourist event (Toyoyoshi, 2006).

Although many event-style festivals are emerging, equally a large number of newly created festivals are disappearing due to the financial burdens and resource shortage in continuing the events (Hasegawa, 2002). As the number of events all over Japan is reaching a saturation point, people have a choice and events that are more attractive win the visitors. In the remote areas where the ageing of residents and depopulation of the communities are major issues, communities are launching various events and festivals as a means of rescuing otherwise 'dying communities'. With limited resources, these community development projects focus on local assets, including regional cuisine as a feature attraction, combined with activities that take advantage of local natural resources.

Regional food today across Japan

Bell and Valentine (1997) define that the 'region' is a product of 'a natural landscape and a peopled landscape' (p. 153). What people consider or imagine as a regional food may not necessarily reflect reality. Bell and Valentine (1997) use the example of Yorkshire pudding and how outsiders' stereotype image of Yorkshire pudding differs from what insiders consider as Yorkshire pudding. Avieli (2005) also emphasizes that the ethnic and regional food are often imagined or invented. Nonetheless the topic of regional dishes is emotionally loaded and sparks regional pride and identity.

Until the railways and road systems connected the remotest parts of Japan, many villages were isolated and developed their own dishes with limited local produce. The mountainous physical features separated one hamlet from another hamlet. Microclimates created by these physical features also differentiated available produce and foodstuff between neighbouring villages. Even if the communities produced the same product, for instance, *miso* (soy bean paste), the quality of water, the quality of soy beans, the type of fermentation agents used and the type of soil soy beans grow in distinguish the type and taste of the end-product, *miso* paste. The closest comparison is the concept of 'terroir' often discussed with wine.

The list of the regional food shown in Table 15.1 was compiled by Rokugo Junior High School students. There is a *Shokuiku* (Food Education) movement today to preserve traditional food ways and Japanese education institutions include a curriculum of understanding regional cuisine. In the Rokugo project, each region's regional government offices or tourism offices nominated the region's most well-known or typical dishes as their 'regional dish'. With such emic pre-sentation of regional dishes, most of the dishes are so-called traditional dishes and not been invented with modern ingredients. Most of the places use rice and cereal, vegetables, and fish (fresh water or sea). Occasionally a special type of sushi is shown as a regional dish. Two exceptions are Hokkaido and Okinawa. Genghis Khan (Mongolian-style barbeque) represents Hokkaido, owing to Japan's colonization of Hokkaido Island with animal husbandry as a new form of farming in the late nineteenth century (MAFF, 2005d; Hokkaido Kinen-hi

Table 15.1 List of the regional dishes

Prefecture		Regional dish	Prefecture		Regional dish
Hokkaido and Tohoku region	Hokkaido	Genghis Khan (grilled mutton), Ishikari hot pot (salmon, tofu, and vegetable)	Kinki region	Mié	Tekone-zushi (tuna, sushi rice), Ise Udon (udon in soy sauce soup)
	Aomori	Ké no shiru (vegetable-rice porridge), grilled abalone with miso souce		Shiga	Funa-zushi (fermented crucian carp)
	Iwate	Cold noodle, Tofu dengaku (grilled tofu with miso)		Kyoto	Hamo dishes (pike conger), Unagi Chazuke (BBQ eel, rice, and tea)
	Miyagi	Zunda mochi (green bean), whale dishes		Osaka	Takoyaki (wheat ball with octopus pieces), Odamaki-mushi (steamed egg with udon)
	Akita	Kiritampo (mochi in chicken, vegetable soup)		Hyogo	Ikanago (Ikanago fish)
	Yamagata	Imoni (potato, taro cooked with meat or poultry soup)		Nara	Kakino-ha zushi (sushi wrapped in persimmon leaf), Cha méshi (rice cooked in tea)
	Fukushima	Ika ninjin (marinated dried squid with carrots)		Wakayama	Mehari-zushi (sishi rice, bonit shavings, pickles wrapped in takana leaf), Sanma-zushi (salted sawry sushi)

(Continued)

Table 15.1 Continued

Region	Prefecture	Regional dish
Kanto region	Ibaraki	Anko hot pot (angler fish), Natto (fermented soy beans)
	Tochigi	Shimo tsukare (salmon head, vegetable, roasted soy beans, sake curd, fried tofu)
	Gunma	Yaki Manju (grilled wheat bun with miso), Okirikomi (soup noodle)
	Saitama	Gyoda Fry (thin crape with pork or dried shrimp)
	Chiba	Namero (chopped sardine or sawry with ginger), sardine dishes
	Tokyo	Hukagawa méshi (rice and corbicula in miso soup), Monja yaki (thin waterly crape)
	Kanagawa	Kenchin soup (tohu, vegetable soup)
Chubu region	Niigata	Noppei soup (vegetable and chicken soup)
	Toyama	Itoko-ni (squash, red bean, and vegetable)
Chugoku region	Tottori	Itadaki (rice and vegetable cooked in fired tofu), Daisen Okowa (glutinous rice dish)
	Shimané	Izumo soba (buckwheat noodle)
	Okayama	Matsurizushi (sushi with shrimp, Spanish mackerel, vegetable)
	Hiroshima	Oyster hot pot
	Yamaguchi	Iwakuni-zushi (Conger eel, lotus root, seasonal vegetable), Itoko-ni (red bean, vegetable)
Shikoku region	Tokushima	Soba-komé Zousui (buckwheat seed porridge)
	Kagawa	Sanuki udon (soup noodle)
	Éhimé	Tai méshi (red snapper rice)
	Kochi	Sahachi dish (combo dish of sashimi, sushi, cooked seafood, vegetable)

Region	Prefecture	Dishes
	Ishikawa	Jubu-ni (duck and vegetable)
	Fukui	Echizen Orishi Soba (backwheat noodle with grated daikon radish), mackerel dish
	Yamanashi	Hoto (Hoto noodle in miso soup)
	Nagano	Sasa-zushi (sushi with seasonal vegetable)
	Gifu	Gohei mochi (grilled mochi with miso), Hebo méshi (wasp/bee rice)
	Shizuoka	Gawa (fresh fish, pickles, vegetable, and miso)
	Aichi	Miso Nikomi Udon (noodle, chicken, and leek in miso soup)
Kyushu and Okinawa region	Fukuoka	Gaméni (chicken and seasonal vegetable), Kurumé ramen (noodle in pork soup)
	Saga	Funa kobu-maki (crucian carp in kelp), Mutsugoro BBQ (mudskipper fish)
	Nagasaki	Nagasaki chanpon (soup noodle with vegetable, pork, shrimp squid), Tai Chazuké (snapper)
	Kumamoto	Buen Zushi (sushi with snapper), Karashi rénkon (mastered filled lotus root)
	Oita	Dango-jiru (wheat gnocchi in vegetable soup), Yase-uma (wheat gnocchi/noodle in soy powder and sugar)
	Miyazaki	Hiya-jiru (cold miso soup)
	Kagoshima	Keihan (rice, chicken, vegetable, covered with chicken soup), Tonkotsu (slow cooked pork on the bone)
	Okinawa	Goya champru (bitter melon and egg), Rafty (slow cooked pork)

Risuto, 2006). Native Ainu dishes use salmon, venison, seal, and dried vegetables and herbs (Haguma, 2002). Okinawa, as a tropical island with a challenge of keeping ingredients fresh, had developed famous pork dishes. The traditional Okinawan formal dishes were developed to entertain Chinese ambassadors since 1400 AD, thus there is a strong Chinese influence on ingredients and cooking techniques (Okinawa Prefectural Government, 2003).

The traditional regional dishes do attract people from outside the region to some degree, particularly when the main ingredient of the dish is unique to the region. For example, oysters are cultivated from Hokkaido to Kyushu; however, Hiroshima prefecture produces more than 71 per cent of the entire oysters harvested in Japan (Yamada, 2002). Therefore, the Hiroshima oyster is best known and its festival draws more visitors than other regions' oyster festivals. One notable point is that the advertisement of food festivals emphasizes the regional ingredients, yet the known regional dishes, which are made from featured ingredients, are less visible in the advertisement.

Food and festivals in Japan

The provision of food and drink is an important part of festivals and entertainment. Many festivals feature 'food' or 'drink' as the main attractions. Depending on the type of festivals, the type of food or drink provided varies. Some festival food used in rituals at shrines are often not the main attraction and they can be a very humble snack such as *édamamé* (green soybeans), *surumé* (dried squid), and grilled chicken (Ashkenazi, 1993). Other festivals such as the Haboro Sea Urchin Festival features freshly harvested sea urchins as well as other seafood dishes (Haboro TV, 2007).

People travelling a significant distance to visit a food festival is a relatively new phenomenon. Until the late nineteenth century, only pilgrims and accidental travellers who happened to be at the right place at the right time had a precious chance to enjoy dishes from outside their own residential region. During the Meiji Era (1869–1912), the railway system spread nationwide. The boxed lunch (*ekiben*) sold at various railway stations were invented based on local food. However, both railway travel and purchasing of *ekiben* were privileges of a handful of elite for nearly 70 years. It was not until after the post-war economic recovery in 1956 when these *ekiben* began to sell regional dishes at various price ranges to accommodate an assortment of customers (Ekiben no Komado, 2007). Although the common people's exposure to regional dishes were relatively early with the development of the *ekiben*, the concept of visiting a food festival outside their own hometown has only been seen in the past few decades. The origin of food festival tours is uncertain; one of the biggest Japanese tour operators suspects the origin was rather hap-hazardous off-season tour packages whose attraction was a regional dish beginning in the 1970s and 1980s (Personal communication, 2007).

With information technology today, it is very easy to find the list of events in Japan. The Ministry of Foreign Affairs supports Web-Japan (http://web-japan.org/atlas/festivals/festi_fr.html), which includes a list of selected events and festivals. Japan Travel Bureau has a web site that can be searched for events as well, and the event search web site (Rurubu.com) has over 130 food events throughout the year listed. Although many events and festivals are on search engines, smaller events and festivals or those in smaller communities are often overlooked in the large database. Each community has its own web site these days or a group of communities share a site. A small but attractive tourist town of Hagi, for example, is not found on any Search Engine's event list, yet it shows its festivals and events for the forthcoming 2 months, along with its culinary traditions and attractions on its own web site (http://city. Hagi.yamaguchi.jp/portal/taberu.sakana/index.html).

Food festival seasons

Selected featured items of the festivals from across Japan are shown in Table 15.2. These featured items are taken from the descriptions of event lists (Rurubu.com, JTB, various prefectures' event lists). Each category includes explicitly identified varieties and excludes the entries that simply describe 'fish', 'aquaculture products', or 'agriculture products'. The list is not exhaustive, yet gives some idea what types of food (food ingredients) are popular as feature items for festivals. Fresh ingredients such as fish and fruit are advertised as 'catch it yourself'/'pick your own', 'eat fresh', 'cooked according to local recipes', and 'buy and send home by a special delivery service'. Tea and rice products from the first harvest of the year are associated with dedication ritual to local shrines. These main items are usually accompanied by other food products, which are also unique to the area.

As shown in Table 15.3, the featured food items of the festivals vary from month to month. The number of festivals is also surprisingly concentrated in October (30 per cent of entire

Table 15.2 Selected feature items of food festivals

Fish	Shell fish	Vegetable/ fruit	Alcoholic beverage	Meat	Other food
Blowfish	Abalone	Banana	Beer	Beef	Gyoza dumpling
Chub	Crabs	Cherry	Doburoku	Duck	Hoto noodle
Salmon	Hokki clam	Mushroom	Saké		Kiritampo, Mochi
Sardine	Isé Lobster	Plum	Wine		Senbei
Saury	Oyster	Potatoes			Soba noodle
Seaweed/ kelp	Scallop	Rice			Somen noodle
Sweetfish	Sea Urchin	Tea			Tofu
Tuna	Tiger prawn	Yuzu lime			Ramen noodle
	Turban shell				

festivals). Autumn is obviously the season of harvest and as the Japanese saying goes 'appetizing autumn (*shokuyoku no aki*)', eating becomes a focus in this season. Popular seafood festivals (24.2 per cent of entire festivals) are spread through September to December. The festivals that feature fresh seafood are determined by the permitted fishing seasons and vary by species. Rainy seasons (May to June in Okinawa; June to July in the rest except Hokkaido) and a hot and humid summer challenge food safety and hygiene at outdoor festivals.

On the other hand, the geographical advantage of having a cold north to a warm south stretches the harvesting seasons, thereby extending festival season. Using the example of the oyster again, Japan boasts both winter and summer oyster seasons. There are over 25 varieties of oysters in Japan alone. Although in the western hemisphere, the known season for the oyster is from September to April. Southwestern Japan enjoys a warm sea temperature and the most popular variety, *Magaki* is in season from December to February (Komatsu, 2001); whilst northern Japan takes advantages of a cold sea temperature and the season is from October to March, but some varieties are in season in Summer (Okhotsk Sanchoku Asaichi, 2003). The well-known summer variety is natural *iwagaki* (rock oyster) from Tohoku, and is best between June and August (Shunshun-do, 2006). Although the possibility of purchasing

Table 15.3   Features of the events by months

Month	Fish	Shell fish	Vegetable/ fruit	Alcoholic beverage	Meat	Others	Total
January	2	1	0	0	0	0	3
February	0	2	0	0	0	2	4
March	1	1	0	0	0	4	6
April	1	0	1	0	1	3	6
May	2	2	1	1	0	2	8
June	1	1	3	0	1	0	6
July	0	0	0	0	1	0	1
August	1	1	0	0	0	0	2
September	5	1	2	3	1	3	15
October	12	3	5	3	4	13	40
November	2	4	3	2	1	5	17
December	5	4	3	1	2	9	24
Total	**32**	20	18	10	11	**41**	132
n = 132	(24.2%)	(15.2%)	(13.6%)	(7.6%)	(8.3%)	(31.1%)	

Notes: Fish category includes: fish varieties and sea weed varieties.
Shellfish category includes: shellfish, lobster/shrimp varieties, and sea urchin.
Vegetable/fruit category includes: vegetable, fruit, tea, and rice.
Meat category includes: meat, poultry, and dairy products.
Others category includes: prepared products (e.g. noodles, soup, rice cakes, tofu, sweets, etc.)
or combination of different categories (no one main feature).
Source: Rurubu.com (2006).

the *shun* (in season) oysters stretches from October to August, the well-known oyster festivals start in October (Hokkaido), and the number of festivals peaks in November. Hiroshima particularly organizes a number of oyster festivals between November and March (Benride Gozaru, 2007) and ending in late May (Hokkaido) (Akkeshi Town, 2007).

Similar to the oyster, the sea urchin's harvesting areas spread all over Japan, and so Sea Urchin festivals are also widespread. Over 100 varieties of sea urchin exist in Japan, nevertheless only 7 varieties are suitable for human consumption (Zenchinren, n.d.). Licensed harvesting seasons vary from one region to another and these staggered seasons allow for all-year-round availability of sea urchin for festivals. Fishing seasons vary by variety of the sea urchin. First, northern Okhotsk (from January), then Kyushu (from April) and then most of the regions start in July. Therefore, the Sea Urchin Festivals are usually in the month of July; Éhimé prefecture's festivals are in September to October. These festivals are event-type festivals, started by local governments or tourism associations. The example of Akuné in the Kyushu area below represents different Sea Urchin Festivals.

The Akuné city government in Kagoshima in collaboration with Akuné Tourism Cooperation launched the Akuné Sea Urchin Bowl Festival in 2007 (Chiran, 2007). The restaurants have been independently hosting similar events in the past; however, this is one of the series of events the City of Akuné intended to establish its own 'Community Development Through Food' project (Chiran, 2007). In this festival, the feature is rice in a bowl covered with 100 grams of purple sea urchin (Akuné Kanko, 2007), Akuné harvests 370 tons of sea urchins per annum (MAFF, 2006). Taking an advantage of being in a warmer region, it hosts the festival from April to May (55 days).

Locations and scales of food festivals

As mentioned above, while there is no comprehensive national listing of food and drink festivals, some selected festivals/ events are available from the Internet and these have been used to generate Table 15.4. As shown in Table 15.4, Hokkaido and Tohoku areas in the north listed 37.5 per cent of total events, followed by 18.7 per cent in the Chubu area. It is not surprising as Japanese seafood-related festivals (fish and shell fish categories in Table 15.3 totalled to 39.4 per cent) in northern regions have a longer seafood season than southern regions. Warmer climates cannot retain the freshness of the ingredients for a long time. However, smaller communities simply did not participate in listing their events and festivals on the Internet or the sites were neglected by web owners. It also depends on the advertising budget of each community for each event and how many visitors the community can handle.

The scale of the festivals and events varies substantially. In Aomori prefecture, Hiranai town's *Hotate Matsuri* (Scallop Festival) attracts more than 117,000 people for this 1-day event, which exceeds the town's population of 14,500 (MAFF, 2006). Shirahige Shrine *Doburoku* festival in Ota village, Oita prefecture draws over 30,000 visitors over 2 days (Kitsuki City, 2007) and Ota village's population is 1,794 (Wikipedia, 2007b); while the Soba Matsuri (buckwheat noodle festival) in Oita attracted 2,000 visitors (Bungotakada City, 2007a). As a comparison,

Table 15.4 Number of events by months and regions

Month	Hokkaido/ Tohoku	Kanto	Chubu	Kinki	Chugoku/ Shikoku	Kyushu/ Kinawa	Total
January	2	0	1	1	0	0	4
February	1	0	1	1	0	1	4
March	0	1	3	1	0	1	6
April	1	0	0	1	1	2	5
May	4	2	3	0	1	3	13
June	2	1	0	2	1	0	6
July	2	0	0	0	0	0	2
August	0	1	0	0	0	1	2
September	11	0	1	0	1	2	**15**
October	17	5	8	4	5	4	**43**
November	11	6	8	5	4	3	**37**
December	3	0	2	2	0	0	7
Total	**54**	**16**	**27**	**17**	**13**	**17**	**144**
n = 144	**(37.5%)**	**(11.1%)**	**(18.7%)**	**(11.8%)**	**(9.0%)**	**(11.8%)**	**(100%)**

Source: Rurubu.com (2006).

when the focus of the event is other than food, the carnival-like street dancing *Yosakoi Soran* Festival in Hokkaido attracts over 40,000 participants (Yosanet, 2007) and a traditional Rice Planting Festival in Tashibunosho in Oita drew 500 visitors (Bungotakada City, 2007b).

While food and drink festivals such as seafood festivals are held all over Japan, other types of food festival are more spatially and temporally limited. For example, Yokohama city in Metropolitan Tokyo will celebrate its 150th year of the opening of Yokohama Harbour in 2009. As part of the 5-year celebration (2005–2009), there will be the annual 'World Gourmet Festival'. The main theme is '*jimoto shokuzai* (Yokohama's indigenous food ingredients)'. Within Yokohama city, participating restaurants and food suppliers are offering a variety of menus, using local ingredients. Occasionally food festivals from other regions are invited to Yokohama. *Umaimono* [Tasty Food] summit was held in Yokohama in 2007 and the main attraction was a food event called '*Shoku no Jin* [Battle of Food]' from Niigata city. Niigata in northern Japan started this event in 1992, to introduce food ingredients and local dishes in Niigata. This event takes place throughout the year, and the biggest winter season (December to March) attracts over 170,000 visitors. *Shoku no Jin* in Yokohama limited the visitors to 20,000 over 2 days, yet the prepared food products were not enough in quantity to satisfy visitors (Niigata Shoku no Jin, 2007; Pacifico Yokohama, 2007). This type of 'visiting' food festivals are often seen as events in the department store or community programme. Department stores host food and drink festivals, highlighting products from across Japan or invite well-known restaurants to participate.

Challenges for festivals in the future

As the number of new food festivals increases, the challenges for the existing festivals are many. Once the festival is established and known, the organizers are divided by tasks, thus weaker communications among the divisions result and the cost of hosting the events including advertisement becomes more and more burdensome. Developing plans to make the festival more attractive without losing the core features is another concern.

Although not a food festival, the example of the *Tanabata* Festival in Shigehara, Chiba clearly shows some of these common dilemmas (Hirai, 2002). The *Tanabata* Festival originated in Chinese legend that a stellar princess and her mortal husband (Altair and Vega) meet once a year. It is celebrated on July 7th (or August 7th if the area follows the lunar calendar). In the city of Shigehara, shops on the street started a festival to attract visitors during low season in 1949. The street festival was very well received and the city and tourist association took over running the event in 1954. At the beginning, the festival hosted about 50,000 visitors over 3 days; around the year 2000, the visitor number increased to 850,000 people over 3 days. The cost of running this festival in 2000 was ¥32 million (approximately US $265,000 or €196,000). The city provides half the sum and sponsorship covers the other half. Approximately ¥5 million was spent on advertising, yet a researcher investigating the change in the festival over time (Hirai, 2002) and who was a resident of the city was unaware of the festival's advertisement activities. The current challenge is that the festival is becoming humdrum and repetitive; small shops are moving out as a wave of large-scale shops in suburban areas are threatening business. Finding funding for the Festival costs is also becoming increasingly harder. The city is hoping that this Festival will involve not only visitors from outside, but also more citizens (participation as well as volunteering) in the near future.

Another example of the challenges is the modification of local festivals when it is re-created as an event. Otake (2002) examined authenticity, aging population, and the changing nature of bureaucracy in terms of how festivals are changing to larger events. The local people considered these events as different from their own festivals: the events attracts a large number of visitors, and therefore the informality and spontaneity of the festival was lost and instead, it is structured and orchestrated, the venue and the route of parades and dancing are fixed, and the type of 'festival' food has changed. Tourists demand cleanliness and comfort when attending these events, therefore modern substitutes for old traditional equipments are needed (e.g. tourists complain about the old-fashioned fishing boat for *Awamori* wine drinking as 'dirty' or 'dingy'). The second point was related to the ageing population in the area in the context of maintaining or participating in the events. Japan's youth population (from 0 to 24 years of age) is continually decreasing. In 2000, the youth accounted for 27 per cent of the total population and they show quite different cultural values and interests (Ministry of Education, Culture, Sports, Science and Technology, 2000). In terms of passing down the history and heritage through festivals, the prospect is bleak. Otake's third finding was with respect to the bureaucracy of regional government employees who are responsible for running these event-type festivals. The person(s) in charge of the festivals will stay in the post for a short time (e.g. 5 years) and their aim is to run the festivals every year without deficits. No innovation, remodelling or changes for better or worse are welcomed. In Japan, there is a saying that the nail that sticks out gets pounded back in, so there is reluctance to make significant changes.

Food festivals and regional identity: concluding remarks

Food and drink are important parts of entertainment in Japan, especially at festivals. Geographical attributes and the historical evolution of regional cuisine helped in the formation of regional identity; and vice versa, regional identify and pride helped further sophisticate regional cuisines. Yet, regional cuisine only became more widely known through two very recent developments. The nationwide railway system spreads regional cuisine across Japan through the *ekiben* lunch box, and the Japanese people have become affluent enough to pursue the pleasure of 'food and drink'. As a reaction to rather humble food practice at home, Japanese consider pursuing gastronomic pleasure in a *Haré* environment something of importance.

The timing was right for the growth of festivals as the average Japanese became wealthy enough to travel around; interests in gourmet food was heightened; and food safety improved at the same time the health of the population faced a new challenge from a more westernized diet. Japanese food festivals today are mostly re-created events. The reasons and motivations behind re-creating these food events are manifold. It is political, it is socio-cultural, and it is economic.

The resurgence of food festivals is political because the Government of Japan feels the urgency of protecting disappearing knowledge and techniques in traditional food ways. It is also concerned about educating younger generations about nutrition, reaffirming a relationship between food production and consumption, and establishing a relationship between health and good eating habits. The Government has on its agenda that the declining primary industry must be protected for the saké of food safety and self-sufficiency. Food events are one of the best ways to promote this political agenda.

The resurgence is also socio-cultural. After a long history, the Japanese established a well-balanced Japanese-style diet, which has nearly been overturned by globalization and western-style convenient food in the last three decades. The Japanese society became excessively affluent and many people pursue the epicurean pleasure of gastronomy. Food is no longer a sustenance of life, but something to indulge one's life in. In another light, for small communities in remote areas, events focused on regional food and unique foodstuffs will put the community on the map. This, consequently, increases the self-esteem, self-efficacy, and pride of the local community population.

Finally, the resurgence of food festivals is economic. Many food festivals emerged in order to rejuvenate a community's economic activities. With various government laws and initiatives, there are a wide range of seed grants and technical support available for communities to start festival projects. Food festivals also lead to potential trade after the events between suppliers and consumers. Japanese household's spending on food and food-related expenses are steadily increasing even after the prolonged economic recession. These trends will enhance the potential of food festivals as an economic engine.

The issues the food festivals themselves face can also be looked at in terms of political, socio-cultural, and economic dimensions. It is political because when political priorities shift, there is no guarantee that the projects through *Omatsuri* Law (Law Concerning the Promotion of Sightseeing and Commerce and Industry in Designated Areas by Organizing

Events Taking Advantage of Traditional Music, Arts and Other Local Cultures) will be supported as much as today. Government officials who are involved in the community projects are usually apathetic and avoid all possible risks of failure. Moreover their involvement in the projects are of a limited term. The socio-cultural challenge is related to the lack of the next generation who are willing to continue traditions. The older generations are ageing and soon will be unable to continue to be involved in the community festivals. Consumer's tastes are also changing over time. How long the food events with the same food products can survive is another challenge. The economic challenge is finding grants and funds to continue and maintain the community events. Food events often require additional activities to keep the visitors in the area.

This chapter has attempted to illustrate the importance of understanding the role of geography, and history in the development of regional identity and cuisines. These form the basis of food and drink festivals in Japan, many of which are undergoing transformations to staged events with the assistance of some government support. While small rural community festivals are very important and hold potential for rural tourism, the changing demographics and social attitudes place some of these festivals at risk over the long term.

References

Akkeshi Town (2007). *Dai 58 kai Akkeshi Sakura/Kaki Matsuri* [The 58th Akkeshi town cherry blossom and oyster festival]. Retrieved from http://info.town.akkeshi.hokkaido.jp/pubsys/public/mu1/bin/view.rbz?cd=584

Akuné Kanko (2007). *Akuné Uni-matsuri Kaisai* [Akuné Sea Urchin Festival is coming]. Retrieved from http://www.kagoshima-mall.co.jp/akune-kanko/pickup.php

Ashkenazi, M. (1993). *Matsuri: Festivals of a Japanese Town*. University of Hawaii Press, Honolulu.

Avieli, N. (2005). Roasted pigs and bao dumplings: Festive food and imagined transnational identity in Chinese–Vietnamese festivals. *Asia Pacific Viewpoint*, 46(3), 281–293.

Bell, D. and Valentine, G. (1997). *Consuming Geographies: We Are Where We Eat*. Routledge, London.

Benride Gozaru (2007). *Hiroshima no Kaki Matsuri* [Oyster Festivals in Hiroshima]. Retrieved from http://benride.gozaru.jp/kaki.html

Bungotakada City (2007a). *Kyo no Dekigoto: Soba Matsuri Daiseikyo* [Today's event: Buckwheat noodle festival a big success]. Retrieved from http://www.city.bungotakada.oita. jp/dekigoto/bungotakadasobamatsuri.jsp

Bungotakada City (2007b). *Shoen no Sato, Tashibono Sho: Otaue Sai* [Tashibono-sho, the manor land: the Rice Planting Festival]. Retrieved from http://www.city.bungotakada.oita. jp/nourin-suisan/tashibunosyou/tasibunosyou_otaue.jsp

Chiran, T. (2007). *Akuné de Hatsu no Unidon Matsuri* [The first Sea Urchin Bowl Festival in Akuné] (2007/03/19). Japan Alternative News for Justice and New Cultures. Retrieved from http://www.janjan.jp/area/0703/0703181873/1.php

Dokkyo University (1998). Images of Japan: *Nipponjin no Shoku-seikatu*. Retrieved from http:www2.dokkyo.cajp/~japan/Japanese/sub4.htm

Ekiben no Komado (2007). *Ekiben Gakushu Shitsu* [Ekiben study room]. Retrieved from http://www.ekibento.jp/

Food Kingdom Miyagi (2007). *Miyagi, Daté-ké to Shokubunka* [Food culture of the Daté Family in Miyagi]: *Miyagi-ken Norinsuisan-bu Shoku-sangyo Shinko-ka* [Food Industry Promotion Section, Department of Agriculture, Fishery and Forestry, Miyagi prefecture]. Retrieved from http://www.foodkingdom-miyagi.jp/date/index.shtml

Fuji Television, (2000). *Iron Chef: The Official Book, edited by the Staff of Iron Chef, Translated by Kaoru Hoketsu*. Berkley Books, New York.

Fujigoko (2007). *Hibino kurashi to Matsuri – Minzoku – : it* [sic] deifies with a daily life – Folk Customs –. Retrieved from http://www.fujigoko.co.jp/yoshida/history/folk.html

Haboro T.V. (2007). Event. Retrieved from http://www.haboro.tv/top.html

Haguma, K. (2002). *Ainu Ryori Repooto* [Report on Ainu dishes]. Retrieved from http://kotahaguma.hp.infoseek.co.jp/ainuCook.htm

Haitani K. (1996). Japanese Law Names. E-Asia, University of Oregon. Retrieved from http://purl.library.uoregon.edu/e-asia/ebooks/read/jpnlawnames.pdf.

Hasegawa, K. (2002). *Matsuri: Ibento-gata to Dento-gata* [Festivals: Event style vs. traditional style]. *2002nendo Shakaigaku Jisshu Hokokusho, Dai 4Sho: Matsuri* [2002 Sociology Field Work Reports, Section 4: Festivals]. Retrieved from http://www.l.chiba-u.ac.jp/~sociology/dep/research/2002/2002report/data/sa02.pdf

Hirai, T. (2002). Maturi no Hensen – sigehara no tanabata matsuri – ibento-teki mature kara dento-teki matsui [Evolution of festival – Shigehara Tanabata Festival – from event-style festival to traditional-style festival]. *2002nendo*

Shakaigaku Jisshu Hokokusho, Dai 4Sho: Matsuri [2002 Sociology Field Work Reports, Section 4: Festivals]. Retrieved from http://www.l.chiba-u.ac.jp/~sociology/dep/research/2002/2002report/data/sa04.pdf

Hokkaido Kinenhi Risuto (2006). *Hokkaido no Mukashi* [Old times in Hokkaido]. Retrieved from http://www.geocities.jp/xxreport/html/theme_h1.html

Inoue, K. (2007). *Shirochizu* [Blank map]. Retrieved from http://www.freemap.jp/php/japan_nurinuri_1_1/japan_nurinuri.html

Kitsuki City (2007). *Hirahige Tahara Jinja no Doburoku Matsuri.* Retrieved from http://www.city.kitsuki.lg.jp/modules/itemmanager/index.php?like=0&level=4&genreid=8&itemid=172&storyid=71

Komatsu, H. (2001). *Iyo-iyo Shun no Kaki, Oishiku tabete, Kokoromo Karadamo Genki n*i [Finally oyster season; enjoy oyster and keep your mind and body healthy]. Retrieved from http://www.kireine.net/tokusyu/toku0058/body.html

Machida (2002). *Haré to Ké ni tsuite* [About 'festive' and 'ordinary'] (2002/9/9.) Retrieved from http://www7.plala.or.jp/machikun/kokoroto6.htm

MAFF (2005a). *Waga Kuni no Shoku Seikatsu no Genjou to Shokuiku no Suishin ni Tuite* [The reality of national food life and recommendation of food education]. Retrieved from http://www.maff.go.jp/syokuiku/kikakubukai.pdf

MAFF (2005b). *Chisan Chisho Suishin Keikaku* [Plans for implementing 'locally grown, locally consumed' movement]. Retrieved from http://www.maff.go.jp/chisanchisyo/jissen_plan.html

MAFF (2005c). *Iikoto Ippaosi Chisan Chisho* (Video clip). Retrieved from http://www2.maff.go.jp/cgi-bin/maff-tv/tv.cgi?ch=6&ptr=0&play=192&player=

MAFF (2005d). *Komakonai Yousui no Chichi*, Edwin Dun. The Ministry of Agriculture, Forestry and Fishery of Japan: Digital Museum of Agricultural Water, Soil and Rural in Japan. Retrieved from http://www.maff.go.jp/nouson/sekkei/midori-ijin/01hkd/01hkd.htm

MAFF (2006). *Waga Machi, Waga Mura – Shichouson no Sugata –* [My city, my village in statistics]. Retrieved from http://www.toukei.maff.go.jp/shityoson/index.html

MAFF (n.d.). What is 'Shokuiku (Food Education)'? Retrieved from http://www.maff.go.jp/english_p/shokuiku.pdf

Makino, T. (2007). *Tabemono Bunka Ko: 'Hare' no hi no shokutaku* [Thinking food culture: Food on a festive day]. Retrieved from http://www.jia-tokai.org/sibu/architect/2007/01/tabemono.htm

Ministry of Education, Culture, Sports, Science and Technology (2000). *Heisei 12-nen do Waga Kuni no Bunkyo Shisaku* [Year 2000 National Policies on Education and Culture]. Retrieved from http://www.mext.go.jp/b-menu/hakusho/html/hpad200001

Mori, T. (1998). Yosakoi Festival in Kochi. Retrieved from http://www.yosakoi.com/jp/AboutYosakoi.html

Niigata Shoku no Jin (2007). Niigata *Shokuno-Jin* [Battle of food]. Retrieved from http://www.shokuno-jin.com/index.html

Okhotsk Sanchoku Asaichi (2003). *Ima ga Shun no Shokuzai* [Food ingredients in season]. Retrieved from http://asaichi.org/01syun/imasyun.html

Okinawa Prefectural Government (2003). Okinawa Cuisine. Retrieved from http://www.wonder-okinawa.jp/026/

Onshindo Pharmacy (2007). Food and Culture No. 3. Retrieved from http:ww7.tiki.ne.jp/~onshin/food13.htm

Origuchi, S. (2004). *Ho to suru hanashi: Matrsuri no hassei sono ichi* [Stories of heart: Origins of festivals, No. 1]. Reconstructed from *Kodai-kenkyu Minzokugaku hen Dai ichi* [Anthropology Volume 1] (1929) and *Origuchi Shinobu Zenshu 2* [Shinobu Origuchi Anthology Volume 2] (1995) for Internet Library Aozora. Retrieved from http://www.aozora.gr.jp/cards/000933/files/13213_14433.html

Otake, Y. (2002). *Matsurino Chuukaisha no Nayami* [Dilemma of festival intermediaries]. *2002nendo Shakaigaku Jisshu Hokokusho, Dai 4Sho: Matsuri* [2002 Sociology Field Work Reports, Section 4: Festivals]. Retrieved from http://www.l.chiba-u.ac.jp/~sociology/dep/research/2002/2002report/data/sa05.pdf

OVOP (n.d.). Oita OVOP International Exchange Promotion Committee. Retrieved from http://www.ovop.jp/jp/index.html

Pacifico Yokohama (2007). *Umaimono Samitto* [Tasty Food Summit]. Retrieved from http://www.pacifico.co.jp/information/archives/information_070201_umaimonosummit.pdf

Plam Record (2002). *Yosakoi Soran towa* [What is Yosako Soran?]. Retrieved from http://www.plamrec.com/yosakoi-dans2.htm

Rurubu.com (2006). *Nippon no ibento sahchi* [Event search in Japan]. Retrieved from http://www.rurubu.com/event/list.asp

Satomi, M. (2005). *Niigata no Doburoku 7-shu o nomi kurabe* [Tasting seven *Doburoku* varieties from Niigata] *Dancyu* 02.03.2005. Issue No. 11. Retrieved from http://www.president.co.jp/dan/special/sake/011.html

Segawa, K. (2001). *Shokuseikatsu no rekishi* [History of foodways]. Kodansha, Tokyo.

Shigeto (2005). *Shoku kiten ni Hito no arikata made* [From food as a starting point to people's ways of existence]. *Kagawa daigaku meiyo kyoju yamano yoshimasa 'Chokubunka to oishisa o kangaeru' semina* [Seminar on Food Way and Tastiness by Prof. Emeritus Yoshimasa Yamano, Kagawa University] (27.01.2005). Retrieved from http://www.palge.com/news/h17/1/seminar20050128.htm

Shunshun-do (2006). *Shonau no Ten-nen Iwagaki wa Natsu ga Shun* [Natural rock oyster from Shonai is Best in Summer]. Retrieved from http://www.ekamo.com/goods/fish/kaki.html

Slow Food Japan (2007). *SFJ ni tsuite* [About us]. Retrieved from http://www.slowfoodjapan.net/about_us/story.html

Sushi Master (2000). *Sushi towa? Sushi no rekishi* [What is sushi? The History of Sushi]. Retrieved from http://sushi-master.com/jpn/whatis/history.html

Suzuki, T. (2003). *Amerika Komugi Senryaku to Nipponjin no Shoku Seikatsu* [America's Wheat Strategies and Japanese Food Life]. Fujiwara-shoten, Tokyo.

Toshi Noson Gyoson Koryu Kasseika Kikou (2007). *'Gyojishoku tte nandarou* [What is event food?]'. *Noson Asbi-gaku Nyumon: Chiiki ni nezashita shoku-bunka* [Introduction to farming village leisure study: Food culture rooted to the area]. Retrieved from http://www.kouryu.or.jp/asobi/2003syoku/d/2.htm

Toyoyoshi, H. (2006). *Hitoaji chigau Naruko: Doburoku senryaklu jimono no aji, shokuno hashirani* [Different Naruko: Doburoku strategy and local cuisine as a culinary pillar]. The Sankei Shinbun Web-site (12.09.2006). Retrieved from http://www.sankei.co.jp/chiho/tohoku/061209/thk06120900.htm

Wikipedia (2007a). Sushi. Retrieved from http://ja.wikipedia.org/wiki/%E5%AF%BF%E5%8F%B8

Wikipedia (2007b). Ota-mura. Retrieved from http://ja.wikipedia.org/wiki/%E5%A4%A7%E7%94%B0%E6%9D%91

Yamada (2002). Oister [sic]. Kagawa Nutrition University Bunka-happyokai 2002 (Takahashi Katsumi Seminar). Retrieved from http://www.eiyo.ac.jp/bunkahappyou/happyou2002/H14HP/tka2/frame.htm

Yonehara, K. (2002). *Matsuri-en ga dekirutoki – 'Yosakoi' o toshite* [When a festival is born]. *2002nendo Shakaigaku Jisshu Hokokusho, Dai 4Sho: Matsuri* [2002 Sociology Field Work Reports, Section 4: Festivals]. Retrieved from http://www.l.chiba-u.ac.jp/~sociology/dep/research/2002/2002report/data/sa03.pdf

Yosanet (2007). Yosakoi Soran Matsuri 16th in Sapporo: History. Retrieved from http://www.yosanet.com/yosakoi/history/outline.php

Zenchinren (n.d.). *Zenkoku Chinmi Shoukougyo Kyodo Kumiai Rengokai* [United Alliance of National Delicacy Business Cooperations]. Retrieved from http://www.chinmi.org/

Zenkoku Joho Gakushu Shinko Kyokai (n.d.). *Shokumotsu no Rekishi* [History of food]. Retrieved from http://www.shikakunavi.net/kids/gika/shokumotu1.html.

CHAPTER 16

The Airey's Inlet Farmers' Market: Where the coast meets the ranges

Anne-Marie Hede

The growth of farmers' markets in Australia during the past 5 years is nothing short of phenomenal. There are now about 80 markets in operation around Australia (Adams, 2007). This case study examines a farmers' market held in the small coastal town of Airey's Inlet, which is located on the Great Ocean Road, in the south-west of Victoria, Australia. The Great Ocean Road, an attraction in itself, has an international reputation, and extends 300 kilometres from Torquay to Warrnambool. It is one the most popular tourist attractions in Australia, attracting over 6 million tourists each year. Towns and beaches are scattered along the Great Ocean Road, some of which are large, such as Torquay and Lorne. Hence, there is no shortage of tourists for Airey's Inlet to attract, but in a competitive marketplace, there is the challenge to actually motivate tourists to stop and spend some time in the town.

Research was undertaken on the Airey's Inlet Farmers' Market using a range of data collection methods including in-depth interviews, participant observation and media analysis, during 2005 and 2006. The farmers' market commenced in late 2005, and was the brainchild of Paul Angeloni, a local resident and tourism operator. He felt that a farmers' market would be sympathetic to the values of the Airey's Inlet community, provide an opportunity to attract tourists to stop in Airey's Inlet on their 'Great Ocean Road drive', and be the conduit for social cohesion within the community. A market committee was formed under the auspice of the Airey's Inlet Hall Committee, and comprised seven local residents with a range of skills. The Airey's Inlet Farmers' Market was set up as a not-for-profit entity, with proceeds made to be channelled back to fund the upgrade of the hall's kitchen to a commercial standard. It was hoped that such an upgrade would enable the community to then use the hall as a venue for a food and wine festival, and other community events, in the future.

The farmers' market produced a number of outcomes for the Airey's Inlet community. Many of these were expected, but as the markets and the research progressed, it became clear that many of these were surprisingly unexpected.

Social outcomes

The markets provided opportunities for people to socialize. This was often nearby to a stall, and most frequently while drinking coffee or listening to the music that was provided. Young children were seen nearby the entertainment, dancing and singing – which very often became the entertainment in itself.

This created a good ambience and a festive atmosphere at the markets. Like other tourism special events, some of the key motives for attending events is to socialize and to be with other people who are also enjoying themselves.

The markets provided a relaxed and friendly atmosphere for people to socialize. Indeed, one of the committee members interviewed for the study of the market talked about the positive emotions felt around the markets. People were happy, friendly and enjoyed the company of others, including attendees and the farmers. He said:

... (The markets are a) bit like your birthday when people bring you presents. There's that look of happiness and expectation what it might be or what it means.

The markets provided an opportunity for attendees and the farmers to exchange information about food and the destination. Farmers at the markets share their knowledge about their produce, and how it should be stored and processed, and were quick to point out the differences between their produce and that available elsewhere at the 'big stores'. Farmers exchanged recipes with attendees, and likewise attendees were doing the same with other attendees.

Not all the social outcomes of the market were positive however. One committee member noted that the market manager, who was a volunteer, put a considerable amount of his own leisure, and work, time into management of the market. This appeared to be at the detriment of his health and his business.

... One of the problems you have with something like this ... like Tim, he's done (all this work) on a volunteer basis and you'll find if you talk to him now, he's a tired man. He's just, he's really almost over it, which is unfortunate because what he's created is so worthwhile (Peter).

Economic outcomes

Without an economic impact analysis, it's almost impossible to determine the economic outcomes of the farmers' market. Some quantitative and qualitative indicators, however, provide some indications that the markets were successful from an economic perspective.

For example, it appeared that many of the attendees at the farmers' markets were shopping rather than simply browsing.

People come and just buy from, you know, three or four or five vendors and they come with the money to do it. They bring their carry bags and you know, they're happy to leave with their carry bags full or several of them. They'll load up and take it back to the car. It's really quite astounding really.

Reports in the media indicated that vendors experienced strong sales at the markets, particularly at the January market. The local newspaper reported that 'one of the standouts was the Afghani Kasoundi ... producers of the product had sold 63 jars in more than 5 hours at another market', but at the Airey's Inlet Farmers' Market, they sold 100 jars in an hour. Furthermore, based on participant observation, one vendor indicated to another vendor that they had sold 200 units of one product which sold for Aus$3.00 per unit. While this is a high volume, but low unit price, product at the market, other produce at the market has a similar profile (e.g. fruit and vegetables). On the other hand, some of the produce at the market is more expensive. For example, the olive oil is priced between Aus$15 and $20 per bottle, as was the wine that was available at the January market.

Environmental outcomes

There is an obvious connection between environmental sustainability and farmers' markets, which very much stems from the connections between farmers' markets and the Slow Food Movement. One key factor contributing to positive environmental impacts of the farmers' markets is the reduction in 'food miles' travelled. As one interviewee indicated 'as a small town, we always have to leave town to find fresh produce'. Residents of Airey's Inlet usually travel to the supermarkets of Geelong, Anglesea, or Lorne, which are approximately 30, 10 and 25 kilometres away, respectively. Like most supermarkets in Australia, the fresh produce available in them is sourced from all over Australia and internationally. Furthermore, many of the farmers and value-adders at the markets would have likely distributed their produce outside of Airey's Inlet, and most likely outside of the Surf Coast Shire, had they not had the opportunity to distribute their produce at the Airey's Inlet Farmers' Market. By reducing the number of food miles that fresh produce travels 'to the plate', a raft of factors detrimental to the environment is reduced. For example, fuel consumption is reduced, not only with regard to delivery of the produce to the consumer, but also with regard to the delivery of waste produce to landfill sites. Furthermore, the packaging of produce at farmers' markets is less substantial than that at supermarkets. Hence, waste is reduced. Overall, there is no doubt that the ecological footprint of those households purchasing at the markets was reduced.

A major outcome of the farmers' market is the development of a fruit and vegetable co-operative comprised around 20 to 25 families in the Airey's Inlet community. Indeed this is a legacy of the markets. The co-operative now sources fresh produce fortnightly, from a farmer in the hinterland of the Otway Ranges, who is also a vendor at the farmers' market. One person from Aireys' Inlet is rostered to collect the produce each fortnight. One interviewee described what is like to be involved in the co-operative:

To make it sustainable, the (delivery person) gets their produce for free and they get paid $20 ... (we get) good access to really great fresh produce, organic produce. And that's been a bit of a spin-off from the market. So the market itself, you know has a really nice relationship with what people in town think, which is important (Eliza).

Reasons for success

A number of reasons contributed to these outcomes, including:

- The role of a champion.
- The compatibility with the Airey's Inlet community and their shared values.
- A strategic management's approach.

These factors seemed to have resulted in the amelioration of a range of potential negative impacts of such an event on a small host community.

The role of the champion played an integral role in the success of the markets. The development of a farmers' market was astute as it seems to have aligned with the values of the Airey's Inlet community. One interviewee thought that a 'farmers' market works, as opposed to any other market in Airey's, rather than some of the busier towns (along the Great Ocean Road) because it is a bit more laid back' (Peter). While this study did not measure community pride, it seems that the markets further established, and perhaps, improved community pride in Airey's Inlet.

A not-for-profit management structure was selected for the Airey's Inlet Farmers' Market. Some farmers' markets in Australia, but not all of them, are managed on a for-profit basis. Such an approach would have been fatal for this particular market, as it is likely that it would have gained very little support from the local community. Furthermore, the committee was aware that a farmers' market, while a seemingly compatible concept for the town, would encounter issues of sustainability. As such, they were able to recognize the signs of 'volunteer burnout', and committee members were able to 'rise to the challenge' in the management of the farmers' market and play a more active role in its management.

The farmers' markets appealed to both local residents and, according to one of the interviewees, a reasonable number of tourists interrupted their journey along the Great Ocean Road to visit the Airey's Inlet Farmers' Market. The farmers' markets seem to have ameliorated the negative impacts of tourism on the town that might have occurred had another type of event been staged by the community.

Challenges and opportunities for the future

Farmers' markets, like all special events, are not easy to organize. In rural and regional areas, in particular, their management, administration and operations are most often undertaken by volunteers, who very often have other equally important commitments. Volunteer burnout is a major issue for events, and farmers' markets unfortunately do not escape this peril. This issue emerged in the Airey's Inlet Farmers' Market, which will undoubtedly continue to be a challenge for the market's continued sustainability.

One other issue that emerged, which is also a challenge for farmers' markets generally, is that it is often very difficult to attract large numbers of farmers to distribute their produce at farmers' markets. There are barriers to participation, such as time. This impacts the range and quantity of produce that is available at farmers' markets. The Airey's Inlet Farmers' Market found it difficult to sustain an optimum number of farmers participating in the markets, which has implications for its continued sustainability.

The future of farmers' markets in Australia and New Zealand seems to be positive. Consumers are increasingly looking for fresh produce, which is grown and/or processed locally. Farmers' markets are an ideal venue to satisfy this shift in consumer values. The sector is establishing networks and standards for farmers' markets. For example, the Australian Farmers Market Association and the Victorian Farmers' Market Association have developed strategic plans for the development of farmers' markets in these regions, which include marketing, training and capacity building initiatives.

Reference

Adams, J. (2007). *Guide to Farmers' Markets: Australia and New Zealand*. R.M. Williams Classic Publications, Mosman.

CHAPTER **17**

Farmers' markets as events for local cultural consumption: The Otago Farmers' Market (Dunedin, New Zealand) explored

Richard Mitchell and David Scott

Introduction

In many ways farmers' markets are a microcosm of the issues that face consumers of food and tourism experiences (or products and services?). In particular, the omnipotent (the ever increasing) influence of globalization on our foodways (Hall and Mitchell, 2001) has lead to arise in demand from within much of the burgeoning middle-class consumer markets of Western society for what is perceived as *local* food. Individuals are attempting to reconnect with the local through their eating habits: seeking out locally produced foodstuffs; dining at restaurants that provide local dishes and use local products; demanding labelling of foods that indicate its provenance, both at retail outlets and sites of consumption. Cook and Crang (1996) suggest that such a connection between the (local) place and food is an attempt to 're-enchant' food products, giving them meaning beyond that of a globalized commodity.

Tourism, by its very nature, is also concerned with the local as it is ultimately about the differences between places (Relph, 1996) and several authors have suggested that food is an important element in creating and reinforcing such differences (e.g. Hjalager and Corigliano, 2000; Hall et al., 2003; Cohen and Avieli, 2004; Quan and Wang, 2004, Hashimoto and Telfer, 2006; Scott, 2006; Mitchell, 2008). Hall, et al. (2003, p. 32), for example, suggest that 'local food and drink networks, the development of food trails, and the rediscovery of farmer's markets – often frequented by daytrippers and tourists are testimony to the importance of the local within the global'. Some have also suggested that local food can ascribe a greater degree of 'authenticity' to the tourism experience (Quan and Wang, 2004; Urry, 2005).

This chapter explores how one market, the Otago Farmers' Market (Dunedin, New Zealand), is constructed as a social space and how this can inform our understanding of the nature of the attraction of farmers' markets for tourists. We suggest here that farmers' markets are dynamic places where different spaces and performances emerge providing different tourist experiences with different meanings. The analysis goes beyond the material world of local food to explore the social and cultural construction of the farmers' market as a place of public performance.

The Otago Farmers' Market

Like the New Zealand Farmers' Market scene more broadly, the Otago Farmers' Market has experienced rapid growth. The

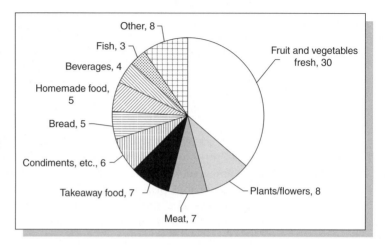

Figure 17.1
Vendor categories at the Otago Farmers' Market
(*Source*: http://www.otagofarmers market.org.nz/vendor_list.aspx)

Otago Farmers' Market was established in Dunedin (a city of 120,000 people in the south of the South Island) in 2003. It is operated by a charitable trust (Otago Farmers' Market Trust) that resulted from the Farmers Market Project Group, which began discussing the possibility of establishing a Farmers' Market in 2001 with the assistance of the Dunedin City Council. The Trust received seed funding from the Dunedin City Council and Otago Community Trust and the first market took place in March 2003 with 23 vendors who took a 'great leap of faith' with the Otago Farmers' Market Trust (http://www.otagofarmersmarket.org.nz/). Less than 4 years later it regularly has 35–40 vendors (up to 75 during the high season) and around 4,000–5,000 people visit the market each Saturday (around double that for the pre-Christmas market). There is now a list of more than 80 vendors that attend the market – some year round and others seasonally – providing everything from fruit and vegetables to cut flowers, tea blended by a local merchant and various outlets selling value-added products such as cakes, hot food and pies (often made from raw materials supplied by other vendors) (see Figure 17.1).

The Trust actively manages the mix of products available at the market to ensure that they '... have plenty of everything but not too much of anything' (http://www.otagofarmersmarket.org.nz/). The Trust consists of five Trustees, a Minutes Secretary, and an Advisory Board (all voluntary) and it employs three part-time staff and a pool of volunteers to assist in the weekly operation of the market and undertake an important public liaison role. Marketing of the market is a key role and this is becoming more sophisticated as its income increases and the Trust becomes aware of the needs of both consumers and vendors. This has included research undertaken on consumers and, more recently, the development of a strategic plan that includes a significant marketing component. As part of its role as charitable trust, the Otago Farmers' Market Trust is now also able to regularly offer prizes and scholarships to horticultural students who take part in sponsorship of the Gardens in Schools scheme and offer grants to local community horticultural initiatives.

There are several indicators of the Otago Farmers' Market's success as a local community initiative including the fact that in its first year of operation it was estimated to contribute at least NZ\$2.25 million to the Dunedin economy (Guthrie et al., 2006 after MacKenzie, 2004). The Otago Farmers' Market Trust also received a community award for 'Heritage and Environment' and the award summary says: 'The Otago Farmers Market Trust benefits the entire community – consumers, vendors, charities and tourists – while adding to the vibrancy of Dunedin's inner city. It is a fantastic initiative and tonight we celebrate its success' (Trustpower Dunedin Community Awards, 2005, p.3). It has also assisted in the transformation of an important heritage precinct surrounding the historical Dunedin railway station. Several other craft and art markets have established alongside the Otago Farmers' Market (some surviving, others not) and it is no coincidence that there have also been some recent residential developments in disused industrial buildings in the immediate area. The railway station is an important hub for some local tourism activities (e.g. a heritage railway excursion, sports museum and art gallery), and the addition of the market on a Saturday adds an important dimension to this area for tourists.

While tourist numbers at the market appear to be low, there is evidence that at least some tourists are present each week. For example a survey of 250 market-goers undertaken in May 2006 (generally considered to be in the low season for tourists) found 8 per cent of those surveyed were from outside Dunedin, including some from overseas (Bastiaans and Mitchell, 2006). Anecdotal evidence suggests that the number of international visitors would be much higher during the high season (November through February) and there are also around 15 per cent of visitors that are students from the University of Otago campus nearby (Bastiaans and Mitchell, 2006), most of whom are temporary migrants to the city for their studies.

Bastiaans and Mitchell (2006) also found, amongst other things, the following key characteristics of the visit for consumers:

- The market was the primary reason for the travelling to the central city that day for 72 per cent of those surveyed.

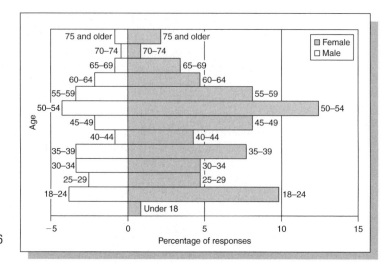

Figure 17.2
Demographic
pyramid for Otago
Farmers' Market
attendees May 2006
(N = 250)

- The 'best things about the market' were (an open-ended question):
  - the atmosphere (15 per cent of respondents),
  - a specific product (14 per cent),
  - the fact that it is 'local' (11 per cent),
  - friendly people (10 per cent).
- When asked to provide three adjectives that described the market the top responses were:
  - fresh (49 per cent of respondents, aside from this, few responses described the food),
  - friendly (21 per cent),
  - variety (15 per cent),
  - vibrant/bustling/busy (14 per cent),
  - great (12 per cent),
  - fun (12 per cent).
- The market was predominantly attended by women, with the largest age group being 50–54 (16.7 per cent) (see Figure 17.2).

The analysis and discussion that follows goes beyond this basic contextual analysis to include a deeper analysis of the data gathered by Bastiaans and Mitchell and observation of the Otago Farmers' Market over a period of 3 years. Observation of the market is informed by several perspectives. Firstly the authors are both academics specializing in the analysis of food and tourism; one from a consumer behaviour perspective, the other a more sociological perspective (although this is obviously a simplification of their ontological and epistemological perspectives). This is also informed by the personal interest of two well-travelled, widely read, gastronomes; one with extensive food and beverage management experience and the other with less formal experience in the area of gastronomy. Lastly it is informed by one 'outsider' who visits the market infrequently and one 'insider' who visits regularly and who was an official advisor to the Otago Farmers' Market Trust for a period of 12 months.

The metamorphosis of the Otago Farmers' Market

In many ways the observations of the Otago Farmers' Market reflect those made almost 15 years prior of the Midville Market in the USA by McGrath et al. (1993). One observation made in both cases is particularly pertinent to this discussion: that pertaining to the way in which they are both performances constructed in time and space. McGrath et al. (1993, p. 299) observe the changing nature of the consumers at the market: starting with the 'Diehards' between 6 a.m. and 7:30 a.m. looking for the 'best and freshest'; then 'The Sociable Diehards' between 7:30 and 9 a.m. who desire good produce and need to meet friends and vendors; to 'The Very Social' between 9 and 11 a.m. who 'spend more time talking with acquaintances than shopping'; and, finally; 'The Late People, Bargain Hunters and Night People' from 11 a.m. until 2 p.m. with no concern for the quality of their purchases or desire for interaction with others.

At the Otago Farmers' Market there is a similar rhythm with early 'diehard' shoppers arriving before the market officially opens at 8 a.m. There can be around 100 of these shoppers and they tend to be drawn from the same group of market-goers who stay for a short period of time and shop at their regular vendors. The number steadily grows over the next hour or so with a mixture of shoppers and socializers until some time during the morning there is a shift in the market experience. This shift sees a turn towards the more sociable market-goer and, in particular, a far greater number of students begin to arrive and the performance of the market begins to change. In a count of market-goers entering the market in May 2006, for example, it was observed that more than one-third (37 per cent) of all students visiting the market arrived between 11 a.m. and 12 noon, so that they accounted for more than one in five people (21 per cent) arriving at that time compared with fewer than 15 per cent at all other times (just two percent prior to 8 a.m.). The market closes between noon and 1 p.m. and few market-goers arrive after noon, but those that do, tend to be similar to McGrath et al.'s final classification who are neither interested in the quality of their purchase nor in social interaction. The changing of the market is gradual and, while more students arrive in the latter part of the morning, it is difficult and perhaps even pointless to suggest any particular time that sees the market move from one space to another. It is perhaps better to suggest that it is a gradual metamorphosis.

Students are clearly important agents in the transformation of the market experience each week. At a purely transactional level, for example, they have a much higher propensity to purchase food and drink to consume at the market (52 per cent doing so compared with 30 per cent of non-students). Students also stay average of 10 minutes longer at the market than others (45 minutes compared with 35 minutes), despite spending around half the amount that others do (an average of NZ$17 compared with NZ$33 by others). Beyond the transactional the presence of students (and other more sociable actors) sees the mood of the market change. Here as the numbers of serious shoppers begin to drop off, the pace becomes a little slower even though the number of people does not and people take time to chat with each other. Something to eat and coffee to wash it down with becomes the excuse for interaction and weekly catch up with friends. As an article in one of New Zealand's leading food and wine magazines (*Cuisine*) put it: 'Come Saturday morning and there's only one place to be in Dunedin – at the Otago Framers' Market in the north car park of the famous railway station. ... by 9 a.m. it is thronging with customers, the aromas of fresh coffee mingling with roast pork, frying bacon, fresh bread, crêpes and whitebait fritters' (Cuncliffe, 2007, p.183). Lengthy waits are normal at the bacon-buttie, coffee and crepe stands and while people wait they wander off to make their purchases or catch up with friends. The few tables that are available become full and conversations occur between groups of (mostly young) people about what they are planning for the weekend and '... isn't the market just fantastic...'. Few discuss the produce and fewer still are purchasing more than a few fruit and vegetables. Conversations with the vendors are rare in this space (except for those visiting the market for the first time or those from out of town). As part of the backdrop, the vendor now becomes an object to be gazed upon and his/her produce grazed on.

In this space one vendor's theatrical manner is an important part of the performance of the market. As Cuncliffe (2007, p.184) observes, the vendor '... entices and cajoles passersby into tasting his farmhouse range with all the energy and verve of a Cockney barrowman. Many is the showman who would be proud of his patter'. This is a larger than life pantomime by a true 'showman' with audience participation rather than engagement between vendor and market-goer. His performance is one that polarizes market-goers, amusing and entertaining to those there to g(r)aze upon the market, but sometimes irritating to those there for serious shopping.

In an interesting corollary to the observations made by these authors, Cuncliffe (2007) describes, with only two exceptions (a mushroom grower and a butcher), vendors that provide value-added food, many of whom are selling their products to be consumed at the market. There is no mention of fruit, vegetables, or fish, but rather pies, breads, bacon butties, roast pork, whitebait fritters, crêpes, organic beer, confectionary and tarts. This is an article targeted at food and wine enthusiasts travelling to Dunedin for a 'foodie' experience and it is directing the tourist to what they should see, taste and smell at the market. It describes a space of performance, social interaction and entrepreneurship not one of farming, fresh produce and retail. To Cuncliffe at least, the tourist's space is that of the performance and not the early morning space of 'diehard' shopper.

The Otago Farmers' Market, then, is a dynamic space whose predominant mood changes through the course of the market. Beginning with the mundane everyday experience of the 'diehards' early in the morning and progressing to a space of spectatorial performance. This is not to suggest that the space of the diehard is not one that is devoid of meaning for the tourist. On the contrary, this is a space of interaction and intersubjectivity; one that is shared by vendor and market-goer in a way that the performance is not.

Earlier in the morning market-goers tend to be efficient with their time, buying what they need and then leaving. The brevity of the visit, however, belies the depth of meaning of this space. The 'die-hard' (for want of a better description) and the vendor create a space based on a sense of community, which has elements of both Holloway and Kneafsey's (2000) 'alternative' and 'reactionary/nostalgic' spaces. Here the market-goer is making a conscious stand against the dominance of the supermarket, where freshness and provenance are paramount. But there is also a very strong sense of nostalgia and relationships between vendors and these serious shoppers flourish. This is a dialogic performance where conversations (some lengthy, but more often than not very brief) will be had, including what is fresh or seasonal (sometimes including what is growing in the market-goer's garden); the best way to prepare or store something (both from the vendor and the market-goer); or advice on the care of plants. The market-goer and vendor are equals in a community where the use of first names is relatively common and knowledge and experience of food is shared. In some cases this nostalgia is more than one of an idealized past and reflects purchases from the farm gate made during a market-goers childhood or earlier years. This is because several of the fruit and vegetable vendors are well-known local market gardeners or orchardists from Central Otago (around two hours away) that operate very popular farm gate operations but which generally began to decline in the mid-1990s. In a very real sense these vendors and market-goers are reliving the relationships of the past.

This is also a space built on trust between the market-goer and the vendor. Market-goers in this space are often loyal to just a few vendors, shopping at the same vendors week-in, week-out (hence the relatively short period of time spent at the market). The absence of a favourite vendor can be quite disconcerting for some in this space and, rather than purchase a similar product from another vendor, they may choose not to purchase that item until the following week.

This, then, is a space (dominant in the early part of the market) that is a construction of the everyday, one built on routine, loyalty and trust. To a number of authors (e.g. Bessière, 1998; Holloway and Kneafsey, 2000; Hall et al., 2003) this is also an 'authentic' space for tourists, somehow 'backstage' (MacCannell, 1976) and engaging. To McGrath et al. (1993) this would be the authentic market, while the performance (dominant in the latter part of the market) would be more representative of the 'artificial' and 'ambient' to be gazed upon (Urry, 1990) by those that visit when this space dominates. This is not to suggest that these spaces are mutually exclusive. Indeed, at some times of the morning (especially mid-morning) market-goers may choose to operate in both spaces. For example, they might engage in discussions with vendors about the produce and make serious purchase decisions early in their visit and then move to the more performance-oriented space, meeting with friends for coffee later in their visit (perhaps taking their shopping to the car in-between). Some may also easily switch from one space to the next with ease (perhaps creating a space in-between), while others may not. In choosing to visit the market early, however, most 'diehards' (especially those visiting before 8 a.m.) are consciously denying the performance space that emerges later in the morning. Thus they delimit this space for themselves and, perhaps, making it more authentic, exotic and 'the other' for the tourist that happens upon the market early on a Saturday morning.

While several of the observations made in this section are not necessarily new, the way in which these two spaces interact is significant for our understanding of the attraction of farmers' markets for tourists. The melding of the everyday and the performance spaces creates a dynamic place full of charm, atmosphere, ambience and authenticity and this is the stuff that tourists desire. So what, then, are the lessons from this case study.

Situating Farmers' Markets as sites of consumable touristic experiences

Farmers' markets can be considered creative spaces; sites where culture(s) transfer food from the stuff of an everyday commodity to the possibilities of the experiences surrounding the culturally embedded nature of the value-added product constructed for ingestion in situ. This is suggestive of the farmers' market as a site of performance. As discussed earlier, farmers' markets have assumed the mantle of sites for the public display of resistance for both consumer and producer. Indeed in the case of many farmers' markets this extends to the (re)appropriation of public space. Changfoot (2006, p.2) suggests, this resistance as allowing 'incursions into public space ..., even if only temporarily, transforming space into theatre that involves citizen participation and engagement, empowering the people represented'. If farmers' markets can be considered as sites of theatricality, then apropos, this may take a number of forms.

It has been suggested that farmers' markets can be considered as falling within two key categories with respect to the performances enacted by the various actors involved. Tiemann (2004a,b) has suggested that farmers' markets might successfully be examined as dichotomous sites of performance. Using Pine and Gilmore's (1999) construct of the experience economy, Tienmann, argues that some farmers' markets may be considered as *experience* markets, whereby the provision of food as a commodity is enhanced through valorization by experiences produced and consumed. Conversely, those farmers' markets that provide food as materiality of the everyday are considered as *indigenous* markets (Tiemann, 2004b). Key amongst the criteria distinguishing performance from indigenous markets is the construction and performance of the *consumer* as a sophisticated individual. This suggests that experienced farmers' markets can be seen as sites that allow the performance of distinction (Bourdieu, 1984), spaces that offer the potentiality for touristic experience of the exotic. Implicit in Tiemann's argument is that the indigenous market is a presentation of the everyday and therefore it cannot add value for the tourist. However, contrary to Tiemann's assertions, if performance of the 'everyday' is seen as an authentic manifestation of culture (Inglis, 2005), the indigenous market becomes exotic to the tourist through the very banality which locates it as the everyday.

The Otago Farmers' Market appears to contradict the experience-indigenous dichotomous classification proposed by Tiemann (2004b). It is clear from the discussion above that the Otago Farmers' Market is indeed, both an experience and an indigenous market: metamorphosing from indigenous to experience over the course of the market. The space of the indigenous market a key component of the use of the market for what is seen as an everyday purchase, is the farmers' market as a space for the (re)construction of social interactions. These take the form of intersubjective performance between stallholder and consumer, consumer and consumer, and stallholder and other stallholders. In effect the farmers' market is enabling the construction of an 'imagined community' (Anderson, 1991) as a response to what Beck (1992) considers the risk inherent in late modernity. This legitimizes the claim for farmers' markets as a postmodern response (Cross, 2000) to the massification and impersonality many consumers associate with supermarkets. As the day progresses the role of the market changes from a place for the (re)appropriation of public space for the performance of 'community', to a place for spectacle. The performances of both stallholders and consumers change and interactions change from being intersubjective to subjective. In this experience space, perhaps more appropriately labelled as a *performance* space, the market changes from a place of engagement to a place to see and be seen and g(r)aze on a (disembodied) material culture through subjective performances. In this space where the consumer is constructed as a modern day version of Beaudelaire's 19th Century Parisien *flâneur* (literally someone who strolls the streets to be seen (Tester, 1994)) and/or *voyeur* (those there to gaze upon others and to g(r)aze upon the market). Moreover, the stallholders' performance indeed, product, changes. Whether intentional or not, the emphasis on selling food as a commodity is gradually replaced with an awareness of the importance of the g(r)azing of the experience market and value-added products come to the fore. The more entrepreneurial of the vendors have added value to their raw product to be grazed upon on site rather than to be taken home and consumed later (e.g. a fishmonger cooking and selling whitebait fritters or a pork producer selling hot roast pork sandwiches in an adjoining stall). In doing so this transforms their product from indigenous ('natural') to experiential ('cultural') thus changing the tourism experience from one that is uncontrived (authentic) to one that is staged (performed). Both spaces are attractive to tourists but their construction, meaning and performance are very different (Hall, 2007).

To speak of the farmers' market as a place of authentic tourist experience is therefore potentially to deny the complexity of the way in which markets are performed: they are dynamic, living places. It is also not wise to categorize markets as 'this type or that', as they may represent different spaces at different times or indeed may be constructing two or spaces simultaneously. As Maclaran and Brown (2005, p. 317) after Casey (1996, p. 27) suggest when discussing the spatiotemporal dynamic of the festival malls '… places are much more than inert geographical loci, they are subject to processes of change. Places take place, so to speak, they occur as events or enactments. 'Places not only are, … they happen' '.

References

Anderson, B.R.O. (1991). *Imagined Communities: Reflections on the Origin and Spread of Nationalism*. London, Verso.

Bastiaans, M. and Mitchell, R.D. (2006). *Otago Farmers' Market: Analysis of 2006 Visitor Survey*. University of Otago, Dunedin. Unpublished report.

Beck, U. (1992). *Risk Society: Towards a New Modernity*. Sage Publications, London.

Bessière, J. (1998). Local development and heritage: Traditional food and cuisine as tourist attractions in rural areas. *Sociologica Ruralis*, 38(1), 21–34.

Bourdieu, P. (1984). *Distinction: A Social Critique of the Judgement of Taste*. Routledge and Kegan Paul, London.

Casey, E.S. (1996). How to get from space to place in a fairly short stretch of time: Phenomenological prolegomena. In Feld, S. and Basso, K.H. (eds.) *Senses of Place*. School of American Research Press, Santa Fe, pp. 13–52.

Changfoot, N. (2006). Local Activism and Neoliberalism: Performing Neoliberal Citizenship as Resistance. *Proceedings of the 78th Annual Conference Canadian Political Science Association (Association Canadienne de Science Politique)*. 1–3 June 2006, York University (Canada). http://www.cpsa-acsp.ca/papers-2006/Changfoot.pdf

Cohen, E. and Avieli, N. (2004). Food in tourism: Attraction and impediment. *Annals of Tourism Research*, 31(4), 755–778.

Cook, I. and Crang, P. (1996). The world on a plate: Culinary cultures, displacement and geographical knowledges. *Journal of Material Culture*, 1(2), 131–153.

Cross, J.C. (2000). Street vendors, modernity and postmodernity: Conflict and compromise in the global economy. *International Journal of Sociology and Social Policy*, 20(1/2), 29–51.

Cuncliffe, S. (2007). City of secrets. *Cuisine*, 124, 178–188.

Dyer, A. (1991). *Decline and growth in English towns, 1400–1640*. Cambridge University Press, 1995, Cambridge.

Guthrie, J., Guthrie, A., Lawson, R. and Cameron, A. (2006). Farmers' markets: The small business counter-revolution in food production and retailing. *British Food Journal*, 108(7), 560–573.

Hall, C.M. (2007). Response to Yeoman et al.: The fakery of 'The authentic tourist'. *Tourism Management*, 28(4), 1139–1140.

Hall, C.M. and Mitchell, R.D. (2001). We are what we eat: Tourism, culture and the globalisation and localisation of cuisine. *Tourism Culture and Communication*, 2(1), 29–37.

Hall, C.M., Mitchell, R. and Sharples, E. (2003). Consuming places: The role of food, wine and tourism in regional development. In Hall, C.M., Sharples, E., Mitchell, R., Cambourne, B. and Macionis, N. (eds.) *Food Tourism Around the World: Development Management and Markets*. Butterworth-Heinemann, Oxford, pp. 25–59.

Hashimoto, A. and Telfer, D.J. (2006). Selling Canadian culinary tourism: Branding the global and the regional product. *Tourism Geographies*, 8(1), 31–55.

Hjalager, A-M. and Corigliano, M.A. (2000). Food for tourists – Determinants of an image. *International Journal of Tourism Research*, 2(4), 281–293.

Holloway, L. and Kneafsey, M. (2000). Reading the space of the farmers' market: a preliminary investigation from the UK. *Sociologia Ruralis*, 40(3), 285–299.

Inglis, D. (2005). *Culture and Everyday Life*. Routledge, Abingdon.

MacCannell, D. (1976). *The tourist: A New Theory of the Leisure Class*. Schocken, New York.

Maclaran, P. and Brown, S. (2005). The center cannot hold: Consuming the utopian marketplace. *Journal of Consumer Research*, 32(2), 311–323.

McGrath, M.A., Sherry, J.F., Jr and Heisley, D.D. (1993). An ethnographic study of an urban periodic marketplace: Lessons from the Midville Farmers' Market. *Journal of Retailing*, 69(3), 280–319.

Mitchell, R.D. (2008). International business, intellectual property, and the misappropriation of place: Food, wine and tourism. In Hall, C.M. and Coles, T. (eds.), *International*

Business and Tourism: Global Issues, Contemporary Interactions. Routledge, London.

Pine, B.J. and Gilmore, J.H. (1999). *The Experience Economy: Work is Theatre and Every Business a Stage.* Harvard Business School Press, Boston.

Quan, S. and Wang, N. (2004). Towards a structural model of the tourist experience: An illustration from food experiences in tourism. *Tourism Management,* 25(3), 297–305.

Relph, E. (1996). Place. In Douglas, I., Huggett, R. and Robinson, M. (eds.), *Companion Encyclopedia of Geography: The Environment and Humankind.* Routledge, London.

Scott, D.G. (2006). *Socialising the Stranger: Hospitality as a Relational Reality.* University of Otago, Unpublished Masters Thesis.

Tester, K. (1994). Introduction. In Tester, K. (ed.), *The Flâneur.* Routledge, London, pp. 1–21.

Tiemann, T. (2004a). American farmers' markets: Two types of informality. *International Journal of Sociology and Social Policy,* 24(6), 44–57.

Tiemann, T.K. (2004b). *"Experience" Farmers' Markets: Conduct determines performance.* Eastern Economic Association Meeting, Washington.

Trustpower Dunedin Community Awards (2005). Recipient Summary.

Urry, J. (1990). *The Tourist Gaze: Leisure and Travel in Contemporary Societies.* Sage Publications, Newbury.

Urry, J. (2005). The 'consuming' of place. In Jaworski, A. and Pritchard, A. (eds.), *Discourse, communication, and tourism.* Channel View Publications, Celevedon.

CHAPTER 18

Case study: The tale of three markets

Jane F. Eastham

Introduction

Recent years have witnessed apparently quite profound reversals in consumer perceptions of 'good food'. Perhaps stimulated by recurrent food scares and crises, consumers appear to be increasingly interested in the provenance of the food they consume. The cause of their interest is wrapped up in a range of mantels including: supporting the farmer, healthy eating, a semantic representation of traditions, ecological issues associated with food miles and carbon foot prints. An increase in the UK sales of local food has been particularly notable since the 2001 outbreak in foot and mouth disease. Claim that local food was the 'new organic' has stimulated consumer interest and local food is now available from a wide range of retail outlets, including multiple retailers, box schemes and of course farmers' markets. As indicated in Chapter 1, the interest in local food has had the effect of increasing the number of farmer's markets from 1 in 1997 to over 450 by 2003.

Seen to be a means of re-connecting consumers with producers (Policy Commission, 2002), farmers' markets have the potential to challenge conventional: production, retail and consumption patterns (Holloway and Kneafsey, 2000). They represent, for some, a significant initiative in the development of an alternative rural economy (Marsden et al., 2000).

Whilst earlier chapters indicate that the number of farmers' markets is now remaining fairly constant and growth of this form of retail has plateaued at around 500, such figures hide the dynamics of this format and the numbers of exits and entrants. Whilst there are a number of studies that claim positive impacts, both in terms of income to farmers and in terms of externalities (NFU, 2002; NEF, 2005), there are limited evaluations of the factors which affect their success or failure. This chapter presents three case studies and then draws upon more extensive research to highlight factors which appear to contribute to the success/failure of farmers' markets within specific geographical locations.

Exhibit 18.1   Marylebone Market

Marylebone Market is situated off Cramers street, between Marylebone High Street and Baker Street in Central London. It opened on Sunday 22nd June 2003, and is surrounded by many individual shops, cafes and restaurants. The market is one of a number run by the London Farmers' Markets (LFA), a member of FARMA.

(Continued)

LFA operate as a small company which was developed to provide Londoners with fresh local food, and better returns to farmers. They manage every aspect of the markets from their conception to the daily running. They allow no 'middle-men' at the markets, and have very strict rules about stallholder's attendance.

They run fourteen markets, which include Blackheath, Ealing, Islington, Notting Hill and Wimbledon Park. LFA estimates that they bring £3 million pounds back to the rural economy each year. They see that they have an important role in promoting the development of links between farmers and restaurants and other food outlets in London. Unlike some markets they insist that all traders should grow, process or bake all the products they sell. There are strict guidelines for each category of product according to permissible criteria.

The Marylebone Market is held every Sunday between 10.00 a.m. and 2 p.m., and is the largest London farmers' market. Customers generally live locally and walk to the market, 36 per cent live within 1 mile of the market, and 79 per cent live within 3 miles. There are in the region of 45 traders as registered stallholders which means that there are around 35 stallholders who are present in each market. The market attracts between 2,000 and 3,500 visitors each Sunday, weather permitting, and traders generate anywhere from £450 to over £1,000 of income on comparable Sundays. Average takings are around £716 per stallholder. All producers must come from within 100 miles of the M25, a more liberal concept of 'local' than found within other areas of the UK. The market annually draws around £1.3 million for traders with a further additional spend at local retailers of £295,000. The market is well marketed with web links to the London Farmers' Markets site.

The Best Western consortium promotes the market to visitors to London, with details of 47 Best Western Hotels being identified as being near to the Marylebone Market.

Customer base

Customers are predominantly drawn from the city of West London which has a population of over 181,286. Average gross incomes within this area are around £41,048, which is within the highest four income levels within the London local authorities. The customer base largely reflects the demographics of the area which is predominantly white middle-class and these make up 96 per cent of the customer base.

Customers in recent surveys appear to be particularly attracted to the atmosphere of the market, spending would appear to reflect this. Customers spend around £10 to £24 in the surrounding cafes and shops per visit. Levels of spends are similar to those found in Ealing Farmers' Market, an area where average incomes are significantly lower than the Marylebone district. Suggestions are that Marylebone customers see the market more as a vehicle of leisure than a source of the next week's meals (Extracted from research undertaken by NEF, 2005).

Exhibit 18.2 Bakewell Farmers' Market

Bakewell Farmers' Market is held at Bakewell's Agricultural Business Centre. Bakewell is one of the major market towns in the Peak District National Park in Derbyshire, Northern England. Opened in July 2000, pre foot and mouth disease, it survived this ordeal to become a highly successful market. In the Peak District, there are approximately 2,000 farms which are predominantly small-holdings, farming dairy, sheep and beef on a total area of approximately 77,500 hectares. Whilst there are 38,000 inhabitants, many of these commute to work in the larger industrial towns that surround the area. There are however over 17 million people who live and work within 60 miles of the Park District and the Park attracts over 30 million visitors to the area each year. Many of these are day visitors from the surrounding urban areas.

The market is run strictly according to FARMA rules, producers predominantly are based within a 30-mile radius from the market although there are a number of exceptions to the rule. The shortage of cheese producers and limited numbers of wine producers within the 30-mile radius mean that producers are drawn from as far away as Stoke on Trent. Initial funding for the market came from the Peak District National Park and the LEADER II scheme. The farmers' market is managed by the market co-ordinator who is specifically employed by Derbyshire Dales county council to organize, and develop the market, in close co-ordination with the Peak District National Park. The market is effectively promoted through its own web site, which links to other events within the area.

Held every last Saturday in the month, the market has around 43 to 50 stallholders who are registered to trade at the market, with a long waiting list. The management of the market involves a careful balance of product types in order to offer maximum choice and interest to the consumers. Turnover per stallholder ranges from £60 to £2,400 per market, with some traders attaining 100 per cent of their income from this and other farmers' markets in the area. The average turnover per week for the market as a whole amounts to £67,500 – approximately £810,000 per year.

Traders have a choice of farmers' markets and word spreads between traders as to which markets are the most lucrative. There are many as 42 farmers' markets held within the month, all drawing draw upon the high concentration of population found within the area. These, depending on the stringency of application of FARMA rules in each market, are easily accessible by traders. One trader with three family members is present at nine markets per week.

The market has offered traders tremendous opportunities for expansion, often through collaborative activities between farmers. Initially instigated by a surfeit of traders for the market, the Bakewell Farmers' Market shop has now been established in the centre of Bakewell offering a permanent point of sale for traders and non-traders at the market. Farmers have also been

(Continued)

encouraged to sell to local shops and hotels, as well as to develop mail order systems and farm shops. A number of traders that are involved in the farmers' market are also part of a small network group; Peak Eats, supplying to holiday cottages, as part of a larger Peak District Foods network.

There has been significant support through the Peak District National Park, Chatsworth Estate and the Duchess of Devonshire, and more recently through EBLEX (English Beef and Lamb Executive-Quality scheme) and the support of the Prince of Wales. In addition many producers hold the Peak District Environmental Quality Mark for businesses which support the National Park's natural assets, or receive financial support from the New Environmental Economy programme.

Customer base

Bakewell draws some 3,000 to 4,000 customers from Manchester, Sheffield, Cheshire and Derbyshire. Customers spend around £5 to £10 per visit, which represents between 5 and 25 per cent of their weekly spend on food. The market is perceived by customers to be predominantly an extension of a day out and only around 10 per cent of the customer base live in the immediate area. Traders recognize the importance of customizing their products and are heavily reliant on feedback from customers at the farmers' market to adjust their offering to consumers needs. Producers have extended their product range, e.g. range of vegetables, packaging and processed products to enhance customer's interest.

Exhibit 18.3 Askern Farmers' Market

Askern Market was first held on the 24th September 2004 and was, for a period of 2 years, held every third Thursday of the month. The project was established by the Doncaster Rural Trust, in conjunction with the local parish council and charities, such as Sure Start, and funded with Objective 1 money. The project was predominantly designed to promote healthy eating for the local community whilst also drawing in outside visitors in order to boost income to the area, and increase income to local farmers. The market now only operates intermittently, with the occasional market at Christmas and Easter.

Askern is a small rural village that is situated 7 miles from Doncaster on the Humber Levels in the North of England. Until the early 1900s, the village was predominantly based on agricultural activity, but whose population grew seasonally due to tourism. A fresh water spring in Askern was said to hold curing properties, and during holiday periods the population of the village doubled as surrounding urban populations came to take the cure. In the early 1900s, the area was found to be rich in coal and the population of

(Continued)

Askern grew as the highly mobile mining communities moved to profit from this new coalfield. During the miners' strikes of the 1980s, the town suffered, and the mine was closed by the 1990s. The area is beset by high levels of unemployment, although there is a strong informal market economy.

Askern is located on either side of the A19, identified as a main tourism route to the coast. The area is also of archaeological interest. The iron age site of Sutton Common nearby was excavated in summer 2003, funded by English Heritage, but little remains are evident and plans to develop a visitor centre were less than successful.

In addition, the location of the village on the edge of the Pennine Trail was seen to offer a point of respite for hikers and bikers, attracting passing trade, particularly in the summer months.

The farmers' market started with around 27 stalls, but had diminished to around 8 at the time of its demise. Average incomes per stall ranged from £100 to £500 at the beginning of the market, although these dropped to less than £200 for even the most profitable stalls as time went on. The market is sited on one of two locations depending on the weather. During winter months, the market has tended to be held within a hall in a council building whilst during the spring, summer and autumn months, it can be found beside a small lake in the centre of the village. The market organizers chose a number of ways to market the event. Flyers were widely distributed in Askern and the surrounding villages, several broadcasts were made on local radio and notices were placed at the entrance to the village; however, little attempt was made to reach a wider audience.

Whilst the village had at one time been prosperous, the closure of the mines in the 1990s had led to a considerable decline in the income within the area, despite the informal economy. The village still supported a co-op, several bakers and other grocery and hardware stores. Many of these stores reported considerable losses in income after the market was opened, suggesting that the market brought little additional income to the area. The market closed in July 2006, some 20 months after its launch.

Customer base

Customers predominantly came from Askern and surrounding villages. Few people from outside the region came to the market. During the 2 years, the market was held regularly, the number of visitors to the area, who had come specifically to attend the market, barely entered into double figures. Customers spend per week averaged at around £10 to 15, and the maximum numbers of customers within the market were around 500. In comparison to the London markets, at its peak the market drew £6,750 per week, and it is unlikely that the market ever generated more than £80,000 a year. The increase in income to farmers was predominantly offset against the decline in income for local businesses.

Discussion and conclusions

The cases examined here show that the nature of the customer base has a significant impact on the value attained by stall-holders. The case studies outline two success stories and one 'failure', which highlight that the ability of a market to target and attract higher income consumers appears to be an essential component.

The industrialization of Britain has, over the last two/three centuries, distanced food production from food consumption, and the materialization of intermediaries to create linkages between farmers and consumers have to a large extent been instrumental in reducing the value attained by farmers. Furthermore, particularly since World War II, consumers have come to expect that food should appropriate a limited amount of their total disposable income. These two factors have a major impact on the value of farmers' markets both as a source of local food and a means of regeneration. The success of farmers' markets is contingent on two factors. Firstly of its ability to bridge the gap satisfactorily between source and consumption and secondly that disposable income of potential consumers is such to provide sufficient income to farmers to make the market a viable option. A failure to do this will result in a downward spiral and eventual failure. The number of farmers' markets means that based on returns farmers can 'cherry pick' the markets that they attend. Markets with fewer customers and lower consumer expenditures will result in a decline in numbers of stallholders, thus making the market less attractive to customers and so on.

It is notable that some of the most financially successful farmers' markets appear to be found in or around commuter belts, for instance, Winchester farmers' market. Other ways in which 'local' food and farmers' markets have proved to be successful have been sometimes in remote rural locations (Eastham, 2003, 2005) where through the development of longer transactional relationships with visitors through box schemes, mail order and Internet sales, farmers have been able to capitalize on their seasonal visitors. In essence, where there is no natural bridge between consumer and source, then there needs to be additional mechanisms to bridge the gap between the consumer and source. Even in Bakewell, where regular influxes of visitors provide income, the longer-term success is dependent upon the development of additional points of access to 'local foods' for consumers, in this case, the farmers' market shop.

The strong contrast between Askern and Bakewell is worth noting. Located not more than 40 miles away, the failure in Askern was predominantly linked to its failure to attract external customers. Its 2 year survival was predominantly due to trade diversion, and as other markets within the area became more successful traders gradually shifted their business from the Askern Market. It is suggested in other chapters that by increasing the impact of farmers' markets through the provision of entertainment, e.g. circus acts, Morris dancing, mystery plays, this can do much to differentiate the market and increase the number of stallholders. However, within Askern, when attempts were made to introduce juggling acts and similar street entertainment, the lack of awareness of potential visitors of the event provided little impetus to the project.

References

Eastham, J.F. (2003). *Farmers' Markets and Rural Policy*. Unpublished Masters Dissertation, New Economics Foundation, London.

Eastham, J.F. (2005). Farmers' markets here to stay. *ICCAS Conference*, Warsaw.

Holloway, L. and Kneafsey, M. (2000). Reading the space of the farmers' market. *Sociologia Ruralis*, 40(3), 285–299.

Marsden, T., Banks, J. and Bristow, G. (2000). Food supply chain approaches in rural development. *Sociologia Ruralis*, 40(4), 425–438.

NEF (2005). *Trading Places and Local Economic Impact of Street Produce and Farmers' Markets Written by John Taylor, Matina Madrick and Sam Collin*. A report by NEF (the New Economics Foundation), November 2005, New Economics Foundation, London.

NFU (2002). Farmers' market business survey, htttp://www.nfu.org.uk/ino/fmbusiness.asp

Policy Commission (2002). *Farming and Food: A Sustainable Future*. Report of the Policy Commission on the Future of Farming and Food. London.

PART V

Conclusions

CHAPTER 19

Food festival research methods and approaches

Howard Lyons

The purposes of this chapter are twofold, to establish the special characteristics that distinguish food and drink festivals from a research perspective and to provide an overview of research methods for those involved with these festivals. Many of the characteristics identified as being peculiar to food and drink festivals may be relevant to other forms of festival, and the reader is invited to further explore the similarities and differences.

The research methods that can be used to research festivals are common to those employed in other disciplines. However, the approach advocated here is to look closely at the unusual characteristics of food festivals as they will have a major bearing on research methods appropriate in any particular situation. The 'causal texture of the environment' was a phrase coined by Emery and Trist (1965). In part their work was applied to an analysis of environmental turbulence, and in part this turbulence was related to the industry in which their studies were conducted. As their work related to the post-World War II era, it is unsurprising that their studies included British coal mining. Their understanding is however transferable. It is that the local or micro industry conditions (my words) are important to understanding a managerial situation. As such, the proposition of the contingent nature of research methods is based firmly in the research literature, and the distinctive characteristics of food festivals are explored in this chapter as a prelude to the consideration of the methods of research, or tools to be used in research.

Special characteristics of food and drink festivals

There are many competent books published that cover research methods for business, the social sciences, leisure, tourism, hospitality, and associated disciplines. This chapter will identify the special characteristics of food and drink festivals with the perspective of highlighting how the general principles and practices of research contained in the literature need to be reviewed in the light of these special characteristics.

The special characteristics of the food and drink festivals relate firstly to 'food and drink', and secondly to 'festivals'. We will begin by looking at what makes festivals 'special'; we do not use the word 'unique' as this would mean that they were a one-off having no points of difference with other activities. Such a proposition of uniqueness would be implausible.

What makes festivals special?

The first attributes that distinguish festivals are that they are a service with all of the characteristics of a service (perishability, heterogeneity, intangibility, inseparability, e.g. Zeithaml and Bitner, 2002) which will be explained later. In addition, these services relate to a consumer product (the festival) that is unlike most others in that it is and can only be experienced briefly, typically for one or a few days a year. Festivals are unlike holidays which are also a typically short experience, but are taken over several days or weeks. Whereas many people take holidays and can be therefore researched both at home and on holiday, festival customers are hard to research other than when at the festival. In many cases there will be no opportunity to use a mailing list for research as even large festivals tend to rely on on-the-door purchase rather than pre-purchases. This differs from large exhibitions where pre-purchases with early booking discounts are typical. Festivals such as York and Ludlow are still typically organized by their own committees which are lay, but may include professionals. In contrast exhibitions such as BBC Good Food are more typically run by professional organizers.

As the festival visit is likely to be short in duration and concentrated in experience, normally research will need to be undertaken at the festival, and will have to be either short if it involves interviews, or take no subject time and be in the form of observational research where people are observed and not interviewed. Off-site research would typically depend on the availability of an address database, possibly generated at the festival.

Many festivals have a seasonal identity. The underlying seasonal nature of food and drink is often reflected in the time of year when the festival occurs. Thus the opportunity to market winter or Christmas-specific products in spring, summer, or early autumn food and drink festivals may be difficult. Hence punch, toddy, gluvine (also Glühwein), Christmas pudding or cake, and turkey would be unseasonable at a summer festival, and may not inspire customers to sample or purchase.

Whereas food and drink exhibitions and shows held in large metropolitan exhibition halls may share a consumer expectation with festivals for seasonality of products, festivals held in more rural surroundings will be more closely linked by history or customer perceptions to the seasons. However, would people buy Easter Eggs at the November BBC Food and Drink Exhibition, despite being held at the large and anonymous

National Exhibition Centre in Birmingham in England's West Midlands region?

Organizers of metropolitan food and drink shows may call them festivals, so the metropolitan or rural location may be more important than the name, be it festival or show, for the purposes of the researcher. Some festivals may coincide with key times in the agricultural cycle, such as harvest or planting of crops. This real or perceived linkage to 'nature' may endow food festivals with attributes that transcend the more mundane characteristics associated with other products or services, and the religious festivals associated with seasons and the equinoxes often have a resonance with food and drink festivals.

For the researcher, these deeper relationships may be an important issue that could be explored, notwithstanding the risk that such an exploration risks the methodological pitfall of leading questions. A leading question is one where, for example, an interviewee may be fed an idea that had not occurred to them, such as the link between the festival and the season.

Turning to the characteristics of services, *perishability* is an important issue. At its simplest, an empty table in a restaurant NOW cannot be sold at another mealtime or on another day. Hence services are even more perishable than the freshest food. For a food festival, perishability is a key concept for researchers. A festival has a carrying capacity of visitors, and these numbers may be negotiated with Health and Safety Inspectors and be limited by licensing authorities (the mechanism for setting actual limits will vary depending on the legal jurisdiction). However, individual elements of the festival will have limits to participants that are perishable. If there is a 'logical' route around the festival stands or exhibits, then the crush of entrants at busy times may make certain stands or exhibits unapproachable. Later in the day they may be accessible, and it is an important research issue to see if visitors will re-trace their path to see things that they missed first time around.

Similarly there are times when visitors will want to purchase meals at the festival, and engineering a mechanism to stagger demand is worthy of research, as the capacity of food service is unlikely to match the total number of visitors at a single sitting. Managing the catering should be such that all who want to buy food will be served, yet significant redundant capacity engineered out of the system.

Free food and drinks are also typical of food and drink festivals and exhibitions. If used, they are provided as a sales promotional tool. As with mass catering, the traders wish to see a festival where visitors are spread across the opening times, and where they have enough time to sample and can be persuaded to purchase. So again the perishability of the service is crucial. As will be argued later, many of the foods that are sampled are also perishable – in that they are subject to melting (ice cream), microbiological deterioration (spoilage of cooked meats and dairy), etc. Hence, whereas perishability is an issue for all services, it is unusually complex to model and manage in food festivals. In an art festival an empty seat at a ballet performance is a loss that is at least easy to comprehend, but there will be rarely a very large number of concurrent events. Whereas a food festival may have hundreds of concurrent opportunities represented by exhibitors, talks, demonstrations, and other activities.

Heterogeneity is a reflection that services are delivered to a person, often by another person. The experience of each customer is therefore truly unique because the relationship between customer and server is inseparable. The two characteristics of heterogeneity and inseparability are distinct but closely linked. A person providing a sample of cheese to a food festival visitor is trying to generate a sale. They are trying to select a cheese for the visitor to sample that they have reason to believe will please them so that they will buy. This is a complex relationship and reflects traditional sales practices rather than those typically found in supermarkets, where the unique experience of shoppers tends to be increasingly designed out of shopping.

At a broader level, the experience of each festival visitor is unique. Researchable sources of heterogeneity include:

- Problems encountered in going to the festival. Thus a bad journey may sour the attitude of a visitor.
- The route followed around the festival. Entering a melee of other visitors at the start of a tour around a festival site may also sour attitudes, whereas following a route where passage is easy and exhibits accessible and interesting is likely to lead to positivity.
- The health and fitness of the visitor. Festivals and exhibitions can be endurance trials that favour the fit and healthy.
- The congestion encountered in the visit. This is closely linked to the route followed around the festival.
- The weather. An outdoor rural festival experienced by visitors in driving wind and rain can be distinctly unpleasant, whereas in fine weather it is a great joy.
- Products sampled. Alcohol can colour the view of visitors, and those who graze their way around a food and drink festival may be sated and happy.
- Products purchased and any problems encountered transporting these around the festival. Thus the urge to purchase

large or heavy products can be counterproductive to over-all enjoyment, unless the vendors or festival organizers facilitate the process, such as with home delivery, shopping crèches, or vendors retaining goods for later collection.

- On-site services such as catering and toilets. Toilets are an issue for many people who evaluate any service offering by the accessibility, comfort, and hygiene of toilets, and for many the quality, accessibility, and price of on-site catering can be a make or break issue, such as in The Times (2007).
- Attitudes of traders. Festival organizers rely on exhibitors having excellent personal skills in dealing with the public. However, crowd management and visitor's expectations covering challenging customers such as the disabled and young children can be managed by organizers.
- Behaviour of any people accompanying or surrounding the visitor … Thus over-imbibing of alcoholic refreshments must be avoided, and general stewarding must be attentive and appropriate, as well as complying with legal requirements.

Inseparability is widely discussed in the context of businesses such as restaurants and hairdressers. However, a food and drink festival is a much more complex environment in which to explore the idea. In a restaurant, the customer may typically meet a waiter and a wine waiter. In a hair dresser they meet the stylist and hair wash person. In a food festival they meet and at some level interact with perhaps scores of exhibitors and officials, and hundreds of other visitors. Yet their experience of the festival is coloured by a mixture of individual encounters plus an overall feel of the event. This is a challenging research area, and my own insights and experience suggests two differ-ent lines of investigation. Firstly at the individual experience level, I have encountered answers to open ended questions, where respondents have highlighted specific experiences such as the positive and helpful attitudes of stewards. In answer to other open ended questions, respondents have commented specifically on the 'buzz' of a festival. Clearly these observa-tions are ad hoc and superficial, and the topic is open to rigor-ous investigation.

Intangibility is another attribute of a service. Hence the cheese that is sampled may be tangible (literally able to be touched), but the visitor's state of mind and propensity to buy cheese is probably generated by their intangible experience of the fes-tival as well of being a function of their relationship with the cheese vendor. I recently sampled some very strong smoked cheese which ruined my next sampling of a subtly smoked salmon. So the immediate experience in the festival has a major impact on purchasing behaviour. Researching the visitor experience so that it can be managed to ensure that they have a propensity to sample and buy is a great challenge for festival organizers and researchers.

So far we have looked at the special characteristics of festivals with an emphasis on food and drink. Next we will consider what makes food special, and reflect on this from a research perspective.

What makes food special?

Just as service is perishable, so too is some of the food supplied to, and sold at, festivals. However, it is not all perishable. In fact the traditional stance of food festivals means that much of what is sold has been subject to traditional forms of food processing and preservation, such as bottling (canning), salting, smoking, preserving with sugar, fermentation, and in alcohol or oil. Some fresh produce is also sold, typically covering traditional (and commonly rare) breeds of animals and var-ieties of fruit and vegetables which are often subject to more modern forms of preservation such as chilling, freezing, and irradiating as with spices.

Hence the level of physical *perishability* of foods is limited, but often the regulatory authorities apply standards to food storage that is appropriate for 'modern foods' that are lower in their salt and sugar content. Examples include salted meats such as ham, where chill cabinet temperatures are required to be set at a level appropriate to factory processed meats rather than those that are traditionally cured. Hence perishability is on occasion a legal rather then an innate concept. A major public health issue and emerging research need is to monitor the understanding of consumers of the storage needs of food-stuffs arising from their innate characteristics. At the extreme, traditional hams are stored in cool ambient rooms for months or years (and sometimes hung from the ceiling in shops and bars). Whereas packaged ham has a short shelf life even in the refrigerator.

Seasonality of food is innate and rooted in natural cycles of sowing and harvesting on land or sea. Religious festivals frequently celebrate these seasons, and emphasize how deeply grounded culture is in natural cycles. However, one major theme of contemporary food supply is that foods are sourced from around the world. Hence any food is available as it is in season somewhere in the world, or in a controlled factory farming environment. Food festivals celebrate those foods that are in season, and how foods are processed at times of glut to ensure that they are available in lean times. Hence the management of perishability through the traditional forms of preservation dealt with above (bottling, salting, etc.) is also typically celebrated. How far contemporary lives mean that customers perceive the underlying natural cycles is an important challenge for those of us who wish to see a return to 'real' and 'local' foods.

This dimension of seasonality is highlighted when we consider that the major religions of the world have festivals that coincide with natural rhythms of sowing and harvesting crops. As these religions are often from the northern hemisphere, they are anachronistic in the southern hemisphere, where seasons are reversed.

Celebration may be at its zenith when encountered as alcohol. Grains, fruits, and occasionally vegetables (such as potato spirits) are fermented when crops are available, and then they are stored and aged for celebration at other times of the year. Sampling such products is an agreeable and popular activity at many food and drink festivals. How purchasing behaviour at festivals is affected by such sampling is a legitimate research activity. Furthermore, the prevalence of sampling alcoholic drinks at festivals means that the role of the researcher is affected by an imbibulous sample. Clearly not all visitors drink alcohol, and many who do are prudent in their consumption. Yet the bonhomie engendered is both a facilitator for the success of the festival, and also a risk for researchers for whom some results may be biased.

'Involvement' is a characteristic that considers the extent which festival visitors are merely 'surfing' the event, and how far they feel an ideological commitment to any espoused values. Typical of these values usually relate to local, whole, rare, and traditional foods. Thus some festival visitors may share an almost religious commitment to the values claimed by some festival organizers, who seek to maintain and develop local food traditions. This may differ from visitors who have a hedonistic drive to visit. Of course many (maybe most) visitors go for a 'good day out'.

Establishing psychographic market segmentation models is a very valid form of theory building research for festival researchers. There are several forms of approach to psychographic segmentation which can be found in most texts on consumer behaviour, typical of which is VALs, standing for Values, Attitudes, and Lifestyles. Clearly knowing the age, gender, and other demographics, and also the socio-economic profile of festival visitors is useful. However, a more complex typology that describes archetypes may be more useful for festival organizers who wish to ensure that visitors' needs are met and that exhibitors are properly briefed.

You may wish to consider several possible research ideas that can be explored in food and drink festivals. These are additional to ideas previously discussed.

Project ideas

- Describe the types of visitor that you would expect to find at a rural food and drink festival. Producing such a typology may help organisers' to improve their advertising.
- Identify the psychographic market segments that a festival addresses using factors such as values, attitudes and lifestyles (Business Dictionary 2007).
- Have a look at multivariate analysis to see some advanced approaches to measuring responses.

So far we have identified possible research themes linked to what makes food festivals a differentiated research site. We next take this into a problem ownership context by considering the special needs of the various interest groups who will either sponsor or facilitate festival research.

A research agenda for food festivals

The many research tools available to any social scientist may be relevant to those who work for food festival businesses. A lack of a large and coherent body of research into food festivals is a barrier to the development of the field, but is typical of new areas of work. However, the rapid growth of the field means that there is a large body of good practice that has been reported, and will be referred to in other chapters in this book.

The focus of this part of the chapter is to suggest ways in which the research base of food festivals can be expanded in a structured way. Normally, new fields develop over a protracted period of time as researchers publish their individual contributions.

What is proposed is that we should develop a tradition of publishing research findings that reflects the work undertaken over decades in medicine. In that field research often took the form of findings being published as case studies in which individual or small numbers of patients were studied. Such studies provided insights, but the purposes of research – model building or model testing – were hard to justify on the strength of such small numbers of observations.

A large body of such published case study findings does, however, provide an opportunity for statistical analysis. Hence researchers undertake what is called cases studies such as in Lyons (2005), where multiple case studies are analysed. For this to be relevant, the provenance of case studies must be clear, and the replicability of studies ensured by developing relevant formats in which data are clearly and precisely outlined. In contemporary medical research, we see the publication of the so-called meta-research studies, in which suites of case study research are aggregated and analysed, and results represent a large number of individual investigations.

The remainder of the article will outline some key research areas and strategies for creating case studies. Reading other chapters in this book will suggest other research topics, and the approach proposed here will be equally relevant.

A problem owner approach

The festival organizer's needs are a useful focus. Their needs revolve around a requirement to have knowledge of their visitors, exhibitors, competitors, and staff (particularly volunteers), alongside research needs associated with local planners and regulatory authorities. We will consider these groups as each may provide research opportunities.

Customers or visitors are most readily researched at the festival. Hence permission from the organizers is essential. What the organizers need to know is, who the visitors are demographically (primarily, age and gender plus the relationship of group members, e.g. a family), because this identifies needs for facilities and helps to inform exhibitors. Next socio-economics are important as they may affect marketing. However, our experience is that the foodie group seems to span a wide range of demographic and socio-economic groups.

Socio-economics are important if measured and evaluated carefully. A question about household income is always sensitive and if asked should be left to the end of any interview. However, care must be taken in evaluating such data. Thus a high salary for a new graduate living at home with parents may be rather poor salary for a family with children, and be moderate for a retired home owner with a small modern house (an old or large house may reduce the retired person to penury).

A surrogate to socio-economic questions is often useful. Thus a car park survey where the value of motor cars used by festival visitors can be helpful particularly if benchmarked against some other festival or supermarkets. This provides a methodology, where sensitive and unreliable questions about income can be avoided, and where objective data can be collected (despite limitations associated with, say, company cars, second cars, etc. be used to visit the festival). At its simplest a car park survey requires the collection of data on the make, model, year, and condition of cars. These data are then used in conjunction with a used car price guide to value vehicles. A comparison of value with other retail activities is a useful method to establish the economic place of visitors. For a more sophisticated analysis it is possible to look at cars as a reflection of VALs such as the prevalence of iconic vehicles such as Volvo's, or life style choices such as 4WD's, and people carriers. Prestige marques may be another indicator as may utilitarian vehicle choices.

Where food and drink festival visitors come from is of great importance as it has implications for accommodation needs of visitors, and for advertising to new or existing geographical areas for visitors. The UK postcode is our preferred method of collecting homes as it links to publicly available databases that also provide socio- and demographic data (e.g. from http://www.upmystreet.com). Similar data exist in other countries, although Michels (2007) denies the value of such data in a company-focused article based on Canada.

New forms of psychographic segmentation are important to festival visitors. A major longitudinal study that we have been involved in is the Ludlow Food and Drink Festival. We have identified that some visitors to the Ludlow Food Festival are what we call 'foodies', whereas others visit because they want a good day out. We have encountered church groups, singles holidays, group reunions, and pub group outings alongside foodies who cannot afford hotels or B&B's, so they camp to afford the goodies, and others who visit both the festival and also local Michelin starred restaurants whilst staying at expensive hotels.

Our own experience of festival on-site research is that conventional market research interviewers (and students) can collect short structured questionnaires, as visitors are generally relaxed and communicative. However, for less structured research and probing, there is a need for mature and experienced researchers. We have collected many hundreds of interviews as mature experienced researchers who are prepared to undertake fieldwork, and our commitment and knowledge to the field mean that the data that we have collected is very rich.

Similarly, we have undertaken many focus groups in which we have explored questionnaire results more fully, which again require experienced interviewers or facilitators.

Supplier or exhibitor research is a little different from customer research because it carries a commercial dimension. Many traders regard their replies as having implications for exhibitor charging, and the allocation of pitches. We have found that on-site research is helpful for probing immediate issues, such as when a new closing time is being piloted. However, exhibitor research is challenging and probably best approached personally by phone or pre-arranged visit at some time other than at the festival. The ethical dimension of researching traders is a little difficult as an outside researcher cannot commit the organizers to not changing their pricing policy of stands based on research data. In fact, the only commitment that the external researcher can be sure of delivering is anonymity. For university researchers, the Research Ethics Code of their university is clearly tested by such studies, as is the professional code of commercial market researchers.

Some festivals depend on volunteers. Where this is the case the individual volunteers may be more crucial to the organizers than individual customers because the pool of prospective volunteers is more limited than festival visitors. Knowing as much as possible about volunteers and their satisfaction with the festival is crucial. The typical volunteer in our study in Ludlow is retired, and how new retirees can be attracted is important as is the recruitment of new people who will serve on committees and in leading the festival.

So far this analysis has been focused on the festival organizer as problem owner. However, the analysis above indicates many of the stakeholders in a festival, to whom can be added the local community (possibly local or regional government authorities) and others such as academics.

At a more abstract level, it is useful to consider the what's and why's of research methods and this is done next.

Food and drink festivals research: what's and why's

Broadly, there are two styles of approach to researching food and drink festivals. Either we may pose a research question or define a soluble problem. Each of these approaches will be discussed next.

A research question typically contains a word such as: who, what, where, when, why, how, followed by a '?'. Often we have a high-level question such as 'what brings visitors to our festival?' which generates a series of more detailed research-able questions which may include:

1. Who are our visitors?
2. Where do these visitors come from?
3. How do they travel to the festival?
4. When do they come and how does where they come from change this?
5. Why do these various types of visitor come?
6. What satisfiers mean that our various types of visitors are happy and likely to return?

This is purely an example of the sorts of questions that we may wish to answer. What is also important is that these are reasonable questions to pose and that we have suitable tools to collect data. A common mistake is made where complex motivational issues are explored based on issues that simply occur to the researchers. Good research is grounded in data. Hence attitudinal questions should be grounded in language used by visitors, possibly captured in a focus group and then further explored in a survey.

The research question approach is typical of academic researchers, although it is found in all sorts of studies which include those of commercial market researchers. A more typical consulting approach is however to pose the issue as a problem, such as 'how can we increase visitor numbers by 50 per cent?'

In practical terms it may be sensible to scope a relevant aspect of a festival using a research question approach in 1 year, and to subsequently develop a problem-solving approach for a further year. This is because the problem solving approach is preceded by a data gathering phase.

If we have answered the research question outlined above, then we can start to identify potential markets that could be tapped into using appropriate advertising promotions. Thus it may be that a geographical region has good transport access to a food festival, but is not in the same administrative region and is therefore not subject to local information about events. It could be that a significant part in the increase of visitors could be generated simply by promoting the festival in the area. In the case of the Ludlow, although located in Shropshire, it is close to the borders of the English counties of Hereford and Worcester, Staffordshire, West Midlands, and to the Welsh county of Powys. As much tourism promotion is developed at the level of administrative counties this means that the Ludlow Festival may miss out on promotion in neighbouring counties. This may be through it being overlooked, but may also be a result of rivalry between destination events and it may overlook the possibilities of lost overnight stays for visitors.

Clearly, the example is overly simplified, but it does make the point that problem-solving is partly a function of scoping and collecting data that is informative for decision-makers.

Qualitative and quantitative data are distinguished in books on research methods. Qualitative data provide richness, but are frequently based on small numbers of respondents collected by interviews, focus groups, and surveys. In contrast quantitative data are perceived by the uninitiated as being statistical and therefore credible. This perception of credibility can be misplaced based on the principle of GIGO – Garbage In Garbage Out. However, complex the statistical analysis, results are only as good as input data quality permits. The abuse of statistical tests when misapplied to inappropriate data is widespread; in fact, many seminal research articles in the social sciences use the wrong statistics. Although good, modern journals no longer publish such work, as a journal reviewer, I am frequently surprised to see how often investigators working today still perpetuate mistakes (such as applying parametric data analysis to non-parametric Likert data). For a fuller explanation see the discussion at the end of this chapter.

Kanji (1999) prefaced a current edition of his textbook with the comment that when he began working as a professional statistician, there were only 12 tests that were required. Now his book focuses on the 100 most important tests, and he invites readers to discuss refining this list. The moral of this is that a prudent quantitative researcher will involve a professional statistician at the design stage of a quantitative survey, and keep them involved throughout. For example, even sample size is a difficult trade-off between accuracy and cost. Accuracy is itself a matter of the consistency of responses. Thus a small survey where people largely agree may well be statistically significant, whereas a large sample with a wide variation of responses may be less statistically significant.

So far the chapter outlines some key issues in food and drink festival research design. In addition, there are several examples of research that people may pursue. Next we have a short overview of some key research studies in the field, some of which are cited elsewhere in this book. This will be followed by the brief annotated reading list of research methods books.

Research methods used in food and drink festivals

The implications of the chapter focus on social sciences research methods, which include both qualitative and quantitative methods including individual and group interviews, focus groups and similar, as well as quantitative surveys. Attitudes and behaviours are both important to social scientists, and can be very different. For example, preferring sausage A to sausage B doesn't mean that A will be purchased in preference to B. Price may be important, and so may appearance, or the anticipated preferences of other family members. Whereas attitudes are explored by asking questions or setting up experiments to test preferences, etc. behaviours can be explored by asking questions or by observing people. Watching how people shop, explore a festival site, and/or exhibitor's displays can be often best explored by watching them rather than asking them. Sometimes people tell you what they think that you want to hear, or they may just misunderstand their own behaviours.

Some of the more useful observational techniques to consider include:

- Assessing the types of visitors at a festival. This may be on different days at a festival, and achieved by working out the value of their cars on the car park. The car value can be taken from published motor trade sources and used as a surrogate for the socio-economic group of festival visitors.
- Observing their search behaviour pattern by seeing how they go around the festival and when they purchase food to eat there and food to take away.
- Watching groups to see how decisions to explore the festival and shop are arrived at.

Throughout the other chapters of the book, the major source of detailed data has been obtained through the use of social science research. The presentation of these data in the book takes several forms, ranging from case studies and shorter scenarios through to statistical reportage.

The research methods used to generate economic impact studies is typically generated through social science research methods, but also applies economic models that apply appropriate methods of factoring multipliers into leverage up the impact of direct expenditure on a food festival within a local economy. What is most important about this approach is that data generated by social science research methods are used as inputs to other processes and do not themselves answer questions such as 'what is the economic value of a food festival to the host community?'

However, not all research on food festivals reported in this book or undertaken elsewhere fits the social science research mould. Some work is concerned with exploring pre-existing documents which are increasingly electronic, but maybe paper based. It is easy for social scientists to define such work as secondary research as it draws in various ways on the endeavours of others. However, much is actually primary research in so far as it provides new understanding and uses research methods more typically previously used in the humanities, rather than the social sciences.

Exploring archives and records that maybe contemporary with an event or written at a later date (such as the New Testament Apostles) is all relevant work in the humanities. However, it shares much with those using contemporary or on-line sources of data. In particular, establishing the authenticity of a record is of absolute importance. Most readers are aware of the computer scams which involve tricksters setting up web sites to look like legitimate banks. However, this extends beyond financial fraudsters to critics of organizations or ideas and to simple tricksters. Meticulous study of records to establish their provenance is always critical. How this may be done varies between subjects and may include some science as in carbon dating artefacts, some statistics such as in seeing if the style of writing of one author is matched in another document such as a play, through to expert testimony from experts who have long worked in a field.

At its simplest writing a case study on a festival based on data published on line or existing in paper or electronic archives is actually primary research and the case study is the output of the research. We must avoid the conclusion of some social scientists who may seek to diminish such publishable output as secondary research, as their view of research is discipline based and fails to appreciate the research tradition of the humanities. Other studies using similar datasets might simply quantify the frequency of occurrence of key terms associated with a festival in various databanks, and report the result as a statistic.

Down to detail

So far we have looked at the broad issues associated with researching food and drink festivals. Now we will consider the reality of what the reader needs to appreciate.

Firstly, there is one very important distinction to be made between the prospective researcher, who is seeking to pass an assessment on an academic course of study, and a person seeking to change and improve a festival.

For the former, the 'truth' of their findings is of passing interest. What is important is to pass the various assessment criteria used on their course. Thus reliance on statistics reported in the trade press is frowned upon in an academic project, whereas as statistics collected by trade bodies and government agencies is approved of, as are data collected by other academics and published in properly blind refereed academic journals. In reality, the officially collected and published data may be of dubious validity, as may the output of the academics. However, the academic researcher may rely on them, whereas a person investing money would be well advised to be more circumspect.

The use of web sites to collect data highlights the problem. Firstly, it can be difficult to even establish the provenance of a web site, and if it genuinely represents the alleged owner – witness many banking scams where a credible web site is created to look just like a proper bank.

Secondly, data published by an interested party is always likely to be biased. Sometimes this means presenting data truthfully, but in a biased form, but it may also include simply lying. Checking up on web sites or other published documents is always important and rarely simple. Even historians often make the point that history is written by the winners, so how can we really know what happened?

Moving on to a practical social science issue, students almost always ask how big their sample should be. Some supervisors provide an answer, a sample size such as (say) 100. Others give the more correct answer that 'it all depends'. Looking at this more closely, the issue unpacks as follows: firstly there is a question as to the statistical significance being sought in an answer. The larger the sample the more significant the answer is likely to be. However, there is a further issue to consider, which is the level of agreement or otherwise between respondents. So if everyone gives the same answers, a very small sample will be statistically highly significant, whereas if answers differ greatly a large sample will be needed. For a student it is often only necessary to prove that you appreciate the correct use of statistics when studying a festival, whereas a person investing money should need greater certainty.

We must not lose sight of how data will be used. So if we want to know if visitors differ over the various days on which a festival happens the question becomes one of defining the appropriate sample size for each day. In the consumer work that I have done with Liz Sharples at the Ludlow Food and Drink Festival, we have normally had samples typically of 120 groups of people on each day surveyed, representing around 1,000 individual visitors for the three days of the festival (as each respondent was typically representing the views of their party of three or so members). However, we had much smaller samples of traders and volunteers when these groups were interviewed, as there are many fewer people in total in each group.

Statistical analysis of data has been mentioned consistently in this chapter. Using an appropriate statistical analysis is of absolute importance. For example, simply saying that 45 per cent of people preferred sausage A (as above) and 55 per cent preferred B does not necessarily mean that B is preferred to A. The percentages are a statistic and not a number, so what is important is if the result is statistically significant? I would not spend my own money on the percentage statistic without the significance test being properly applied. As a general principle always seek expert advice on collecting and then using statistics, and that means talking to a practicing statistician and not relying on someone who passed an exam in statistics or research methods 10 or 20 years ago!

Selecting books to support your research

I had initially proposed to review a selection of good texts for readers to use if they wish to undertake research into food and drink festivals. However, I have been doing some research into the subject which has alerted me to the variety of users that I may be addressing, and the wide range of contexts in which you may be working.

For those in large universities working in research you will, like me, enjoy a breathtaking range of formal and informal support in the form of computing packages, and more specifically expert colleagues who usually generously share their time and experience.

Other readers will be entry level students who are being assessed on their ability to design work unaided. Whilst some readers will be festival organizers or volunteers working without free access to a resource rich university environment.

I have therefore decided to produce a checklist for readers to check the suitability of books for themselves. There are two over-riding questions to answer in selecting a book:

1. Does the book seem to be acceptably accessible, notwithstanding it containing some scary technical looking stuff?
2. Is the book up to date and technically competent?

You will have to decide your own answer to the first question, but assistance can be provided with the second. In that context remember that research like everything else is developing rapidly and ideas are changing.

Is a book up to date and technically competent: some tests

You do not need to understand the meaning of these detailed points to apply these tests, any more than you need to know how a car works to drive it. However, reading the research methods book should enlighten you.

Test 1

Firstly look to see if the book is clear on there no longer being a competition between qualitative and quantitative research in the social sciences research community. Excellent projects typically start with a qualitative study such as focus groups to define what to survey, continue with a quantitative study such as a survey, and finish with further qualitative study such as in-depth interviews to probe the meaning of survey results.

Test 2

Check the clarity of the book when describing the nature and use of quantitative data. The different types of data that you can collect need different forms of statistical analysis. A book should define these data in a simple and understandable way. Here is the contents of a teaching slide that I use for this; see if the book is clear on the points.

Types of quantitative data

- *Nominal* (typical statistical test, chi-squared)
  - named categories, e.g. favourite TV channel
- *Ordinal* (typical statistical test, Wilcoxon, Mann–Whitney)
  - ranked categories, e.g. social class
- *Interval* (typical statistical test, parametric stats)
  - score categories, e.g. IQ, temperature with no real zero
- *Ratio* (typical statistical test, parametric stats)
  - similar to interval, but with a real zero e.g. length

Test 3

Check up that the book is correct in its recommendations on the nature of data. If the book mentions a form of question using something called a 'Likert scale', check up that the analysis of the results include the calculation of the median or mode as acceptable 'averages', not the mean. Likert data are ordinal (as in test 2 above) but often inappropriately treated by some authors as interval.

Test 4

If the book suggests the use of a computer in analysing quantitative data, for the non-expert user, it is probably important that you are advised that a modern spreadsheet program like Microsoft Excel can be used. If the use of expensive specialist programs like SPSS is required then the book will not be of great use to the inexpert or person working outside of a research organization for a food festival.

References

Business Dictionary (2007) at http://www.businessdictionary.com/definition/Values-Attitudes-and-Lifestyles-System-VALS-2.html accessed 26.11.2007.

Emery, F.E. and Trist, E.L. (1965). The causal texture of organizational environments. Human Relations.

Kanji, G. (1999). *100 Statistical Tests*. Sage Publications, London.

Lyons, H. (2005). Food industry case studies: A suitable medium for publication. *British Food Journal*, 107(9), 702–713.

Michels, C. at http://extranet.mapinfo.com/common/library/geodemographic_fundamentals_august_2003.pdf, accessed Wednesday, 07. 03.2007.

The Times (2007). Bee, P. Talking Dirty, August 28.

Zeithaml, V.A. and Bitner, M.J. (2002). *Services Marketing*, 3rd edition. McGraw-Hill, New York.

CHAPTER 20

Future issues and trends: Food events, festivals and farmers' markets

C. Michael Hall and Liz Sharples

Previous chapters and cases have illustrated the wide range of themes and agendas surrounding the area of farmers' markets and food and wine festivals. This is a topic of research which cuts across many disciplines and fields and, as such, is of interest to academics and practitioners researching or working in food/wine production and distribution, food policy, gastronomy, destination marketing, regional development and urban/rural regeneration. This discussion is also relevant to individuals involved in events and festival management. The successful execution of food and wine events is dependent on an understanding, or at least an appreciation of, key skills and competencies associated with event planning such as logistics and programming. This is particularly relevant in the organization of major or hallmark food and wine festivals, where a 'common sense' or community volunteer approach may not be sufficient.

Due to this multi-disciplinary nature and the number of complex factors which impact on the management of these food events on an almost daily basis, it is difficult to accurately forecast trends regarding the size and nature of the farmers' markets/food events market in the future. For example, the incidence of a number food scares in the UK between 2000 and the current day (BSE, foot and mouth, avian flu) have had a major impact on the public's interest and commitment to local food with a clear provenance which, in turn, has helped generate interest not only in farmers' markets, but also in more general food and wine events (Sassatelli and Scott, 2001; FARMA, 2006). This trend would have been hard to predict 5 or 10 years earlier. Indeed, as noted in several chapters in this volume, it is increasingly difficult to disaggregate the development of food events from broader concerns with sustainable food and agriculture and alternative food systems. For example, the Slow Food Movement is instrumental not only in supporting large-scale international events, but members are often strongly involved in community food festivals and farmers' markets (see Exhibit 20.1).

Exhibit 20.1 Slow Food, Salone del Gusto and Terra Madre

The Slow Food Movement originated in Italy in 1986 under the inspirational leadership of Carlo Petrini and now has over 80,000 members involved with over 850 'Convivia' (local chapters) worldwide. The philosophy of the movement is founded on the concept of 'eco-gastronomy', in other words, a recognition of the strong relationships that exists between 'plate and planet'

(Slow Food, 2007). The Slow Food Movement believes in 'good, clean and fair' food, i.e. that 'food should taste good; that it should be produced in a clean way that does not harm the environment, animal welfare or our health; and food producers should receive fair compensation for their work' (Slow Food, 2007).

The international movement stages a considerable number of food events throughout the year, at convivium, national and international level with an aim to link small/local food producers with other food producers and to showcase their products to consumers. The most impressive of these events is the Salone del Gusto, which was launched in 1996 and is now held bi-annually at the end of October in Turin. In 2006 this event was organized by the Slow Food movement, the Piedmont Regional Authority and, for the first time, the Turin City Council.

The event has some commercial aims of encouraging producers to network, but also has an educational objective in allowing the public to see, taste and learn about artisan products which are little known. The concept of preserving the heritage and culture associated with these food stuffs is gaining in popularity and in 2006 over 150,000 visitors were attracted to the event (Salone del Gusto, 2007).

The 5-day event is staged in 50,000 square metres of exhibition space at the Lingotto Fiere Exhibition centre and includes 125 institutional stands, 600 exhibitors from 80 countries, 270 stands of Italian and foreign 'presidia' (endangered food products that are being promoted and safeguarded by the Slow Food movement). The hall also houses tasting areas and restaurants, and there are a comprehensive number of cookery demonstrations, taste workshops and educational events on offer for children and adults. Many well-known chefs from around the world are involved with the event. The event is sponsored by a number of companies and organizations including Lurisia, De Cecco, Lavazza, Consorzio Parmigiano-Reggiano, Consorzio Prosciutto di San Daniele and Sanpaolo Imi (Salone del Gusto, 2007).

In 2004 the movement staged for the first time the 'Terra Madre', an international food communities meeting, which was repeated in 2006 to run alongside the Salone. This event is not open to the public, but brings together producers and other members of the food and agriculture sector to debate about key issues which are pertinent to the theme of sustainability within the global food chain. This world meeting brought together 9,000 people in Turin; 4,803 farmers, breeders, fishermen and artisan food producers from 1,583 food communities and 150 nations; 953 cooks, 411 professors and representatives from 225 universities, 2,320 observers and guides and 776 volunteers (Terra Madre, 2007).

Sources: Derived from Salone del Gusto (2007): http://www.salonedelgusto.com Slow Food (2007): http://www.slowfood.com and Terra Madre (2007): http://www.terramadre2006.org

Of course this is not to suggest that the Slow Food or organic movements are the only reason why growth in food events has occurred. But the growth of these movements parallel to that of the growth of food events is no accident and reflects broader societal concern in many developed countries not only about the qualities of the food we are consuming, but also how about rural regions and communities, agricultural practices and lifestyles and certain forms of small-scale retailing can continue to survive if not prosper.

In many developed countries such as the UK and the USA, some agricultural regions have attempted at least a partial shift from wholesale production to service-oriented agritourism to mitigate the impacts of economic globalization, urbanization and corporate agribusiness on small farms, and to develop a stable niche for local food products within their communities (Food System Economic Partnership, 2006). For example, owners of small farms in western and northern Michigan have worked to develop a regional identity to attract new customers to their farms through tourism-related direct retail and entertainment ventures (Che et al., 2005). However, it is also apparent that access plays a major role in the relative success of food events, and that the most successful agricultural and food tourism ventures benefit from being located within regions with strong place-based identities located near large, urban, visitor-generating areas (Che et al., 2005). Events are therefore extremely important because at a variety of scales they help to reinforce the 'sense of place' with respect to food and community pride, while they also serve to help promote place and help brand foods and their qualities (Hjalager and Corigliano, 2000; Hall et al., 2003). Such promotion is significant at local and regional level and, for the larger events, at a national and international level. For example, wine festivals and events typically go hand-in-hand with awards and promotions that are integral to the marketing strategies of many wineries and their regions (Hall and Mitchell, 2008).

The substantial growth in the number and variety of food events and festivals (Emmons, 2001; Hall et al., 2003; Çela et al., 2007) is matched by the growth of farmers' markets (Brown, 2002; Payne, 2002; FARMA, 2006; see Chapter 13, this volume). In a number of locations, many small-scale agricultural producers have transitioned from selling at farmers' markets for supplemental income to establishing these direct sales opportunities as their primary retail operations. In addition, the entrepreneurial skills and networks established at farmers' markets can provide an opportunity for some producers to develop new distribution and sales channels, even including export (Guthrie et al., 2006).

'When vendors work cooperatively instead of competitively, these retail outlets help to foster informal networks and provide social benefits such as the sharing of information and education through personal interactions between consumers and producers' (Food System Economic Partnership, 2006, p. 2).

Networking has been recognized as integral to the success of many food tourism ventures. Although it should be stressed that the networks within which food events are embedded usually consists of a number of other agritourism and/or wine and food tourism ventures and products in addition to agricultural production (Telfer 2001; Hall et al., 2000, 2003). Lynch and Morrison (2007) highlight the fact that businesses in the wine and food tourism network identified by Telfer (2001) in the Niagara region of Canada work together to improve the quality and diversity of the regional wine tourism product, as well as undertaking joint marketing of the region. Hall (2004) also notes that as food and wine networks develop over time they can further reinforce notions of place, thereby creating further positive feedback in relation to the hosting of food events and farmers' markets (see Chapter 2).

Connection between accommodation providers and events is also an important part of network development. The concept of offering a short break package where a farmers' market experience is combined with overnight hotel accommodation is gaining in popularity. Sometimes this is a simple deal where guests are just provided with return transport to the market from the hotel, but other packages have added value. For example, the Bonham Hotel promotes a 'farmers' market cooking experience', which includes two nights at one of Edinburgh's top boutique hotels, escorted trips to the market with Bonham's executive chef, and several opportunities to watch one of the hotel chefs cook for the group using the local ingredients (Bonham's, 2007).

As with food events in general farmers' markets can also provide substantial regional economic and environmental benefits, and are increasingly being turned to as a means of local economic development in agricultural regions. In economic terms farmers' markets, as well as many community-based food events, help retain monies in the local economy for a longer period thereby assisting in the maintenance of local employment. In environmental terms, they can also assist in the maintenance of traditional farming practices and product varieties that also help maintain rural landscapes and biodiversity. Both economic and environmental localism as embodied in farmers' markets help combine with other local marketing practices to promote local branding and reinforce local identity.

Such measures may then be utilized by producers in their own marketing. In addition, markets and festivals can provide an outlet for farmers to experiment with new products, gain customer feedback and also help educate interested consumers or, as noted above, to transition to larger ventures or new markets at minimal risk.

Yet, arguably, farmers' markets in many situations have evolved in to something far more than a community-based food event as they have become focal points for the encouragement of sustainable consumption and the development of alternative economic systems and distribution channels. Research also suggests farmers' markets as institutions and many of their vendors place emphasis on the values and norms that reflect their ethics, honesty, and co-operativeness in their selling environment and willingness to serve their customers (Baber and Frongillo, 2003; Food System Economic Partnership, 2006). While this is the case, there also appears to be opportunities to grow the contribution of farmers' markets to local food systems development via attracting larger volumes of customers where practical and increasing the proportion purchased at markets through improved marketing practices such as:

- branding;
- guarantee/point-of-origin labels;
- greater varieties of available products where possible;
- extending the length of opening season for the farmers' market where possible;
- educational opportunities such as cooking demonstrations and free samples of uncommon products;
- improving accessibility for elderly, disabled and low income populations (Griffin and Frongillo, 2003; Thilmany, 2005; Food System Economic Partnership, 2006).

However, a key issue that becomes apparent in examining food festivals and farmers' markets as expressions of local food systems means that because of their community foundations and relatively decentralized nature they are often 'reinventing the wheel' when it comes to marketing and planning practices. This is particularly with respect to the small businesses that participate in such events, and their understanding regulatory requirements, customer needs and how the event and/or market fit within their wider business strategy – assuming that they have developed one. Such concerns are important for small businesses so that they can best use their scarce financial and human resources in the most effective manner to achieve business and personal goals. Moreover, at a regional level such concerns are also important because of the relative balance that regions need to address with emphasis on events, festivals and farmers' markets, as part of their overall product mix for tourism and distribution and retailing of produce, including adding value through the restaurant and foodservice sector or other means.

Despite a lack of clear direction for many events and regions, there is a wealth of discussion and literature emerging from a number of interested parties: academics, government departments, campaigning organizations, university extension services and interested individuals which should be useful in supporting the development of the sector in the short/medium term (e.g. Payne, 2002; Oberholtzer and Grow, 2003; Thilmany, 2005; Stephenson et al., 2006). Despite some of the stakeholders having different aims and objectives with respect to the hosting of food events and their utilization for tourism purposes, there is a positive commitment to the farmers' markets/ food event concept. For example, in the UK, several government departments have the topic of farmers' markets and food festivals firmly on their agenda. The Department of Food and Rural Affairs (DEFRA) has published a number of reports since 2000 (DEFRA, 2001a, 2002, 2003), which have commented on the value of farmers' markets/food festivals as tools of reconnection within the food supply chain. Other reports produced by the same department support the importance of events as a mechanism for regeneration in rural areas (e.g. DEFRA, 2001b), and there is a keen governmental interest in the maintenance and support of market towns as strong and vibrant communities in which to live (DEFRA, 2000, 2004).

DEFRA also has a strong commitment to education, and an initiative 'The Year of Farming and Food in Education' was launched in September 2007 (DEFRA, 2007). This project aims to give young people in England direct experience of the countryside and the food chain. One of its aspirations for the year is to encourage every school to participate in local food procurement activities. Farmers' market and local/regional food events are ideal locations for this learning to take place.

The Department of Health also has an interest in the production and distribution of good quality food as a key driver in the health of the nation. In their latest action plan on 'Delivering Sustainable Development' (Department of Health, 2007), which builds on an earlier report from 2005, there is an identification of the need to encourage consumption of good food in the context of sustainable farming, a commitment which sits well with the farmers' market ethos. The UK initiatives with respect to access to healthy foods, particularly for lower income groups, are also replicated in the US context although, as in the UK, there is significant variation between regions with respect to the effectiveness of such a strategy (e.g. Conrey et al., 2003; United States Department of Agriculture, 2002).

There are several well-established campaigning groups who also have an interest in the future of farmers' markets and local food initiatives. For example, in the UK The Soil Association (2003), an organization committed to the promotion of organic food, and Friends of the Earth (2000a, b, 2001, 2002), an environmental charity which calls for a 'greener' planet, have produced several reports which support farmers' markets as good practice within sustainable communities. Sustain, an organization which advocates 'food and agricultural policies and practices that enhance the health and welfare of people and animals, improve the working and living environment, promote equity and enrich society and culture' (Sustain, 2007) have also been champions of local food initiatives for the last decade (Sustain, 2003, 2004), and it is likely that they will continue to have an interest in their future. The National Trust who clearly establish their position through their food and farming policies (National Trust, 2007a) also have a keen interest in farmers' markets and food festivals (National Trust, 2007b). Events held at their properties enable their tenant farmers and local food producers to bring produce to market, but in the longer term the Trust has a firm belief that food events have an important educational role to play about sustainable food production. In the USA, University Extension Services are arguably one of the most important forces in supporting grower direct marketing initiatives along with farmers' market associations themselves.

It is also important to acknowledge the role of food events in more urban settings and several organizations including the Association of Town Centre Managers (ATCM) in the UK have identified the importance of events in supporting the life, health and vibrancy of town and city centres. They advocate the development of 'event space' in town planning and have clearly articulated the benefits that farmers' markets and food events can bring to an urban environment (ATCM, 2007).

Finally, farmers' market associations, such as FARMA, the official body which represents farmers' markets across the UK, are key contributors to discussions about the future. A conference held in November 2007 (FARMA, 2007) brought together experts from the world of food and farming to discuss the development of farmers' markets. Key themes that were debated included quality, funding, marketing, certification and education. An examination of information that has emerged from these organizations alongside findings that have been articulated in academic papers suggests a number of key areas of long-term importance to food events and farmers' markets.

Product life cycle

There appears to be a marked difference between the maturity of the market with regards to farmers' markets and other types of food events. This is not necessarily concerned with the length of time that individual events have been inexistence, or for how long the sector can continue to develop, but more to do with our understanding of the sector. With regards to farmer's markets, there is a reasonably well-accepted concept in many countries of what constitutes a farmers' market and through organizations such as FARMA (2007), it is possible to reach a reasonably good comprehension about the size and nature of the market.

Through this information it is evident that, in some countries where the farmers' market renaissance first occurred as in the USA and the UK, the food event market is reaching quite a mature stage. For example, in the UK, the number of new farmers' market sites that are now being opened up has softened over the last 2 years following the rapid growth in 2001 to 2003. It is predicted by FARMA (2007) that markets will continue to be opened at a steady rate, but the overall market is likely to become saturated by the time there are a total of 800 sites in operation.

Stephenson et al.'s (2006) research on farmers' markets in Oregon also highlights the need to understand the complexities of a more mature market for food events such as farmers' markets. In the period 1998 to 2005 of the 62 markets that opened, only 30 continued to be open at the end of the 2005 season, therefore the total number of markets grew from 38 to 68. Of the 32 markets that closed, 15 markets (nearly 47 per cent) did so following their first season. Thirty of the 32 markets (94 per cent) closed after operating 4 or fewer years. As Stephenson et al. (2006, p.4) noted, 'the high failure rate for markets, especially younger ones, is startling. The two older markets that closed after 11 and 22 years respectively demonstrate that this is not just an issue with new markets'.

The markets that are already in existence, and especially those who have been in operation for some time, are now looking at ways of extending/developing their product in order to provide variety and interest for their customer base.

They appear to be doing this in two ways. Firstly some market organizers have chosen to offer the market more frequently, such as once a week rather than once a month, as in the case of Edinburgh, Scotland (Edinburgh Farmers' Market, 2007), whilst others have decided to offer an augmented product by providing additional benefits to their customers. This may be in the form of entertainment at the market, children's activities, cookery demonstrations or competitions. Another common trend is to offer 'one-off' specialized markets at several points throughout the year. These take a range of formats, for example, a seasonal celebration, such as Easter or Christmas markets, or themed markets such as Medieval markets and Continental markets. Another strategy may be to link farmers' markets to the food events. For example, when the Savour New Zealand food event was held in Christchurch in 2007, a special farmers' market day was held in the city's Cathedral Square by vendors from the city's various farmers' markets.

Definitions of what is meant by a 'food event' are less well established and as such there are no national organizations, such as FARMA, which can easily collate information and set standards. At the present time, it is a complex task to gather meaningful statistics to illustrate the size, nature and scope of this sector. What is known is that there appears to be rapid growth in this area with many new food festivals and events, under a range of formats being established and actively promoted in many countries around the world. Host organizations include governmental bodies, charities and interested groups/individuals. However, the relative survival rate of such food event initiatives is unknown. Nevertheless, the interest that currently exists in food events and farmers' markets has also created a renewed awareness of some of the longer established food festivals. For example, in the UK, ancient food festivals such as The Whitstable Oyster Festival in Kent have had something of a renaissance. It is difficult to predict growth patterns or when the market will become saturated, but at the present time there are no indications that the market is slowing down.

Certification and licensing

In many countries, the whole subject of policy, regulation and market certification is a key debate in the future development of farmers' markets and food events (Payne, 2002). For example, in the USA, it is widely recognized that farmers' markets began to re-emerge (after years of decline) only after the passage of the *Farmer-to-Consumer Direct Marketing Act of 1976*

(Thilmany, 2005), and revisions in 2002 and 2006. Nevertheless, regulatory issues differ from jurisdiction to jurisdiction. As Chapter 12 noted in California farmers' markets are defined under state law, although in most other jurisdictions such markets are self-defined with regulation and quality assurance usually being maintained by farmers' markets associations themselves.

With reference to the UK farmers' markets, for example, FARMA are keen to ensure that, as many markets as possible are certified and listed with their organization with an aim to protect the quality of delivery and maintain the concept of local sourcing. Unfortunately there are always operators who are ready to seek financial gains from a good idea, and there have been repeated reports of markets being run that do not comply with the farmers' market ethos, often selling cheaper, poor quality or non-local food (e.g. Kelleher, 2007). This trend is hard to regulate and control against, but if the true farmers' market concept is to survive, it may be up to consumers to boycott these markets and to continue to push for high standards or for government to take a stronger regulatory interest in markets.

Licensing legislation, with regards to the sale of liquor and the inclusion of entertainment at an event, also throws up a challenge for the food event organizer. Licensing legislation is constantly being updated and organizers have to be vigilant if they are to avoid prosecution. This is a challenge for farmers' markets organizers who may wish to extend their product by offering a more sophisticated model. For example, if a market is set up in a church hall selling fruit, vegetables, cheeses, jams, chutneys and cakes, and then decides to expand and involve a wine producer and cider producer, who will offer sampling, the licensing arrangements will have to be carefully reviewed. Similarly, licensing law is also a major issue for any food event that focuses on alcohol, whether it be beer, cider, wine or spirits, even if such events do have a strong regional beverage focus.

Ancient market charters, held by some towns and cities in the UK, and elsewhere in Europe, are another limiting factor on the future expansion of farmers' markets. These charters, often held by the local council, prevent markets from being established in a certain geographical area without permission from the charter holder. This is a good way of monitoring and maintaining the standards of markets that are being set up, but it does mean that the charter holder in a way has a monopoly situation. This situation could stifle creativity from the lack of new players being involved in the region.

Development of permanent sites

If individual farmers' markets become successful, then one direction that some choose to adopt is to trade more frequently. Several markets have taken this a stage further, through the establishment of a permanent site, which houses a farmers' market each day. The question that then arises is, 'Is this still a farmers' market'? One example of this is the Goods Shed in Kent (The Goods Shed, 2007), which complies with farmers' market guidelines and has a good following. Likewise, if we look at other types of food events and festivals, as they develop in scale, it is likely that some of these may need to use more permanent locations. Two of the largest agricultural shows in the UK, The Great Yorkshire Show (2007) and The Royal Show (2007) have become so big that they now take place on purpose-built showgrounds, which is a model that has long been used in Australia and New Zealand.

More formalized management styles

As markets mature and food events become more established, it is also likely that there will be an adoption of more formalized management structures. For example, at Ludlow Marches Food Festival, there has been a gradual move from a very informal casual committee arrangement which was set up 13 years ago by a group of individuals. Due to the size and complexity of the festival, there is now a board of directors who are responsible for the strategic development of the event (Ludlow Marches Food Festival, 2007). The 12 London farmers' markets are also run by a company arrangement which was established to ensure a consistent approach across the city (London Farmers Markets, 2007). Other models also exist such as at the Whitstable Oyster Fair where a paid event organizer was recently employed to manage their event (Whitstable Oyster Fair, 2007). This more formalized approach is necessary when events reach a certain size to achieve organizational and financial control. Although as Stephenson et al. (2006) have reported with respect to their research, it is also a way of ensuring the survivability of events and markets.

Branding of events

The increased popularity of food events in recent years has encouraged a number of individuals and companies to launch a series of events under a brand name. One of the first people in the UK to do this was the food writer, broadcaster and consultant Henrietta Green (Celebrity Chef UK, 2007). Her 'Food Lovers fairs' have been very popular and have been influential in raising awareness of British food. It was one of her fairs that helped to launch the refurbished Borough Market to the public. One of the most recent 'brands' to be promoted is the 'Taste' brand of events which are sponsored by Channel 4 television. Taste of London was a 4 day gourmet festival that took place in Regents Park during the summer of 2007. Other Taste events were held at Bath, Birmingham, Dublin and Edinburgh (Taste Festivals UK, 2007). Such events are also significant as they demonstrate the increasing strong relationship between food media, such as television (especially food channels and shows) and specialist magazines. However, the longer-term implications of such relationships for events and markets may affect the relationship of events to the locations in which they originated. For example, Savour New Zealand was held in Christchurch every 2 year years from 2001 to 2007 with Cuisine magazine as a sponsor as well as support from the Christchurch City Council. From 2008 the privately owned event moved to Auckland, where it was planned to be held annually and featured a new official media partner in the form of Dish magazine. Such shifts in place as events seek greater returns also highlight some of the difficulties for local governments in providing financial support for events, as they may be concerned that money invested in developing an event will be wasted if it then moves to another location.

Conclusions

This book has highlighted some of the major issues that face food events in developed countries and the way that they have become part of broader strategies of regional and product promotion and development. As noted in Chapters 1 and 2, food events are different from other events in that although they share some of the same management, marketing and planning concerns, they are inseparably bound to issues of food localization and globalization, alternative regional food systems, sense of place and terroir and the communities in which food is produced and consumed. Food events and farmers' markets therefore have sets of issues that need to be addressed differently from some of the standard event management strategies, although the wider field can still be useful for informing food event decision-making and management.

Arguably, food events therefore have specific sets of expectations on them with respect to their role in promoting more specific forms of economic development, lifestyles and local products which may at times be difficult to achieve. Increasing concern over the quality of food we eat also means that food events, and farmers' markets in particular, are also seen as important avenues of food and health education and quality assurance with respect to what we eat, as well as a means of sustaining communities and heirloom food products and varieties.

Food events are therefore not just there for tourism and external promotion of regional produce, as important as these concerns may be, but are often part of contemporary local responses to modern food system impacts of environmental degradation, food security and economic instability and decline. As Chapter 2 noted, food events and farmers' markets have become integral part of local 'foodsheds' and alternative agricultural networks. However, the extent to which such developments have become part of broader consumer understanding or has influenced the larger food and economic system is not as well understood as it could be.

One recurring problem that has been identified in various alternative regional food system models is the challenge of marketing the system and its components, including food events and farmers' markets. Objectives such as business survival while maintaining ethical food production may be confounded by changing consumer trends as well as competition with large food retailers, especially supermarkets, which may co-opt some elements of local food production as well as utilize their market and media power to retain their existing customer base and influence on consumer purchase. Moreover, it can be argued that there is a need for a broader understanding of event and market visitors anyway, particularly as each event is likely to have its own particular profile.

Even given the relatively limited understanding of the area, it is hoped that this book and the range of cases and profiles it provides of food events is at least a part of beginning to understand their place within contemporary consumption and lifestyle, and the potential contribution that they may have with maintaining rural landscapes and production. Given contemporary concerns over global environmental change, food security and the increasing costs of energy, it is increasingly the case that food events and farmers' markets are not just regarded as worthwhile business developments, but are also becoming integral to the development of more sustainable forms of production and consumption.

References

Association of Town Centre Managers (2007) at http://www. atcm.org

Baber, L.M. and Frongillo, E.A. (2003). Family and seller inter-actions in farmers' markets in upstate New York. *American Journal of Alternative Agriculture*, 18, 87–94.

Bonham's (2007) at http://www.thebonham.com/citybreaks/farmersmarket.html

Brown, A. (2002). Farmers' market research 1940–2000: An inventory and review. *American Journal of Alternative Agriculture*, 17(4), 167–176.

Çela, A., Knowles-Lankford, J. and Lankford, S. (2007). Local food festivals in Northeast Iowa communities: A visitor and economic impact study. *Managing Leisure*, 12(2/3), 171–186.

Celebrity Chef UK (2007) at http://www.celebritychefsuk.com/chefs.asp?id=33

Che, D., Veeck, A. and Veeck, G. (2005). Sustaining production and strengthening the agritourism product: Linkages among Michigan agritourism destinations. *Agriculture and Human Values*, 22, 225–234.

Conrey, E.J., Frongillo, E.A., Dollahite, J.S. and Griffin, M.R. (2000). Integrated program enhancements increased utili-zation of farmers' market nutrition program. *The Journal of Nutrition*, 133(6), 1841–1844.

DEFRA (2000). Rural white paper, http://www.defra.gov.uk

DEFRA (2001a). Policy commission on the future of farming and food, http://www.defra.gov.uk

DERFA (2001b). Tackling the impact of foot and mouth disease on the rural economy, rural task force, http://www.defra.gov.uk

DEFRA (2002). The strategy for sustainable farming and food: Facing the future, http://www.defra.gov.uk

DEFRA (2003). Local food: A snapshot of the sector, report of the working group on local food, http://www.defra.gov.uk

DEFRA (2004). Rural strategy paper, http://www.defra.gov.uk

DEFRA (2007). Year of food and farming in education, http://www.defra.gov.uk/schools/yff.htm

Department of Health (2007). Delivering sustainable develop-ment: DH action plan 2007/08, http://www.dh.gov.uk

Edinburgh Farmers' Market (2007) at http://www.edinburghcc.com/farmersmarket

Emmons, N. (2001). Festivals are salivating while celebrating food. *Amusement Business*, 113, 24–26.

FARMA (2007) at http://www.farma.org.uk

Food System Economic Partnership (2006). *Alternative Regional Food System Models: Successes and Lessons Learned: A Preliminary Literature Review*. Food System Economic Partnership, Michigan.

Friends of the Earth (2000a). The economic benefits of farmers' markets, Friends of the Earth, London.

Friends of the Earth (2000b). Farmers' markets: Actions needed by local authorities, Friends of the Earth, London.

Friends of the Earth (2001). Get real about farming: Friends of the earth's vision for the future of farming in the UK.

Friends of the Earth (2002). Local food: Future directions.

Griffin, M.R. and Frongillo, E.A. (2003). Experiences and perspectives of farmers from upstate New York farmers' markets. *Agriculture and Human Values*, 20, 189–203.

Guthrie, J., Guthrie, A., Lawson, R. and Cameron, A. (2006). Farmers' markets: The small business counter-revolution in food production and retailing. *British Food Journal*, 108(7), 560–573.

Hall, C.M. and Mitchell, R.D. (2008). *Wine Marketing: A Practical Approach*. Butterworth-Heinemann, Oxford.

Hall, C.M., Johnson, G.R. and Mitchell, R.D. (2000b). Wine tourism and regional development. In Hall, C.M., Sharples, E., Camboourne, B. and Macionis, N. (eds.) *Wine Tourism Around the World: Development Management and Markets*. Butterworth-Heinemann, Oxford, pp. 196–225.

Hall, C.M., Mitchell, R. and Sharples, E. (2003). Consuming places: The role of food, wine and tourism in regional development. In Hall, C.M., Sharples, E., Mitchell, R., Cambourne, B. and Macionis, N. (eds.) *Food Tourism Around the World: Development, Management and Markets*. Butterworth-Heinemann, Oxford, pp. 25–59.

Hall, C.M. (2004). Small firms and wine and food tourism in New Zealand: issues of collaboration, clusters and lifestyles. In Thomas, R. (ed.) *Small Firms in Tourism: International Perspectives*, Elsevier, Oxford, pp. 167–181.

Hjalager, A-M. and Corigliano, M.A. (2000). Food for tourists: Determinants of an image. *International Journal of Tourism Research*, 2(4), 281–293.

Kelleher, L. (2007). Customers being duped by rip-off farmers' markets. The Independent, http://www.independent.ie/national-news/customers-being-duped-by-ripoff--farmers-markets-1222493.html

London Farmers Markets (2007) at http://www.lfm.org.uk

Lynch, P. and Morrison, A. (2007) The role of networks. In E. Michael (ed.) *Micro-clusters and Networks: The Growth of Tourism*. Elsevier, Oxford, pp. 43–62.

Ludlow Marches Food Festival (2007) at http://www.food festival.co.uk

National Farmers' Retail and Markets Association (FARMA) (2006). *Sector Briefing: Farmers Markets in the UK; Nine Years and Counting*. National Farmers' Retail and Markets Association, Southampton.

National Trust (2007a). Food policy, http://www.nationaltrust. org.uk/main/w-chl/w-countryside_environment/w-food_ farming.htm

National Trust (2007b). Farmers' markets, http://www.national trust.org.uk/main/w-chl/w-countryside_environment/ w-food_farming/w-food_farming-farm_foods-farmers_ markets.htm

Oberholtzer, L. and Grow, S. (2003). *Fresh from the Farm: Overview and Characteristics of Producer-Only Markets in the Mid-Atlantic Region*. Henry, A. Wallace Center for Agricultural and Environmental Policy, Arlington.

Payne, T. (2002). *US Farmers' Markets – 2000: A Study of Emerging Trends*. Agricultural Marketing Service, United States Department of Agriculture, Washington, DC.

Sassatelli, R. and Scott, A. (2001). Novel food, new markets and trust regimes: Responses to the erosion of consumers' confidence in Austria, Italy and the UK. *European Societies*, 3(2), 213–244.

Stephenson, G., Lev, L. and Brewer, L. (2006). *When Things Don't Work: Some Insights into Why Farmers' Markets Close*. Special Report 1073. Oregon State University Extension Service, Corvallis.

Sustain (2003). Feeding the future: Policy options for local food. A discussion paper, Sustain, London.

Sustain (2004). Capital eats: An analysis of London's food economy, Sustain, London.

Sustain (2007). Policy statement, http://www.sustainweb.org. Sustain, London.

Taste Festivals UK (2007) at http://www.channel4.com/life/ microsites/T/taste/visitors.html

Telfer, D.J. (2001). Strategic alliances along the Niagara wine route. *Tourism Management*, 22(1), 21–30.

The Goods Shed (2007) at http://www.made-in-kent.co.uk/ producers/the-goods-shed.html

The Great Yorkshire Show (2007) at http://www.greatyork- shireshow.com

The Royal Show (2007) at http://www.royalshow.org.uk

The Soil Association (2003). Developing local food economies: Soil association policy recommendations, http://www.soil association.org

Thilmany, D. (2005). *Planning and Developing a Farmers Market: Marketing, Organizational and Regulatory Issues to Consider.* Agribusiness marketing report, Department of Agricultural and Resource Economics, Cooperative Extension, Colorado State University, Fort Collins.

United States Department of Agriculture (2002). *Improving and Facilitating a Farmers Market in a Low-Income Urban Neighborhood: A Washington, DC, Case Study.* Agricultural Marketing Service Transportation and Marketing Programs, Wholesale and Alternative Markets, United States Department of Agriculture, Washington, DC.

Whitstable Oyster Fair (2007) at http://www.whitstableoyster festival.co.uk

Index

Plate 1
The Queen Victoria Market, Melbourne. Based on a permanent site the weekly markets have become a major tourist attraction as well as a significant shopping opportunity for locals.

SINGAPORE CHILLI CRAB

Unofficially known as Singapore 'national dish', the Chilli Crab has many incarnations.

Some are packed with fresh spices like galangal, ginger, and tumeric, some are sweet-sour and rosy with tomato, others are ribboned with beaten egg, and still others carry the sting of chilli oil. All are meant to be attacked with gusto - and a nutcracker to tackle thick shells, plus a few slices of French bread and Mantou (Chinese Buns) to help soak up every drop of the delicious sauce.

Plate 2
Singapore has increasingly been using food and food events to promote itself to international visitors and reinforce its heritage and identity. Picture shows a banner in Bugis Junction shopping and hotel complex that is used as part of a food festival promotion.

Plates 3 and 4
The outdoor waterfront markets of Helsinki are an important part of the culture of the city as well as an important visitor attraction in the summer months. In autumn it is possible to purchase herring as well as other seasonal produce from the back of fishing craft. The markets are co-located with a permanent indoor market building.

Plate 5
The autumn local farmers and organic market of Umeå in Sweden is an important community event as well as a means of supporting local producers.

Plates 6 and 7 (cont'd)

Plates 6 and 7

Vancouver's Granville Island Public Markets help make the island one of the major tourist attractions of the city as well as being a fresh food source for the local communities. Although a permanent market with around 50 permanent stallholders, the market also has more seasonal stalls as well, including a farmers' truck market in July and a gardeners' truck market in May. To emphasize the seasonal nature of produce special themed events and promotions are also held during the year.

Plate 8
The Waipara Valley Farmers' Market held at Pegasus Bay Winery in north Canterbury in New Zealand is a seasonal market which insists that stallholders sell local produce similar to UK definitions of farmers' markets. Although such an approach helps ensure that the market is genuinely local in character and reduces food miles, it may also restrict the range of produce offered.

Plate 9
The Lyttleton Farmers' Market in New Zealand is a successful year-round market that has developed in conjunction with the gentrification of the port town. Although a number of its stallholders would not qualify under UK or Californian definitions of farmers' markets, it continues to attract custom for its excellent range and quality of produce.

Plate 10
The Otago Farmers' Market, New Zealand is a year-round Saturday market that utilizes a car park at a railway station that no longer has scheduled passenger services and therefore helps utilize existing public infrastructure.

Plate 11
Stall selling ostrich burgers at the Stirling Farmers' Market in Scotland. Markets are a very good mechanism to educate consumers and sell customers local but otherwise exotic foods.

Plate 12
Preparing fresh chickens on the meat floor of the Macau markets. Macau is increasingly promoting its food culture to visitors as a means of broadening its attractiveness to tourists.

Plate 13
This picture shows the busy Via dei Dolci (Sweets and Spirits Lane) at the Salone del Gusto in 2006. Photo is from the Slow Food Movement Archives

Plate 14
Delegates from around the world attending the Terra Madre in Turin in 2006. Photo is from the Slow Food Movement Archives.

Plate 15
Stalls at Wallington Food and Craft Festival, Northumberland, England in 2007. Photo produced by kind permission of the National Trust Wallington/Peter Sword.

Plate 16
Early morning visitors to the farmers' market in Newcastle upon Tyne, England. Photo produced by kind permission of Newcastle upon Tyne City Council.

Plate 17
A colourful Christmas food Market in Nice, France in 2005. Produced by kind permission of Keith Sharples Photography.

Plate 18
A local wine festival at Clermont L'Herault, Languedoc, France. Produced by kind permission of Kathy Sharples.

Plate 19
Visitors to the Ludlow Marches Food and Drink Festival, Shropshire, England, enjoying a spot of wine sampling. Photo produced by kind permission of the Ludlow Marches Food Festival committee.

Plate 20
The Ludlow Marches Food and Drink Festival has a wonderful setting. This photo shows the marquees in the Outer Bailey of the town's historic castle situated at the end of the market square. Photo produced by kind permission of the Ludlow Marches Food Festival committee.